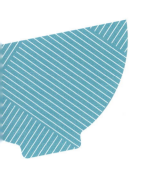

FOOD TRAILS

PLAN 52 PERFECT WEEKENDS IN THE WORLD'S TASTIEST DESTINATIONS

Explore the secret
cicchetti bars of
Venice's backstreets:
see page 134

© Susan Wright

INTRODUCTION

Whether we realise it or not, food is one of the key ways in which we experience a place when travelling. That secret locals' tapas bar you stumbled across down a backstreet; that briny-fresh seafood you saw hauled straight from the sea and onto the barbecue; that heartwarming family recipe you were privy to one time. Ingredients evoke landscapes, recipes recall history and certain dishes can unlock the very essence of a place and its people.

This book is a gastronomic tour of the world in 52 short breaks. We've scoured the globe for the greatest food experiences worth planning your travels around – not just fine dining, but also the best regional specialities, the most atmospheric street food spots, and the most memorable cooking courses.

What's clear is that food tourism is booming, making it easier than ever to get under the skin of a place. In many countries you'll find communities are reconnecting with heritage dishes and reinventing traditions. Farm-to-table, nose-to-tail and locavore principles have also become popular buzzwords for exciting food destinations. Local culture is there for the tasting; so bring your plate to the table and dig in.

Chef Dan Hunter picking
fruit at Brae restaurant,
Australia: see page 28

Check out the pintxos
scene in San Sebastián,
Spain: see page 268

CONTENTS

MALAYSIA

↓

Penang **190**

MOROCCO

↓

Fez & Middle Atlas **196**

NEW ZEALAND

↓

Auckland & Around **204**

OMAN

↓

Muscat **210**

PERU

↓

Lima **216**

PORTUGAL

↓

Porto **222**

RUSSIA

↓

St Petersburg **228**

SCOTLAND

↓

Outer Hebrides **234**

SEYCHELLES

↓

Mahé **240**

SLOVAKIA

↓

Bratislava & Around **244**

SOUTH AFRICA

↓

Cape Town & West Cape **250**

SOUTH KOREA

↓

Seoul **256**

SPAIN

↓

Catalonia **262**

San Sebastián **268**

THAILAND

↓

Chiang Mai **274**

TURKEY

↓

Istanbul **280**

USA

↓

New York **286**

New Orleans & Cajun Country **290**

Texas **296**

Maine **302**

Hawaii **308**

VIETNAM

↓

Hanoi **314**

Map labels:

BELGRANO 08

COLEGIALES PALERMO

05

Río de la Plata

RECOLETA

07 RETIRO

VILLA CRESPO 02

ALMAGRO 03 LA CITY 09

CABALLITO BALVANERA 06

MONTSERRAT PUERTO MADERO

BOEDO 01

SAN TELMO 04

LA BOCA

ARGENTINA

Argentina

MEAT FEAST IN BUENOS AIRES

Cattle-rearing gauchos and waves of European immigrants have shaped the culinary landscape of Argentina, and turned Buenos Aires into a world-class city for meat lovers.

Beef, empanadas, ice cream and more beef, washed down with wine: such is a typical weekend in a place where the very essence of the city is the smell of barbecuing meat. The food scene in Argentina's capital owes everything to the verdant pastures of the Pampas grasslands that lie beyond it, where generations of gauchos tended the cattle on which the country was built. Ships transporting Argentinian beef to Europe passed those making the opposite journey, bringing immigrants from Italy, Spain, France, Germany and elsewhere to Buenos Aires.

Attracted by the promise of food and lodgings on arrival, and help to find work, between 1880 and 1930 some six million Europeans fled the problems of poverty and persecution in their homeland in search of a better life in Argentina. Today, the city's cuisine is an eclectic mix of the traditions these European immigrants brought with them: Italian-style ice cream, empanadas from Spain, wine from vineyards planted by the French, and German-style sausages and cheeses.

The residents of Buenos Aires, known as porteños (people of the port), are certainly a carnivorous lot. In fact, Argentinians consume more beef per capita than any other country in the world except for neighbouring Uruguay. The meat is usually grilled over an open flame on a *parrilla*, a heavy duty barbecue found in steak restaurants (themselves known as parrillas), and in private homes and roof terraces, where families and friends gather for *asados* (barbecues). But not even a porteño could eat steak for every meal. Empanadas – oven baked pastry parcels with various fillings – are another staple of the porteño diet. Not only are they the local equivalent of a lunchtime sandwich (a mealtime portion is usually three), empanadas can be eaten anywhere, any time.

NEED TO KNOW
This 3-day trail is best done Thu-Sat, as Sunday closures affect many restaurants, cafes and shops in BA.

(02)

02 Matt Munro © Lonely Planet

01 MERCADO DE SAN TELMO

Step off a cobbled side street into the city's oldest fresh produce market and you'll find Buenos Aires' culinary scene laid out under one roof, ready to explore. Butchers slice cuts of meat to order from whole carcasses hanging behind the counter, while neighbourhood *señoras* bemoan the day's prices as they wait in line. Fruit and vegetable stalls overflow with produce, most of it grown in Argentina – La Verduleria de Henry is one of the best.

For freshly baked bread don't miss the *panadería* (bakery) Angelito, a neighbourhood favourite that has been a market fixture for more than 50 years. Owner Rosa puts the bread's popularity down to the fact that it is baked in a traditional oven; most *panadarías* use rotary ovens these days.

San Telmo is one of the city's oldest and most atmospheric neighbourhoods, the birth place of the Argentine tango and a hub of antiques shops, Bohemian bars, street art and fading grandeur. Come in the morning when the market is buzzing and take time to wander among the stalls and talk to the vendors, soaking in the sounds and smells of everyday porteño life.

Stop for a brew at Coffee Town, a tiny, understated coffee cart in the middle of the market that has one of the city's best selections of beans. Ask the baristas – trained at the local Centre for Coffee Studies – for a taste of the latest blend. Most market vendors speak a little English, but a Spanish phrasebook will be useful for those who don't.
Carlos Calvo 430, San Telmo; Mon-Sat 8am-9pm, to 8.30pm Sun

02 EL CUARTITO

This old school pizzeria, a short bus ride and walk from San Telmo market, can't have changed much since it first opened in 1934. It's an atmospheric joint where every space on the wall is covered with photographs and posters of football teams and boxers, and the framed shirts of Argentina's football heroes - including 'El Diego' (as Maradona is known locally), who chose to feast on pizza from El Cuartito at his wedding reception.

But forget pizza; El Cuartito is the place to come for empanadas. The house speciality is the *empanada de atún* (tuna), a satisfying snack to eat standing up at the bar.
Tel +54 11 4816 1758; Talcahuano 937, Barrio Norte; Sun-Thu 12.30pm-1am, Fri & Sat to 2am

'Butchers here cut, slice and bag around 1000kg of meat a day, with much of it sold to top restaurants'

01 Argentinian meat feast

02 Tango on BA's streets

03 A homage to beef outside a restaurant in central BA

04 El Cuartito restaurant

03 PARRILLA PEÑA

Don't be put off by the fluorescent lighting; what this no-frills neighbourhood restaurant lacks in glamour it more than makes up for with steaks so tender you can cut them with a spoon. Meat-lovers come to Parrilla Peña for good value, generous portions of reliably top-quality *bife de lomo* (tenderloin) or *ojo de bife* (rib eye) steak, served with fries and malbec wine and followed by a portion of flan (set custard covered with caramel sauce).

This is a traditional place where the waiters don crisp white shirts and bow ties, with a mostly local clientele. To join them for dinner don't even think about turning up before 9pm. *www.parrillapenia.url.ph; tel +54 11 4371 5643; Rodríguez Peña 682, Barrio Norte; Mon-Sat noon-4pm & 8pm-midnight*

04 EL OBRERO

The next day, continue your meat marathon at El Obrero. Tucked away in the working-class neighbourhood of La Boca, not far from the stadium of Boca Juniors football club, this *bodegón* (a low-key restaurant serving hearty, homestyle cooking) is the perfect place for lunch.

El Obrero (meaning 'the worker') began as a canteen-style eatery popular with locals looking for a good feed that was tasty, filling and cheap, but gradually gained a reputation extending well beyond the neighbourhood boundaries. Although these days you're as likely to see luxury cars parked outside El Obrero as overalled workers dining inside, the restaurant still has an authentic feel.

This is an excellent place to try traditional local cooking, such as *milanesas* (breaded meat cutlets);

steak lovers should try the *asado de tira* (short ribs) with a side order of chips.

If you happen to be here on the 29th of the month order *ñoquis*, a cheap meal of doughy dumplings that originated in Italy (where it is known as gnocchi) traditionally eaten on the last day before payday; dine like the locals and put a ARS$100 bill under you plate while you eat, for luck. Don't miss the brightly coloured houses of nearby Caminito (take a taxi to get there as it's not safe to walk), a living museum that showcases the traditional housing of La Boca's Italian immigrant ship workers, with tango dancing street performers and tourist souvenir stalls. *Tel +54 11 4362 9912; Agustín R. Cafferena 64, La Boca; Mon-Sat lunch & dinner*

03 Y. Levy © Alamy

04 Contributor © Insights

05 PROVEEDURIA PIAF

Given that the average Argentinian consumes nearly 60kg of beef a year, it's no surprise that in Buenos Aires meat-buying is a serious business. And while most porteños have their own trusted neighbourhood butcher, those in the know buy their *vacío* (flank steak), *entraña* (skirt steak) and *asado de tira* (short ribs) at Piaf, a bus ride from La Boca into the neighbourhood of Colegiales.

Run by brothers Gustavo and Hernan Mendez, Proveeduria Piaf is always busy – the butchers here cut, slice and bag around 1000kg of meat a day, with much of it sold to some of Buenos Aires' top restaurants.

The friendly staff are happy to talk you through the cuts on offer; as well as beef, Piaf also sells free-range chicken and other meat, such as buffalo, llama, duck and wild boar. Piaf even runs courses in butchery, usually held one evening a month.
www.proveeduriapiaf.com.ar; tel +54 11 4777 4279; Avenida Dorrego 1605, Colegiales; Mon-Sat 8am-8pm

06 HELADERIA CADORE

In a city crammed with *heladerías* (ice-cream shops), the place to go for ice cream has to be Cadore – a busy little place in central BA named after the region in Italy where the Olivotti family honed their gelato-making skills before moving to Argentina in 1957.

Located amid the theatres of Avenida Corrientes, Cadore's busiest time is between 10pm and 1am. The ice cream here is creamy and smooth, with new flavours added every few months. Be sure to try the local speciality: dulce de leche, an exquisitely rich and intensely flavoured ice cream made by boiling dulce de leche for 14 to 16 hours. Cadore is in between Uruguay and Callao Subte stations.
www.heladeriacadore.com.ar; tel +54 11 4374 3688; Avenida Corrientes 1695, Barrio Norte

07 LUCIO

Lucio might look like a regular neighbourhood pizzeria, but hidden inside is one of Buenos Aires' best kept secrets: tray loads of the most delicious freshly baked *medialunas* (croissants) in town. Porteños aren't big on breakfast – it's usually just a cup of *café con leche* (milky coffee), sometimes with a *medialuna de manteca* (butter croissant with a sweet glaze) or *de grasa* (savoury, flaky croissant made with lard). Mouth-wateringly spongy and moist in the middle, Lucio's *medialunas* are generously sized and the perfect cure for any Sunday morning Malbec-induced grogginess.
Avenida Raúl Scalabrini Ortiz 2402, Palermo; +54 11 4831 5513; Sun-Thu 7am-midnight, Fri & Sat to 1am

08 LA TABLITA

You don't have to spend long in Buenos Aires to hear mention of a *picada*, a wooden board covered with a range of *fiambre* (cold cuts) and cheeses, usually accompanied by bread and wine and shared among friends. For lunch, head to the neighbourhood of Belgrano, where for more than 30 years La Tablita has been tempting local residents with its delicious *jamón crudo* (cured hams), fiambre, artisanal cheeses, homemade salamis and selection of wines – all the components of a good picada. But besides the unrivalled selection of produce crammed into this inviting little store, it's the friendliness of the staff that makes it so special.

Locals know better than to make a quick call into La Tablita for one item – once through the door you will be plied with samples of hams and cheeses so divine that you will spend hours tasting, and leave with bags full.
www.fiambrerialatablita.com.ar; tel +54 11 4782 5393; Vidal 1726, Belgrano; Tue-Fri 9.30am-1pm & 4pm-8.30pm, Sat & Sun 9.30am-1.30pm & 4.30pm-8.30pm

09 CARRITOS DE LA COSTANERA SUR

For one more mega-hit of meat, make a pit-stop at one of the roadside parrillas that line the edge of the Reserva Ecologica in Puerto Madero. This is street food Buenos Aires style: brightly coloured carritos (mobile barbecue carts) selling choripan (sausage sandwiches) and bondiola (pork) sandwiches, with self-service Tupperware containers of garnishes and salads. Dine at the plastic tables and chairs laid out on the pavement.

Locals favour Mi Sueño, where the generous servings of meat oozing out of a crusty bread roll the length of your forearm will sate even the most ravenous. The carritos are on the Costanera Sur, a 15-minute walk heading east from Plaza de Mayo.
Avenida Int Hernan M Giralt, Puerto Madero; open 24 hours

WHERE TO STAY
HOTEL BOCA
Taking the idea that Argentinians live and breathe football to new heights, Hotel Boca is a sophisticated, upscale place that's billed as the world's first football-themed hotel. Each room has an image of one of Boca Juniors' star players on the doors (no prizes for guessing that 'Maradona' is the penthouse suite), while the team colours – blue and yellow – are used in the interior design.
www.hotelbocajuniors. com; Tacuari 243, Monserrat

1555 MALABIA HOUSE
Built as a convent in 1896 and converted into one of Palermo's first boutique hotels in 1997, 1555 Malabia House has bags of character, natural light and staff who'll make you feel at home.
www.malabiahouse.com.ar; Malabia 1555, Palermo

WHAT TO DO
Don't miss Recoleta Cemetery, the final resting place of a host of Argentina's most illustrious figures whose elaborate tombs and dusty mausoleums occupy a prime patch of one of the city's most salubrious neighbourhoods. Try to find the tomb of Eva Perón, who fought for women's suffrage during her time as the First Lady of Argentina (hint: look for a crowd). There are free tours in English on Tuesdays and Thursdays at 11am. After dark, watch some tango and have a go yourself at one of the city's milongas (tango dance halls) – one of the most atmospheric and welcoming to beginners is La Catedral, which also offers nightly classes. (www.lacatedralclub.com)

CELEBRATIONS
LA RURAL
To delve deeper into the world of beef you can get a true taste of country life at the annual exhibition of the Argentinian agricultural society, La Rural, a two-week farming show held in July or August. It's packed with gauchos on horseback, prize-winning cows and other livestock, as well as stalls selling fresh country produce. (www.exposicionrural. com.ar)

Ø5 Tray of empanadas

Ø6 Mercado de San Telmo

01

Australia

FARM TO TABLE IN SOUTHERN TASMANIA

Tasmania's pure environment at the very southern extreme of Australia has cultivated a special community of green-loving farmers, producers and local food champions.

There was a time when Tasmania felt overlooked. A tiny (by mainland standards) triangular island dripping from the bottom of Australia's east coast, often forgotten by map makers, economically challenged, shunned by sun-loving holidaymakers, a backwater known for its violent convict past and... apples.

Hobart was originally settled by the British in 1804. Surrounded by sea stretching straight to Antarctica on one side and impenetrable wilderness on the other, the land around Hobart made a perfect natural prison. More than 70,000 men, women and children were transported to Van Diemen's Land (as it was then known) as convicts.

Early settlers noticed the vast numbers of whales in the bays around Hobart, and whaling became an engine for the colony's development. Like the penal colonies, it too had virtually come to an end by the 1850s. It's pleasurably mind-bending now to contemplate, while slurping incomparably fresh oysters pulled from the D'Entrecasteaux Channel, that this was once the gory site of a whaling station.

It's also nicely symbolic. Australia's Green movement was forged here in the 1980s, in a bitter fight between mining interests and eco-warriors driven by a vision of what Tasmania could be. In seeking out small sustainable producers and passionate landholders, you find the spiritual descendants of the early Greens, harnessing Tasmania's other natural resources – clean air, pristine waters, a climate perfect for growing grapes and berries (and apples!), lush farmland.

It's the end-of-the-worldness, the wildness and isolation of Tasmania that make it special today. A pure environment, surrounded by some of the world's cleanest ocean, home to people driven to a gorgeous extreme in their search for perfection, for authenticity. And, no queues.

NEED TO KNOW
Start this 3-4 day trail on a Saturday to hit both the markets, and hire a car as public transport is scant.

01 Courtesy of the Museum of Old and New Art

NEW NORFOLK

Derwent River

SORELL

02

08

04

05

03

HOBART

DUNALLEY

AUSTRALIA

01

KINGSTON

Storm Bay

WOODBRIDGE

06 07

01 SALAMANCA MARKET

Kick off your Tassie adventure on Hobart's waterfront with a visit to this vivacious market. Lined with dusky yellow sandstone warehouse buildings dating from the whaling era's 1830s peak, Salamanca Place breathes history, and the 300-stall market is a showcase of island abundance.

Producers from all over descend each week – elderflower farmers from the Derwent Valley, apiarists from the Huon Valley, and regional winemakers. Depending on the time of year, you'll find a dazzling array of berries from blue and black to logan and silvan, or the 'Apple Isle's' organic signature fruit. You may even get a tantalising whiff of the budding black truffle industry. After the market, explore the old warehouses that hide a warren of crafts and gourmet goodies. *www.salamanca.com.au; tel +61 3 6238 2843; Salamanca Place, Hobart; 8am-3pm Sat*

'Australians don't share the northern hemisphere squeamishness about eating oysters during their summer spawning season'

02 MONA

From the port near Salamanca Place, hop on the ferry to the Museum of Old and New Art (MONA), 30 minutes up the Derwent River. It's hard to overstate the effect this art gallery, housed in a $AUD75 million building that has become an icon of Tasmania, has had on Hobart since it was opened in 2011 by art lover and professional gambler David Walsh. Tourism has surged and the local cultural scene electrified by the eccentric, boundary-pushing collection.

Enhance your art appreciation by touring and tasting at the gallery's on-site Moo Brew artisan brewery and Moorilla Estate winery (cool-climate wines; try the riesling and the pinot noir). Top it off with dinner at The Source, also within the gallery grounds, for spectacular views, an impressive wine list and a menu that, like the art collection, stuns with unexpected flavours.

Don't underestimate the enchantment spun by this Disneyland for grown-ups – the combination of avant-garde art, excellent feasting and stunning setting can easily occupy you for a whole day. *www.mona.net.au; tel +61 3 6277 9900; 655 Main Rd, Berriedale, Hobart; 10am-6pm Wed-Mon*

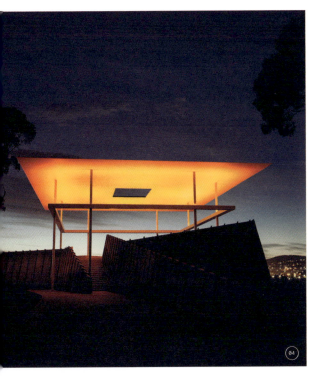

01 Dine at the Museum of Old and New Art

02 Bill Lark, of Lark Whisky Bar & Distillery

03 Farm Gate Market in Hobart

04 *Amarna* by James Turrell at the Museum of Old and New Art

03 FARM GATE MARKET

While big, bustling Salamanca Market struts its delicious stuff to Hobart's growing crowds of visitors, the Farm Gate Market is the foodie heartbeat of the community. Founder Madi Seeber-Peattie says it's about relationships between the locals and Tassie's food producers – more than 70% of the customers are locals.

The focus is on small and family producers, working close to the land to grow and rear food they care about. Like the small, 25-acre holding where former chef Ross O'Meara runs rare-breed pigs to make Toulouse sausages, pork pies, smoked trotters and other porky delights. Or the luscious summer berries that come from the Clarke family's Westerway Raspberry Farm.

'See you Sunday' has become a Hobart cliché, says Madi – no need to specify where, everybody knows. Lunch on what some call Australia's best sushi made by Japanese sushi chef Masaaki Koyama, who travels 60km from his restaurant in Geeveston to attend the market each week. Made with locally grown wasabi root and wakame, and fish pulled fresh from the rivers and bays of the Huon Valley, it's another of Tasmania's surprising secrets.

www.farmgatemarket.com.au; tel +61 3 6234 5625; Bathurst St, Hobart; 8.30am-1pm Sun

04 LARK WHISKY BAR & DISTILLERY

With its rich barley fields, pure soft water, highland peat bogs and the ideal climate, Tasmania has all that's required to make a world-class single malt. That's what whisky lover Bill Lark realised, and when he established Lark Distillery it marked a resurgence in distilling that has since spread. In 2014 a Tasmanian distillery called Sullivan's Cove took the award for world's best single malt at the World Whiskies Awards – a first for a whisky from outside Scotland or Japan.

At Lark they smoke their barley using peat from their own bog, and use small casks that give more oak contact and a rapid, robust maturation. The distillery's methods mean a small output that competes on quality, not quantity.

Taste its rarefied wares (along with other local drops) at the atmospheric Whisky Bar – all corrugated iron and ancient wooden beams – then board the 'Drambulance' for a trip to the distillery in the Coal River Valley for a privileged inside look at how it's done. *larkdistillery.com; tel +61 3 6231 9088; 14 Davey St, Hobart; 9am-7pm Sun-Thu, to 10pm Fri & Sat*

05 DUNALLEY FISH MARKET

Locals say these are the best fish and chips in Tasmania. Set in a ramshackle, quirky old shed, this is seafood at its sparklingly fresh, unpretentious best, and at disarmingly reasonable prices.

A seafood 'basket' (actually everything comes wrapped in newspaper, *à la* tradition) might contain salmon, trevally, striped trumpeter, flake (shark), scallops, calamari, baby octopus... whatever the boats brought in that day. You can buy fresh fillets to cook yourself on the barbecue outside and, if you're lucky, local crayfish or fresh oysters.

Sit in the shed and enjoy the collection of old photos and fishing paraphernalia, or outdoors with a glorious view over Norfolk Bay, where you might spot the resident seal, or enormous stingrays gliding past the pier. Plan ahead and bring a bottle of chilled local wine, and enjoy a quintessential Tassie moment. *11 Fulham Rd, Dunalley; tel +61 3 6253 5428; 9am-6pm daily*

06 BRUNY ISLAND CHEESE CO

From Kettering, a 30-minute drive south of Hobart, the ferry leaves for Bruny Island. Bruny is a windswept, sparsely populated isle with magnificent coastal scenery and abundant wildlife (penguins, echidnas, mutton birds). Here in a bush oasis you'll find Bruny Island Cheese Co – the product of Nick Haddow's travels and training in the great cheese-producing regions of France and Italy, with a distinctly Tasmanian character.

Nibble on cheeses such as OEN – a soft, fudgey cow's milk cheese, washed in Pinot Noir and wrapped in vine leaves to mature – under the eucalypts then take a look at the traditional cheesemaking going on inside, to see Nick's manifesto in action: 'We believe people ate better a hundred years ago than they do today. We don't understand cheese awards. We often do things the hard way.'
www.brunyislandcheese.com.au; 1807 Main Rd, Bruny Island; tel +61 3 6260 6353; 10am-4pm Mon-Thu, to 5pm Fri-Sun

07 GET SHUCKED

Some of the best bivalves in the Pacific come from these parts. At Get Shucked, they're reared in the pristine waters of the D'Entrecasteaux channel until they're plump, sweet and bursting with saline goodness. Australians don't share the northern hemisphere squeamishness about eating oysters during their summer spawning season, and these are at their creamy best during the warmer months from December to February.

Sit on the homey decking and sample the pride of Great Bay done any number of ways – Kilpatrick (lightly grilled, topped with Worcestershire sauce and Bruny Island bacon), or panko-crumbed, poached in Asian flavours – but, for our money, they need nothing more than a squeeze of lemon juice. If you're an oyster-lover, prepare to be wowed; if you're not, prepare to be converted.
www.getshucked.com.au; tel +61 429 933 954; 1735 Main Rd, North Bruny; 9.30am-6.30pm daily (reduced winter hours)

08 AGRARIAN KITCHEN

Experience paddock-to-plate philosophy up close at The Agrarian Kitchen, a farm-based cooking school in the picturesquely rural Derwent

Valley, 45 minutes from Hobart. Rodney Dunn and his wife, Séverine Demanet, run a five-acre organic farm with vegetable and herb garden, orchard and berry patch, plus rare-breed pigs, chickens, milking goats, geese and honeybees. Amid this bucolic bliss, classes are conducted in a 19th-century schoolhouse.

Rodney, a former chef who apprenticed with legendary Sydney chef Tetsuya Wakuda, designs menus to show off the farm's seasonal bounty and leads students in harvesting and preparing a multi-course feast. In winter, the renowned two-day 'Whole Hog' course begins with a rare-breed pig carcass and takes students from nose to tail. Book well ahead. *www.theagrariankitchen.com; tel +61 3 6261 1099; 650 Lachlan Rd*

05 Windswept beaches at The Neck, Bruny Island

06 Picking raspberries, The Agrarian Kitchen school

WHERE TO STAY

HENRY JONES ART HOTEL
This super-swish restored jam factory is in a prime spot on Hobart's waterfront. It oozes both history – remnant bits of jam-making machinery and huge timber beams – and sophistication, with modern art adorning the walls, and a classy cocktail bar and restaurant. *www.thehenryjones.com; tel +61 3 6210 7700; 25 Hunter St*

MONA PAVILIONS
It's possible to stay on-site at MONA in the gallery's own ultra-modern five-star accommodation. With panoramic views of the Derwent River, each pavilion has its own wine cellar and is decked out with valuable Australian art: it's super-flash luxury. *www.mona.net.au/mona/accommodation; tel +61 3 6277 9900; 655 Main Rd, Berriedale, Hobart*

WHAT TO DO

PORT ARTHUR HISTORIC SITE
Between 1830 and 1877, this 'natural penitentiary' – the peninsula is connected to the mainland by a strip of land less than 100m wide – was a grim home to 12,500 convicts doing hard, brutal prison time. Now a World Heritage site, it's an important, if sombre, historical experience, best seen on a guided tour. (www.portarthur.org.au)

MT WELLINGTON
Overlooking Hobart, it's possible to drive to the summit of Mt Wellington, from where there's an unbelievable view. Don't be deterred if it's overcast – the peak often rises above cloud level to look out over a carpet of cottony clouds. You can also take a hike or a mountain-bike tour down its slopes.

CELEBRATIONS

THE TASTE OF TASMANIA
Try hard to time your visit for the few days either side of New Year's Eve, when Hobart's waterfront hosts a refined Bacchanalia. Hundreds of food and wine producers from across the island create the ultimate street-food market. With the yachties and excitement of the Sydney-to-Hobart Yacht Race arriving over these days too, it's without doubt Hobart's annual high point. (www.thetasteoftasmania.com.au)

Australia
MOD-OZ IN MELBOURNE

Melbourne's famed gastronomic allure has spread way beyond the big city, into country farms and coastal villages around the Great Ocean Road and Bellarine Peninsula.

Winding past spectacular beaches, dramatic ocean vistas and scenic rainforest detours, Victoria's Great Ocean Rd in southeast Australia is one of the world's most famous coastal drives. However it's also a drive that rewards folk prepared to take some less-touristy paths. Here you'll uncover true culinary highlights, with some of Australia's finest restaurants hidden away in sleepy coastal hamlets, and a string of local producers specialising in organic, gourmet foods from mussels, soft cheeses and berry farms to olive groves and Belgian chocolate. Combine this with wineries, breweries and even a single-malt distillery, and it confirms this region's credibility as a top epicurean destination.

The coastline arches from Melbourne to Geelong before jutting around the Bellarine Peninsula and stretching its way to the Great Ocean Rd: this is where Country Victoria meets the sea, and local produce thrives here.

A number of food-themed itineraries have been launched to showcase the region's specialities, all easily combined into a weekend of indulgence. No food itinerary of Victoria would be complete, however, without first visiting the state's capital city, Melbourne. Home to a world-renowned gastronomic scene, where top chefs are household names, Melbourne has its finger on the pulse for the latest food trends. It can pull off anything, whether it be cutting-edge or homegrown specialities, as well as an impressive array of multicultural cuisine. Indigenous ingredients are increasingly common elements on menus, which has long been overdue. Melbourne has also earned a reputation among coffee aficionados as one the world's best cities for speciality beans. Grab a coffee to go and stroll Melbourne's art-filled laneways, 19th-century European-inspired arcades and grand Gold Rush–era architecture.

NEED TO KNOW
The Great Ocean Road is classic road-tripping territory: count on 2-3 hours behind the wheel each day.

01 Joon Wei Ooi © 500px

01 PROUD MARY

While Australia's claim to coffee fame may be the flat white, these days it's all about single origin. One of the best of Melbourne's many specialist roasters who've set up shop over the past few years is Proud Mary. In the industrial backstreets of Collingwood – one of inner-Melbourne's hippest suburbs – Proud Mary is passionate about its coffee. Directly sourcing its own green beans from farmers in Africa, Asia and the Americas, it has played a big role in Melbourne's third-wave coffee revolution, redefining how coffee is sourced, prepared and appreciated.

Knowledgeable baristas are briefed to inform, and are experts in pour-overs, siphons, aeropress, slow-drips and espresso. One interesting point of difference here is Proud Mary's nitrogen-charged cold brew on tap, produced by a beer brewer in 20L kegs. As well as coffee, it's popular for breakfasts and light meals, such as ricotta on sourdough or pork belly sandwiches.

For coffee tasting/appreciation head to its cellar door, Aunty Peg's, which hosts a variety of brewing classes, cupping and roasting sessions. *www.proudmarycoffee.com.au; tel +61 3 9417 1333; 172 Oxford St, Collingwood; 7am-4pm Mon-Fri, from 8am Sat & Sun*

02 CHARCOAL LANE

Spend mid-morning wandering hip Smith St and Fitzroy's Brunswick St before lunch on Gertrude St, a once rough-and-tumble strip, now gentrified and lined with boutiques. When people attempt to define Australian cuisine, most will inevitably focus on post-colonial British-influenced dishes. Charcoal Lane is on a mission to change this perception, with its menu dedicated to flavours from native Australian flora and fauna, the basis of what's been eaten by indigenous people for millennia.

The food here is a must for anyone interested in uniquely Australian flavours, with head chef Greg Hampton's background in botany invaluable in sourcing such ingredients as lemon myrtle, wattleseed, pepper leaf, sea parsley, strawberry gum, saltbush and coastal succulents.

The chef's tasting platter is highly recommended, allowing you to sample oysters speckled with caviar-like native finger lime or wattleseed-infused hummus. Delicious seasonal mains can include emu fillet with beetroot and lemon-myrtle risotto, Parma-ham wrapped wallaby or paperbark smoked veggies.

Charcoal Lane is a non-profit

01 An atmospheric
Melbourne laneway

02 Street art in hip
Collingwood

03 The smart interior
of Cumulus Inc

04 Melbourne at night

organisation run by Mission Australia, employing indigenous staff and cooks, and assisting local Aboriginal communities in Victoria. *www.charcoallane.com.au; tel +613 9418 3400; 36 Gertrude St, Fitzroy; noon-10.30pm Tue-Sat*

03 BAR AMERICANO

From Fitzroy, walk off lunch with a brisk half-hour stroll, or a short jaunt by tram, into the city's Central Business District (CBD) to hit Melbourne's laneways. Once grimy, seedy and rubbish-strewn no-go zones, these narrow alleys are now tourist attractions, decorated in street art and home to restaurants and bars.

Hidden down a nook off a laneway, finding the divey hole-in-the-wall Bar Americano is a challenge even for locals. An old-school dark-wood polished cocktail bar, it specialises in recipes lifted from vintage cocktail books dating from the early- to mid-20th century. This is an intimate affair, with only 10 people allowed in at any given time, giving it an air of exclusivity minus the pomp. Its low-key Italian theme is matched by the bar's signature Negroni, the perfect tipple for a pre-dinner apertif. *www.baramericano.com; tel +61 3 9939 1997; 20 Presgrave Pl, Melbourne CBD; 5pm-1am Mon-Sat*

04 CUMULUS INC

Wandering the laneways, you'll soon hit Flinders Lane, Melbourne's most fashionable street – home to the city's hottest restaurants. When you see the queues you'll know you've arrived at Cumulus Inc.

Long regarded as one of the city's best, Cumulus is run by Andrew McConnell, one of Melbourne's most respected chefs; everything he touches turns to gold and he has a number of critically acclaimed restaurants around town.

Grab a stool at the marble bar overlooking the open kitchen within this smart NYC-style industrial space. Start off with freshly shucked oysters and cured meats from its charcuterie. Seasonal mains are shared dishes, such as slow roasted lamb shoulder or a heaped bowl of charred yabbies (small freshwater crayfish) drizzled with aioli. It's also a very popular breakfast spot, known for its full English breakfast with slab bacon, blood sausage, smoked tomatoes and eggs. There's also a loft wine bar upstairs, Cumulus Up, that offers tasting plates. *www.cumulusinc.com.au; tel +61 3 9650 1445; 45 Flinders Ln; 7am-11pm Mon-Fri, 8am-11pm Sat & Sun*

05 JACK RABBIT

The next day leave Melbourne and head down the coast. A 1.5-hour drive from the big city, the Bellarine Peninsula is so impressive for its local produce and wine-growing industry that the community has its own Bellarine Taste Trail (www.thebellarinetastetrail.com.au) mapping the area's artisanal producers, local restaurants, wineries, provedores, cheesemakers, mussel farms, olive groves and berry farms.

One of the highlights is Jack Rabbit in Portarlington, a restaurant/winery with sublime 180-degree bay views. The House of Rabbit cafe is for more casual dining, where you can get a bowl of Portarlington mussels with fries, a grazing plate of Bellarine produce or Flying Brick–cider battered fish to go with its award-winning wine selection.

Its more upmarket restaurant also utilises local produce in more sophisticated dishes, such as local kingfish ceviche with squid ink mayo and duck breast with blueberries picked from nearby Tuckerberry Hill. All are matched superbly with Jack Rabbit's cool-climate shiraz, pinot noir and chardonnays.

Also try its Flying Brick cider, either here or at its nearby cider house (www.flyingbrickciderco.com.au) enjoyed on its grassy lawn. *www.jackrabbitvineyard.com.au; tel +61 3 5251 2223; 185 McAdams Ln, Bellarine; 10am-5pm Mon-Thu, to 11pm Fri, 9am-5pm Sat & Sun*

06 BRAE

Moving on from the Bellarine, you'll pass through the Surf Coast, including well-known surf spots Torquay and Bells Beach. Soon you'll officially be on the Great Ocean Rd, with its justly famous ocean views.

At Lorne take a turn-off into the Otway Ranges and head for the charming town of Birregurra, home to Brae – a bucket-list restaurant headed by maestro chef Dan Hunter, who moved here from one of Australia's most highly awarded restaurants (Royal Mail Hotel) in late 2013.

In a rural homestead on a 30-acre property surrounded by gum trees and grazing cattle, it's a scene of classic Australiana. The restaurant grows most of its own produce, with orchards of pistachio, mulberry trees and many vegetables, including crimson-flowered broad beans. The tasting menu comprises 16 dishes with distinct flavours that mix indigenous ingredients with Asian and European influences.

Like the Bellarine Peninsula, the Otways has put together its own taste trail (www.otwayharvesttrail.org.au), on which Brae is the star stop: once you're done here, hang around and check out other well-loved spots, such as the Forrest Brewing Company. *www.braerestaurant.com; tel +61 3 5236 2226; 4285 Cape Otway Rd, Birregurra; lunch from noon Mon-Fri, dinner from 6.30pm Thu-Sat*

07 TIMBOON RAILWAY SHED DISTILLERY

Synonymous with the Great Ocean Rd, the Twelve Apostles rock formations are the pin-up image for this stretch of coast but the area is also home to a host of small producers and another locally conceived food trail: the 12 Apostles Gourmet Trail (visit12apostles.com.au).

Along with cheese, chocolate and wine tastings or berry-picking, don't miss Timboon Railway Shed Distillery: part restaurant, part whisky distillery. Set within a designer corrugated-tin shed, its breakfast and lunch menus feature local produce such as Apostle Whey cheeses and Timboon Fine Ice Cream, and the restaurant serves inventive wood-fired pizzas.

A producer of single malts, its on-site whisky distillery is inspired by Timboon's 19th-century illegal bootlegging distilleries. The Shed continues the legacy, producing a very decent dram that's world class. *www.timboondistillery.com.au; tel +61 3 5598 3555; 1 Bailey St, Timboon; 10am-4.30pm Mon-Thu, to 11pm Fri, 9am-4.30pm Sat & Sun*

05-07 Beautiful Brae restaurant, started by star chef Dan Hunter

WHERE TO STAY

BROOKLYN ARTS HOTEL
Located in arty Fitzroy, close to many bars and restaurants, this family-run bohemian hotel attracts a hip crowd. Rooms are well priced and full of colour and character. *www.brooklynartshotel.com.au; tel +61 3 9419 9328; George St, Fitzroy*

ATHELSTANE HOUSE
This boutique guesthouse dates from 1860 and fits into historic Queenscliff's streetscape beautifully. It's a 15-minute drive from the wineries of the Bellarine Peninsula. *www.athelstane.com.au; tel +61 3 5258 1024; 4 Hobson St, Queenscliff*

BRAE
Designed by acclaimed Melbourne architects Six Degrees, Brae's on-site hotel has full eco-credentials. Guests are treated to a rustic breakfast using produce from the restaurant's garden and homebaked sourdough bread. There's also an in-room cocktail bar and record player with vinyls. *www.braerestaurant.com; tel +61 3 5236 2226; 4285 Cape Otway Rd, Birregurra*

WHAT TO DO

FEDERATION SQUARE
Melbourne's ultra-modern architectural landmark is the site of Ian Potter: NGV Australia, a gallery showing eminent Australian painters, including key indigenous artwork. There's a free daily tour of the site.

OTWAY ECO TOURS
Tucked away in the Otway Ranges in the tiny township of Forrest, join a canoe trip on Lake Elizabeth to spot platypus, or sign up for guided mountain-bike tours and walks. (www.otwayecotours.com.au)

CELEBRATIONS

MELBOURNE FOOD & WINE FESTIVAL
Held annually in March, this is the high point of Australia's foodie calendar when Melbourne – and the rest of the state – gets to show off its world-class food credentials. The festival features tastings, classes and themed dinners, drawing top chefs from Asia, Europe and the Americas. Book well in advance for pop-up dining events held by international chefs across town. (www.melbournefoodandwine.com.au)

The map shows locations labelled: PERTH, FREMANTLE (01), (02), (03), MANDURAH, INDIAN OCEAN, AUSTRALIA, BUNBURY (04), (05), EAGLE BAY (06), YALLINGUP, BUSSELTON, MARGARET RIVER (07)

Australia

A TASTE OF AUSTRALIA'S WILD WEST

Heading south from Perth, this remote region of southwestern Australia is a surprising foodie destination, thanks to a dedicated community of chefs and producers.

Isolated at the remote edge of Australia – state capital Perth is closer to Bali than it is to Sydney – Western Australia (WA) celebrates an independent and maverick spirit. Local chefs and food producers proudly support each other thousands of kilometres from the big cities of Australia's eastern seaboard, and a strong focus on organic and sustainable ingredients also imbues WA's restaurants and markets. Blend in the culinary influences of immigration and close proximity to Southeast Asia, and the region's food scene emerges as a vibrant and multicultural marvel.

To the north and east of Perth, the state's spectacular and singular red dirt landscapes soon emerge, but south from the city is very different. Towns and cities including Fremantle, Bunbury and Busselton hug the coast, local seafood is plentiful, and just a

few hours from Perth the Margaret River wine region combines a rural ambience and spectacular beaches with a sophisticated food scene.

Artisan food producers dot narrow country lanes fringed by grapevines, craft beer is emerging as an innovative challenger to Margaret River's stellar wine scene, and chefs showcase local meat, seafood and produce in stylish vineyard restaurants and relaxed cafes. Marron – a freshwater crayfish – is popular on menus during summer, and the restaurant at the Vasse Felix winery often showcases the local delicacy with custard apple and buckwheat.

And unlike other parts of the state – everything you've heard about Western Australia's massive size is definitely true – southwestern WA is a compact area that is ripe for road-trip exploration.

NEED TO KNOW
This is a 3-day roadtripping trail: be sure to end on a Saturday to catch the Margaret River Farmers Market.

01 WILDFLOWER

If you want to taste Western Australia, head directly to Wildflower. The serious fine diner, housed in glass atop the city's most elegant hotel, pays homage to indigenous culture by framing the menu around the six – not four - seasons observed by the Noongar people. Elegant use of on-trend bush herbs such as citrusy Geraldton Wax leaf, tart riberry and piquant saltbush justifies the hype over native ingredients like freshwater marron or smoked kangaroo. Sit on the open-air terrace, or inside on grey velvet chairs facing city and Swan River views. Choose from the a la carte menu, or break the bank with a wine-matched degustation.
www.wildflowerperth.com.au; tel +61 8 6168 7855; Level 4, State Buildings, 1 Cathedral Ave, Perth; 12pm-2.30pm Tue to Fri and 6pm-late; 6pm-late Sat.

02 BREAD IN COMMON

From Perth it's a 30-minute drive to Fremantle, a relaxed port town worth lingering in, with a well-preserved heritage precinct. Restaurants, cafes and pubs dot the historic townscape filled with Victorian and Edwardian architecture, and Bread in Common fills a high-ceilinged brick warehouse with a wood-fired bakery, shared tables, and one of Fremantle's longest bars.

Platters of house-made charcuterie and West Australian cheese are served with crunchy slabs of warm sourdough bread, and shared plates harnessing seasonal WA produce include chargrilled chicken with sweet potato and chilli, or octopus with black beans and cajun spices. Return the morning after for a fresh brioche and coffee.
www.breadincommon.com.au; tel +61 8 9336 1032; 43 Pakenham St, Fremantle; 9am-10pm

03 RAW KITCHEN

It's an easy walk through historic King's Sq to The Raw Kitchen. Reflecting Fremantle's bohemian vibe, vegan, organic and sustainable ingredients all punctuate the menu, served in yet another hip brick-lined space. Raw ingredients are harnessed – but not used exclusively – and gluten-free Billabong Pale Ale and biodynamic and organic wines are available.

Healthily virtuous dishes include pad thai using zucchini noodles, and a zesty yellow curry with quinoa and tempeh made of Margaret River lupins (a flowering Mediterranean legume). Leave room for dessert of refined-sugar-free salted caramel ice cream.
www.therawkitchen.com.au; tel +61 8 9433 4647; 181A High St, Fremantle; 11.30am-3.30pm Mon-Thu, to 9pm Fri-Sat

04 HAPPY WIFE

From Fremantle, it's a two-hour drive south to Bunbury. The redeveloped port area features restaurants, cafes and a microbrewery, and 2km east of Bunbury's historic centre, The Happy Wife has views of sleepy Leschenault Inlet, a relaxed Cape Cod-style interior and is one of Western Australia's best cafes for home baking – don't go past the macarons – while the lunch menu includes a hickory-smoked chicken salad.
www.thehappywife.com.au; tel +61 8 9721 7706; 98 Stirling Street, Bunbury; 6.30am-3.30pm Mon-Fri, 7.30am-2.30pm Sat

05 EAGLE BAY BREWING CO

The wine-making credentials of the Margaret River region are impeccable, but with more than six microbreweries the area is also developing a great craft beer scene. Eagle Bay Brewing Co, 78km southwest of Bunbury, combines rural and ocean views with a savvy selection of beers. Partner the refreshing Kölsch with squid and snapper tacos, and ask if Eagle Bay's seasonal Cacao Stout – crafted in conjunction with Margaret River chocolatiers Bahen & Co – is available.
www.eaglebaybrewery.com.au; tel +61 8 9755 3554; Eagle Bay Rd, Dunsborough; 11am-5pm

06 WILDWOOD VALLEY COTTAGES & COOKING SCHOOL

A pleasant 15km rural drive from Dunsborough, the final section of the journey through Wildwood Valley's bush-fringed 50 hectares often includes laid-back kangaroos sunning themselves beside the driveway. The big attraction for travelling foodies is cooking classes with Sioban and Carlo Balducci, whose CVs include Australia's highly regarded Longrain Thai restaurant, and cooking and living in Italy. Their wood-fired cooking classes – turning out fabulous pizza – take place around an alfresco traditional oven shaded by the towering trees. Booking ahead is highly recommended. Outside of the cooking school season, Wildwood Valley offers luxury cottage accommodation. *www.wildwoodvalley.com.au; tel +61 8 9755 2120; 1481 Wildwood Rd, Yallingup; Jan-Mar*

07 MARGARET RIVER FARMERS MARKET

Around 50 artisan producers gather at this Saturday morning farmers market on the fringes of Margaret River township. Kick off the day with great coffee and super-fresh baked goods from Yallingup Woodfired Bread. While you're here, stock up on Swiss-style cheese from Koonac Goat Farm and herb-crusted pastrami from The Farm House for a picnic on one of Margaret River's brilliant beaches. Also check out Lotus Blue, which sells fortifying chai blends using local wattleseed, an edible seed from the acacia tree traditionally eaten by indigenous Australians. Some of the stallholders can be visited around the region in the week, too. *www.margaretriverfarmersmarket. com.au; tel +61 8 9757 9095; Lot 272 Bussell Hwy, Margaret River; 8am-noon Sat*

01 Surfers Point, near Margaret River

02 Vines in Margaret River

03 Eagle Bay Brewing

WHERE TO STAY

HOUGOMONT HOTEL
In central Fremantle, this boutique hotel has a cosmopolitan ambience, and complimentary snacks and drinks every afternoon. The best of Fremantle's craft beer pubs are a short walk away. *www.hougoumonthotel. com; tel +61 8 6160 6800; 15 Bannister St, Fremantle*

BURNSIDE ORGANIC FARM
These earthy bungalows are the perfect rural retreat after a day exploring the wine and food attractions of Margaret River. Produce from Burnside's organic gardens can be used in the guest kitchens. *www.burnsideorganic farm.com.au; tel +61 8 9757 2139; 287 Burnside Rd, Margaret River*

WHAT TO DO

BUSSELTON JETTY
Originally built in 1865, Busselton's timber-piled jetty is now fully restored and it's a great 1.8km walk to the end. (www. busseltonjetty.com.au)

KOOMAL DREAMING
Join a tour with local Wardandi man Josh Whiteland to explore the Ngilgi Cave, or go bushwalking and learn about indigenous culture. (www. koomaldreaming.com.au)

CELEBRATIONS

MARGARET RIVER GOURMET ESCAPE
Rick Stein and Marco Pierre White are two of the international chefs that have attended this three-day foodie celebration in mid-November. (www. gourmetescape.com.au)

Courtesy of Eagle Bay Brewing

Brazil
SIZZLING SÃO PAULO

Brazil's largest city is carving its niche on the world culinary stage, but out on the streets it is Portuguese bakeries, Bahian soul food and unique Japazillian fusion that hold sway.

Monstrous São Paulo is the largest city in the Southern Hemisphere, which no doubt generates endless howls of complaints from the locals: The traffic! The noise! The pollution! But the one thing about which Paulistanos never utter a word in protest? The food.

Thanks to the rise of local chefs, such as Alex Atala (D.O.M.) and Helena Rizzo (Maní) – both represented on San Pellegrino's World's 50 Best Restaurants list – contemporary gourmet Brazilian cuisine is having a moment on the world's culinary stage. The city's smart bistros and gourmet restaurants have stamped São Paulo as one of few world-class Latin American food destinations; gourmands have taken note, and for good reason. *Sampa*, as São Paulo is known to locals, has gained worldwide attention as Brazil's high-gastronomy epicentre in recent years, but the city has a long history dedicated to simpler

01 © Moses Hallberg

NEED TO KNOW
Do this 3-day trail Saturday to Monday to make the most of São Paulo's weekend culture, fairs and markets.

culinary arts, jump-started by various waves of Japanese, Italian and Syrian/Lebanese immigration that have made Brazil's biggest city home to the largest immigrant populations in the world of these three gastronomically rich cultures. The tasty results are evident throughout the city's organic fairs, urban markets, Portuguese-style bakeries and small holes-in-the-wall that pepper nearly every kerbside around town. It's not unheard of to see as much culinary care going into a street snack such as *pastel* (a stuffed fried pastry said to originate when Japanese immigrants tweaked Chinese wontons), as any dish heralded on San Pellegrino's coveted list.

Eating in São Paulo is a daunting proposition: spread over a metro area of 1500 sq km, it offers more dining venues and eating options than most other cities in the world (11 have Michelin stars). In other words, you won't go hungry. In *Sampa*, the soup is always on.

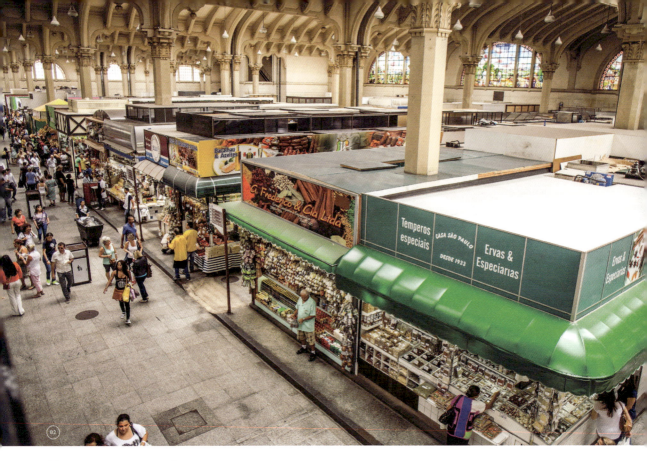

02 © Adam Hester

01 PADOCA DO MANÍ

While not known for a distinct breakfast cuisine, Brazilians take the most important meal of the day as seriously as anyone and that can only mean one thing: popping into a *padaria*. These hyper-bakeries are a cultural tradition originally imported from Portugal, but taken to an entirely new level in Brazil.

Some 3.2 million *padarias* dot the São Paulo cityscape, but not just any will do. Opened in 2015 and voted the city's best by local food bible *Veja Comer & Beber*, Helena Rizzo's Padoca do Maní in Pinheiros – the city's most recent up-and-coming foodie neighbourhood – offers an elevated start to your day. Like Brazilians, keep it simple: start your tour on Saturday morning with *pão na chapa* (grilled toast) and a *cafezinho* (espresso).

www.manimanioca.com.br; tel +55-11-2579-2410; Rua Joaquim Antunes 138, Pinheiros; 8am-7pm Tue-Fri, to 2pm Sat-Sun

02 FEIRA PACAEMBU

São Paulo street fairs are some of the best places to pick up produce, legumes, spices and other goodies direct from producers. One of the best and most traditional is the Feira Pacaembu (aka Sumare Moderno), a quick taxi ride 4km northeast of Pinheiros. Get there early and wander the lively stalls of exotic fruits, organic veggies and regional hot peppers, and throw yourself into the boisterous environment – worth a look-see in and of itself.

Need a snack? Head straight to Pastel de Maria, consistently awarded one of the city's best *pastels* (sweet or savoury stuffed pastries fried on the spot in large, drum-like fryers of soybean oil). Japanese immigrant Maria Kuniko Yonaha has frizzled these traditional 'Japazillian' street snacks for more than 35 years. *Carne* (minced beef with lime zest) is the most popular. Pair it with freshly crushed *caldo de cana* (sugar-cane juice), another ubiquitous street-fair must. *Praça Charles Miller, Pacaembu; from 7.30am Tue, Thu & Sat*

03 FEIJOADA DA LANA

Saturday lunch in Brazil means *feijoada*, as this is commonly the traditional day for serving the country's most coveted national dish. *Feijoada* is a bean stew of various salted beef and pork cuts seasoned with garlic, onions and bay leaves, served over rice alongside fried manioc, sautéed kale, orange slices and farofa (manioc flour).

century, giving the city one of the largest Italian populations in the world outside Italy and one of South America's best-kept culinary secrets.

Pizza Paulistana is as much a part of the city's cultural tapestry on Sundays as church and *futebol*. Perfect order: an appetiser of steaming *pão de calabresa* (sausage bread) dipped in spiced olive oil, followed by a Fosca pizza (smoked ham, catupiry cheese, mozzarella and tomato sauce), all washed down with a Brazilian Brahma lager *chope* (draft beer). *www.brazpizzaria.com.br; tel +55-11-3037-7973; Rua Vupabussu 271, Pinheiros; 6pm-midnight Sun-Thu, to 11.30pm Fri-Sat*

06 MERCADO MUNICIPAL

Begin your second morning strolling the senses-seizing aisles of São Paulo's Mercado Municipal, an architectural confection of stained glass and vast domes overseeing a bounty of fresh and colourful fruits, vegetables, spices, meats, poultry, seafood and gourmet goodies (a short walk from Luz metro station in Centro).

On weekends, it's a full-on foodie frenzy as locals and tourists alike comb more than 10,000 sq m of epicurean expanse, housed in one of the city's most stunning architectural gems, dating to 1933.

Food stalls and restaurants dot the space as well, with Bar do Mané drawing legions of followers for its take on the epic mortadella sandwich, one of São Paulo's most entrenched culinary legends – a skyscraper stack of pan-fried mortadella (an Italian cured sausage) and melted cheese between two slices of crusted *pão frances* (Brazil's beloved bread of the people). *www.oportaldomercadao.com.br; Rua da Cantareira 306, Centro São Paulo; 6am-6pm Mon-Sat, to 4pm Sun*

01 São Paulo, the mega city, by night

02 people eating and shopping inside of Mercado Municipal

03 Stained glass window at the cavernous Mercado Municipal

04 Pastel de bacalhau in Mercado Municipal

Though some restaurants serve individual portions at the table (*na cumbuca*, or 'in the bowl'), the more atmospheric choice is self-serve style, with up to 12 or so piping hot cauldrons of various cuts on offer.

Lana, a journalist by trade, offers her hugely popular version inside a smallish Vila Madalena house. In our humble opinion – and Anthony Bourdain's – it's the best *feijoada* for the buck in the city. Lana's place is 4km southwest of Pacaembu and best reached by a short taxi ride. *Rua Aspicuelta 421, Vila Madalena; tel +55-11-3034-4770; noon-3:30pm Tue-Fri, 12:30- 5pm Sat & Sun*

04 A QUEIJARIA

Stroll through bohemian Vila Madalena, the city's most foot-friendly neighbourhood. While you're there, pop in to meet the city's first

artisan cheesemonger, A Quejaria, just 400m northwest of Feijoada da Lana.

Brazil is not known for its cheeses (neither domestic nor imported), but this fabulous cornucopia of *quiejo* has flipped the script on that reputation. It features small-production artisanal and farmstead cheeses, mostly from Brazil's Minas Gerais and São Paulo states; and you'll often find the cheesemakers in-house, hawking their wares personally and shooting the cheese with customers. Time for a nap? Probably. *www.aqueijaria.com.br; tel +55-11-3812-6449; Rua Aspicuelta 5, Vila Madalena; 9am-8pm Mon-Sat*

05 BRÂZ PIZZERIA

End your evening back in Pinheiros by diving into the city's beloved pizza culture. Swarms of Italian immigrants settled in São Paulo in the late 19th

03 © Mechika / Alamy

04 Eli K Hayasaka © Getty Images

07 LAMEN KAZU

Sampa is home to the largest Japanese diaspora in the world and the bustling downtown neighbourhood of Liberdade is at its core, a short metro ride from Luz. The gritty *bairro* is still lined with traditional Japanese shops and eateries and is full of hidden Asian cultural gems. Praça da Liberdade hosts a vibrant market on weekends as well.

Tucked away down an uneventful side street is Lamen Kazu, the best of the city's traditional Japanese noodle shops and the perfect spot to immerse yourself in 'Japazillian' culture. Grab a spot at the counter, order up the Kara Misso Lamen (seasoned pork in a spicy broth with bamboo shoots, bean sprouts, seaweed, sesame and *kimuchi*) and relish Brazil's most interesting subculture, the result of a massive early-20th-century immigration to search for a better life on booming Brazilian farms and coffee plantations.
www.lamenkazu.com.br; tel +55-11-3208-6177; Rua Tomás Gonzaga 51, Liberdade; 11am-3pm & 6-10.30pm Mon-Sat, 11am-3pm & 6-9pm Sun

08 VELOSO

Take a stroll around Liberade after lunch before hopping back on the metro and heading a few stops to Ana Rosa station, from where it's a short walk to one of the city's best happy hours. If you want to sit, get to Veloso before it opens; otherwise it's a standing room-only street party.

The order at this trendy *boteco* (neighbourhood bar) is unarguable: a half-dozen *coxinhas* (battered and fried croquettes of shredded chicken, catupiry cheese and spices, served with Brazil's best house-made pepper sauce) chased by what are consistently the city's best caipirinhas (*jabuticaba*, starfruit and basil, or tangerine with *dedo-de-moça* pepper will do nicely).
www.velosobar.com.br; tel +55-11- 5572 0254; Rua Conceição Veloso 54, Vila Mariana; 5.30pm-12.30am Tue-Fri, from 12.45pm Sat, 4-10.30pm Sun

09 PATUÁ DE BAHIANA

Dinner tonight is one for the ages. It's meant to be a 'secret', but the experience at this underground restaurant inside the home of Bá, a Bahian legend, is just too priceless to omit.

You must call ahead and know someone who knows someone. If Bá takes a liking to you, she'll be the perfect host and treat you to a night of scrumptious specialities from the heavily African-influenced northern state of Bahia, her home turf.

She chooses what you eat, not you, but a typical menu will likely include some of the country's most delicious and iconic dishes, such as *acarajé* (black-eyed pea fritters stuffed with *vatapá*, a creamy paste of shrimp, peanuts, coconut milk and palm oil, and dried shrimp); *moqueca* (a fiery, coconut milk-based seafood stew); or *bobó de camarão* (shrimp in manioc sauce).

You'll remember this night for a long time to come.
www.facebook.com/patuadabaiana; +55-11-98312-5302; Rua Luis Barreto 74A; by reservation

⑩ RECEITARIA

Come Monday, it's time to learn how to recreate some of Brazil's food highlights for yourself. Receitaria cooking school offers all manner of culinary courses in Portuguese as well as a nearly four-hour basic intro to Brazilian cooking (in English).

You'll learn how to prepare some serious local staples, such as *coxinhas*, *bobó de camarão*, *brigadeiro* (a sickly-sweet chocolate truffle) and, of course, the country's most famous cocktail, the caipirinha.

Group classes run on Mondays every 15 days or so, while private classes are available if you making a booking in advance.
www.receitaria.com; tel +55-11-2892-0031; Rua Fradique Coutinho 600, Pinheiros

05 Street dining São Paulo-style

WHERE TO STAY

GUEST 607
With just six rooms, this playful guesthouse inside a converted two-storey townhouse is close to Rua Oscar Freire (Brazil's ritziest shopping street). It's also just around the corner from top *Sampa* restaurant Arturito, and has its own small bistro. Rooms aren't large, but the place packs in a lot of personality.
www.guest607.com.br; +55 11 3081-5030; Rua Lisboa 493, Pinheiros

HOTEL EMILIANO
São Paulo's most discerning boutique hotel occupies prime real estate in the city's upmarket neighbourhood, Jardins. Besides refined service and stylish trimmings, it throws a decadent, don't-miss weekend brunch that's a destination meal for locals.
www.emiliano.com.br; tel +55 11 3069 4369; 384 Rua Oscar Freire, Jardins

WHAT TO DO

SP FREE WALKING TOUR
This free tour condenses more than 450 years of *Sampa* history into a long but fascinating 'Old Downtown' walk, held three times a week at 11.30am. (www. spfreewalkingtour.com)

MOSTEIRO SÃO BENTO
Step inside this gorgeous monastery, dating to 1598, to view its impressive stained glass. Masses (7am weekdays, 6am on Saturday and 10am Sunday) include Gregorian chanting. There's a legendary, culturally rich brunch of local delicacies from top chefs, and cakes and breads from the monastery's own monks, held on the second and last Sunday of each month; book well in advance. (www.mosteiro.org.br; email brunchnomosteiro@ multiplaeventos.com.br)

CELEBRATIONS

During São Paulo Restaurant Week, more than 100 restaurants offer special menus and promotional prices for two weeks, twice a year in spring and autumn. (www. restaurantweek.com.br; check the website for annual dates)

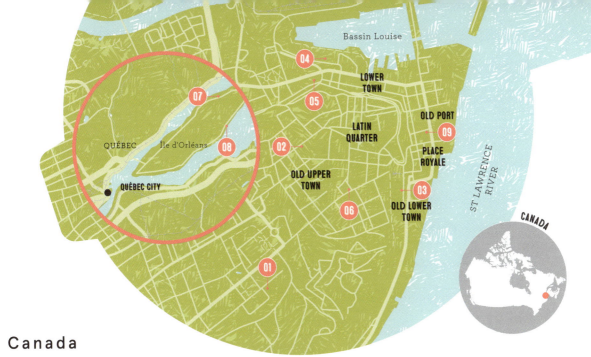

Bassin Louise

LOWER TOWN

04

05

LATIN QUARTER

OLD PORT

09

PLACE ROYALE

07

QUÉBEC   Île d'Orléans

08

02

ST LAWRENCE RIVER

03

OLD UPPER TOWN

OLD LOWER TOWN

QUÉBEC CITY

06

CANADA

01

Canada

COSY WINTER EATING IN FRENCH CANADA

Wild hunting flavours from fur-trading days form an unlikely alliance with French cuisine in Québec, best experienced in winter/spring when maple and carnival mayhem descend.

Few cultures on earth celebrate winter as whole heartedly as the French Canadians. When the thermometer plunges, the *Québécois* welcome the snow and ice with open arms – while taking refuge in hearty fare that offers a perfect antidote to the bone-numbing chill. Deeply rooted in French culture and completely distinct from the rest of Canada, the province of Québec proudly embraces its language and European heritage. Here, in the New World's largest francophone community, traditional French influences blend seamlessly with indigenous ingredients from the North American continent – wild game, smoked fish, wild berries and the ubiquitous maple syrup.

French traditions are especially strong in Québec City, the provincial capital. Dating back to 1608 and drenched in Old World atmosphere, the walled city of Vieux-Québec (Old Québec) is a Unesco-listed maze of

narrow cobbled streets, mansard-roofed houses and pretty parks overlooking the St Lawrence River. In winter, the city takes on an especially romantic air, with charmingly lit squares and a host of intimate restaurants, *boulangeries* (bakeries), *traiteurs* (French-style delis) and wine bars offering hints of Parisian panache.

French-Canadian cuisine derives not only from these refined French roots but also from the wild-sourced fare favoured by legendary *coureurs de bois* – the adventure-seeking fur traders who roamed Québec's backwoods in the early days, learning Native American skills for living off the land by hunting wild game and harvesting blueberries, cranberries and other native plants.

The best times to do this trail are February, during Québec City's winter carnival – the world's largest – or March/April during the annual maple sugaring season. It may be freezing, but hearty food will never be far away.

NEED TO KNOW
To visit Québec's sugar shacks on this 2-day trail, you'll need a car. Temperatures can hit −30°C in winter.

01 Vlad G @ Shutterstock

01 WINTER CARNIVAL

Nothing epitomises the Québécois' love of winter like Québec City's exuberant Winter Carnival. The city lets loose for 17 days every January or February, celebrating the joys of snow and ice. Bonhomme, the giant smiling snowman and official Carnival mascot, presides over the festivities in his ceremonial *tuque* (hat) and *ceinture fléchée* (waist sash), the same garb traditionally worn by Québec's *coureurs de bois* (fur traders).

Carnival-goers merrily stave off the sub-freezing temperatures with special winter treats sold at stands throughout the fairgrounds. Especially popular are *queues de castor* (beaver tails)—paddle-shaped mounds of yeasted fried dough topped with anything from cinnamon-sugar to Nutella or Grand Marnier. Heat-seeking revellers also indulge liberally in winter carnival's official drink: *caribou* – a fortified,

'Tire d'érable is Québec's tradition of making maple taffy by pouring hot maple syrup over snow, then rolling it onto wooden sticks'

hot spiced wine; buy it in glasses made of ice, or follow the locals' lead and pick up a *canne*, a hollow plastic cane festooned with Bonhomme's likeness, which can be filled with *caribou* at stands dotted around the fairgrounds – and used as a walking stick when your gait goes wobbly. *www.carnaval.qc.ca; Battlefields Park*

02 PAILLARD CAFÉ-BOULANGERIE

Before prowling the Old City's romantic snowy streets, stop in at this quintessential French-style *boulangerie-pâtisserie* (bakery). There's nothing like starting your

morning with a huge bowl of *café au lait* (milky coffee) or *chocolat chaud* (hot chocolate), accompanied by fresh-baked croissants, *chocolatines* (the same chocolate-filled pastries known as *pain au chocolat* in France) or *tentations* (luscious pastries loaded with local wild blueberries).

Afterwards, meander through the Upper Town to the iconic 19th-century Château Frontenac hotel, where you can enjoy an exhilarating toboggan ride before descending by funicular to the Lower Town. *www.paillard.ca; tel +1-418-692-1221; 1097 Rue St-Jean; 7am-9pm Sun-Thu, to 10pm Fri & Sat*

01 Snow fun with a view of Québec City's Chateau Frontenac

03 Dish preparation at Aux Anciens Canadiens restaurant

02 Rug up for Québec's Hôtel de Glace

04 One of Québec's ubiquitous sugar shacks

03 LE LAPIN SAUTÉ

Lapin (rabbit) plays a starring role at this cosy eatery near the foot of the funicular, in dishes such as rabbit cassoulet or rabbit-mushroom pie. Alternatively, consider indulging in French Canada's classic comfort food: poutine. Since its invention in the 1950s, this carb-loaded concoction of fried potatoes and cheese curds slathered in brown gravy has become as iconic to the *Québécois* as hamburgers to Americans.

Poutine is sold at humble *casse-croûtes* (roadside snack bars) throughout Québec province, and even at McDonald's, where it has already earned its own Twitter hashtag (#McPoutine, naturally)! The version sold at Le Lapin Sauté is more refined, with hormone-free rabbit from the Besnier Farm in nearby Beauce, top-quality cheddar curds from the city's venerable Fromagerie Perron, and a two-mustard sauce

replacing the usual beef gravy. *www.lapinsaute.com; tel +1-418-692-5325; 52 Rue du Petit-Champlain; 11am-10pm Mon-Fri, 9am-10pm Sat & Sun*

04 MARCHÉ DU VIEUX-PORT

Window-shop your way through the Rue St-Paul antiques district to this heaving covered market, where dozens of regional food and drink specialities are sold. Most vendors come from nearby Île d'Orléans, a 190-sq-km island in the St Lawrence River that's renowned for its farms, orchards and vineyards.

The local produce on offer includes blackcurrant wine, honey, smoked salmon, sausages, chocolates and maple products. You'll also find one of Québec's proudest homegrown innovations: *cidre de glace* (ice cider). Invented at orchards south of Montreal in the 1990s, it's made from apples that are allowed to stay on the

tree after the first frost, then pressed and cold-fermented for months. The taste is sweeter and more concentrated than regular hard cider.

Also don't miss La Fromagère, a shop that sells an impressive selection of Québécois cheeses, from Fromagerie du Presbytère's decadently creamy Laliberté to the Roquefort-like Bleu Bénédictin produced by the monks at Fromagerie Saint-Benoît-Du-Lac. *www.marchevieuxport.com; tel +1-418-692-2517; 160 Quai St André; 9am-6pm Mon-Fri, to 5pm Sat & Sun*

05 LÉGENDE

Offering a modern twist on *cuisine boreale* (cuisine of the far north), chef Frédéric Laplante's classy eatery manages to pull off the improbable, serving a predominately Québec-sourced menu even in midwinter. Ingredients drawn from the province's vast woodlands and offshore waters

include oysters, mackerel, Arctic char and elk carpaccio, complemented by obscure northern fruits, such as pembina (a sour red berry) and sea buckthorn, as well as root vegetables like celeriac and Jerusalem artichoke.

French mainstays including duck and foie gras also make an appearance, alongside artisanal Québécois cheeses and speciality ingredients, such as birch syrup, fiddlehead ferns and wild mushrooms. www.restaurantlegende.com; tel +1-418-614-2555; 255 Rue St-Paul; 5-10pm Sat-Tue, 11.30am-10pm Wed-Fri

06 AUX ANCIENS CANADIENS

The historic Jacquet House (built in 1676) is home to this well-worn tourist destination specialising in robust country cooking served by waitstaff in historic garb. It's an atmospheric spot to sample such traditional *Québécois* dishes as *tourtière* (a meat pie typically served at Christmas and New Year), bison in blueberry wine sauce, venison or wild caribou filet mignon.

The original 17th-century rooms have been left intact, creating several small, intimate dining spaces. www.auxancienscanadiens.qc.ca; tel +418-692-1627; 34 Rue St-Louis; noon-9.30pm

07 ÉRABLIÈRE BOILY

For a first-hand look at maple syrup production, head 35 minutes east of Québec City to this sugar maple farm near Île d'Orléans' eastern tip. Friendly owners Richard Boily and Nicole Gosselin lead visitors through the groves, showing how sap is collected in buckets and slowly boiled down to syrup (30 to 50 gallons of sap for each gallon of syrup). Free tastings of syrup and creamy maple butter are offered, and maple products are sold for half the price you'd spend in Québec City.

During peak sugaring season (March and April), try your hand at *tire d'érable*, Québec's tradition of making maple taffy by pouring hot, concentrated maple syrup over snow, then rolling the congealed syrup onto wooden sticks.

The tradition of tapping maples

dates back to the Native Americans, who collected sap in birch bark containers, discarding the ice that formed each night or boiling off the water with hot rocks until the remaining liquid yielded a high concentration of sugar; by the 18th-century, French explorers were already boiling sap in metal kettles, in a process that foreshadowed today's production techniques.

Nowadays, Québec is far and away the world's most important maple syrup producer: neighbouring Vermont, the United States' maple capital, produces only one tenth as much. www.erabliereiledorleans.qc.ca; tel +1-418-829-2874; 4739 Chemin Royal, Sainte-Famille, Île d'Orléans; 9.30am-5.30pm mid-Mar-Oct, by appointment rest of year

08 LA SUCRERIE BLOUIN

For another time-honoured Québécois experience, follow the main road 15 minutes southeast to the Blouin farm, picturesquely perched beside the St Lawrence River. For

countless generations, Québécois maple sugar makers have spent late winter days sitting, chatting and eating by the wood-stove as the newly running sap boils down into syrup.

This family operation is typical of the dozens of commercial *cabanes à sucre* (sugar shacks) around Québec City and Montreal that open their doors to visitors in March and April. Visiting a *cabane à sucre* is a festive affair where families sit at long tables, chowing down on a calorie-rich, all-you-can-eat menu of *oreilles de crisse* (deep-fried pork jowls), *pâté à la viande* (meat pie), *fèves au lard* (baked beans), oven-baked omelettes, pea soup, pancakes and maple-cured meats, all drenched in maple syrup.

At dessert time don't miss the classic *tarte au sucre*, a sweet, golden brown maple sugar pie. Afterwards, take a horse-drawn sleigh ride or dance to traditional fiddle and accordion music.
www.sucrerieblouin.com; tel +1-418-829-2587; 2967 Chemin Royale, St-Jean, Île d'Orléans; lunch & dinner daily by advance reservation Mar-Apr

09 PANACHE

Cap off your visit with a meal at this Québec City foodie institution, celebrated for its imaginative cuisine and top-notch service. Dinners and well-priced midday *tables d'hôte* (set menus) feature such locally sourced ingredients as maple-glazed halibut, Appalachian red deer with wild berry sauce and spit-roasted duck. The restaurant is set in a stone-walled 19th-century maritime warehouse, with rustic wood beams and a blazing fireplace.
www.saint-antoine.com/panache; tel +1-418-692-1022; 10 Rue St-Antoine; 7-10.30am, noon-2pm & 6-10pm daily

05 Québec City's winter carnival

06 Ahhh, maple sugar pie

WHERE TO STAY
HÔTEL DE GLACE
Québec City's famous Ice Hotel is like stepping into a wintry fairy tale. Nearly everything here – the desk and chandelier in the reception area, the sink in your bathroom, the bed – is made of ice. Guests sleep on frozen slabs draped in thick, cosy animal furs and sip drinks from glasses made of ice beside the roaring fireplace at the atmospheric in-house bar. *www.hoteldeglace-canada .com; tel +1-418-623-2888; 143 Rte Duchesnay, Jan-Mar*

AUBERGE SAINT-ANTOINE
One of Canada's finest hotels, this Old Town favourite offers phenomenal service and luxurious amenities. Plush, spacious rooms come with high-end linens and goose-down duvets, while the halls resemble an art gallery, filled with French colonial relics discovered during excavations to expand the hotel. Panache restaurant, a darling of Québec's fine-dining scene, is located next door. *www.saint-antoine.com; tel +1-418-692-2211; 8 Rue St-Antoine*

WHAT TO DO
Québec City's biggest attraction is its beautifully preserved Old Town. Perfect places for a picturesque stroll include the narrow, boutique-lined Rue du Petit-Champlain, the vast Terrasse Dufferin boardwalk with its magnificent St Lawrence River views, and the pretty Parc de l'Esplanade. Or hop aboard a horse-drawn *calèche* (old-fashioned carriage) and go clippety-clopping over the cobblestones, as your driver recounts tales of the city's rich history.

CELEBRATIONS
TOURNOI INTERNATIONAL DE HOCKEY PEE-WEE
For a uniquely *Québécois* cultural experience, visit in February during this extravagant ice hockey tournament, which brings together the best 11- and 12-year-old players from Canada, the United States and Europe for 12 days of skating and puck-slapping action. With more than 2000 participants and tens of thousands of spectators, it's the world's biggest youth ice hockey competition. (www. tournoipee-wee.qc.ca)

Chile

LIVING OFF THE LAND & SEA IN PATAGONIA

An isolated area for adventurers and hikers, Patagonia also has a fascinating food heritage from cowboys and early settlers that is being enhanced by new organic farming efforts.

01 Matt Munroe © Lonely Planet

Who hasn't noticed that aromas sharpen, appetites awaken and food tastes better far from the hum of civilisation? For places still defined by their landscape, far on the sidelines of global commerce, eating remains all about geography.

For Chilean Patagonia and Palena province within it, it's a geography of the extreme. Ferries and unpaved roads lead you through this narrow country hemmed between the emerald Andes and the blue Pacific. In the early 20th century it was settled by Chilean pioneers who took on near-total isolation in exchange for its fertile valleys and vast waterways. The tradition of fishing and small family farms continues, though adventure tourism – trekking, whitewater rafting, and fly-fishing – have become vital additions.

A hearty diet of potatoes, seafood, berries and lamb feeds this humble populace. On the coast, expect a heavy culinary influence from the island of Chiloé, with

NEED TO KNOW
Chilean Patagonia is accessed via the domestic airport at Chaitén; the tourist season is Nov-Mar.

fragrant seafood stews such as *paila marina* (a bit of everything) or *caldillo de congrio* (conger eel soup), a favorite of Chilean Nobel Prize-winning poet Pablo Neruda. Flame-roasted lamb comes from the many family farms strung along the hillsides.

Don't skip an invitation for *mate*, a bitter tea served in gourds. Popularised by Chilean ranch hands who found work in the large Argentine *estancias*; its ritual is one of friendship. Fried bread known as *sopapillas* is another influence of cowboy culture; a reminder of when pioneers lacked ovens.

The move in 2016 to turn Palena into Chile's first Provincia Agroecológica – a designated area of sustainable and organic agriculture – is reinvigorating local food culture. Spend four days hiking Parque Pumalín's wild temperate rainforest, rafting the world-class whitewater of the Futaleufú River, and taking in flavours as you go. Because here, eating is one more form of exploration.

CHILE

01 CALETA GONZALO

02

CHAITÉN

03

04

CHILE

ARGENTINA

06

05 FUTALEUFÚ

01 CAFÉ CALETA GONZALO

Start with breakfast at the Parque Pumalín cafe, an attractive lodge with stunning black-and-white nature photography and crackling fires on chilly mornings. The homemade *kuchen* is a German tradition brought to the region two centuries ago – these cakes are baked with local berries including *murta* (a tart red fruit). Hikers can order lunchboxes to go.
Caleta Gonzalo; 9am-10pm

02 COCINERÍAS COSTUMBRISTAS

Apron-clad *señoras* in tiny kitchens serve up piping-hot seafood empanadas, fish platters and shellfish stew in a shared dining hall here in Chaitén. Dense crowds form at lunchtime but that's exactly the moment to go. This women's co-operative started as a community job initiative to help empower local ladies, but early success showed just how important the food is to the local community. Home cooking is a highlight of the region. This is everywoman's food: piping hot and ultra-fresh, the perfect introduction to this spirited coastal town.
Tel +56-9-7574-1892; 8.30am-midnight; Portales 258, Chaitén

03 HUERTA FUNDO LAS LOMAS

This first-class holistic garden and greenhouse caters to the micro-economy of the region, which starts with eating local. Set up by Tompkins Conservation, the gardens help reduce the footprint of food consumed in the region, and bring healthier options to a remote area long dependent on infrequent shipments of non-perishables and focused on meat.

Residents contribute compost in exchange for fresh fruit, such as strawberries and blueberries, and such vegetables as lettuce, zucchini and tomatoes. The initiative also innovates with vermicompost (using earthworms to turn organic matter into high-quality compost), intensive cultivation and natural pest deterrents. The greenhouses themselves are constructed from recycled wood and materials.

Visitors can explore the garden and staff can explain some of the workings of the project. On Sundays in summer (December to March, 2pm-5pm), the project also supplies a farmers market at the El Amarillo Junta de Vecinos (community house) with cheese, cakes and produce for sale. An on-site teahouse and cafe featuring local produce is in the works for the future. It's on the main road out of Chaitén, 23km southeast. *www.tompkinsconservation.org; tel +56-65-220-3107; Carretera Austral km 23; 8am-6pm Mon-Sat*

04 PUMA VERDE

In the El Amarillo sector, Puma Verde is a park-run general store and gas station, but this is no 7-Eleven. On sale are organic and natural products developed by Parque Pumalín to promote sustainable agriculture. One of the must-tries is its organic honey, Pillán Organics. Renowned for its purity, it's dark and dense, with a distinctive caramel flavour from Ulmo trees native to the Valdivian rainforest in and around the park. Puma Verde is located 25km southeast of Chaitén. *www.parquepumalin.cl; Carretera Austral km 25; 10am-8.30pm*

05 LA CASA DE CAMPO

Barbecue is as sacred as Sunday in Patagonia. At a rustic homestead overlooking Lake Espolón, hosts Anibal and Elma serve it Patagonian-style – perfect for a leisurely lunch. Local lamb is butterflied and slow-cooked for hours over a wood fire, served with steaming potatoes, *pan amasado* (fresh rolls) and garden salad. These lingering countryside meals are the essence of the region and can't be missed. Stoke your appetite casting a line for trout.

The homestead is reached via a signposted dirt offshoot from the main road just before Futaleufú. *www.lagoespolon.cl; tel +56-9-7721-9239; Puerto Espolón; reserve ahead*

06 MARTÍN PESCADOR

Finally head to the mountain town of Futaleufú for a taste of the new Patagonia with a special dinner. Martín Pescador delivers a modern, organic take on regional delicacies – chef Tatiana Villablanca has been a driving force in this region's sustainable agriculture movement.

Traditional and local produce are fundamental to the seasonally changing menu. Think exquisite morel mushrooms gathered in the mountains in springtime, and rosehips that proliferate in the summer fields. The setting is a log-cabin *quincho* – a circular dining space. Sample the wild hare pasta, tender house greens and pancakes made with native blue potatoes. There's also a good wine selection and a 10-course tasting menu available on Sundays. *Tel +56-65-272-1279; Balmaceda 603, Futaleufú*

01 Grazing guanacos

04 Chilean gaucho

WHERE TO STAY

CALETA GONZALO CABAÑAS

Smart yet cosy, these irresistible shingled cabins overlook the fjord in Parque Pumalín. An adjacent restaurant provides healthy, home-cooked meals. It's at the ferry landing in Caleta Gonzalo, 55km north of Chaitén. *www.parquepumalin.cl; tel +56-65-225-0079*

LA ANTIGUA CASONA

Every polished detail of this refurbished settler's barn expresses the loving attention of its Italian and Chilean owners. For passers-by, there's an inviting cafe with a shaded terrace. It's on the east side of the plaza in Futaleufú. *Tel +56-65-272-1311; silvanobmw@gmail.com; Rodriguez 215, Futaleufú*

CARA DEL INDIO

With a spectacular riverfront setting, this adventure camp offers scenic camping and cabins in the countryside with a wood-burning sauna. It's 35km from the Carretera Austral turn-off. *www.caradelindio.cl; tel +56-02-1962-4240; road to Futaleufú, open Nov-April*

WHAT TO DO

PARQUE PUMALÍN

Whether you're walking through ancient Alerce forest, under waterfalls or to the puffing crater of Volcan Chaitén, this is one magnificent destination. It's a remarkable conservation project created by the late American Doug Tompkins, and among the largest private parks in the world. (www.parquepumalin.cl)

WHITEWATER RAFTING FUTALEUFÚ RIVER

Dubbed Futa or Fu, the aquamarine waters of Futaleufú River flow fast through Patagonia's lush forest and offer world-class whitewater rafting. Bio Bio Expeditions is an ecologically minded tour operator and pioneer in the region, offering descents down the river. (www.bbxrafting.com)

CELEBRATIONS

In early February, Fiesta Costumbrista takes over the town of Chaitén with live folk bands, and it's a good opportunity to taste regional foods. FutaFest in late February honours the mighty Futaleufú River with rafting, parties and general mayhem.

China

BEIJING IN THE FOOTSTEPS OF EMPERORS

Look beyond Beijing's modern skyscrapers and you'll find a staunchly traditional cuisine served in the hutongs, once reserved exclusively for emperors of the Forbidden City.

Big, brash and boisterous, Beijing makes headlines these days by flexing its political muscles as one of the world's dominant superpower cities, but it is also, let's not forget, an ancient citadel of some note, with a millennium's worth of history and as many Unesco World Heritage sites as most countries are able to boast in their entirety. Old temples, royal parks and the once-lavish courtyard homes of former aristocracy dot Beijing's narrow lanes – known as *hutong* – which criss-cross the more traditional parts of the city centre, while further afield, in Beijing's mountainous outskirts, scattered stretches of the majestic Great Wall snake their way across the landscape.

At the centre of it all is the Forbidden City, the world's largest surviving palace complex and the one-time home of 24 consecutive Chinese emperors, spanning two imperial dynasties. Perhaps unsurprisingly, these all-powerful emperors had a tendency to keep the best things for themselves, and food was no exception. Peking duck, the juiciest of roasted platters and now an institution in China, was once reserved exclusively for the imperial court – as were the kingdom's best sweets, snacks and loose-leaf teas. Fortunately, the long-guarded secrets of the royal kitchens eventually found their way out of the Forbidden City and onto the dinner tables of the masses.

True to its north-China roots, Beijing food is warming, fatty and filling, with meat featuring highly and generous amounts of garlic eclipsing the spicier flavours found in food further south. This heartiest of food trails will take you from little-known back-alley snack shops to the grandiose former hunting grounds of the imperial court, via a teahouse, a duck restaurant and more than 500 years of Chinese history.

NEED TO KNOW
This 2-day trail is designed to be done using Beijing's subway and then mainline train out to Chéngdé.

01 WEN YU CUSTARD SHOP

(Wényǔ Nǎilào Diàn, 文宇奶酪店,)
Custard drinks were a favourite with
emperors back in the day; certain
types were reserved exclusively for
the imperial court during the Qing
Dynasty (1644-1912) before eventually
becoming a sweet sensation among
ordinary Beijingers.

These days you can find plenty
of custard-drink specialists dotted
around the capital, but if the queues
at this place are anything to go by,
Wen Yu's creamy delights get local
taste buds salivating more than any.

Wen Yu's is half way along
Nanluoguxiang, an historic *hutong*
(narrow lane) which has become a
wildly popular market street. Join the
queue of thirsty punters who line up
before doors open at noon to get
your hands on the first batch of the
day, then continue your stroll south
along the lane, before turning right
onto equally historic Mao'er Hutong,

which leads towards Shichahai
subway station. En route, you'll pass
the former home of Wan Rong, at
No 37, who lived here before she
married China's last emperor, Pu Yi.
*Tel +86 10 6405 7621; 49
Nanluoguxiang, 南锣鼓巷49号;
noon-4pm*

02 LIQUN ROAST DUCK RESTAURANT

(Lìqún Kǎoyādiàn, 利群烤鸭店)
No dish represents Beijing's imperial
roots more strongly than Peking
Duck; a truly regal roast once
reserved for emperors (some
things are just too good to share),
but whose recipe was eventually

'Peking Duck was once reserved for emperors, but its recipe was eventually smuggled out of the Forbidden City by a royal chef'

smuggled out of the Forbidden
City by a royal chef. These days
Peking Duck restaurants tend to
be grand, overly lavish affairs, but
Liqun's is one of Beijing's most
intriguing duck restaurants, given its
down-to-earth surroundings and
back-alley location.

Tucked down the *hutong*
immediately southeast of Tian'anmen
Sq, this small, slightly run-down
courtyard restaurant, managed
by chef Zhang Liqun, greets you
with the mouth-watering sight of
rows of honey-glazed ducks glowing
in the ovens. These ducks are so in
demand you'll have to get someone
to call ahead to reserve you one

01 A hutong
street scene

02 Liqun's back-alley
Peking Duck restaurant

03 Traditional
moon cakes

04 Chinese tea-drinking
dates back 2000 years

in advance.
Liqun's is a subway ride from
Wen Yu's and then a 10-minute walk
from the station.
*Tel +86 10 6702 5681; 11 Beixiangfeng
Hutong, 北翔凤胡同11号; 10am-10pm)*

03 TIAN FU HAO

(Tiān Fú Hào, 天福号)
Wiggle through the *hútòng* to the
recently rebuilt, Qing-style shopping
street of Qianmen Dajie, where you'll
find this branch of Tian Fu Hao – a
much-celebrated braised pork
specialist that's been knocking out
delicious *jiàng zhǒuzi* (酱肘子; soy-
marinated braised pork knuckle) for
more than 250 years. The secret of its
success is its fabulously flavoursome
sauce – enriched through extra-long
braising – which won the royal seal of
approval from Empress Dowager Ci Xi
in the late 1800s.

This is a shop, rather than a
restaurant, but with clever use of

the electric kettle in your hotel
room, you can whip up your own,
restaurant-quality pork knuckle to
snack on between meals. Simply drop
the sealed packet into your kettle
and boil it for a few minutes before
emptying the cooked contents into a
bowl. Well, we can't all be waited on
like an emperor, can we?
*www.tianfuhao.com.cn; tel +86 10
6303 5726; 19 Qianmen Dajie, 前门
大街19号; 9am-7pm*

04 DAO XIANG CUN

(Dào Xiāng Cūn, 稻香村)
Though Western-style bakeries are
rising in popularity, none has yet
been able to generate the deep-
rooted fondness locals have for
Dao Xiang Cun, a Beijing pastry
store whose origins stretch back to
imperial times. The first Dao Xiang
Cun opened its doors in 1895, the
20th year of Emperor Guangxu, and
Beijingers have been going crazy for

its sweetmeat pastries ever since.
They're the perfect accompaniment
to Chinese tea and can be boxed
up to take away. Fillings to look
for include buttery Chinese date
(huángyóu zǎoní bǐng, 黄油枣泥饼),
honeydew melon (mìguā sū, 蜜瓜酥)
and fresh rose petal (xiānhuā méiguī
bǐng, 鲜花玫瑰饼). There are branches
all over town. This one is 100m from
Andingmen subway station.
*www.daoxiangcun.com; tel +86 10
6422 6368; 212 Andingmen Waidajie,
安定门外大街212号; 8am-5.30pm*

05 BELL TOWER TEAHOUSE

(Zhōnglóu Cháguǎn, 钟楼茶馆)
When it comes to tea, the Chinese
know their stuff. By the time the
world's second most popular drink
(after water) wound up on the silver
tea trays of the British aristocracy,
the Chinese had been drinking it for
almost 2000 years. Some teas were
so highly regarded by particular

03 LPavo Real © Alamy

04 Matt Munroe © Lonely Planet

emperors they were afforded the status of *gòng chá* (tribute tea) and offered to the imperial court as a form of tax payment. This little-known teahouse, secreted away on the ground floor of the city's historic Bell Tower, gives you the chance to sample numerous types of tea as part of a traditional tea ceremony.

Don't miss climbing the tower to see its 600-year-old, 63-tonne bell. The Bell Tower is a half-hour stroll through the *hutong* from Dao Xiang Cun. *Tel +86 10 6400 2452; Zhonglouwan Hutong, 钟楼湾胡同 ; 9am-4pm*

06 NAJIA XIAOGUAN

(Nājiā Xiǎoguǎn – Zhíwùyuán diàn, 那家小馆 — 植物园店)

As evening approaches it's time for a proper royal banquet. For this, head out to the edge of the city towards the Summer Palace, where the royal court used to retreat to escape Beijing's midsummer heat. Nestled beneath the cooling, tree-shaded slopes of the Fragrant Hills is Najia Xiaoguan; a former residence of the Na family, who once worked as court physicians and who, over time, inherited the secrets of the imperial kitchen.

Many of the dishes are so-called *yào shàn* (medicinal cuisine), which was traditionally served as a dietary staple for the Chinese royalty because of the health benefits associated with the various ingredients. You'll find thick Manchurian soups alongside deer tendons, honey-coated prawns and Chinese yams soaked in osmanthus-flower sauce; a feast truly fit for a king. The royal court used to travel out this way by boat, stopping off en route to lay tributes at the dozens of temples that once lined Beijing's canals; you'll have to take a taxi. *29 Xiangshan Yikesong, 香山一棵松 29号; +86 10 8259 8588; 10.30am-9.30pm)*

07 DA QING HUA

(Dà Qīng Huā, 大清花)

With your appetite whetted for imperial travel, there's only one place to head on day two: Chéngdé. Located four-and-a-half hours northeast of Beijing by train, this once-forested location was the royal hunting ground for the Manchu court and is now a low-key city dotted with temples.

Back in the 17th century, Emperor

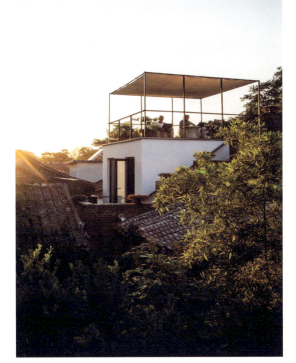

⑥

Kangxi had become accustomed to attending numerous Mongol dinner parties in the grasslands, and felt the need to receive these nomads in a proper imperial setting, so he ordered the creation of the Imperial Summer Residence (Bìshǔ Shānzhuāng, 避暑山庄) at Chéngdé.

Once you've seen its magnificent grounds, follow your nose to Da Qing Hua, a restaurant opposite the main entrance. Here you'll find a regal platter of wild-game 'Emperor Dishes' such as venison and pheasant, as well as some unusually colourful dumplings. Natural ingredients, such as carrot or spinach or tomato, are added as dough dyes to produce orange, green or red dumplings, as well as the standard flour-white variety. *Tel +86 314 203 6111; 21 Lizhengmen*

05 Beijing's Forbidden Palace

06 Roof terrace, the Orchid hotel

WHERE TO STAY

ORCHID

This delightful courtyard hotel in Beijing is within walking distance of Wen Yu's Custard Shop, the Bell Tower Teahouse and Dao Xiang Cun bakery. Rooms are cute and cosy, and come with modern shower rooms and Apple TV home-entertainment systems. The real draw though, is the roof terrace cafe area with distant views of the Drum and Bell Towers. *www.theorchidbeijing. com; tel +86 10 8404 4818; 65 Baochao Hutong,* 宝钞 胡同65号

MOUNTAIN VILLA HOTEL (SHĀNZHUĀNG BĪNGUǍN; 山庄宾馆)

Mountain Villa Hotel is opposite the main entrance to the Imperial Summer Residence in Chéngdé. Avoid the cheapest rooms: go for one of its 'standard' or 'deluxe' rooms, which are large, comfortable and carpeted, albeit not quite as luxurious as the resplendent lobby area promises. *Tel +86 314 209 5500; 11 Lizhengmen Dajie,* 丽正门大街11号

WHAT TO DO

Either before or after your visit to Li Qun Roast Duck or Tian Fu Hao, don't miss seeing the iconic Tian'anmen Sq, where in 1949 Chairman Mao proclaimed the birth of modern China, 40 years before the now infamous student protests in the square resulted in hundreds of civilians being killed by the Chinese military. Come evening, the *hutong* are dotted with cute back-alley bars. Try Jiang Hu (at 7 Dongmianhua Hutong, just off Nanluoguxiang) for some live-music action in a converted courtyard.

CELEBRATIONS

If you're here during any of China's major festivals, allow yourself plenty of extra queueing time at Dao Xiang Cun pastry store. Locals line up round the corner for moon cakes (during Mid-Autumn Festival), glutinous sweet dumplings (during the Lantern Festival) and sticky rice cakes (during the Dragon Boat Festival). Just beyond the pastry store is Ditan Park, which holds a huge temple fair during Chinese New Year.

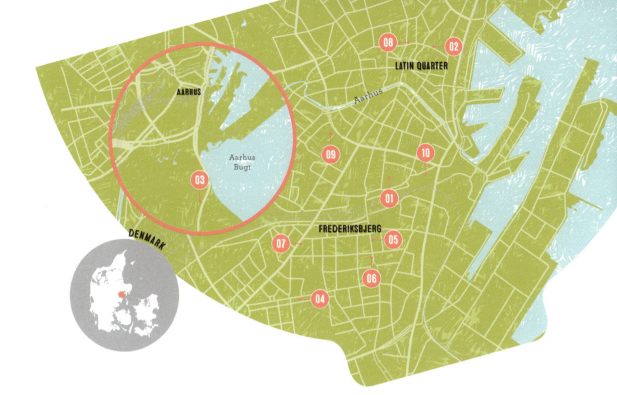

Denmark

THE RISE OF AARHUS

Denmark's second city is stepping out of Copenhagen's shadow and emerging as a quirky destination for hyper-local dining with a flair for turning tradition on its head.

Long labouring in Copenhagen's shadow, Viking-founded Aarhus on the Jutland peninsula is emerging as a European destination for city-breakers, festival-goers, art and food fans, and those looking beyond the capital-city conga. It's an ideal place to investigate how and why Denmark has gone from dowdy dining destination to full-blown culinary darling in little over a decade. Copenhagen steals the international headlines (on all fronts, not just food-related), but a recent charge by Aarhus, Denmark's second city of 320,000 people, is bearing fruit and it has been accruing some weighty accolades to shore up its appeal: in 2017 the spotlight shines upon Aarhus as European Capital of Culture and a European Region of Gastronomy (combined with broader central Denmark).

In the past few years, Aarhus has added loads of noteworthy attractions. On the food scene it's taking some of its cues from Copenhagen (wouldn't you, given the capital's stratospheric rise?), but it's also forging its own identity. There is a strong focus on invention in the kitchen, supported by excellent local produce. Aarhus' surrounds – the bay, the forests and the fields – provide a rich larder of hyper-local ingredients, from excellent pork, beef, game, dairy and seafood to root vegetables, wild berries and herbs. Organic farmers and orchardists are promoting their wares, supplying to an ever-increasing number of butchers, bakers, microbrewers and more. New markets and provedores are wooing the public with star ingredients and the produce of small-scale local operators.

In restaurant kitchens, New Nordic cuisine is heading in new directions, classic traditional recipes continue to be rediscovered and reinterpreted, and the resurgence of food culture continues. Move over, Copenhagen – it's time to share your spotlight.

NEED TO KNOW
Aarhus has a small international airport but Billund, 95km away, is a bigger hub. This 3-day trail is mostly walkable.

01 AARHUS CENTRAL FOODMARKET

One of Aarhus' shiny new accoutrements is the super-central Foodmarket. It's a revamped small square on the town's pedestrianised high street, which begins opposite the main train station and leads a meandering 850m to the 12th-century cathedral.

Inspired by Copenhagen's Torvehallerne, it is an ode to the fresh, the tasty and the artisanal, its stalls selling seasonal berries, smoked meats, seafood, cheeses and more. Roam, taste-test, chat with vendors, or enjoy a sit-down meal. Check if there are activities planned in the green-tinged outdoor area, which hosts seasonal concerts and open-air cinema.

www.aarhus-central-foodmarket. dk; Sankt Knuds Torv; open daily

02 HAUTE FRITURE

In the cobbled blocks north of Aarhus' central landmark cathedral you'll find plentiful pit stops. Snack time? Classic Danish street food is the *pølse* (hot dog), sold from ubiquitous carts. These cheap, mass-produced frankfurters are pretty standard: grilled and served in a bun with rudimentary toppings (pickles, crispy-fried onions, ketchup, mustard, remoulade).

Ripe for a gourmet makeover, the guys behind grill-bar Haute Friture have done just that. Their Asian-inspired 'hot duck' is a revelation: confit duck is fried in pastry (spring-roll style), then served on homemade bread with lashings of coriander, chilli and garlic. The Dogg1 (with a name inspired by Dokk1, Aarhus' showpiece harbourside development) is a French chipolata sausage accessorised with

a sharp, delicious relish of beetroot, horseradish and parsley.

www.facebook.com/hautefrituredk; tel +45 32140095; Graven 16; noon-8pm Sun-Thu, to 9pm Fri & Sat

03 RESTAURANT FREDERIKSHØJ

When serious gourmands spoke of Michelin's duty to cast its net beyond Copenhagen, this is the restaurant most had in mind. Michelin finally heeded the call, and in 2015 Frederikshøj got its first star; pundits believe two-star status is on the cards. Bookings are essential to experience the stylish restaurant's forested setting just outside the centre, and to savour the gastronomic wizardry of Beirut-born owner-chef (and TV personality) Wassim Hallal.

A variety of menus are offered, from three courses of long-

01 Herb and vegetables gardens on ARoS rooftop, beneath Your Rainbow Panorama walkway

02-03 Kähler Spisesalon

04-06 Frederikshøj – Aarhus' first Michelin-starred restaurant

Smørrebrød generally consists of a slice of rye bread topped, for example, with roast beef, tiny shrimp or a fish fillet, and finished with garnishes. The final, artfully sculpted products often look too good to eat. Kähler Spisesalon wins plaudits for its masterful modern spin on traditional *smørrebrød* – two or three *stykker* (slices) make a perfect lunch.

Standout toppings include salted cod with crushed potatoes, dressed with a salad of pink grapefruit and fennel, or chicken salad topped with pickled green tomatoes and vegetable crisps.

www.spisesalon.dk; tel +45 86122053; MP Bruuns Gade 33; 9am-10pm Mon-Sat, from 10am Sun

06 SOCIAL FOODIES

The Danish language has a number of shibboleths – words almost unpronounceable to non-Danes. A favourite is *flødeboller*, translated as 'cream balls' – these dome-shaped sugar bombs have a base of marzipan or wafer biscuit and a body of soft, velvety marshmallow, all coated in chocolate. They are a quintessential Danish treat, beloved of kids and adults.

You can buy them in cheap-and-cheerful multipacks in supermarkets, or head to a confectioner's for a handcrafted version (perhaps with a flavour injection, such as fruit, caramel or even liquorice). In social-media adjudications the *flødeboller* of Social Foodies were judged the finest in Copenhagen, and in 2016 the company opened a branch of its socially minded store in Frederiksbjerg.

Social Foodies is strongly committed to positive engagement with its suppliers in Africa, and supports a number of aid and environmental projects. Stop by for *flødeboller*,

established favourites to a 10-course extravaganza. Hallal transforms fine ingredients (local, but not exclusively so) into edible artworks, with a penchant for such high-end headliners as lobster, caviar, oysters and foie gras. *www.frederikshoj.com; tel +45 86142280; Oddervej 19-21; 6pm-midnight Wed-Sat*

04 INGERSLEV TORV PRODUCE MARKET

A fine way to kick off Saturday is with a stroll around the market anchoring the cool Frederiksbjerg neighbourhood. This pocket south of the train station brims with cafes, bars, food stores and boutiques. Ingerslev Torv is where small-scale producers congregate twice a week (year-round) to sell their wares: organic farm-fresh veggies, fresh and smoked fish, locally made cheeses,

freshly baked bread, and coffee carts doling out warmth on cool mornings. Spring sees the market at its photogenic best, with blooming daffodils and tulips alongside just-picked new potatoes and asparagus. *www.ingerslevtorv.dk; Ingerslevs Blvd; 8am-2pm Wed & Sat*

05 KÄHLER SPISESALON

When the raw ingredients have worked up your appetite, head here in Frederiksbjerg to experience Aarhus at its cosy best. The 'salon' charms with plants, lamps, vintage photographs and cute, colourful ceramics (made by Kähler, a 175-year-old ceramic company with its flagship store just a few doors down).

It puts on a fine weekend brunch buffet, but for out-of-towners it is a perfect place to sample *smørrebrød*, Denmark's famed open sandwiches.

handmade ice cream or fair-trade chocolate. Or sign up (in advance) for a *flødeboller*-making class. *www.socialfoodies.dk; tel +45 23637392; MP Bruuns Gade 60; 10am-8pm (til 10pm in summer)*

07 RESTAURANT HÆRVÆRK

Hærværk means 'vandalism', and this is one of Aarhus' new breed of creative spaces looking to challenge the establishment with new ideas. It's succeeding in its mission, if a Bib Gourmand gong is any measure of success. Bib Gourmands are awarded by Michelin to highlight restaurants offering star-quality food at reasonable prices, and Hærværk's five-course set menu for under €50 deserves the accolade.

The buzzing, industrial space in hip Frederiksbjerg is run by four friends (three are chefs) and wears its non-traditional approach as a badge of honour: its set menu changes from day to day – sometimes from table to table – and varies with the raw material available, sourced locally and preferably from small producers. Pay a premium to pair the food with wine and you've still scored a unique, top-flight meal without the hefty price tag. *www.restaurant-haervaerk.dk; tel +45 50512651; Frederiks Allé 105; 5.30-11pm Wed-Sat*

08 EMMERYS

In Denmark the sweet, sticky pastry known elsewhere in the world as a 'Danish pastry' is called *wienerbrød* ('Vienna bread', ironically). True to their collective sweet tooth, Danes often eat them for breakfast. Stop by Emmerys in the Latin Quarter to grab a coffee and some freshly baked morning treats. Shapes and flavourings are numerous and range from circular *spandauer*, with a custard or jam filling in the centre, to pretzel-like *kringle* topped with icing and chopped nuts. But it's hard to go past a good *kanelsnegl* (cinnamon snail) drizzled with chocolate.

Emmerys was the city's first modern-style cafe-bakery-deli and its success saw it grow to become a chain; it's also known for its all-organic bread (Danes take bread – especially *rugbrød*, or rye bread – very seriously). *www.emmerys.dk; tel +45 51857697; Guldsmedgade 24; 7am-7pm Mon-Fri, to 6pm Sat, to 5pm Sun*

09 AROS FOOD HALL

While out exploring it's hard not to have your head turned by a rainbow-hued walkway atop a large red cubist building. This is ARoS, the city's magnificent art museum; pay a visit and you can combine cultural sustenance with a stop by ARoS' top-floor lunch restaurant.

Provenance is everything at ARoS Food Hall, where the menu of small dishes utilises produce from the museum's rooftop kitchen gardens and beehive, and 90% of the meat comes from Troldgaarden, a nearby organic farm (a maturation cabinet for the meat is on display). The menu lists some 18 dishes divided into herbs, sea, garden, smoker, meat, bees and art, with some dishes taking their cue from artworks on display downstairs. *www.aros.dk; tel +45 87306650; ARoS Allé 2; 10.30am-3pm Tue-Sun, also dinner Wed & Thu*

10 FOLKETS SPISEHUS

Few fine-dining restaurants are open on Sundays, making this the perfect time to chill out over casual eats and drinks. Make a beeline for another new addition to the local scene: the permanent, indoor street food market by Aarhus' bus station, inspired by such places as Copenhagen Street Food and London's Borough Market. The formula seems clear: take a disused industrial space, pack it with food trucks and stalls, hipster baristas and a chilled-out bar or two, and voila.

The emphasis is on fresh, affordable food, and flavours span the globe – you can dine on Thai noodles, French crêpes or spicy tacos here. Portions aren't huge (all the better for sampling from a number of vendors) but quality is high. *www.facebook.com/folketsspisehus; Ny Banegårdsgade 46; daily*

07 Fishing boats, Aarhus harbour

WHERE TO STAY

HOTEL GULDSMEDEN
In a plum Latin Quarter location, this boutique base has organic breakfasts, bikes for rent and a cool courtyard garden. *www.hotelguldsmeden. com; tel +45 86 13 45 50; Guldsmedgade 40*

VILLA PROVENCE
This small, chic hotel has a pronounced French accent, from the movie posters to the bed linen to the wine list. Its loveliest feature is the cobbled courtyard, full of flowering blooms and fairy lights. *www.villaprovence.dk; Fredens Torv 12; tel +45 8618 2400*

CITY HOTEL OASIA
Handy for the restaurants of Frederiksbjerg, Oasia is streamlined and modern, showcasing fine Nordic design. *www.Hoteloasia.Com; tel +45 87323715; Kriegersvej 27*

WHAT TO DO

Danish cities are primed for two-wheeled exploration, so rent a bike and cruise the cycle lanes with the locals. Aarhus' reinvigorated harbourfront shows off fabulous new public spaces such as Dokk1 (home to Scandinavia's largest library) as well as show-stopping apartment developments best exemplified by the photogenic Iceberg. ARoS captivates with a multicoloured rooftop walkway known as Your Rainbow Panorama.

CELEBRATIONS

FOOD FESTIVAL
Wrapping up the 10-day Aarhus Festival (the city's biggest annual party), this tasty weekend in September celebrates Nordic produce and innovation. There are tastings, workshops, activities, and a showdown to claim the title of the year's best hot dog (www.foodfestival.dk).

VIKING MOOT
The 'moot' is a meet, where the Viking era springs to life over a weekend in late July. Costumed folks? Check. Craftsmanship and authentic food such as spit-roasted meats and mead? Absolutely. Warrior and cavalry displays? Oh yes! (www.moesgaard.dk)

England
REVIVING OLD LONDON

London may be a truly multicultural world city, but engrained in the big smoke there's still a class of traditional cafes and bars that have one foot stuck firmly in the past.

London has always fancied itself at the cutting edge of everything – fashion, music, art, you name it – and Londoners have exactly the same attitude to food. If it's trendy, innovative and never-been-seen-on-a-plate-before, Londoners will queue around the block to eat it. But we want to turn back the clock to an older, more innocent time, before all the molecular gastronomy and breakfast cereal cafes. Because there's another side to foodie London, based on the simple, home-grown flavours that saw the city through two world wars and one sexual revolution.

For the longest time, English food was the butt of continental jokes, for its reliance on rudimentary ingredients and pretty much two dishes – roast beef and fish and chips. This was, however, always a little unfair. English cuisine was hobbled by the forced austerity

NEED TO KNOW
London is serviced by 5 airports. Once in the city centre, use the tube and your two feet for this 2-day trail.

of WWII, when many ingredients vanished completely from menus, thanks to blockades at sea and a generation of farmers going away to war. Luckily, a new generation of London cooks are reviving vanished ingredients and ways of cooking that haven't been seen since the time of Charles Dickens and Oliver Twist.

Of course, some dishes never really went away. London was home to the first ever fish and chip shop, and the fillets are still frying 150 years later. And East Enders are still slurping down pies and eels, just as they did when Britannia ruled the waves, despite the influx of Hoxton hipsters. We shouldn't be too hard on the hipsters though – the revival of vanished London traditions like sipping artisan gin is largely thanks to the hipster love affair with all things Victorian. This trail starts in their favourite 'hood, inner East London, and then heads into pockets of central south and west areas.

'Pie is an institution borne of necessity – the East End's slum inhabitants needed cheap fast food to fill their bellies'

(02)

01 E PELLICI

Give a Brit a choice of breakfasts and you won't find many who choose orange juice and a croissant. The Full English – an epic fried breakfast of bacon, sausage, egg and a host of side orders – is a national institution, to the lament of cardiologists across the country. Everyone has their own favourite line-up (black pudding, fried tomato, mushrooms, chips, baked beans, you name it) and it's the favourite follow-up to an evening of excess the night before.

By a quirk of 20th-century immigration, many of the 'greasy spoon' cafes that serve this quintessentially English breakfast are actually run by Italians, which has the added bonus of ensuring a decent cappuccino on the side. Set within easy striking distance of hip Hoxton and Columbia Road Flower Market, E

Pellici has been run by the same Italian family since 1900 and its charmingly nostalgic art deco interior is Grade II listed. Behind the chromed frontage you'll find the Full English in all its glory, served at Formica tables with a healthy side serving of cheeky banter. *Tel +44 20 7739 4873; 7am-4pm; 332 Bethnal Green Rd, E2*

02 F COOKE

Having indulged in an English breakfast, it pays to burn off a few calories exploring the eastern fringes of the City, browsing for funky junk and retro fashions in Spitalfields Market and along Brick Lane. Your lunchtime destination, though, is north of the hipster hang-outs, tucked away in the authentically East End Hoxton Market.

Behind an old-fashioned shopfront, F Cooke has been serving

old-fashioned pie and mash to generations of proper East Enders. This classic dish is an institution borne of necessity – the inhabitants of the slum tenements of the East End needed cheap, fast food to fill their bellies, and pies filled with minced-up beef, made from flavoursome off-cuts, fit the bill perfectly.

The other magic ingredient was eels, originally yanked wriggling from the Thames (though now, sadly, almost extinct; the eels are imported these days), whose boiled down jelly forms the basis for the parsley-flavoured 'liquor' poured generously over pies and mashed potatoes.

Today, F Cooke is one of a dying breed, but the pie and mash still attracts a loyal local following. *Tel + 44 20 7729 7718; 150 Hoxton St, N1; 10am-7pm Mon-Sat*

01 Old juxtaposed with new in London's East End

02 Sipsmith

03 Borough Market

04 A Borough Market vendor

03 ST JOHN

For supper, head back into the City to Smithfield Market, London's bustling wholesale meat market, where one of London's most carnivorous restaurants has been reacquainting Londoners with the wriggly bits found alongside their favourite cuts of meat. Nose-to-tail eating is the motto at St John Smithfield, and yep, that means offal, in all its fascinating and flavoursome guises.

Housed in a vintage smokehouse, St John celebrates the visceral tastiness of meat, from roasted bone marrow to fried pig skin, heart and kidneys. We concede that it's a little gory, but the menu is a fascinating window back in time to the days before meat came in sanitised supermarket packets. St John has become an established stop for London food lovers, so expect upmarket food at upmarket prices, but its meaty ingredients are spectacularly fresh, having travelled just a few metres across Charterhouse St from Smithfield Market. *www.stjohngroup.uk.com; tel +44 20 7251 0848; 26 St John St, EC1; noon-3pm & 6-11pm Mon-Fri, 6-11pm Sat, 12.30-4pm Sun*

04 MONMOUTH COFFEE

After the fried excesses of the preceding day, start day two the right way with a wholesome breakfast of hot coffee and buttered toast. Although London first caught the coffee bug way back in the 1700s, Monmouth Coffee was one of the pioneers of Britain's 20th-century coffee renaissance, and it has been roasting coffee from small producers for nearly 40 years, though it's only recently that good coffee went mainstream in London. Covent Garden's Monmouth St was the company's first premises, but its Borough Market location is the perfect place to start a morning of foodie browsing and sampling.

As well as espresso-based beverages prepared using the house beans, the breakfast menu runs to flaky pastries and thumb-thick slices of artisan bread, topped with butter and marmalade. This is just the kind of light breakfast you need, considering you'll spend the next few hours sampling cheeses, olives and charcuterie. *www.monmouthcoffee.co.uk; tel +44 20 7232 3010; 2 Park St, Borough Market, SE1; 7.30am-6pm Mon-Sat*

05 BOROUGH MARKET

Suitably fired up with toast and coffee, you'll be ready to hop across the street and dive into the maze-like precincts of Borough Market. Today,

this is the centre of the world for London's 'urban peasants' who love everything wholesome, rare breed, artisan and organic.

The market has a history dating back to at least 1276 but it was only in the 1990s that the market made the leap from bog-standard fruit and veg mart to gourmet phenomenon. These days, you'll find stalls piled high with meats from rare breeds, artisan olives, apples in every colour under the sun and more wheels of cheese than a convoy of delivery trucks from Cheddar Gorge. Many stalls will let you sample before you buy. *www.boroughmarket.org.uk; tel +44 20 7407 1002; 8 Southwark St, SE1; lunch only Mon & Tues, full market 10am-5pm Wed & Thurs, to 6pm Fri, 8am-5pm Sat*

06 GOLDEN HIND

Fish and chips has an oft forgotten history in London. It was here in the capital, in the 1860s, that a Jewish migrant named Joseph Malin opened the first fish and chip shop in Britain, introducing the nation to its national dish. Blindingly simple in concept, fish and chips is just deep-fried chipped potatoes and fillets of fish, traditionally cod from the North Sea, fried in beer-based batter, typically served with lurid green mushy peas (marrowfat peas, allowed to mature in the field, then boiled down with sugar and salt).

Our favourite fish and chip shop is the Golden Hind – an unexpectedly down-to-earth find on swanky Marylebone Lane in the West End. Despite the location, you won't pay through the gills for an old-fashioned

platter of haddock – now used instead of cod, which has been severely over-fished – in fantastically crispy and grease-free batter, with a mound of chips and a lake of mushy peas. *Tel +44 20 7486 3644; 73 Marylebone Ln, W1; noon-3pm & 6pm-10pm Mon-Fri, 6-10pm Sat*

07 SIPSMITH

When William Hogarth etched his famous *Gin Lane* in the 18th century, satirising the debauched life of London's impoverished alcoholics, he could never have imagined that gin would be transformed from the comfort of the masses into the favourite quaff of London's affluent. In 2009, Sipsmith Distillery was granted the first new distillers' licence in 200 years, bringing the authentic taste of

London gin to a whole new generation and starting a craze for boutique micro-distilleries and gin bars.

The Sipsmith experience started, in true hipster style, in a garage in Shepherd's Bush, but it now has its own dedicated premises in the upmarket western enclave of Chiswick, where gin buffs can see the process from start to finish on distiller-led tours, and sample the produce of its three gleaming stills in a Victorian chemistry lab-like bar. Produced in small batches, the house gins are a homage to old London in a glass, infused with hints of juniper, sloe berries, tea leaves and herbs. www.sipsmith.com; tel +44 20 8747 0753; The Distillery, 83 Cranbrook Rd, W4; distillery tours 6.30-8pm Mon-Wed

05 Preparing eels for pie & mash at F Cooke

06 Brick Lane

07 Nose-to-tail dining at St John

07 © The Washington Post. 06 Eddy Galeotti © Getty Images

WHERE TO STAY

HOXTON HOTEL
A hotel for the hipster generation, with boutique rooms at budget prices and a great Hoxton location close to the East End. There's even a morning delivery of granola! thehoxton.com; tel +44 20 7550 1000; 81 Great Eastern St, EC2

CITIZEN M
Tech-heads will love Citizen M, where everything is controlled by tablet. Expect cool lounges full of designer furniture, sleek bedrooms and enough tech to satisfy the most demanding gadget lover. www.citizenm.com; tel +44 20 3519 1680; 20 Lavington St, SE1

BROWN'S HOTEL
At London's oldest hotel, you get five stars and 180 years of history, all in a stunning location within penny-rolling distance of Piccadilly and the Royal Academy of Arts in London's prestigious West End. www.roccofortehotels. com/hotels-and-resorts/ browns-hotel; tel +44 20 7493 6020; Albemarle St, W1

WHAT TO DO
The British capital has some of the world's finest museums and galleries: try the British Museum, Natural History Museum, Science Museum, Victoria & Albert Museum, National Gallery and Tate Modern. It also has some of the world's most famous monuments, the Tower of London and Houses of Parliament take centre stage, but St Paul's and Westminster Abbey are close behind. When you need a breather, head to the parks. An impressive 47% of London is given over to open green spaces, from sprawling Hyde Park to beloved local suburban hang-outs, such as Hampstead Heath and Richmond Park.

CELEBRATIONS
The Notting Hill Carnival is a bona fide phenomenon, with riotous Caribbean costumes, bombastic sound systems and abundant jerk chicken attracting more than 1 million people a year, and the buzz is similarly lively (though more intimate) at Field Day (up-and-coming bands), Lovebox (dance music) and Born & Bred (beats, roots and grime).

01

ATLANTIC
OCEAN

03 ◦ SELWORTHY   CHEDDAR ◦

◦ BARNSTAPLE   01

◦ KNOWSTONE   02
04   ◦ SOUTH
      PETHERTON

08   ◦ EXETER
      ◦ EXMOUTH
PADSTOW ◦   10
07 ◦ BODMIN   BUCKFASTLEIGH   ◦ TORQUAY
    MOOR   ◦ BRIXHAM
    ◦ PLYMOUTH   05   06
TRURO ◦   09

ENGLAND

England
A SEAFOOD & CIDER CRAWL

England's bucolic southwest, encapsulating Somerset, Devon and Cornwall, has many claims to foodie fame, and local kitchens and cafes like to keep nature close to heart.

The gangly green peninsula of Southwest England has long been a bastion of rural bliss. It hoards the country's most conducive climate for agriculture, a stunning coastline and an array of moors and wetlands that have conspired to keep it cut off from the rest of Britain – and with some singular foodie traditions intact. Here, much of the UK's dairy herd is reared, and apples hang ruddy in the orchards. Much-prized fare from the seas has been catching the eyes of such celebrity chefs as Rick Stein since the 1970s.

The fertile grazing land translates onto the plate in the form of phenomenal cheeses, including world-famous Cheddar. The orchards have long supported the greatest and most eclectic cider making industry in the world, with the Somerset region having England's best terroir for cider apple cultivation. Brixham, near Torquay, is the most significant fishing port in England and Wales in

terms of catch landed, and some of the country's best seafood restaurants festoon the shores here.

But the Southwest's unique culinary zenith is best epitomised in an afternoon snack: the cream tea. Partaking of just-baked scones slathered in locally made jam and the region's famous clotted cream, washed down by tea, in one of the many idyllic tea gardens hereabouts is a not-to-be-missed experience. In so doing, you'll be continuing a tradition harking back almost a millennium: monks in Tavistock Abbey were allegedly wolfing down bread with jam and cream as early as the 11th century.

And perhaps therein lies this area's greatest appeal. It's about placement just as much as product: sitting down to dine on organic food just plucked from the undulating fields behind the farm restaurant; tucking into lobster as the waves of a fairy-tale cove crash outside.

01 Myles New © Lonely Planet

NEED TO KNOW
Bristol is the nearest airport to Cheddar, the start of this 3-day trail. The Southwest is great driving terrain.

01 CHEDDAR GORGE CHEESE COMPANY

The village of Cheddar is renowned for two things: its spectacular gorge scenery and its cheese. Cheddar cheese has been produced here for over eight centuries, traditionally matured in the nearby caves to perfect its strong, rich taste: King Charles I numbered among the eager customers who ordered cheese direct from Cheddar.

Stipulations of true cheddar cheese are that it is made from the milk of cows grazing in the area's pastures, and with every part of the process carried out by hand. This outfit is the only cheese-makers left in the village, thus flying the flag for Cheddar-made cheddar all by itself. Visitors can watch the whole cheddar production process (cheddaring) unfold at the factory, then decamp to the taster bar where samples of the company's cheeses await.

www.cheddargorgecheeseco.co.uk; tel +44 1934 742810; The Cliffs, Cheddar, Somerset; 10am–4pm

02 SOMERSET CIDER BRANDY COMPANY

From Cheddar, it's a 25-mile sojourn south to Burrow Hill and the Somerset Cider Brandy Company. There are three cider apple terroirs – optimum conditions for growing the fruit – in England, and all three are in Somerset. This distillery sits plum in the middle of one, on the slopes of photogenic Burrow Hill, with panoramic views over the plains of the Somerset Levels.

One hundred and fifty years of cider production have elapsed at this award-winning artisan enterprise, where you can meander on a guided orchard trail, check out the cider stills and purchase take-home bottles in an atmospheric shop bedecked with old cider-making apparatus. Rustically quaint it appears, but ciders from here have graced the world's best restaurants.

www.ciderbrandy.co.uk; tel +44-1460-240782; Burrow Hill, Stembridge, Martock, Somerset; 9am–5.30pm Mon-Sat

03 PERIWINKLE TEAROOMS

An enthralling vista of purple-brown Exmoor moorland looms out at customers as they follow a corkscrewing path through the thatched cottages of this 19th-century model village to Somerset's loveliest garden tearoom, 44 miles northwest of your last stop, dishing up one of the Southwest's finest cream teas. Go for whortleberry jam with the saucer-sized scones: the juicy berry is an Exmoor speciality, not found in such abundance in many other locales in Britain.

www.nationaltrust.org.uk/holnicote-estate; Selworthy Green, Selworthy, Somerset; 10.30am–5pm late Mar-Oct

04 MASON'S ARMS

The countryside tavern is the de facto dinner stop across the region, but this 13th-century thatched, oak-beamed watering hole stands out from a character-rich bunch, as it now sports a Michelin-starred restaurant with frescoed ceiling. Partake of the gourmet Somerset and Devon goodies on the menu or grab one of its picnic hampers (order 48 hours in advance) and hit the hills of Exmoor, which rear up outside.
www.masonsarmsdevon.co.uk; tel +44 1398 341231; Knowstone, Devon; noon-2.30pm & 6-11pm Tue-Sat, noon-2.30pm Sun

05 RIVERFORD FIELD KITCHEN

An hour and a half's drive south, Riverford made its name delivering organic fruit and veg boxes around the UK, but here in Devon it also operates a wonderful restaurant sequestered up a sleepy farm lane. Ensconced in rolling fields chock-a-block with its fabled produce is this airy pine-furnished farmhouse kitchen. Here, straight-from-the-soil staples such as griddled butternut squash with walnut and blue cheese, or celeriac, onion and white bean pie, celebrate the Southwest's diverse homegrown delights. Guests can factor in a 1.5-hour audio tour of the farm, too (wellies provided).
www.riverford.co.uk; tel +44 1803 762074; Wash Farm, Buckfastleigh, Devon; lunch 1pm daily, dinner 7.30pm most evenings

06 BRIXHAM FISH MARKET

40 different types of fish are landed and auctioned off every day at nearby Brixham Quay, the most important fishing port in England and Wales. Getting a gander at good old-fashioned commercial haggling over everything from hake to scallops, before the rest of town awakes, is surely the region's most authentic seaside experience. Brixham Trawler Agents host tours, which are necessary to go behind the scenes, winding up at the Fisherman's Mission for breakfast.
www.englishriviera.co.uk/whats-on; The Quay, Brixham, Devon; tours (arrange in advance) 3-5 times monthly Jun-Sep

07 CAMEL TRAIL TEA GARDEN

A fairy-tale orchard garden sets the scene for one of Cornwall's most magnificent cream teas – and one of its most needed, situated as it is on the Camel Trail, one of the UK's most popular cycle routes. The tea garden is a 65-mile drive west into Cornwall, or leave the car at Bodmin and hire bikes to cycle to this stop and the next via the Camel Trail.

04 AL Hedderly © Getty Images

05 Alfresco seating at
Camel Trail Tea Garden

06 Michelin-starred
Devon dining,
Mason's Arms

07 Rick Stein's Cornish
Seafood Restaurant

Cyclists and afternoon tea aficionados will find the high tea to be the best fuel, combining a cream tea topped with the county's renowned Rodda's clotted cream and Cornish crab finger sandwiches. Locally manufactured yarg (a tangy cheese with an almost mushroomy taste) and Cornish blue make up the divine cheeseboard. The tearoom comes with the further sparkle of one of England's best Bruts, from the award-winning Camel Valley vineyard just down the road. The Cornish, incidentally, do cream tea the opposite way around to Devon folks: here it's jam first then cream on your scones. *www.cameltrailteagarden.co.uk; tel +44 1208 74291; Nanscarne, Nanstallon, Bodmin, Cornwall; 10am-5.30pm Mar-Nov*

08 THE SEAFOOD RESTAURANT

In the pretty North Cornwall port of Padstow, 10 miles further along the Camel Trail, this is the joint often credited with putting Southwest England's seafood on the gourmet map. Over 40 years after opening, it's still hooking diners by the boatload. Owned by TV chef Rick Stein, not only does a lot of the fish served here get brought ashore outside the door but the restaurant has a central bar where you can witness the likes of langoustines and lobster being prepared. There is also a seafood school, where you can learn to rustle up marine delicacies yourself. *www.rickstein.com, tel +44 1841 532700; Riverside, Padstow, Cornwall; noon-2.30pm & 6.30-10pm*

09 TREGOTHNAN TEA

English tea was never really English – it was not grown in England – until this company started their tea plantation at Tregothnan near Truro in 1999. Now this grand old estate, cultivating teas including Earl Grey, eucalyptus, manuka and myrtle, tempts devotees of the great British brew-up with everything from plantation tours to tea lectures and a tea-maker master class. The estate, 25 miles south of Padstow, has Cornwall's most extensive landscaped gardens, which are open to the public one day per month; otherwise, by prior appointment. *www.tregothnan.co.uk; tel +44 1872 520000; Merther, Tregothnan, Tresillian, Cornwall*

10 DELIMANN

The weather is often erratic, and opening hours equally so, in the countrified Southwest. Delimann, a Devon-based delicatessen, specialises in delivering gourmet Devon afternoon teas right to the door of your accommodation, wherever that should be (and not just in Devon!).

The deli prides itself on stocking the county's finest products – choose from just-baked scones and cakes, Devonshire-made clotted cream, West Country blended tea, Devon-roasted coffee and organic cider in a greater array of combinations than any tearoom currently offers. The owners have pooled 130 years' worth of family experience running a deli in the small town of Bovey Tracey into this now exclusively online venture. *www.delimann.co.uk; +44 1626 854793, deliveries Mon-Sat, fresh-baked goods delivered Tue-Fri*

WHERE TO STAY
GIDLEIGH PARK
A glorious timber-framed manor hotel on the edge of Dartmoor in south Devon, Gidleigh Park is home to the Southwest's only two Michelin-starred restaurant, as well as a legendary afternoon tea. *www.gidleigh.co.uk; +44 1647 462367; Gidleigh Park, Chagford*

OLD SCHOOL HOUSE
This rural self-catering retreat sits in river-rimmed farmland next to a ruined church, in the grounds of the Tregothnan Estate, where England's only tea is grown. *www.tregothnan.co.uk; see main text*

WHAT TO DO
CHEDDAR GORGE
The emerald hills of North Somerset rise up to form the country's most impressive gorge – a paradise for hikers, climbers and also cavers. There are three show-caves here, plus many more challenging speleological adventures (www. cheddargorge.co.uk).

CAMEL TRAIL
This gentle 18-mile cycling/hiking trail, following the delightful River Camel between Wenford Bridge and Padstow along old railway lines, has become one of the country's most popular pedalling routes. Bodmin Bikes rents out bikes from Bodmin (www. bodminbikes.co.uk).

CELEBRATIONS
SOMERSET CHEESE & CIDER FESTIVAL
This is a weekend-long June celebration of Somerset's proudest culinary exports. Cider mixologists will be in attendance, and events include a speed butter-making contest and a farmers' market, accompanied by lots of live music (www. somersetciderandcheese fest.co.uk).

NEWLYN FISH FESTIVAL
In late August, this Cornwall seaside town hosts the UK's largest celebration of fish: expect gig (small boat) racing, a fish-themed 'cook-off', and a fish auction. (www. newlynfishfestival.org.uk)

07 TravelCollection © Alamy

France

FALLING FOR PARISIAN PÂTISSERIE

Decadent sweet creations are a hallmark of France, and Paris inspires modern pastry chefs with a pâtisserie love affair quite unlike any other city on the planet.

With its architectural icons, fashionable boutiques and world-class art, Paris has a timeless familiarity hard to resist. Its reputation for excellent dining precedes it, and whether you end up in a packed neighbourhood bistro or a Michelin-starred temple to gastronomy, the French capital delivers exquisite preparation and presentation of quality produce.

But the true seductress of gourmet Paris is *pâtisserie*. From simple preserved fruits, jellies and wafers in the Middle Ages to such sumptuous 19th-century showpieces as caramel-kissed pyramids of rich choux-cream puffs, sophistication and zany creation have always been hallmarks of French *pâtisserie*. The cheeky glean of a glazed *éclair*, the decadence of a boozy *baba au rhum*, the pleasing crunch of a made-to-order *millefeuille*: yes, this is a European city that creates pastries to swoon over.

No other place exalts its *pâtisserie* with such passion and inbuilt panache as Paris. Like French fashion designers, the finest pastry chefs create new collections each season. Some of the world's best work here: celebrity *haute-pâtissier* Pierre Hermé even hosts catwalk shows with tray-bearing waiters waltzing down the red carpet to show off new-season masterpieces.

Zany maybe, but French *pâtisserie* never forgets its roots. Iconic cakes like the *éclair*, *millefeuille*, *tarte au citron* and *macaron* are known the world over, but it is only really in Paris that *pâtissiers* dare – indeed have the right from birth – to revisit and reinvent these century-old sweets using exotic fruits, flower blossoms, unexpected savoury flavours and other contemporary trends. One bite into a Pierre Hermé *macaron*, perhaps flavoured with olive oil and mandarin orange or matcha green tea and black sesame, says it all.

NEED TO KNOW
This 2-day trail is best experienced travelling by foot and on Paris's convenient metro system.

① LA CUISINE PARIS

Second-hand booksellers peel back the wooden lids of their weathered stalls. Fountains at the neo-Renaissance Hôtel de Ville spring into action. And down the road at La Cuisine Paris, ovens are fired up for aromatic trays of rich buttery croissants. This cooking school's morning croissant workshop is a real treat – few Parisians dare make the impossibly flaky French breakfast staple at home.

The greatest irony is the origin of the French croissant. Introduced to Paris in the 19th century, it was inspired by an Austrian who opened a Viennese bakery at 92 rue de Richelieu in 1837. Local bakers imitated his Kipferl (crescent-shaped pastry) and all too soon France's croissant was born. *www.lacuisineparis.fr; tel +33 1 40 51 78 18; 80 quai de l'Hôtel de Ville, 75001 Paris; metro Hôtel de Ville*

② BLÉ SUCRÉ

Pastry chef Fabrice Le Bourdat traded in the glamour of Michelin-starred, palace-hotel cuisine for his own kitchen in 2006. The lavish cakes and desserts he gets up at 2am each morning to craft in his neighbourhood *boulangerie-pâtisserie* near Bastille remain five-star. But appropriately, his pièce de résistance is the humblest French cake of all – the Madeleine.

Immortalised by 19th-century French novelist Marcel Proust in *Remembrance of Things Past*, the petite scallop-shaped tea cake is a simple mix of flour, eggs and sugar, sweetened after baking with a delicate orange-sugar glaze. Proust ate his mother's homemade Madeleines dipped in a cup of linden-flower tea, but chic Parisians snack on them at any opportunity

these days – including at the end of a simple quiche or savoury tart lunch on Blé Sucré's pavement terrace overlooking leafy Square Trousseau. Follow suit. *Tel +33 1 43 40 77 73; 7 Rue Antoine Vollon, Bastille; 7am-7.30pm Tue-Sat, to 1.30pm Sun*

③ LA CHOCOLATERIE DE JACQUES GÉNIN

After lunch head to the foodie Marais neighbourhood for an enticing exploration on foot. Taste chestnut honey nougat, ginger caramel, rhubarb or pumpkin fruit jellies and other novel flavours in the chic loft lab of self-taught, chocolate-and-caramel wild child Jacques Genin. This hugely creative chef's basil-and-lime-laced tarte au citron (lemon tart) and made-to-order millefeuille (flaky, cream-filled vanilla slice) are

02 © Giovanni Simeone

03 Matt Munroe © Lonely Planet

01 Macaron flavours
are inexhaustible in Paris

02 Haute-couture
pâtisserie from
L'Éclair de Génie

03 Blé Sucré pastry
chef displaying his
Madeleines

04 Gardens of
Le Marais

05 Epicure's signature
dessert at Le Bristol

sensational avant-garde retakes on two great French classics.
www.jacquesgenin.fr; tel +33 1 45 77 29 01; 133 Rue de Turenne, Le Marais; 11am-7pm Mon-Sat

04 L'ÉCLAIR DE GÉNIE

Strut the fashionista's catwalk south along rue Vieille du Temple to this dazzling white space where a rainbow of miniature *éclairs*, arranged with military precision beneath glass, hogs the limelight.

This shop – the work of bold pastry chef Christophe Adam – is haute-couture pâtisserie at its finest. Trends and seasons decide flavours: think a plump finger of choux pastry filled with velvety cream and glazed with chocolate ganache or shiny sugar icing and a crazy assortment of fresh fruit, chocolate orange slivers, caramelised pecans,

Madagascar vanilla... Anything goes in fact, which definitely would not have been the case when *éclairs* first graced Parisian tables in the 19th century. Pop a toothpaste tube of Christophe's other-worldly salted caramel into your shopping basket for good measure.
www.leclairdegenie.com; tel +33 1 42 77 85 11; 14 Rue de Pavée, Le Marais; 11am-7pm Mon-Fri, 10am-7.30pm Sat & Sun

05 DESSANCE

For dinner, turn to pastry chef Christophe Boucher at the city's only fine-dining dessert restaurant.

This is a flavour alchemist who knows how to impress. He was previously at Le Grand Véfour at Palais Royal, dining hot spot for the Parisian glitterati since 1784, and his innovative and unexpected pairings of

sweet flavours with vegetables are executed with precision and brilliance.
www.philippebaranes.com/ dessance; tel +33 1 42 77 23 62; 74 Rue des Archives, Le Marais; noon-11pm Wed, Thur & Sun, to midnight Fri & Sat

06 LA PÂTISSERIE DES RÊVES

Next day head west, beyond the steel-laced silhouette of the Eiffel Tower, to the posh 16e arrondissement for breakfast at The Pastry Shop of Dreams.

Head *pâtissier* Philippe Conticini revisits *pâtisserie* classics and his Paris-Brest is Paris's best. The choux pastry wheel, filled with hazelnut praline cream, was created in 1910 to celebrate the Paris-Brest bicycle race – cyclists devoured the cake upon arriving in the French capital

04 Ming Tang-Evans © Lonely Planet

05 Courtesy of Bristol Paris

from Brittany. La Pâtisserie des Rêves conveniently divides the wheel into six bite-sized choux puffs, and spikes the frothy hazelnut cream inside with shock pockets of liquid praline that explode in your mouth.

Or indulge in a timeless Saint Honoré in honour of the French patron saint of pastry chefs and bakers. The small pyramid cake, traditionally piled high with cream puffs and caramel, is re-crafted here as a more manageable oblong so foodies can revel in the combined taste and texture of caramel-coated choux puffs, crunchy puff pastry and different flavoured silky creams in each glorious mouthful. *www.lapatisseriedesreves.com; tel +33 1 47 04 00 24; 111 Rue de Longchamp, Eiffel Tower Area; shop* 10am-7pm Tue-Fri, 9am-7pm Sat & Sun; tea room noon-7pm Fri, 9am-7pm Sat & Sun

07 GALERIES LAFAYETTE

The city's *grande dame* of department stores opened in 1912, with art nouveau staircases and a stained-glass cupola rising dizzily above the shop floor. Wander from the main store to its Maison & Gourmet annex where epicureans drool over a lavish feast of luxury food products, designer chocolates, *bonbons* (candies), cakes, pastries and breads in Lafayette's opulent food hall. It fills two entire floors. *http://haussmann.galerieslafayette. com; 35 Boulevard Haussmann, Grands Boulevards; 8.30am-9.30pm Mon-Sat*

08 EPICURE

Your lunch date, a 10-minute walk away, is one of Paris's most gastronomic addresses (advance reservation essential). Cocooned in luxurious palace hotel Le Bristol, Éric Fréchon's triple Michelin-starred kitchen is an ethereal culinary exaltation of French produce and tradition, climaxing with unique desserts from his outstanding pastry chef Laurent Jeannin. The signature dessert is a vivacious, sunflower-yellow lemon from Menton on the sun-blessed French Riviera, infused with pear and candied lemon, and glazed in Limoncello frosting. *www.lebristolparis.com; tel +33 1 53 43 43 00; 112 Rue du Faubourg St-Honoré, Champs-Élysées; noon-2pm & 7-10pm daily*

06 © Francesco Carovillano

09 LADURÉE

Polished smooth and round like giant smarties, eggshell-fragile *macarons* (nothing to do with coconut) are the icon of French *pâtisserie*. Contemporary *macaron* master Pierre Hermé shares the maestro baton with traditional favourite Ladurée whose signature, pale green boxes are the last word in Parisian romance

Louis Ernest Ladurée, a miller from southwest France, started serving tea in his chintzy, Second Empire pastry shop near the new Garnier opera in 1871 – a 10-minute walk from Le Bristol. Nineteenth-century cherubs and winged fairies flutter across its frescoed ceiling, and glass cabinets display neat rows of colourful *macarons* – a legacy of Catherine de Médicis who came to France in 1533 with an entourage of Florentine cooks and pastry chefs adept in the subtleties of Italian Renaissance cooking. *Macaron* flavours are inexhaustible (cherry blossom, yoghurt and grapefruit, rose and quince...) and any marriage of tastes is possible. Buy a beautifully packaged box for home. *www.laduree.com; tel +33 1 42 60 21 79; 16 Rue Royale, Champs-Élysées; 8.30am-7.30pm Mon-Thu, to 8pm Fri & Sat, 10am-7pm Sun*

10 JEAN-PAUL HÉVIN

Five minutes away on rue St-Honoré, the city's sexiest chocolatier Jean-Paul Hévin invites you to afternoon tea in his beautifully bittersweet *salon de thé* (tea room). Chocoholics be warned: his purist, all-chocolate tartlets are to die for. Exquisite almond- and chocolate-sanded pastry cradles a polished pool of oven-baked, dark chocolate ganache. *www.jeanpaulhevin.com; tel +33 1 55 35 35 96; 231 Rue St-Honoré, Louvre-Tuileries; 10am-7.30pm Mon-Sat*

06 The stained-glass cupola of Galeries Lafayette

WHERE TO STAY

HÔTEL DU PETIT MOULIN
Dressed from head to toe by French designer Christian Lacroix, this lovely 17-room boutique hotel in the Marais lies inside a bakery dating from the time of Henry IV. *www.hoteldupetitmoulin. com; tel +33 1 42 74 10 10; 29-31 Rue du Poitou*

HÔTEL LE BRISTOL
This 1920s palace hotel evokes the grandeur and elegance of yesteryear Paris with its lavish Louis XV and Louis XVI furniture, rich vintage-inspired fabrics and impeccable service. The breakfast buffet is possibly Paris' most lavish. *www.lebristolparis.com; tel +33 1 53 43 43 00; 112 Rue du Faubourg St-Honoré*

WHAT TO DO

Food-and-wine themed treasure hunts organised by THATLou (www.that lou.com) offer tourists a unique chance to eat their way around wine-swilling Bacchuses and 17th-century Dutch baroque still-life paintings in the Louvre. For non-art lovers, there is nothing more romantic – or tasty – than a lunch or dinner cruise along the Seine with Bateaux Parisiens (www.bateauxparisiens. com) or Bateaux-Mouches (www.bateaux-mouches. com). It is one of the most wonderful ways to get a quick introduction to the city's main monuments – while eating to boot.

CELEBRATIONS

No food fest explores new culinary trends and celebrates upcoming chefs quite like Omnivore Paris (www.omnivore. com), a three-day festival in March dedicated to celebrating, sharing and honouring the *jeune cuisine* of young chefs in Paris and worldwide. France's three-day Fête de la Gastronomie in late September is the other fabulously foodie moment to take on Paris.

DORDOGNE

France
RURAL RICHES OF THE DORDOGNE

Duck, goose and black truffles form the backbone of this southern region of France and its sumptuous local cuisine, which prizes tradition and seasonality.

No region in France reflects the essence of its world-renowned cuisine and culinary *art de vivre* quite like the Dordogne (Périgord in French) and neighbouring Lot in southwest France. In this sun-rich, rural backwater wrapped around the twists and turns of the mighty Dordogne River and a thousand and one historic châteaux, time stopped a century ago. The natural cycle of agriculture – viticulture, walnuts, strawberries and tobacco production – reassuringly charts the seasons, as it has always done. But what is sensational for foodie travellers is the passion, tenacity and gusto with which culinary tradition is respected and exalted. Ancient recipes passed down between generations form the backbone of contemporary cuisine, while cooks insist on a very personal, experiential relationship with the products they use: Michelin-starred chefs select their own seasonal fare

01 Andrew Montgomery © Lonely Planet

NEED TO KNOW
Bergerac and Bordeaux airports are both 90 minutes away from the start of this trail: rent a car to get around.

at the morning markets, farmers invite you in to their rustic kitchens to share culinary secrets, third-generation producers beg you to taste and enjoy at every opportunity.

Three of France's most luxurious food products – duck, goose and black truffles, the quality of which is unmatched elsewhere – form the holy trinity of Dordogne cuisine. Any dish *à la périgourdine* almost certainly contains black truffles, a precious pig-ugly fungus in season from late October to January. No part of the duck or goose is wasted. Joints are simmered in their own fat and preserved in glass jars to make confit. Their fattened livers, soft pink from a goose and red from a duck, are eaten fresh or conserved as *pâté de foie gras*. The sublimely silky paste is indulged in at Christmas all over France – and far more frequently in this privileged, joyfully gourmet neck of the French woods. *Bon appétit!*

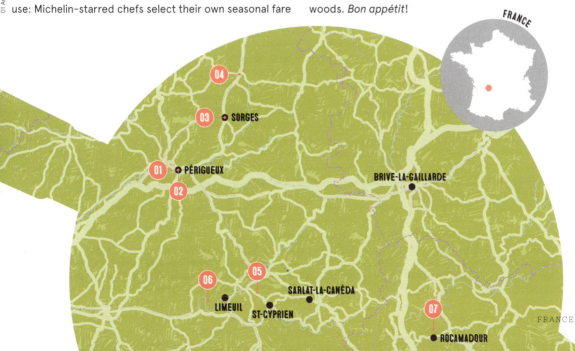

FRANCE

04

03 ○ SORGES

01 ○ PÉRIGUEUX

02

BRIVE-LA-GAILLARDE

05

06

SARLAT-LA-CANÉDA

LIMEUIL

ST-CYPRIEN

07

ROCAMADOUR

① PÉRIGUEUX MARKETS

No town bristles with gourmet energy quite like Périgueux on market day – the perfect first stop to get your culinary curiosity *à la périgourdine* into top gear. Twice a week, farmers pour into the small Roman town to sell their produce.

The *marchés* (markets) have been here since the Middle Ages and little has changed. Cars are banished and wooden trestle tables, charged high with fresh produce, fill the cobbled cathedral square instead – much to the joy of locals and foodies (the two are synonymous) who forge their way indulgently, bite by bite, around the chaotic aromatic stalls. *Dégustation* (tasting) is sacred.

At the *marché alimentaire* (food market) savour syrupy Gariguette strawberries and sun-filled summer figs, salivate over zingy walnut and hazelnut oils milled by eight generations of the Elias family at the

nearby Moulin de la Veyssière, sip a Bergerac red, enter gourmet heaven.

Or go for the kill and gawp in uneasy fascination at heaps of goose and duck carcasses flopped on tables in the nearby Marché au Gras, a poultry market heaving with pallid-white thighs and pinions, giblets, goose necks skinned and unskinned; every existent fowl part, in fact.

A third-generation farmer caresses a swollen pale-pink mass like a magnificent jewel. 'This is a fresh fattened goose liver' he mumbles with deep pride. 'I love it raw but you can salt and pepper it, fry it gently and serve with lemon'. On the other side of the market tent, air thick with furtive negotiation over

'I love goose liver raw, but you can salt and pepper it, fry it gently and serve with lemon'

prized birds, *sanguettes* (dried-blood pancakes) are selling like hot cakes.

Poultry and black truffles are a natural match in this epicurean region, hence the foodie excitement that ushers in Périgueux's Marché aux Truffes (Truffle Market). The overpowering perfume of the 'black diamond' sure beats the smell of butchered birds.

Marché Alimentaire, Place de la Clautre, Place de l'Ancien Hôtel de Ville & Place St-Silain, 8am-12.30pm Wed & Sat; Marché au Gras, Place St-Louis, 8am-12.30pm Wed & Sat Nov–mid-Mar; Marché aux Truffes, Place de l'Ancien Hôtel de Ville, 8am-12.30pm Wed & Sat Dec-Feb

01 Pretty waterside
village of Beynac-
et-Cazenac

02-05 Périgueux
on market day

(04)

(05)

02 L'ESSENTIEL

Recover from the noise, commotion and sensory overload of the market with the perfect antidote – an elegant bistro lunch at L'Essentiel. In his tiny kitchen near the cathedral, Michelin-starred chef Éric Vidal venerates the Dordogne's rich gastronomic heritage with a creative, wholly regional cuisine.

In the early 19th century French food writer Anthelme Brillat-Savarin wrote 'La cuisine, c'est quand les choses ont le goût de ce qu'elles sont (Cooking is when things taste of what they are)' and this is precisely what Vidal does so well. Order warm soufflé with black truffles, or foie gras de canard served dans sa graisse (in its fat) with apple and ginger lemon vinegar, to experience grass-roots cooking at its best.
www.restaurant-perigueux.com; tel +33 5 53 35 15 15; 8 rue de la Clarté, 24000 Périgueux; noon-1.30pm & 7.30pm-9.30pm Tue-Sat

03 ÉCOMUSÉE DE LA TRUFFE

Motor 20km north to Sorges, a gold-stone village with an edible heritage most gastronomes would fly to the moon and back for: this is the world capital of black truffles. 'Suave, unforgettable, subtle and utterly enchanting' is how chef Pierre Corre, who cooks with them in Sorges' celebrity Auberge de la Truffe hotel, describes the strange aroma of the knobbly, veined fungus.

Each year dogs unearth 100 tonnes – that's 10% of France's total black truffle harvest – here. Devote the afternoon to learning about the elusive fungus that 19th-century farmers crumbled over acorns in the hope of spawning 'truffle-friendly' saplings: truffles grow in symbiosis with oak tree roots and cannot be cultivated, hence the tuber melanosporum being the world's most expensive food.

End with an uplifting (and aromatic, if you're lucky) walk along the

Sentier des Truffières, a trail behind the museum that ribbons for 3km through vineyards, walnut groves and truffle orchards).
Tel +33 5 53 05 90 11; Le Bourg, 24420 Sorges; 9.30am-6.30pm mid-Jun-mid-Sep, 10am-noon & 2-5pm Tue-Sun rest year.

04 MAISON DU FOIE GRAS

Keep your tasting cap on in Thiviers, 14km north. This town is another gourmet holy grail on the Dordogne map, where passions run high. Controversially, ducks and geese on farms today are force-fed with unnatural amounts of boiled corn to triple the size of their livers, although traditionally this wasn't the case.

In the 11th century, when the English and French were fighting tooth and nail over this medieval chateau town, local farmers slaughtered the farm goose then plucked out its liver and soaked it

in warm milk to ensure a succulent swollen liver, ripe for feasting on with a chilled glass of sweet Monbazillac white. The history of foie gras is told in the Maison du Foie Gras, an excellent little museum with tasting opportunities and a small shop. *www.maisondufoiegras.jimdo. com; tel +33 5 53 55 12 50; 8 place Foch, 24800 Thiviers; 9am-1pm & 2.30-6.30pm Mon-Fri, 9am-1pm & 3-6.30pm Sat, 9.30am-1pm Sun Jul & Aug, shorter hours rest year*

05 PÉCHALIFOUR

On day two, make the pilgrimage by car to Péchalifour, a remote hamlet in the hills above St-Cyprien. Hunting for truffles here with Monsieur Aynaud and his dog Farah is exhilarating. The

skill with which the Labrador sniffs out the gastronomic bounty, buried 5cm to 10cm underground, is astonishing – as is her ability not to go for the kill when Monsieur Aynaud prises out the walnut-sized truffle from the chalky soil with a blade and his bare hands: pigs, the traditional truffle hunter, scoffed the lot, as would wild boar if they had the chance.

Hemmed in with an electric fence, the four-hectare *truffière* – a poacher's paradise – is a mix of oak, pubescent oak, hazelnut and hornbeam trees carefully chosen to encourage the growth of milder-tasting *truffes d'été* (summer truffles) and winter's exalted 'black diamond of the kitchen'. The latter sells for €800 to €1100 per kilogram. Pre- or post-

hunt, indulge in its magical texture, aroma and flavour over a kitchen lunch prepared by Madame Aynaud – think *brouillade truffée* (truffle scrambled eggs), sautéed goose liver with truffle shavings and truffle mashed potato. Don't hesitate to ask her for cooking tips and buy a Périgord black truffle of your own to gorge on back home. *www.truffe-perigord.com; tel +33 5 53 29 20 44; 24220 St-Cyprien, Péchalifour; visits by appointment*

06 LE VIEUX LOGIS

Bon vivant Bernard Giraudel is fiercely proud of his native Dordogne. At the grand old age of 90-something, this self-proclaimed *marchand de bonheur* (merchant of happiness) passes his days in Trémolat discussing the nuances of local gastronomy with guests at Le Vieux Logis, his old family home. The foliage-draped property was a priory in the 16th century and later a tobacco farm, hence the dining room with beamed ceiling where air-dried tobacco was hung to cure.

The gastronomic cuisine by Michelin-starred chef Vincent Arnould – a contemporary reinterpretation of *périgourdine* dishes using local produce – is equally dazzling. Tuck in using a classic wood-handled Nontron knife, sculpted locally from box wood and traditionally used at lunchtime by farm labourers working in the fields. *See Where to Stay; dinner daily, closed Wed & Thu mid-Oct–mid-Apr*

07 LA BORIE D'IMBERT

To complete your trail, take a side trip to Rocamadour in the Lot, home to a creamy goats cheese that has such a meticulous maturation process and strict ingredient requirements that it has been certified as *Appellation d'Origine Protégée* (AOP) produce.

The maturation process insists on the delicate cheese rounds – 6cm in diameter and 1.6cm thick – being turned daily for six days. At La Borie d'Imbert farm, cheesemaker Marc Vilard does just this. Watch cheese being made each morning, see goats milked at 5pm, and if you're really lucky, catch a birth in the nursery.

Linger afterwards in the farm shop to taste and buy its products – heavenly picnic fodder, and bars of artisanal goat-milk soap. Rocamadour itself, a two-hour drive east from Trémolat, is an ancient pilgrimage destination where cliff-clinging architecture defies gravity. *www.laboriedimbert.com; tel +33 5 65 33 20 37; 46500 Rocamadour; 10am-noon & 2-6pm Mon-Fri, 10am-6pm Sat & Sun, goat milking 5pm*

06 Rocamadour in the Lot – famed for cheese and pilgrimage

WHERE TO STAY

AUBERGE DE LA TRUFFE
Complete with truffle restaurant, this mid-range Logis de France hotel is perfect for gourmets keen to stagger straight from the dinner table into bed. Runs truffle-themed cooking courses. *www.auberge-de-la-truffe. com; tel +33 5 53 05 02 05; 14 rue Châteaureynaud, 24420 Sorges*

LE VIEUX LOGIS
This luxurious rural inn spoils guests with country-chic suites, manicured French gardens and a summertime pool. Service is discreet and superb. *www.vieux-logis.com; tel +33 5 53 22 80 06; Le Bourg, 24510 Trémolat*

CHÂTEAU DE LA TREYNE
Multilingual host Stéphanie Gombert makes guests feel at home in her stunning 14th-century fairy-tale castle, built on a cliff edge on the Dordogne's river banks near Rocamadour. It also has a Michelin-starred restaurant. *www.chateaudelatreyne. com; tel +33 5 65 27 60 60; 46200 Lacave*

WHAT TO DO

Arrange a canoeing expedition on the Dordogne River, hike along its banks or hot-air balloon above it. Admire some of the world's finest prehistoric cave art at Lascaux, a Unesco World Heritage site in the Vézère Valley (www.lascaux.culture. fr). In the Lot, the subterranean caves and waterways of Gouffre de Padirac are a dramatic sight. (www.gouffre-de-padirac.com)

CELEBRATIONS

The medieval market town of Sarlat-la-Canéda is always a delight to mooch around, but its web of quaint golden-hued streets really comes into its own in January during the town's Fête de la Truffe (Truffle Festival) – a lavish weekend of tasting, buying and consuming local black truffles. The Fest'Oie (Goose Fair) in early March is equally entertaining and mouth-watering. (www.sarlat-tourisme.com)

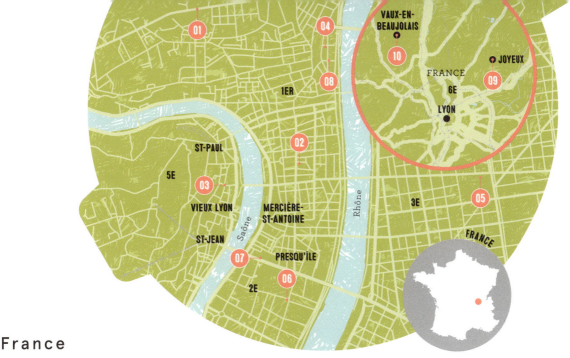

On the map:
- 01
- 04
- VAUX-EN-BEAUJOLAIS
- 10
- JOYEUX
- 08
- FRANCE
- 09
- 1ER
- 6E
- LYON
- ST-PAUL
- 02
- 5E
- 03
- Rhône
- VIEUX LYON
- MERCIÈRE-ST-ANTOINE
- 3E
- 05
- Saône
- ST-JEAN
- FRANCE
- 07
- PRESQU'ÎLE
- 2E
- 06

France

BOUCHONS AND BEAUJOLAIS IN LYON

Honest bistro cuisine with working-class origins has become a secret recipe for success in this food hotspot, revered by the French as a capital of gastronomy.

France's second largest city is a multilayered place rich in history, famed for the clickety-clack of Jacquard looms during its 19th-century heyday as Europe's silk-weaving capital. Today, Lyon is revered throughout France for its cuisine and boasts one of the nation's densest concentrations of eateries.

At the heart of the culinary scene are its *bouchons*: cosy, convivial bistros that date back to the 19th century, when in-house cooks for bourgeois families began going into business for themselves. The *mères* (mothers), as these enterprising women were known, attained widespread popular fame for their straightforward, well-prepared and reasonably priced dishes built on fresh ingredients from Lyon's fertile hinterlands. Early on, the *mères* fed humble silk weavers but by the 1930s they had gained the attention of international celebrities, including renowned French food writer Curnonsky, who dubbed Lyon the world capital of gastronomy.

Dozens of traditional *bouchons* survive in Lyon, their menus filled with colourfully named dishes that reflect their working class origins. Sausages and other meaty delicacies also play a starring role, including *pieds de cochon* (pig trotters), *andouillette* (sausage made from pigs' intestines) and *boudin noir aux pommes* (blood sausage with apples). Everything comes accompanied with free-flowing local Beaujolais, Côtes du Rhône or Mâcon wine – typically served in a heavy-bottomed 46cl glass bottle known as a pot. These days, Lyon's claim to culinary fame goes well beyond its *bouchons*. A flurry of big-name chefs – including the granddaddy of Lyon's gastronomic scene, chef Paul Bocuse – presides over a sparkling restaurant line-up that embraces all genres: French, fusion and international.

NEED TO KNOW
Set aside 3 days for this trail: hire a car for the last day, when Beaujolais wine country calls.

01 MARCHÉ DE LA CROIX-ROUSSE

For a neighbourhood perspective on Lyon's food, climb to the former silk weaver's district of Croix-Rousse – a hilltop arrondissement that retains a bohemian small-village feel. The elaborate Jacquard looms that once wove Marie Antoinette's gowns and made Lyon the silk capital of Europe have mostly gone silent, but Croix-Rousse's six-day-a-week market, sprawling across several city blocks, remains as vibrant as ever.

Gregarious vendors hawk seasonal fruit and veggies, meat, fish, and a rainbow of flowers, while the largely Lyonnais crowd weaves between the market stalls and the adjacent cafes along Blvd de la Croix-Rousse.

The best days are Tuesdays, Saturdays (when there's a dedicated organic section) and Sundays (when

a brass band provides musical accompaniment).
Blvd de la Croix-Rousse; 6am-1pm Tue-Sun

02 LE MUSÉE

For pure *bouchon* bliss, nothing beats this convivial eatery, housed in the stables of Lyon's former Hôtel de Ville on the narrow Presqu' Île peninsula between the Rhône and Saône Rivers. Diners crowd in elbow-to-elbow at long tables draped in chequered tablecloths, while chef-owner Luc Minaire circulates among them, reading off the daily-changing menu.

Meat-heavy mains, such as *joues de porc à la lyonnaise* – pork cheeks simmered in white wine, onions and vinegar – jostle for position alongside veggie-centric treats like roasted peppers stuffed with goat's cheese. Or there's ethereal Lyonnais classics

such as *quenelles de brochet*— feather-light flour, egg and cream dumplings served in a creamy crayfish sauce. End with a slice of Lyon's iconic *tarte aux pralines*, a brilliant rose-coloured confection made with silky *crème fraîche* and crunchy toasted almonds coated in pink sugar.

After the meal, Luc escorts diners to visit the network of *traboules* (secret interior passageways) behind the restaurant. Lyon has hundreds of these hidden walkways, which snake through inner courtyards and underneath buildings all around the city. Originally intended to allow silk weavers to transport their fabric without exposing it to inclement weather, the *traboules* later became an important resource for WWII resistance fighters eluding the Nazis.
Tel +33 4 78 37 71 54; 2 Rue des Forces; noon-2pm & 7.30-9.30pm Tue-Sat

(04)

03 TERRE ADÉLICE

Cross the Saône River into Vieux-Lyon, the city's charming medieval quarter, where Lyon's best ice cream shop offers 100-plus flavours, ranging from the daring to the divine. Play it safe with Valrhona dark chocolate, experiment gently with organic chestnut, honey-rosemary or lavender, or take a walk on the wild side with a scoop of Roquefort or foie gras.

Along with three dozen fruit flavours, there are many others incorporating vegetables (cucumber, fennel, red pepper, pumpkin), herbs (thyme-lemon, tomato-basil, summer savoury), flowers (violet, rose, geranium), wines (sparkling Clairette de Die) and liqueurs (absinthe, Grand Marnier, or shocking-green Verveine du Velay).

www.terre-adelice.eu; tel +33 4 78 03 51 84; 1 Place de la Baleine; 10am-midnight

04 LA MÈRE BRAZIER

Permanently enshrined in Lyonnais culinary lore, this restaurant on the slopes below Croix-Rousse is named for founder Eugénie Brazier, who rose from humble origins to become Michelin's first triple-starred female chef in 1933. Nearly a century later, double-Michelin-starred chef Mathieu Vianney has reinvented this mythical restaurant, doing admirable justice to Brazier's legacy with personal interpretations of her finest recipes.

Tuck into such timeless specialities as *fonds d'artichaut au foie gras* (artichoke hearts with fatty duck liver) or *poularde demi-deuil* (slow-poached Bresse chicken stuffed with black truffles), all accompanied by an impressive wine list. A copy of the original 1933 Michelin guidebook is still proudly displayed up front, and the adjacent street was renamed

in loving memory of Mère Brazier herself in 2001.

www.lamerebrazier.fr; tel +33 4 78 23 17 20; 12 Rue Royale; noon-1.30pm & 7.45-9.15pm Mon-Fri, closed Aug

05 LES HALLES DE LYON PAUL BOCUSE

Lyon's ultimate temple to fine cuisine is this famed indoor market packed with about 50 gourmet groceries, *boulangeries*, *pâtisseries*, *charcuteries*, *fromageries* (cheese shops) and *cavistes* (wine shops). It's a supremely satisfying place to shop for foodie gifts. On Sunday mornings, join local families here for a classic Lyon brunch of oysters and Mâcon blanc wine, then browse the shops to your heart's content.

No trip to Les Halles is complete without a visit to legendary Lyonnais cheesemonger Mère Richard, famous

for her creamy St Marcellin, a mould-ripened cow's milk cheese that's also a staple at Lyon's *bouchons*.

Next, take a crash course in Lyonnais sausages at Charcuterie Sibilia, a local institution since 1925. Discover *rosette de Lyon*, the city's classic dry-cured sausage; *Jésus de Lyon*, traditionally a Christmas speciality, larger in diameter and made with high-quality cuts of pork; the *saucisson brioché*, a sausage baked in brioche dough; and the *saucisson à cuire* – usually served with boiled potatoes. The latter has variants studded with *cervelas pistaché* (pistachios) or *cervelas truffé* (black truffles).
www.hallespaulbocuse.lyon.fr; tel +33 4 78 62 39 33; 102 Cours Lafayette; 7am-10.30pm Tue-Sat, to 4.30pm Sun

06 L'ECOLE DE CUISINE DE L'INSTITUT PAUL BOCUSE

Paul Bocuse's latest venture is this cooking school for amateur chefs, smack in the heart of Lyon.

Half- and full-day courses cover every aspect of French cooking that you can think of. Try your hand at making croissants, tarts or chocolate desserts, accompany your chef-instructor on a shopping trip to the nearby Marché St-Antoine or dive into the mysteries of preparing the perfect duck.

Afterwards, peek in next door at L'Institut restaurant, where giant windows offer glimpses of student chefs from Bocuse's professional culinary arts academy apprenticing in the kitchen.
www.ecoledecuisine.institutpaul bocuse.com; tel +33 4 78 37 03 00; 20 Place Bellecour

07 IN CUISINE

This foodie bookshop on Place Bellecour is the perfect spot to pick up Lyonnais recipes, with its astonishing array of culinary, gastronomic and wine titles. It also offers tastings and cooking courses, sells cooking utensils and serves lunch in its tearoom.
www.incuisine.fr; 1 Place Bellecour; 11am-6.30pm Mon, 10am-7pm Tue-Sat

08 L'OURSON QUI BOIT

On the fringes of Croix-Rousse, this intimate eatery is emblematic of the new wave of fusion restaurants taking root in Lyon. Deftly balancing Asian and traditional French influences, Japanese chef Akira Nishigaki creates his own splendid flavour combinations in offerings from *bavette de boeuf* with plum sauce to green-tea crème brûlée, all accompanied by plenty of locally sourced fresh vegetables.
Tel +33 4 78 27 23 37; 23 Rue Royale; noon-1.30pm & 7.30-9.30pm Mon, Tue & Thu-Sat

09 LA BICYCLETTE BLEUE

A 40-minute drive into the countryside north of Lyon leads to La Dombes, a pond-studded region that supplies abundant fish and frogs for the French table. Stop in at this relaxed family-run eatery on the sleepy D61 and sample Vincent and Anne Sophie Liegeois' famous *grenouilles fraîches en persillade* (frogs' legs in butter and parsley), or the *bouchée de la reine Dombiste*, featuring local pike, crayfish and smoked carp. Afterwards, rent a bicycle on-site to explore 12 mapped circuits of the surrounding lakelands. www.labicyclettebleue.fr; tel +33 4 74 98 21 48; Le Pont, Joyeux; noon-1.30pm & 7.30-9pm Thu-Mon

⑩ AUBERGE DE CLOCHEMERLE

Continue 50 minutes west to this charming inn, surrounded by the rolling vineyard-clad hills of France's Beaujolais wine country. The restaurant here proudly bears a Michelin star for its exquisite preparation of local crayfish, eel, pigeon, sole and rosy tenderloin of Charolais beef (France's best), along with fresh vegetables, such as parsnips, wild mushrooms and asparagus.

The concept here is a menu surprise: chef Romain Barthe invites you to select your favourites from the day's list of freshly sourced ingredients, and then constructs a 'made-to-order' multi-course meal, accompanied by his hand-picked wine pairings.

This region is synonymous with its fruity reds, especially its 10 premium crus, and the Beaujolais Nouveau, drunk at the tender age of six weeks. Renowned wine-producing villages within easy striking distance include Beaujeu, Villié-Morgon, Fleurie, Moulin-à-Vent, Juliénas and St-Amour. A loop through all of these will steer you towards the autoroute for a return trip to Lyon.
www.aubergedeclochemerle.fr; tel +33 4 74 03 20 16; Rue Chevallier, Vaux-en-Beaujolais; noon-1.30pm & 7.30-9.30pm Wed-Sun

06 Grape picking in Beaujolais wine country

07 Inside La Mère Brazier

08 Sarmentelles de Beaujeu celebrations in Lyon

WHERE TO STAY

HÔTEL DE PARIS
This centrally located Lyon hotel in a 19th-century bourgeois building features themed rooms. The spacious, front-facing double with bouchon-inspired decor and chequered bedspreads is among the best. www.hoteldeparis-lyon.com; tel +33 4 78 28 00 95; 16 Rue de la Platière

HÔTEL DES CÉLESTINS
Just north of central Place Bellecour in Lyon, Hôtel des Célestins is a cosy, classy hotel surrounded by designer boutiques. The priciest rooms have gorgeous views of the 19th-century Célestins theatre, the cheaper ones face a quiet courtyard. www.hotelcelestins.com; +33 4 72 56 08 98; 4 Rue des Archers

WHAT TO DO

Explore Lyon's ancient roots in the hilltop district of Fourvière at the Musée de la Civilisation Gallo-Romaine (www.musees-gallo-romains.com) and its adjacent Gallo-Roman amphitheatre. Learn about Lyon's silk-weaving heritage and watch restored Jacquard looms at work at Maison des Canuts (www.maisondescanuts.com) in the Croix-Rousse neighbourhood. Finally, catch a boat down the Saône River to the Confluence (www.lyon-confluence.fr), where you'll find audacious architectural projects.

CELEBRATIONS

SARMENTELLES DE BEAUJEU
At the stroke of midnight as it hits the third Thursday in November – as soon as French law permits – the libération (release) or mise en perce (tapping, opening) of the first bottles of cherry-bright Beaujolais Nouveau is celebrated. This giant street party kicks off the day before, ushering in five days of wine tasting, live music and dancing (www.sarmentelles.com).

NUITS DE FOURVIÈRE
This diverse programme of open-air theatre, music and dance concerts is atmospherically set in Lyon's ancient Roman amphitheatre from early June to late July (www.nuitsdefourviere.com).

The map shows locations marked:

01 BADEN-BADEN
STRASBOURG
02
FRANCE
03
04
BAIERSBRONN
05
GERMANY
ALPIRSBACH
06
GERMANY
TRIBERG
07
08

Germany

TOTAL INDULGENCE IN THE BLACK FOREST

Villages sprinkled with Michelin stars, rich ingredients and passionate producers have created a food scene in this fairy-tale forest that goes far beyond its namesake gateau.

Sidling up to France in the west and Switzerland in the south, the Black Forest is a sylvan region of southwest Germany that's as deep and dark as its namesake gateau and every inch the Grimm's fairy-tale blueprint. Hills rise steep and wooded above church steeples, half-timbered villages, enormous cuckoo clocks and a crochet of tightly woven valleys.

In a region so remarkably in tune with the outdoors, it stands to reason that restaurants play up seasonal, locally sourced flavours. Nose-to-tail and farm-to-plate, organic and locavore – these approaches to food were second nature here long before they became trendy. Along curve after beautiful winding curve you'll see the tell-tale signs – small distilleries producing kirsch, hills striped with pinot vines, rambling farmhouses selling delicious smoked ham and honey, families out foraging in the woods, and farmers markets heaving with locals.

Menus here sing of the seasons: white asparagus and wild garlic in spring, chanterelles and cep mushrooms in late summer and early autumn, followed swiftly by the earthy delights of pumpkins and locally shot game. Hearty Swabian-style dishes, such as *maultaschen* (giant pasta pockets stuffed with pork and onions), *kässpätzle* (noodles topped with cheese) and *zwiebelkuchen* (onion tart with cream, speck and caraway seeds) will send you rolling out of that beamed, cosy rural inn. And you'll never forget your first forkful of real Black Forest gateau.

If you're seeking a more gourmet experience – *herzlich wilkommen*! This region has one of Germany's highest concentrations of top tables. The village of Baiersbronn alone shimmers with eight Michelin stars. Here chefs wow the critics with tasting menus that elevate natural, integral flavours with a pinch of culinary magic and a nod to neighbouring France.

NEED TO KNOW
This 3–4 day trail is best covered by car. The nearest airports are Baden-Baden and Stuttgart.

01 Matt Munroe © Lonely Planet

01 KAFFEESACK

Nuzzled deep in the wooded folds of the northern Black Forest, the swish little spa town of Baden-Baden has always had an appetite for the finer things in life, coffee included. Where to find the perfect cup? Kaffeesack, *natürlich*. Here the barista freshly roasts coffee from all over the world, using fair-trade beans from Kenya to Brazil, India to Guatemala.

The retro-rustic cafe is a chilled spot to sip a cup of joe prepared with love and a creative flourish. They take their beans seriously here, so anything you want to know – be it the subtle nuances of aroma or the roasting process – just ask.
www.kaffeesack.de; tel +49 7221 3979187; Hirschstrasse 6, Baden-Baden; 9am-6pm Mon-Sat

02 REBSTOCK WALDULM

It's an easy drive south to Kappelrodeck, where the hills are

'Baking a Black Forest gateau isn't rocket science, but it takes time, patience and fresh ingredients. And I follow the recipe religiously'

ribboned with vines and orchards. In autumn the leaves turn crimson-gold and the tang of new wine hangs in the air; springtime is when the cherry trees blossom. Karl Hodapp mans the stove at Rebstock Waldulm, a gorgeous half-timbered, 250-year-old farmhouse that looks as though it has been plucked straight from the pages of a children's bedtime story. Karl earned his culinary stripes working in a string of Michelin-starred restaurants and this – coupled with his pride in careful, seasonal sourcing – shines through in Baden-style dishes with a nod to neighbouring Alsace.

Noble pinots from his own vineyards

strike a perfect balance with such flavours as cream of snail soup with wild herbs, and quail terrine in a black pudding crust with plum compote. A shot of Karl's homemade kirsch rounds out a memorable meal in the dark-timber, lamplit restaurant.
www.rebstock-waldulm.de; tel +49 7842 9480; Kappelrodeck/Waldulm; 5.30-11pm Mon & Tue, 5-11pm Wed, 11.30am-2pm & 5-11pm Thu & Fri, 11.30-11pm Sat & Sun

03 RESTAURANT BAREISS

Lushly wooded mountains rise above dinky, red-roofed villages as you follow the twists and turns of

the highways east to Baiersbronn. Baiersbronn! The mere mention of this village sends food lovers into raptures: with a population just shy of 16,000 and a staggering eight Michelin stars – including two three-star restaurants which, gastronomically speaking, puts it on a par with London – this is the Black Forest's food capital.

Helming the kitchen at three-star Restaurant Bareiss is Claus-Peter Lumpp, who walks the culinary high-wire with his inimitable blend of ingenuity, meticulousness and artistic flair. Each dish sings of the seasons and tastes profoundly of its prime ingredients – be it turbot with Périgord truffle or Alsatian pigeon with five-spice glaze and sweet chestnuts. Book well ahead, opt for the tasting menu, let sommelier Jürgen Fend pair the wines, and prepare for the meal of a lifetime.

www.bareiss.com; tel +49 7442 470; Baiersbronn-Mitteltal; noon-2pm, 7-9.30pm Wed-Sun

04 WILD HERB WALKS

You only need to take one look at the forests of spruce and larch around Baiersbronn to imagine what rich pickings they hide in the way of wild herbs and mushrooms. Indeed, the entire Black Forest hums with basket-wielding foragers, particularly from late spring to autumn when wild herbs, berries and mushrooms – including apricot-hued chanterelles and glossy, nut-brown ceps – begin to pop up on the forest fringes and in mossy glades.

Finding them, however, is pot luck and you need to know what you're looking for. If you're a beginner, consider hooking onto one of Baiersbronn's three- to four-hour guided walks from April to October in search of wild herbs, berries and mushrooms; some of which are free with a guest card. See the tourist office website for dates. *www.baiersbronn.de; tel +49 7442 841 40; Rosenplatz 3, Baiersbonn*

05 PFAU SCHINKEN

When you smell the tantalising aroma of Schwarzwälder Schinken, the local ham, you know you've arrived at Pfau, which gives a fascinating insight into the ham curing and smoking process on its guided tours (2.30pm and 4.30pm Tuesdays, 11.30am Saturdays).

The Black Forest ham here is the real deal – we're talking seriously good charcuterie. Locally reared ham is rubbed with salt and spices, such as coriander, garlic and juniper berries, then dry-cured for four to 12 weeks, before being cold-smoked over fir wood and left to mature for

a few weeks to retain its intensely smoky, woody flavour. Pfau, a 20-minute drive east of Baiersbronn, also operates a shop that is ideal for stocking up on picnic provisions; besides ham, other specialities available here include wild garlic, venison and kirsch-laced salami. www.pfau-schinken.de; tel +49 7445 6482; Alte Poststrasse 17, Herzogsweiler; 7.30am-12.30pm & 2-6pm Mon-Fri, 7.30am-12.30pm Sat

06 ALPIRSBACHER KLOSTERBRÄU

From Pfau, the B roads thread through gentle hills and meadows to bring you to Alpirsbach, presided over by its former Benedictine monastery. Lore has it the town was named after a quaffing cleric who, when a glass of beer slipped from his hand and tumbled into the river, exclaimed: *All bier ist in den*

bach! (All the beer is in the stream!). A prophecy, it seems, as today Alpirsbacher Klosterbräu is one of the Black Forest's finest beers, brewed from pure local spring water.

Daily guided tours at 2.30pm whizz you through the brewing process, and two beers are thrown in for the price of a ticket (€7). Even if you miss the tour, it's worth nipping into the shop for tipples such as the brewery's eponymous hoppy, full-bodied beer, which has scooped gold at the World Beer Awards, Or the smooth, malty Kleiner Mönch (Little Monk). www.alpirsbacher.de; tel +49 7444 671 44; Ambrosius-Blarer-Platz 6, Alpirsbach; 10am-6pm Mon-Fri, to 5pm Sat, 11am-5pm Sun

07 CAFÉ SCHÄFER

A slow drive southwest passing the Kinzig Valley takes you through one of the Black Forest's loveliest stretches,

with cute-as-a-button half-timbered villages, castle-topped hillsides and shingle-tiled farmhouses that snuggle among fir forests.

The thunder of Germany's highest waterfall and the chime of the world's biggest cuckoo clocks announce your arrival In Triberg. Give the crowds the slip and head down the high street to Café Schäfer, where Claus Schäfer is the heir to Josef Keller's handwritten 1915 recipe for Schwarzwälder Kirschtorte. Yeah, we know – Black Forest gateau has had a rocky ride over the years, but trust us: this one will restore your faith.

'Baking a Black Forest gateau isn't rocket science, but it takes time, patience and fresh ingredients. And I never cut corners – I follow the original recipe religiously', says Claus. His gateau is a multilayered masterpiece: shortcrust pastry with a hint of marzipan, moist chocolate

05 Andy Christiani © Shutterstock

06 MyImages - Micha © Shutterstock

sponge, tart morello cherry compote, kirsch-laced whipped cream and dark chocolate shavings. It's a winning recipe that has won over everyone from the Sheik of Dubai to roaming British TV chefs the Hairy Bikers – one forkful and you'll see why. *www.cafe-schaefer-triberg.de; tel +49 7722 4465; Hauptstrasse 33, Triberg; 9am-6pm Mon-Tue & Thu-Fri, 8am-6pm Sat, 11am-6pm Sun*

08 HÖHENGASTHAUS KOLMENHOF

Heading south from Triberg on the B500, it's a 20-minute drive up to the top of Martinskapelle where your next stop awaits. The final steep road climbing this 1100m peak, topped by a medieval chapel, negotiates some pretty hairy switchbacks – but it's worth it. These steeply forested slopes, with views sprawling as far as the Alps on cloud-free days, attract walkers in summer and cross-country skiers when the flakes fall in winter.

Fitting neatly into this rustic picture is Höhengasthaus Kolmenhof, a restaurant and hotel run by the third generation of the Dold family. Out front is the brook that flows into the Breg – the main source of the Danube. This accounts for the winningly fresh trout, which is served whole with almond butter and salted potatoes or poached in white wine.

For good old-fashioned Black Forest home-cooking, this place delivers, with a menu playing up regional grub, such as beef broth with *flädle* (pancake strips) and pork roast with buttery *spätzle* (egg noodles). *www.kolmenhof.de; tel +49 7723 931 00; Neuweg 11, Martinskapelle; 8am-8.30pm daily*

05 King of the Black Forest gateau, Claus Schäfer

06 The world's largest cuckoo clock in Triberg

WHERE TO STAY

REBSTOCK WALDULM

Nestled among vineyards and orchards and producing its own wine and schnapps, family-run Rebstock Waldulm is a delightful hotel, with bags of half-timbered charm. *www.rebstock-waldulm. de; tel +49 7842 9480; Kappelrodeck/Waldulm*

HOTEL BAREISS

This Baiersbronn hotel offers every imaginable luxury – plush rooms and suites, beautiful grounds, its own wine cellar and children's club and a spa. *www.bareiss.com; tel +49 7442 470*

BAIERSBRONN-MITTELTAL PARKHOTEL WEHRLE

Hemingway once waxed lyrical about this 400-year-old hotel in Triberg, which has beautiful antique-furnished quarters, a superb spa and a highly regarded restaurant. *www.parkhotel-wehrle. de; tel +49 7722 860 20*

WHAT TO DO

This is one big forest, so plan your time wisely. In Baden-Baden, take in its neoclassical pump room and star-studded collection of modern and contemporary art at the Museum Frieder Burda (www.museum-frieder-burda.de), and linger for a nude splash in the thermal waters of the cupola-topped Friedrichsbad (www.carasana.de). In Triberg, gawp at the world's biggest cuckoo clock at Eble Uhren-Park (www.uhren-park.de) and hike up the seven tiers of Germany's highest waterfall, the 163m-high Triberger Wasserfälle.

CELEBRATIONS

Dubbed the 'fifth season', Swabian-Alemmanic Fasnacht is a 500-year-old rite to banish winter and indulge in pre-Lenten parades, feasting and late-night drinkathons. Find it in towns and villages including Rottweil, Schramberg and Elzach. Stuttgart hosts its own take on Oktoberfest, the Cannstatter Volksfest (cannstatter-volksfest. de), in late September/early October. Christmas markets bring festive sparkle, mulled wine and gingerbread to almost every town and village in December.

Greece

SECRETS OF THE CRETAN DIET

Crete's farm-to-table cuisine is a way of life that has been handed down through generations, and today the island is focusing on its authentic food with renewed gusto.

Much has been made of the Cretan Diet, notably in American physiologist Dr Ancel Keys' *Seven Countries Study* in the 1950s. It found that men in Crete's mountainous villages had excellent longevity and very low instances of heart disease and cancer. Locals will downplay the Cretan Diet (heavily based on olive oil – even more so than mainland Greece – pulses, vegetables, nuts, fish and honey), noting there is nothing new about their seasonal way of living. In fact, it is more of a philosophy than a 'diet': the ancient Cretans had organic principles before the word was even applied to food.

The countryside is fragrant with wild herbs: sage, oregano, rosemary, thyme, 'immortal basil', marjoram and parsley. Villagers scour the mountains for *horta* (wild greens), taught over generations which are poisonous and which are nutritious. Nothing is wasted: herbs are used not just in cooking but in revitalising mountain tea, known

NEED TO KNOW
Crete's international airport is in Iraklio, at the start of this trail. Allocate three days to do this trip justice; hire a car.

for anti-inflammatory and healing properties. Cretan peasants were hunting and gathering high-protein *kohli* (snails) and eating more of them than France (without culinary fanfare) for millennia. And while plenty is eaten fresh, on Crete fruits are also preserved, meat and fish is smoked, vegetables are marinated and pickled: the people have always been resourceful, aware they're at nature's mercy.

Greece's economic crisis has only served to reinforce this 'take from the land, give back to the land' ethos of respect and hard work. Today, Crete's restaurants are renewing their focus on the island's authentic cuisine, with the Greek Academy of Taste certifying restaurants that both preserve the nature of the Cretan diet and promote positive cultural identity. Surrounded by water, predominantly mountainous with a goldmine of natural resources, Crete is, simply, the healthiest place to eat in the world.

01 Sivan Askayo © Lonely Planet

01 Classic Greek cuisine

02 The charming courtyard at Avli

03 Classic Cretan landscape

04 Cretan Olive Oil Farm

01 IRAKLIO MARKET

Your best introduction to the many ingredients Crete has to offer is along pedestrianised 1866 St in the centre of Iraklio. The market is a prime opportunity to chat to a fishmonger about the catch of the day, try thyme honey with *graviera* cheese, or nibble on stuffed olives.

Stock up for a picnic, for edible souvenirs to take home or just settle in one of the cosy *kafeneia* (traditional cafes), which still hosts plenty of locals enjoying strong Greek coffee, pastries and an animated chat.
Odos 1866; 8am-2pm Mon-Sat

02 CRETAN OLIVE OIL FARM

Take the scenic seaside drive about an hour east from Iraklio to Havania where, right by the Bay of Mirabello, you'll find Cretan Olive Oil Farm. The farm has been in its current peaceful location since 2010. It was established by Anastasios Spiridis and is now run with the help of his son, Costas, who is working with his father to reinstate disappearing Cretan farming traditions.

Since 2014 Costas has (with assistance from the occasional WWOOF – World Wide Opportunities on Organic Farms – volunteer) restored his family's ancient olive oil press, originally built in 1882 – one of only two on the island in which olive oil is painstakingly made by hand. Anastasios played a big role advising the authors of two best-selling books about the secrets of Cretan cuisine; and a tour of his beautiful farm and gardens is an eye-opener, not just about olive oil but also the power of Cretan herbs and nutrition.

Watch the video of the first 2014 experiment of hand-grinding the olives in the stone mill, and first pressing with the 135-year-old wooden press, then taste the 'healing oil', as Hippocrates called it.
www.cretanoliveoilfarm.gr; tel +30 28410 24319; Havania, Agios Nikolaos; open 9.30am-7pm Mon-Sat, 10am-2pm Sun Apr-Oct, on request Nov-Mar

03 ELIA & DIOSMOS

Return to Iraklio and head south towards Knossos. In the little village of Skalani you'll find Argiro Barda, an elegant one-woman dynamo who oversees this sprawling, stylish taverna that pays homage to the seasons.

Elia & Diosmos translates as 'olive and mint', and the name encapsulates everything she has in her garden. 'All of Skalani is my garden!' she half jokes, as she buzzes in and out, working with what nature has given her that day: producing homemade

fennel pies, stoking fires at one of the outdoor patio ovens, kneading fresh pasta to go with lamb broth or dishing up her sister's pickled sweet quince over *halva* (a slice of semolina).

She's non-stop, but pull up a wooden chair and try to catch her for a chat. Try whatever she recommends ('these dolmades are with shrimp, no not normal, not normal, but is the season') because with such respect for her ingredients, there's no better judge of a daily special.
www.olive-mint.gr; tel +30 28107 31283; Dimokratias 263, Skalani; lunch & dinner Tue-Sun

04 KRITAMON

A short drive south of Skalani, right in the middle of Iraklio Wine Country, lies the enchanting village of Archanes. Among the maze of pretty, flower-filled alleys veering off from the main square is Kritamon, a restaurant presided over by Dimitris Mavrakis – local boy turned protégé of Michelin-starred chef Alain Ducasse – who plates up delights of the season sourced from his farm or local producers.

There is huge respect here for rustic Cretan cooking (*kritamon* means 'fennel of the sea', a forgotten Mediterranean vegetable with ancient Greek origins) yet the chef's experienced touch is evident. Whether it's the oozing, smoked saganaki encrusted in sunflower seeds served with *petimezi* (a grape syrup) or smoked pork chop with sage, vegetables and orange olive oil sauce, everything is enticing. Don't miss the wild *horta*, the famous Cretan greens that Dimitris harvests from nearby Mt Juktas, drizzled with lemon juice.

It's incredibly easy to linger in the garden courtyard with homemade raki (Crete's ubiquitous spirit, made from grape skins and must), deliciously infused with mint, thyme and lemon verbena.
www.kritamon.gr; +30 28107 53092; Vathy Petrou 4, Archanes; dinner daily, lunch Sat-Sun

05 ELEONAS TAVERNA

Head back via Iraklio following breathtaking twists and turns to the village of Zaros, located at the foot of Mt Psiloritis (Crete's highest mountain) and home to the island's spring water supply. Just 1.5km away, you'll spot the *eleonas* (olive groves) and your first hint of this gorgeous taverna, which is in a truly scenic spot with 360-degree views over the valley.

Here you can eat traditional Cretan recipes made by Koula (the mother of the owner, Manolis Saridakis) who,

along with a local chef, prepares meals for diners at the taverna. She collects fresh vegetables and herbs from the gardens, eggs from the chickens, and while you sip *malotira* (Cretan mountain tea) or local wine, you'll be overwhelmed by the heady aromas, whether that be the lamb *kleftiko* (a dish originating from the Turkish occupation of Crete), *pilafi* (a rice dish, perhaps with meltingly tender goat), *stamnagathi* (a wild mountain green), or potatoes with *anthotyros* cheese.

Overnight guests at Eleonas can also partake in cooking lessons in the kitchen with Koula for an interactive insight into her magic work. *www.eleonas.gr; tel +30 28940 31238; Zaros; lunch & dinner daily in summer, Fri-Sun in winter*

06 AVLI

Head west to the small city of Rethymno, with its Venetian-Ottoman coastal charm. A feast for all the senses awaits at Avli where meticulous, multitasking owner Katerina Xekalou runs cooking classes and is a font of knowledge about Cretan cuisine.

Avli means 'the yard'; a nostalgic reference to Katerina's summer childhoods in Crete and the time she spent in her grandparents' huge courtyard surrounded by her cousins, aunts and uncles, while her grandmother regularly cooked for up to 30 people. When you take one of her classes, it's clear Katerina has inherited the hostess gene: book a place on the 'Introduction to Cretan food culture', where she provides a historical overview of the fascinating

philosophy behind the Cretan way of life. You'll get to take home a customised recipe book following your sumptuous, beautifully presented banquet. You won't want to leave the utterly charming surroundings. *www.avli.com; tel +30 28310 58250; Xanthoudidou 22*

07 PESKESI

Head east along the coastal road to Iraklio for a final meal at Peskesi, a converted cottage secreted away down a tiny lane. A relative newcomer to Crete's fine-dining scene, Peskesi is the brainchild of owner Dr Panagiotis Magganas, who has researched Cretan gastronomy for more than 10 years. Its menu is a joy: such care and attention to detail is given to the explanation of dishes, the dedication to reviving

forgotten, pure products of the land – even from Minoan times – and championing their nutritional value.

Take the warm hand towel infused with *sarantavotano* (a concoction of 40 herbs) and the card telling its touching story: it's an old recipe of balneotherapy using endemic aromatic plants with healing properties. Order one of the refreshing raki cocktails, which might involve spearmint, homemade thyme, honey and lavender syrup. Salivate over a pork chop smoking over thyme and sage at your table. Here is where the lessons from your trip come together: you are truly worshipping the resurgence of authentic Cretan cuisine.
www.peskesicrete.gr; tel +30 28102 88887; Kapetan Charalampi 6-8, Iraklio; from 10am

05-06 Cretan farmers and artichokes in a market

WHERE TO STAY

ELEONAS COTTAGES
Popular with hikers and cyclists (mountain bikes are available), as well as foodies who just want to get back to nature, this is a real family affair. Owner Manolis presides over this eco-friendly paradise of private hillside cottages. His father works the olive farm and extensive gardens, his mother is in the kitchen preparing the breakfast buffets of home-grown cuisine, and his cheesemaker brother's magnificent *mizithra* is among the traditional local produce available.
www.eleonas.gr; tel +30 28940 31238; Zaros

GALAXY HOTEL
A five-star hotel, Galaxy also boasts a five-star location, just 3km from Iraklio airport and within walking distance of the city centre. The staff are charming and genuine, and there's an extraordinary variety of healthy Cretan specialities available at breakfast, with a constantly changing buffet denoting local sources of origin.
www.galaxy-hotel.com; tel +30 28102 38812; 75 Dimokratias Ave, Iraklio

WHAT TO DO

The ruined Palace of Knossos, 5km south of Iraklio, is Crete's most infamous and elaborate archaeological site; some 4000 years ago it was the capital of ancient Minoan Crete. The palace has been partially reconstructed to reveal layer upon layer of invention and decadent living. Many of its original frescoes and findings are now housed in the Museum of Archaelogy in Iraklio, so a combined visit (purchase a ticket at either site) is the best way to do history justice. Do take a guided tour at Knossos to deepen your understanding.

CELEBRATIONS

For a truly authentic Cretan celebration, befriend a local and get a word-of-mouth invitation to a village event, whether that be a farmer's party to celebrate a successful olive harvest, the end of sheep shearing season, a baby's birth or a bit of grape stomping. Or seek out some grass-roots events, such as the Zaros International Competition of Traditional Cuisine (contact Eleonas Taverna for details) in late March.

NORTH
ATLANTIC
OCEAN

STYKKISHÓLMUR

02

03 RIF

05

BÚÐIR

04

05

01 ERPSSTAÐIR

BORGARNES

06

REYKJAVÍK 07

08

ICELAND

Iceland

FJORDLAND FOODS & ARCTIC BOUNTY

Tradition collides with innovation on Iceland's cultural West Coast, where Reykjavík and its surrounding villages pay homage to local produce in experimental cuisine.

Coined 'The Land of Fire and Ice' for its vistas of notorious volcanoes and frost-ridden glaciers, Iceland is an island nation that never disappoints – geysers gush, mud pots gloop, stone towers rise from the sea, and arctic gales swish through the merciless tundra. For nature-lovers, it's pure nirvana.

But Iceland is so much more than an artist's palette of snowy whites, mossy greens and cool Caribbean blues. It is home to a culture unlike any other on the planet – one that has lucidly scrawled its dramatic evolution in thousand-year-old tomes, and has set the bar high as a modern trailblazer in everything from progressive politics to innovative architectural design.

While the majority of the island embraces its arctic assets, west Iceland has become the hotbed for the nation's cultural pursuits.

This of course includes a sophisticated palate for elaborate, refined cuisine – not unlike that of the island's Scandinavian brethren.

A journey along the region's coast reveals bustling sheep, horse, and dairy farms in the north, which produce top-class meats for the restaurant tables and local cheese and yoghurt; fjords full of delicious shellfish; and cottages serving homespun fare by the spoonful.

The shoreline wends through buzzing Reykjavík, the capital city, where you can sip top-shelf tipples and see stars in the kitchen – maybe of the Michelin variety one day.

Further south the coast peters off along the stark Reykjanes Peninsula. Here, among the lava fields, is the country's international airport at Keflavík, and main entry point to this fairy-tale foodie nation.

NEED TO KNOW
This trail fits neatly into a 2-day weekend: Reykjavik is walkable but, outside town, life's easier with a car.

01 ERPSSTAÐIR DAIRY FARM

In the top recesses of the Dalir region along Iceland's upper west coast, the Erpsstaðir dairy farm appears like a mirage for sweet-toothed wanderers along Rte 60. Park at the grey barn and you can tour the farm, greet the buxom bovines, then gorge on a signature scoop of 'Kjaftæði', or 'Bullshit', the brand name of the scrumptious ice cream made on site and sold all over the country.

The farm also makes skýr (protein-rich yoghurt) and cheese – try the oddly shaped konfekt (which is meant to look like an udder, but possibly bears more resemblance to a suppository) – a delicious dessert made from a hard white chocolate shell that encases thick yoghurt-y skýr in the middle.

www.erpsstadir.is; tel +354-868-0357; Buðardalur; 1-5pm June–mid-Sept

02 BJARNARHOFN

As Rte 54 burrows through the jagged lava fields on the Snæfellsnes Peninsula, pass the turn-off to the adorable township of Stykkishólmur to find the farmstead at Bjarnarhöfn marked by a large metal sculpture of a shark. Smell that? It's rotting flesh – the farm is the region's leading producer of hákarl (putrid shark meat), a traditional Icelandic dish.

The on-site museum details the fragrant history of this culinary curiosity by displaying restored shark fishing boats, harpooning tools, and explaining the fermenting process. Each visit to the museum comes with a complimentary nibble of the delicacy in question along with a piece of rye bread to wash it down. Some say it tastes like a sponge dipped in ammonia, but that tang could also be old cheese.

Before you leave, ask about the drying house out back. If you're lucky you'll see hundreds of dangling shark slices being attacked by zealous flies (you'll be glad you tried the shark meat before visiting the drying house!).

www.bjarnarhofn.is; tel +354-438-1581; Bjarnarhöfn; 9am-6pm

03 GAMLA RIF

Further down Rte 54, under the shadow of the Snæfell glacier near the tip of the peninsula is the blink-and-you'll-miss-it village of Rif. Pull off the main road to find the old white house where two fishermen's wives make a mean homemade fish soup (from their husbands' daily catch) with notes of curry and tomato.

If you're feeling extra-peckish, they've also perfected a variety of

> '`Chemists say the water at Snæfellsnes is practically a delicacy – the most naturally rich potable fluid on the planet`'

01 The scenic Snæfellsnes peninsula

02 Sun Voyager sculpture, Reykjavík

03 Street art in Reykjavík

04 Prized lamb dogs at Bæjarins Beztu Pylsur

05 Kaldi craft beer bar, Reykjavík

traditional snacks, such as *kleinar* (doughnuts), and dispense local travel tips with a smile.
Háarif 3; tel +354-436-1001; 12-8pm Jun-Aug

04 HÓTEL BÚÐIR

Windswept, lonely and very romantic, Búðir, on the peninsula's southern side, is primarily an inn but its restaurant has long been a beacon for dinnertime twists on traditional Icelandic dishes.

The restaurant also celebrates local produce: finish your day's explorations with a meal that might include blue mussels from a nearby fjord, trout from a neighbouring lake, and local lamb fresh from the farm down the road; look out for pesto made from Icelandic algae and seaweed.
www.budir.is; tel +354-435-6700; Búðir; 6-10pm

05 SNÆFELLSNES GEOTHERMAL WATERS

The next day drive south along the southern shore of the Snæfellsnes. A stark contrast with yesterday's northern jaunt, here the mountainous spine of peninsula gracefully arcs down into lonely beaches dotted by a smattering of steaming vents.

The pockets of warm air that mingle with the cool Arctic breeze are the quiet clues to a secret network of mineral-rich water that circulates beneath the earth. The island's geothermal activity is perhaps the most defining element of Icelandic culture: myths and legends revolve around seismic events; the elaborate bathing culture focuses squarely on natural 'hot pots'; and the source water itself – now exported all over the globe – gives vitality to thirsty locals.

The farm at Ökelda (which means 'mineral spring' in Icelandic), near Staðarstaður on Rte 54, allows passers-by to stop on the property and fill up their water bottles full of what chemists say is practically a delicacy – the most naturally rich potable fluid on the planet. It's common courtesy to leave some pocket change for the convenience, and if you're so inclined there's a swimming pool full of the magic water down the road at Lýsuhólslaug. It's fenced in at the area's elementary school, but open every afternoon in the summer months (June to August).

06 FRIÐRIK V

Head to Reykjavík, Iceland's capital, where Chef Friðrik and wife Adda hold court as champions of Iceland's proud local food movement. Friends with a slew of nearby farmers and

04 Radharc Images © Alamy

05 Icelandic Photo agency © Alamy

ranchers, they create nightly medleys with their produce in this 32-seat mom-and-pop restaurant.

With only one seating per evening, they take great care in preparing their set menus (wine pairings also available), which boast lamb, fish, fowl and greenhouse-grown veggies. Diners delight in the so-called Wall of Fame, a corkboard showing the photos of the individuals and animals responsible for cultivating the ingredients found in the nightly dishes, like Begga the cow, who made the colostrum in the crème brûlée (yes, colostrum).
www.fridrikv.is; tel +354-461-5775; Laugavegur 60; 5.30pm-close Tue-Sat

07 KALDI

Partying is such a crucial component of modern Icelandic culture that the locals even have a special name for it: djammið. And in the summer months, when the sun never sets, it's easy to while away an entire evening bouncing between the capital's bars and clubs.

Rather than scorching the tonsils with a shot of *brennivín* – meaning 'burnt wine' – Iceland's version of aquavit, try a stop at Kaldi for sips of eight varieties of its eponymous beer; Iceland's foremost local brew.

Tours of the factory are available to those willing to log 400km in the car to reach the facility along Eyjafjörður, but this bar just down the road from Friðrik's is a much easier option for a laid-back flight of samples with an expert bartender on hand.
www.kaldibar.com; tel +354-581-2200; Laugavegur 20b; 12pm-1am Sun-Thu, 12pm-3am Fri-Sat

08 BÆJARINS BEZTU PYLSUR

As evening turns to morning, walk down to the harbour to coat your stomach with one of the most celebrated and essential nibbles in modern Iceland: the hot dog.

Reykjavíkers love their fast food, probably due to the decades of American influence from the US

naval base nearby (which effectively shuttered in 2006), but these wieners are truly special.

Hawked from a wooden shack in a seaside parking space (look for the inevitable long line), these lamb-based dogs are boiled in beer, which gives them their uniquely savoury flavour. Order it 'med öllu' (with everything) and you'll find delightful little crunchy onions on top as well.
www.bbp.is; tel +354-511-1566; Tryggagata, near Kolaportid; 10am-1am Sun-Thu, to 4.30am Fri-Sat

06 Michael Dwyer © Alamy

07 Brytta © Getty Images

08 Arctic Images © Getty Images

WHERE TO STAY

HOTEL EGILSEN

If fisher-chic were ever a trend, its undoubted genesis is this adorable inn, set in a merchant's refurbished timber manse in the heart of seaside Stykkishólmur. Complimentary iPads and a locally sourced breakfast sweeten the deal. *www.egilsen.is; tel +354-554-7700; Aðalgata 2, Stykkishólmur*

ICELANDAIR HOTEL REYKJAVÍK MARINA

This stylish hotel in a renovated factory comes up trumps for its clever design and convenient location for all of the capital's major attractions, including the scenic harbour. A swanky cocktail bar in the lobby and fjord views add to the allure. *www.icelandairhotels. com/en/hotels/marina; tel +354-444-4000; Mýrargata 2, Reykjavík*

WHAT TO DO

SETTLEMENT MUSEUM

The west coast Settlement Centre in Borgarnes offers a fascinating insight into the history of Icelandic settlement and the Viking Saga era through interactive exhibits. Relive the adventures of anti-hero Egil – of Icelandic Saga literary fame – and then head to the on-site restaurant to try one of its traditional Icelandic dishes, such as *plokkfiskur* (a buttery fish-and-potato mash). *www.landnam.is; tel +354-437-1600*

WHALE WATCHING

Of all of Iceland's big-ticket attractions, whale watching is quite possibly the only activity that offers both a truly memorable experience and directly benefits the local environment, as locals increasingly appreciate the value in keeping these great creatures alive. Eco-friendly cruisers depart from both Reykjavík (try Elding; www.elding.is) and Grundarfjörður further north (www.lakitours.com) in search of the graceful beasts that raise their fins and puff plumes of water above the waves.

CELEBRATIONS

During the month of October, farmers across Iceland organise what is known as the *rettir*, or round-up, during which they ride through hills by horse and walk through the tundra with their dogs to gather their sheep before the first frost. Travellers can volunteer to help herd the sheep and afterwards you'll be treated to a very local lamb stew for lunch. Ask at the tourist information centre in Borgarnes for details. (www.westiceland.is)

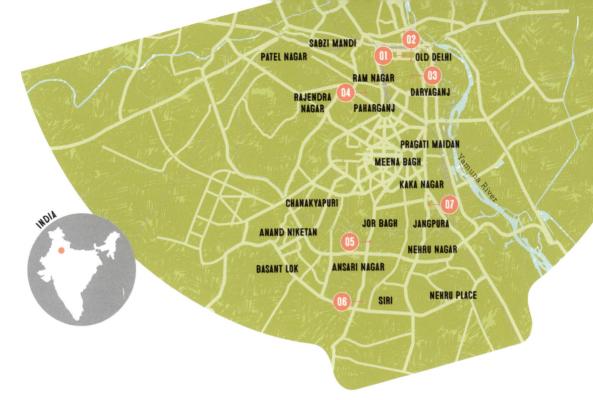

India

HAWKERS OF DELHI CHAAT

The streets of India's pulsating capital are home to a unique network of hawkers who are experts in just one dish: follow them to get under the skin of India's diverse cuisine.

Delhi is India's bamboozling capital, a cacophony of crowds and traffic, medieval-seeming bazaars and brightly hued temples, but with surprising pockets of calm in the form of Mughal tombs, lakes and tranquil parks. Amid all this, street food provides its own special culinary alchemy and moments of joy. Eating on the street is a great leveller, bridging, if only momentarily, the chasm between rich and poor. Delhi is especially renowned for its snacks or 'chaat' sold by the roadside. You'll find some of the world's most tantalising morsels to eat in this city, its creative innovations wrapping an explosion of different flavours up in one bite, rather like the city itself.

In India, anywhere there are people passing, you'll see street food hawkers. Every street corner seems to have something happening foodwise – be it sizzling, wrapping, bubbling, deep-frying, kneading or grilling – with hawkers

deftly creating what is usually their single speciality. Different cultures within the city have brought their own traditions, such as *chana bhatura* (spicy chickpeas with an inflated light-as-air fried bread) from the Punjab, or *bhelpuri* – a cavalcade of spicy yet sweet vegetarian flavours, which originates from Gujarat.

Most of these are produced from hand carts or hole-in-the-wall booths, which occasionally have a couple of seats, but more often you'll eat standing up, having queued with a few dozen other eager customers awaiting something fresh from the fire.

There are hundreds of hawkers around the city, some of which have been plying their trade for generations. You could easily spend two or more days meandering through the older parts of the city, which are particularly good for discovering mind-blowingly good *dilli ka chaat* (Delhi street food).

01 Mint © Getty Images

NEED TO KNOW
Delhi is big and this trail traverses the new and old city districts, so use the gleaming metro to get about.

01 GALI PARANTHE WALI

The most famous of Delhi's street food stops are found in the teeming bazaars of Old Delhi, which lie just off the *Wacky Races*-crazy boulevard of Chandni Chowk. Here, among the lanes selling bobbins, ribbons and glittering robes, a narrow alley is famous for a single speciality, the *paranthe* (fried flat bread).

Gali Paranthe Wali dates from the time of the Mughals and is thought to be up to 300 years old. Clustered along here are hole-in-the-wall places where you can sample *paranthe* with many different fillings, such as mashed potato spiced with cumin. The breads are usually served with cooling curd – a foil to the gentle spices of the filling.
Gali Paranthe Wali, Old Delhi

02 JALEBIWALLA

Fancy something sweet after a *parantha*? Something like a golden spiral of syrup-drenched fried

wheat batter? You're in the perfect place. This is an opportunity not to be missed. Turn back on to busy thoroughfare Chandni Chowk, whose name evokes the mirrorlike waterway that once ran along the centre of this imperial approach, which reflected the moon. Now the street is a constant hooting-tooting, gridlocked traffic tangle of rickshaws, taxis, pedestrians, cows and piled-high trolleys.

This is where, on a busy corner, you can see and taste the golden spirals of Jalebiwalla. The hawker is raised above street level and sits opposite a huge vat of bubbling oil. All day he freshly fries wheat batter into magical-seeming golden yellow-orange spiral shapes, which are then steeped in sugar syrup. There's a perpetual crowd waiting for the tooth-tingling sweets, which are cooked in batches and then snapped up immediately.
Chandni Chowk

03 KARIM'S

A sugar rush is the ideal way to prepare for a launch off into the frenetic bazaars, which are divided into sections according to the wares for sale. Ribbons, lace and decorations fill Kinari bazaar, while in the surrounding lanes you can buy *jootis* (leather slippers) and clothes. When you're ready for lunch, in the shadow of Delhi's Jama Masjid (Great Mosque), lies one of Old Delhi's gastronomic institutions – Karim's.

This is one of the icons of Muslim cooking in Delhi. The highly carnivorous icon may not look like much, with its wipe-clean tables and fast-and-furious service, but it's famous throughout the city and has some of the capital's finest meat dishes. There are several branches across town, but this is the oldest, the best, and most atmospheric. Its story begins when the son of a former Imperial cook decided to

01 Jalebiwalla's sweet golden spirals on Chandni Chowk

02 Fruit seller takes a roadside break

03 Gali Paranthe Wali – fried bread lane – in Old Delhi

04 Delhi's Red Fort

open a food stall outside the Red Fort to cash in on the visit of King George V and Queen Mary in 1911, offering just two dishes – mutton with potatoes and lentil curry.

A few years later he opened the Karim Hotel (one of the 99 names of Allah in Islam, meaning generous and bountiful) in a permanent location, and today it still specialises in Mughal cooking, with recipes passed down from the time of the Islamic imperial court in Delhi – they still use the secret spice combination created by the original Mughal chef, and serve dishes such as slowly cooked, velvety *nihari* (beef) stew (traditionally eaten for breakfast) and the fragrant, marinated *seekh* kebab. If you're not yet ready for more food, simply step inside to observe the frenetic theatre of the open-sided kitchen.
www.karimhoteldelhi.com; tel +91 11-2326 9880; Gali Kababian, Jama Masjid, Old Delhi; 9am-12.30am

04 SITA RAM DIWAN CHAND

On your second day of exploring Delhi's street food, start with a breakfast of *chana bhatura*, spicy chickpeas served with fried puffs of bread, light and hot.

One of the best places in Delhi to sample this is, surprisingly, Paharganj, Delhi's backpacker district, better known for its people-pleasing globe-encompassing menus than for its local cooking. However, Sita Ram Diwan Chand is renowned Delhi-wide and its stainless-steel, no-fuss interior accommodates hoards of people during the day, queuing for the delicious yet cheaply priced snack.

As with all Delhi's street food: if you're only going to do one dish, do it well.
Tel +91 11-2358 7380; 2243 Rajguru Marg, Chuna Mandi, Paharganj; 8am-6pm

05 INA MARKET

Next, take Delhi's gleaming metro over to INA Market, which has its own eponymous metro stop. Standing for Indian National Army Market (because it lies alongside the residential colony maintained by the Airports Authority of India) this is Delhi's most sumptuous and colourful food bazaar selling both local and imported produce, spreading into many tentacles of narrow lanes.

As in Old Delhi's bazaars, each specialises in a particular type of produce. It's in an upmarket area and the stalls seethe with better produce than you'll find anywhere else in the city; it's a great place to wander and explore Delhi's food culture. Piles of fresh fish gleam silver, roosters stalk about and chickens huddle in cages, haunches piled high on meat stalls. There are heaped spices, and fresh fruit and vegetables, with a rainbow of carefully stacked pyramids.

Favoured by Delhi's expat community, the stallholders encounter many different nationalities, and so they speak multiple languages, often including French, German, Japanese, and more.
Sri Aurobindo Marg, INA Colony, South Delhi; 10am-8.30pm

06 SAFFRON PALATE

Having grazed your way around the city, it's time to try making some food for yourself. Saffron Palate is run by Neha Gupta and is based at her family home in the South Delhi arty suburb of Hauz Khas.

The enclave is full of small independent bars, restaurants and boutiques, and borders a rambling park containing several domed, red-stone tombs and a lake that reflects the surrounding greenery and the sky. Neha's corner house faces an 800-year-old temple and tomb.

Neha's lessons teach homestyle North Indian cooking, but are also a chance to immerse yourself in a classic Indian family set-up – rarer and rarer in India's big cities because of the confines of urban living: here there are four generations spread across three storeys of the house.

Neha teaches dishes that are easy to cook at home, such as *saag paneer*, butter chicken, *mutter rogan josh*, and *aloo gobi*; and also Delhi street foods such as *pakora aloo tikki*, and *gol gappas* (puffed fried bread filled with a mixture of flavoured water, chutney, chilli, masala, potato, onion and chickpeas). Ask Neha for tips on eating street food safely in Delhi and you'll find she's a mine of information: 'The cooking part should be in a covered area. There should be plenty of customers, and it should not seem the oil is being reused over and over again. You should avoid dishes that have water in them – for example *gol gappas* – better to have things that are freshly fried.'
saffronpalate.com; tel +91 4100 3049; Block R21, 1st Floor, Hauz Khas Enclave

07 NIZAMUDDIN

For dinner, head over to the Muslim area of Nizamuddin – a back-in-time place with a mosque seemingly on every corner and a maze of narrow streets cobwebbing out from around the shrine devoted to the resting place of the sufi saint Hazrat Nizamuddin

Dargah. Thousands of pilgrims come here nightly and the shrine itself is a whirl of colour, incense and confusion. There are nightly *qaawaalis* (traditional devotional prayers) sung, which draw the most crowds on Thursday evenings at sundown.

However, any night of the week there are also carnivorous delights on offer, serving the busy flow of pilgrims in the narrow lanes around the shrine. You can buy sizzling, divine-tasting kebabs on skewers from the many food stalls, watching them cooked by the flames that shoot up from the grills on handcarts. Made from buffalo meat, they're velvety soft, succulent, and delicately spiced. *Lodi Colony Kebab Stands, Hazrat Nizamuddin Dargah, Nizamuddin West; noon–11pm*

05 Street vendor hawks candy floss

06 Frying up paranthe bread

07 Whirls of colour at Nizamuddin

WHERE TO STAY
SCARLETTE
A serene escape from Delhi's perpetual bustle, Scarlette is a French-owned boutique guest house, with a beautiful sitting-dining room and four spacious bedrooms, sparingly and thoughtfully decorated with Indian textiles and vintage photographs *scarlettenewdelhi.com; tel +91 8826 010278; Safdarjung Enclave*

ROSE
This small, white-painted hotel is a tranquil retreat in the Hauz Khas enclave, between the narrow lanes of the commercial district and the raggle-taggle village around the outskirts. The rooms are decorated in earthy, pale colours, with beautiful Indian furnishings. *www.the-rose-guest-house.new-delhi-hotel. net/en; tel +91 6568 0444; T40 Hauz Khas Village*

WHAT TO DO
Where do you start? Having immersed yourself in the street life of Old Delhi, you're perfectly placed to visit the Mughal Red Fort – a still-mighty, if depleted, palace and fortress, which was later used as a barracks by the British. Nearby is Old Delhi's 17th-century Great Mosque, which lives up to its name, with capacity for 25,000 faithful. In South Delhi you can visit the serenely symmetrical Mughal Humayan's Tomb, one of Delhi's pockets of tranquility and which provided architectural inspiration for the Taj Mahal. Head further south to see the site of Qutb Minar, where you'll find extraordinary architecture and India's first mosque (constructed out of broken Hindu temples).

CELEBRATIONS
Every festival in Delhi is accompanied by special things to eat, such as a profusion of *mithai* (sweets), made with dried fruits and often wrapped in edible silver, particularly at Diwali – the festival of lights – celebrated in October to November each year. To really immerse yourself in street food, time your visit for the National Street Food Festival (www. nasvinet.org), which takes place over several days in December.

India

A VEGETARIAN PILGRIMAGE TO CHENNAI

India's southern city of Chennai is dominated by a fiery cuisine that puts lentils, potatoes and tomatoes centre stage, challenging perceptions of humdrum vegetarian food.

India's north–south divide is an integral part of the national psyche. Being from the north, or from the south, is a badge of honour and a fierce source of personal pride. Predictably, both sides claim to be the 'real' India, but when it comes to food, the south has the most convincing claim to being the spiritual home of Indian cuisine. The word 'curry' was derived from the Tamil word *kari*, meaning spicy sauce, placing the birthplace of Indian cooking firmly in the cook pots of the steamy south.

As you traverse the country from north to south, place names get more exotic, temples become even more vividly colourful, and meat vanishes from the menus, replaced by a taste-bud tingling selection of vegetables in fiery sauces.

By the time you reach Chennai, the bustling capital of

NEED TO KNOW
This is a 2-day city trail: until the Chennai Metro is completed, you'll need pre-paid taxis to get around – or use your feet.

South India, 'non-veg' is almost a dirty term, and 'veg' and 'pure-veg' (which is even veggier – so no eggs, fish and often no onions or garlic) proudly take centre stage. Even the most hardened carnivore will be turned after just a few mouthfuls.

The foundation stone of South Indian cooking is the tamarind and lentil dipping sauce known as sambar, which is used to dunk everything from crispy dosas (rice flour pancakes) to vada (lentil-flour doughnuts), but chefs are ceaselessly inventive when it comes to finding ways to transform commonplace vegetarian staples, such as lentils, potatoes and tomatoes into gastronomic sensations.

Also look out for dishes made from exotic crops like okra, coconut, green mango and jackfruit, the fleshy state fruit of Kerala and Tamil Nadu.

VEPERY
04
05
CHETPET
EGMORE
PUDUPET
Kuvam River
06
CHEPAUK
NUNGAMBAKKAM
TRIPLICANE
02
GOPALAPURAM
Bay of Bengal
TEYNAMPET
T NAGAR
01
ALWARPET
MYLAPORE
03

INDIA

01 MURUGAN IDLI SHOP

Foreigners always seem a little taken aback the first time they have curry for breakfast, but in Chennai no breakfast would be complete without the zesty zing of sambar. Tamarind and lentils give sambar its sour but mellow tones, and curry leaves, mustard seeds and dried red chillies add punctuation marks of flavour, waking up the senses for the day ahead. The yang to sambar's yin is coconut chutney, a deceptively mild-looking white relish that packs a hidden chilli punch. It's such a perfect combo that you rarely see the two of them apart.

All manner of south Indian dishes come with sambar and chutney, but at breakfast time there's really only one choice: idli – pale, puffy, lightly fermented full-moons made from steamed rice and husked black lentils.

For anyone nervous about the idea of curry for breakfast, the light, fresh taste of idli will ease you in gently. Everyone in Chennai knows that T Nagar's Murugan Idli serves the very best in town, and the dining room is busy morning noon and night. So order, rip and dip into the spicy sambar, and prepare yourself for the frenetic pace of life in the Tamil Nadu capital. *www.muruganidlishop.com; tel +91 44 2815 5462; 77-1/A, GN Chetty Rd, T Nagar; 7am-11.30pm*

02 JUNIOR KUPPANNA

Chennai is a city that loves to lunch, and vast, multi-dish thalis are so close to the city's heart that locals just call them 'meals'. And what a meal! The average thali – as if any could truly be called 'average' – is a degustation sampling platter of south Indian flavours. Rice, chapattis, sambar, chutneys, *rasam* (tamarind-flavoured broth), an assortment of *sabzi* (vegetable) curries and cool curd (yoghurt), to douse the fiery chilli heat so beloved of south Indian cooks.

The best thalis are served not on plates but on giant banana leaves, so you'll have the added satisfaction of not contributing to the workload of the kitchen staff when it comes to washing up. A short rickshaw ride north from Murugan Idli, on the far side of Panagal Park, Junior Kuppanna serves one of the city's best and most flavoursome banana-leaf thalis from its spotless kitchen with, unusually for Chennai, a choice of veg or non-veg. Locals also go bananas for its Pallipaliyam-style fried chicken with coconut and dried chillies. *Tel +91 44 3318 5195; 4 Kannaiya St, off North Usman Rd, T Nagar; 11.30am-4pm & 6.30-11pm*

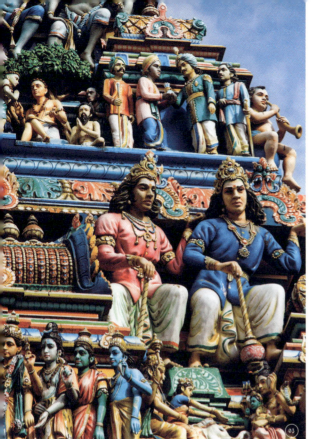

03 DAKSHIN

While in Chennai, it would be foolish not to take advantage of favourable rupee exchange rates to splurge on a lavish five-star dinner. Fine dining in India usually means hotel dining, and Chennai's five-star hotels have restaurants of jaw-dropping excellence. A rough-and-ready thali at a street-side mess may score highly for atmosphere, but the thali at Dakshin, the swish South Indian restaurant at the Crowne Plaza Adyar Park, takes things to a whole other level. It's routinely voted Chennai's best restaurant, and for good reason; to get here, just jump in an autorickshaw from T Nagar.

Dakshin's chefs are pure-veg ninjas, drawing on the rich culinary heritage of the six southern states: Tamil Nadu, Kerala, Karnataka, Andhra Pradesh, Telangana and the Union Territory of Puducherry (Pondicherry). The house veg thali is crammed to overflowing with lavishly spiced sauces, soups and *sabzi*, plus a bowl of curd to cool things down. It all arrives, northern-style – on a polished steel tray – but there's a banana leaf on the bottom to remind you where you are. Non-vegetarian diners can feast on seafood and meat thalis, as well as Chennai's most delicious *appams* (rice flour and coconut milk pancakes).
Tel +91 44 2499 4101; Crowne Plaza Chennai Adyar Park, 132 TTK Rd; 12.30-2.45pm & 7-11.45pm

04 SOUTH INDIAN COFFEE

Nothing could replace chai – sweet, milky Indian tea – in the hearts of 1.3 billion Indians, but in Chennai, coffee comes a very close second. Around a quarter of a million small coffee plantations are scattered across the southern states of Karnataka, Kerala and Tamil Nadu, and the bulk of the beans are served as *kapi* – filter coffee made with finely ground Indian beans, milk, sugar and chicory, for slightly nutty tones that offset the bitterness of the coffee. You can thank the French trading concessions on the Tamil Nadu coast for the chicory – they took the same idea to New Orleans.

When it comes to finding a perfect brew, forget the ever expanding selection of Western-style chain coffee houses (that's right Café Coffee Day, Barista, Starbucks – we're talking about you). Instead, seek out Chennai's best coffee on the streets, prepared by roadside baristas using old-fashioned polished steel coffee urns, and

served with a long pour and a flourish from dawn til bedtime. Historic George Town is a good place to start, before you wander off to explore the streets that once housed the British colonial administration.

05 HOTEL SARAVANA BHAVAN

It's a short autorickshaw ride from George Town to Egmore's most popular fast-food house, part of a home-grown chain that has an almost religious following in Chennai. The vegetarian food at Hotel Saravana Bhavan is nothing short of spectacular; here, legions of cooks whisk up all the flavours of the Indian south, from great *idli* and *kapi* in the morning, to lunchtime thalis and tasty after-work *vada* (spiced lentil-flour doughnuts) to set you up for the

commute home. Our tip is to make a meal of it, ordering a bit of everything – particularly the house dosas – deliciously crisp, rice flour pancakes served with the obligatory sambar and coconut chutney.

If this is your first dosa, push the boat out and try some of the myriad varieties of this legendary South Indian treat. Masala dosa – stuffed with spicy potato curry – is just the start; consider rava dosa, made with spices, curry leaves, ground nuts and semolina flour; kara dosa, made with a whole family tree of different types of lentils; or set dosa, soft, spongy dosas stacked in a tower. Order them topped with onions, *palak* (spinach) or *ghee* (melted butter), or enjoy the lightest, crispiest dosa of all, the paper dosa, which comes as thin as

parchment and as large as a rolled up copy of the *Times of India*. *www.saravanabhavan.com; tel +91 44 2819 2055; 21 Kennet Ln, Egmore; 6am-10pm*

06 MARINA BEACH

A short autorickshaw ride from Egmore, Marina Beach is where Chennai comes to escape the chaos, and you can almost hear the sigh of relief as people step onto the sand. This is the second longest urban beach in the world, stretching for more than 13km.

Though the waters can look quite inviting, swimming is banned because of the undercurrents, but locals are happy to wander in up to their ankles and then amble along the sands, haggling for trinkets, consulting

fortune tellers, and munching on plates of *chaat*, India's vast family of spicy vegetarian salads.

Some travellers are apprehensive about *chaat* because of worries about hygiene, but busy stalls are normally busy because the food is clean and tasty. Technically, this is going off-piste, as most *chaat* recipes come from Mumbai and other cities further north, but when you sample the remarkable variety of textures and flavours, you won't mind.

Two essential salads to try are Mumbai-style *bhelpuri*, with crisp noodles, shreds of green mango and sour tamarind, and *panipuri* – like savoury vol-au-vents stuffed with tamarind chutney, potatoes, onion and chickpeas. Vendors along Marina Beach are open from dawn to early evening.

01 Chennai's Government Museum

02 Sizzling dosas

03 Kapaleeswarar Mandir temple

04 Chef Praveen Anand at Dakshin

05 Local fisher casts a net at Marina Beach

06 Kaleidoscope of juices, Saravana Bhavan

07 Heaped spices in a Chennai market

WHERE TO STAY
BROADLANDS LODGE
A hippy stalwart that has hardly changed since the 1960s, with flaking paint, pale-blue balconies, and leafy courtyards where travellers like to gather and swap tales from the road. *Tel +91 44 2854 5573; 18 Vallabha Agraharam St, Opp Star Theatre, Triplicane*

FOOTPRINT B&B
There are just nine rooms at this low-key B&B in a calm apartment building in South Chennai, but they're lovingly cared for by hosts Rucha and Ashish, who also knock up an impressive breakfast. *www.chennaibedand breakfast.com; tel +91 9840037483; Gayatri Apartments, 16 South St, Alwarpet)*

VIVANTA BY TAJ CONNEMARA
The only heritage hotel in town, set in the former residence of the British governor. For high rates, you get gorgeous rooms set in a gleaming art deco villa. *www.vivantabytaj.com/ connemara-chennai; tel +91 44 6600 0000; Binny Rd*

WHAT TO DO
At the Government Museum in Egmore, galleries are piled high with a pantheon of deities in stone, wood and bronze. From here, it's a short autorickshaw ride to Fort St George, with its fading colonial buildings, and the endless sands of Marina Beach. Temples are plentiful – make time for the Parthasarathy Mandir and the rainbow-coloured Kapaleeswarar Mandir in Mylapore – and drop into San Thome Cathedral, to view the spot where the Bible's Doubting Thomas allegedly met his end.

CELEBRATIONS
The most important date on the Chennai calendar is Pongal in mid-January, when Chennai's already pampered cows get to feast on pots of rice boiled with milk and jaggery (palm sugar) – the pongal that gives the festival its name. Winter is also time for the fabulous Chennai Festival of Dance & Music, with a month of performances of Carnatic dance and music that will have you performing your own 'screwing in the lightbulb' dance before you realise what you are doing.

Indonesia

BALI'S LOCAVORE REVOLUTION

Changes are afoot in Bali's cultural capital, Ubud, where chefs are returning to their roots with traditional dishes that celebrate locally grown, sustainable produce.

Ubud has always been renowned as the cultural capital of Bali, hidden away in the centre of the island, surrounded by tumbling rice terraces and lush jungle. With its ancient temples and palaces, renowned dance troupes and vibrant artistic communities, visitors have long been drawn to this area of the Indonesian island. But today there is a revolution taking place, transforming it into Bali's food capital as well.

Rather than importing foie gras from France, Australian beef and oysters harvested in New Zealand, a new generation of chefs in Ubud are looking local rather than global, turning towards an abundance of superb ingredients available in Bali – partly the result of a movement to encourage sustainable small farmers to concentrate on seasonal organic produce. Now, chefs can choose from a cornucopia of high-quality vegetables and fruits, meat and locally caught fish and seafood.

The revolution is affecting all layers of the local food scene – even simple *warungs*. An integral part of daily life in Bali, these family-run cafes are open from breakfast for *burbur ayam* (chicken rice porridge) to late-night plates of satay. Ubud's *warungs* have long been cooking what they think the tourists want, from pizza and pasta to burgers, but things are changing. As one local chef explains, 'the Balinese have rediscovered their own delicious traditional cooking and stopped trying to turn out bland comfort grub for foreigners.' And it does not take long to discover the fundamental role food plays in Balinese life; there's the cycles that follow the planting, growing and harvesting of the island's life crop, rice. Or see each family making daily offerings of delicate food packages to the temple, and whole villages cooking together to prepare elaborate ceremonial dishes for the never-ending religious festivals that shape the calendar.

NEED TO KNOW
Flights to Bali arrive at Denpasar; this trail focuses on Ubud, 40km north – easily reached by bus or taxi.

01 MOZAIC

If there is one undisputed pioneer of Ubud's culinary renaissance it is Chris Salans, the French-American chef who opened his landmark Mozaic restaurant back in 2001. A splash-out meal in Mozaic's magical candlelit tropical gardens is a memorable journey through dishes that combine subtle European influences with the Balinese food and spices that so enthrall Salans; plump Indian Ocean prawns are paired with pickled radish and ginger flower, while yellow fin tuna is seared with Balinese long pepper, *kemangi* (lemon basil) and pomegranate. And for dessert, his signature potent mix of durian fruit and chocolate, baked in thin pastry with a fermented black rice sauce. *www.mozaic-bali.com; tel +62 361 975768; Jalan Raya Sanggingan, Ubud*

02 LOCAVORE

This revolutionary restaurant has taken Ubud by storm. 'Ubud was the only place we wanted to open our restaurant,' recounts Indonesian chef Ray Adriansyah, who cooks side by side with Dutch chef Eelke Plasjmeijer at Locavore. 'Locavore means we only use local, organic ingredients; from vegetables and fruit, to beef and sheep bred just outside Ubud or scallops and seaweed harvested by fishermen off Lombok. No imported produce – that is our rule.'

Ray and Eelke direct their team of chefs like orchestra conductors, so prepare for a remarkable tasting menu, paired with wine, craft beer and cocktails. Dishes might include thinly sliced squid with hot fennel consommé and seaweed, accompanied by a light rum cocktail with toasted fennel seeds; followed by homemade rabbit and mustard sausage with *arak* (a local spirit made from coconut palm or rice) and ginger-glazed carrots, paired with a dark wheat Bali-brewed beer.

Book two to three weeks ahead and if you have problems getting a reservation try Locavore To Go instead; its no-reservation diner and takeaway deli across the road. *www.locavore.co.id; tel +62 361 977733; Jalan Dewa Sita 10, Ubud*

03 SENIMAN COFFEE STUDIO

One of the greatest pleasures in Ubud is stopping at a tumbledown *warung* for a cup of pitch-black Balinese *kopi*, finely ground locally grown coffee beans mixed directly in the cup with hot water, leaving a thick muddy residue not dissimilar to Turkish coffee. Given the freshness of

'We only use local, organic ingredients. No imported produce – that is our rule'

01 Ubud's Monkey Forest Sanctuary

02 Locavore chef at work

03 Rice paddy fields surround Ubud

04 Workshop at Seniman Coffee Studio during Ubud Food Festival

03 Pete Seaward © Lonely Planet

04 Courtesy of Ubud Food Festival

the beans, it's littler wonder the global coffee revolution (and its bearded baristas) has taken Ubud by storm.

At the cool Seniman Coffee Studio connoisseurs can get a fix of single-origin organic beans sourced from fair-trade Indonesian farmers, dark or light roast, hand-pulled or siphoned. Seniman also runs coffee workshops, covering tasting, roasting and brewing.

What you won't find at Seniman is *kopi luwak*, the controversial Balinese coffee made from the beans of coffee berries that have been eaten by the civet cat and then passed through its digestive system. This process is said to remove enzymes that then leave the coffee smooth, mild and with a sweet aftertaste, but in recent years the drink's production methods have come under fire due to animal rights issues. *www.senimancoffee.com; tel +62 361 972085; Jalan Sriwedari 5; from 8am*

04 UBUD ORGANIC MARKET

To really appreciate how the locavore food scene is profoundly changing Ubud, drop in at the twice-weekly organic market near the centre.

The market is a cooperative of local organic farmers selling not just vegetables and fruits but soy milk, artisan-baked bread, honey, spices, rice vinegar and coconut oil. You can find chocolate flavoured with ginger, cinnamon and lemongrass, traditional herbal remedies, plus Bali's renowned facial and body scrubs, made from perfumed combava (kaffir lime), pandan leaves and jasmine flowers.

Several farmers with stands at the market offer visits to their farms, and at Sari Organik's Ubud smallholding there is a health food *warung* overlooking its rice terraces. The market is located just outside the centre of town; at Warung Sopa

(Jalan Nyuhkuning 2) on Wednesdays and outside Pizza Bagus (Jalan Raya Pengosekan) each Saturday. *www.ubudorganicmarket.com; 9am-1pm Wed, to 2pm Sat*

05 BIG TREE FARMS CHOCOLATE FACTORY

A 20-minute drive south of Ubud leads to an astonishing chocolate factory with the feel of a Willy Wonka wonderland, housed in an immense cathedral-like structure built entirely from woven bamboo. This is the headquarters of Big Tree Farms, founded by American idealists Ben and Blair Ripple as a small vegetable farm back in 2000.

Lately it has been transformed into Indonesia's largest fair-trade organic food company, aiding thousands of smallholder farmers to practice sustainable agriculture. Although it

produces everything from cashew nuts to Balinese sea salt, the core crop is the cacao bean, which is transformed into intense 70% chocolate, slightly sweetened with coconut-palm sugar.

Tours begin with a cup of Coco Mojo hot chocolate and then follow the whole bean-to-bar process, which involves breaking up cacao beans in ancient Heath-Robinson cartoon-like type machines, then grinding them for hours and finally blending the paste with coconut sugar.

Chocoholics will find it impossible to resist the goodies in the boutique and chocolate cafe.
www.bigtreefarms.com; tel: +62 361 846337; Jalan Raya Sibang Kaja, Desa Sibang Kaja; tour 2pm Mon-Fri

06 WARUNG RAI PASTI

This hole-in-the-wall *warung* is an oasis of calm in the middle of frenetic Monkey Forest Rd, with a romantic vista over idyllic rice paddies and an owner, Rai Pasti, who's full of surprises. She is one of Ubud's most skilled tailors and the *warung* used to house her sewing machines, but she loves cooking and five years ago moved her tailors across the road so that she could turn her attention to food.

Now she conjures up an eclectic mix of Balinese delicacies and such backpacker favourites as classic *nasi goreng* (fried rice). Forget the global comfort food on the menu and order (24 hours in advance) one of Bali's signature dishes; *babi guling* (to-die-for crispy suckling pig) or *bebek tutu*

(succulent 24-hour roasted duck). The *babi guling* is exceptional as Rai gets it direct from her sister, Ibu Oka, known as the Queen of Babi Guling, whose Ubud restaurants draw crowds of tour buses every day.
Tel +62 361 973259; Monkey Forest Rd; 9am-10pm

07 PEJENG KAWAN NIGHT MARKET

The traditional *pasar* (night market) is the life and soul of Bali and an assault on the senses with the pungent aroma of *kretek* (clove cigarettes) offset by fragrant wafts of satay grilling over red-hot charcoal, a cornucopia of vegetables, exotic fruits, live ducks and chickens, grisly open-air butchers and fish stalls.

Ubud's grand marketplace at Gianyar has become a tourist trap, so for a real slice of local life take a 20-minute cab ride and plunge into the unforgettable night market in the tiny village of Pejeng Kawan. Be prepared for adventure, because the market is grubby, noisy and smoky.

Colourful *gerobak* (food carts) set up outside the covered market hall offer such iconic street food dishes as *bakso* (meatball soup), *soto ayam* (a soothing chicken broth), *sayur asem* (vegetable soup) and the totally delicious *otak-otak* – a spicy fish paste grilled inside perfumed pandan leaf. *5-8pm*

08 PUTERI MINANG PADANG FOOD

Located on Ubud's busy high street, the stacks of appetising dishes piled high in the window of Puteri Minang are a magnet to anyone interested in food. Welcome to the gastronomic feast that is Masakan Padang, the halal cuisine of the muslim Minangkabau people from Sumatra, a very different world from Balinese cooking.

The system here is simple: a huge portion of steamed rice is scooped onto your plate and then it is self-service from the 20-odd freshly cooked dishes. There are several Padang eateries around Ubud, but Puteri Minang is outstanding for veggie dishes, and serves *lindung* (fried baby eels) fished from the rice paddies.

Although there is no pork, nose-to-tail enthusiasts can choose from *paru goreng* – fried beef lung, and tripe cooked in a rich *gulai* (coconut milk stew). Seafood ranges from fish-head curry to spicy sambal prawns, while veg dishes include tasty yellow jackfruit curry and purple aubergine fried with pungent *belacan* (shrimp paste).
Tel +62 361 975577; Jalan Raya Ubud 77; 10am-10.30pm

Ø5 Balinese rice paddies

WHERE TO STAY
FIBRA INN
Balinese dance diva Sri Utari has welcomed travellers to her simple family compound for more than 30 years. An oasis of peace, Fibra has a luxuriant tropical garden and relaxing spa.
Tel +62 361 975451; Jalan Monkey Forest, Ubud

SANDAT GLAMPING
The first glamping site to open in Bali, Sandat offers five luxury safari tents hidden away in the midst of rice fields, each with a private plunge pool.
www.glampingsandat. com; tel +62 821 44081998; Banjar Sala, Pejeng, Ubud

BAMBU INDAH
Guests at Bambu stay in stunning 100-year-old teak houses, and can visit the nearby Kul Kul farm, an educational project for sustainable organic agriculture.
www.bambuindah.com; tel +361 977922; Banjar Baung, Ubud

WHAT TO DO
Take in a captivating Balinese dance, performed in candelit temples and palaces every night, as Ubud comes alive to the spellbinding chimes of gamelan orchestras. The town has dozens of spas, yoga and wellness centres, and at the simple Warung Sopa (Jalan Nyuhkuning 2, Pengosekan) a massage or yoga class can be followed by a tasty vegetarian meal.

CELEBRATIONS
The Balinese New Year festival, Nyepi, is a unique moment in the middle of March when not one person, tourists included, is allowed out on the streets for 24 hours and the day is spent in silent meditation. Following the international success of the Ubud Writers & Readers Festival, the Ubud Food Festival began in 2015 and already attracts more than 6000 foodies for cooking masterclasses, workshops and food tours each May (www. ubudfoodfestival.com).

Ireland
CONNEMARA SEAFOOD TRAIL

Ireland's windswept west coast has a special relationship with the sea, enshrined in Celtic mythology. Here you'll find smokehouses, mussel farms and overflowing seafood menus.

You can feel the Atlantic's raw energy all along Ireland's west coast but in Connemara it combines with stark, moody mountains, desolate, sweeping bogs and stunning beaches in a 'savage beauty' much admired by Oscar Wilde. Although this sparsely populated corner of Ireland offers poor farmland for many types of agriculture, its generous seas have provided seaweed to enrich the soil, and fish and seafood to sustain large families for thousands of years. Life here is still intimately entwined with the sea, and local people have a real affinity with the ocean and the land they farm. Today, traditional culture and local expertise combine with modern technology to make the region's mussel farms, smokehouses and restaurants justly famous for their seafood.

Salmon, mackerel, mussels, lobsters and oysters are staples on every menu and you'll quickly discover that the fish and seafood here are among the best in the world. Along with a host of fine restaurants and artisan food producers, there's a variety of food festivals, and a hearty seafood chowder awaits in nearly every village pub.

Bookended by two of Ireland's most vibrant towns renowned for their traditional music, this route from bohemian Galway to Georgian Westport runs along the stunning Connemara coast. As you drive past the patchwork of white sand beaches and sheltered coves, trees are bent double by the wind and a new view is revealed at every turn.

Inland, wild valleys and black lakes shelter between quartzite peaks, labyrinthine stone walls creeping up their slopes. This raw landscape makes Connemara an ideal escape for hiking, sea kayaking, kite-surfing, diving and deep-sea fishing, with plenty of colourful little villages and cosy pubs to provide shelter along the way.

NEED TO KNOW
Ireland West Airport Knock is 90km from Galway; hire a car at the airport for this 2-3 day trail.

01 MC DONAGH'S

Set on Galway's colourful Quay St with its tiny houses, numerous shops and a swathe of pubs and restaurants, Mc Donagh's is a local institution, part fish shop, part takeaway, part restaurant, run by the same family for four generations.

You can buy all manner of fish and seafood here, opt to eat local oysters, prawns and mussels in the restaurant with its cosy clutter of model ships, nets and buoys, or, like all the locals, plonk yourself down on one of the long benches in the takeaway where the fish and chips are some of Ireland's finest and the passage of life before you is quintessential Galway.
www.mcdonaghs.net; tel +353 91 565 001; 22 Quay St, Galway; takeaway Mon-Sat noon-11pm, Sun 2-9pm; restaurant Mon-Sat 5-10pm

02 OSCAR'S SEAFOOD BISTRO

Wander around Galway's bohemian streets, sip a pint in the half-light of one of the many pubs and work up an appetite before crossing the bridge from the Spanish Arch into what is known as Galway's cultural quarter. Here you'll find Oscar's Bistro, another much-loved Galway eatery where chef Michael O'Meara combines fish and seafood with the best local produce to create a stunner of a menu featuring flavours from around the world.

It's a fun, flamboyant sort of place and, despite its numerous awards, Oscar's remains a defiantly unpretentious restaurant where the portions are generous and the food is excellent value. Enjoy such delights as Bearna lobster or brown crab, Clare Island salmon tartare and Galway oysters, all simply cooked and served with such delicacies as dillisk butter

(also known as dulse – a dark-red edible seaweed), a bed of seaweed or local farmhouse cheeses.
www.oscarsseafoodbistro.com; tel +353 91 582 180; Dominick St Lwr, Galway; Mon-Sat dinner (book ahead)

03 CONNEMARA SMOKEHOUSE

Drive west on the scenic coastal R336 to Ballyconneely, where, perched on the battered bulk of Bunowen Pier, the Connemara Smokehouse looks out over the Atlantic rollers.

This family-run business was established in 1979 and is run by Graham Roberts and his wife Saoirse, who are mindful of the near mythical place of salmon in Irish culture. 'Salmon have long been a valuable food source', explains Graham, 'but they also mark the passing of the seasons and in Celtic mythology embody a mystical knowledge of the world.'

'Salmon mark the passing of the seasons and in Celtic mythology embody a mystical knowledge of the world'

01 Kylemore Abbey &
Victorian Walled Garden

02 Dessert at
Delphi Lodge

03 An Port Mór
restaurant in Westport

04 Derryclare Lough
with Connemara
National Park in the
distance

05 Mussel farming on
Killary Fjord

Graham and Saoirse respect this rich heritage by hand-filleting all their fish and using traditional smoking methods handed down through the generations.

Quality is extremely important to Graham, as is this specific location. 'We're literally on the edge of the world', he explains. 'We have the purest, cleanest waters, which provide us with the finest fresh fish to work with.' Along with wild, organic and farmed salmon, tuna, mackerel and herring are smoked over slow-burning beechwood shavings for a velvety smooth colour and flavour.

Pop in to the pier-side shop for a sample and they'll explain the whole process in person or if you're visiting between June and August, there's a weekly guided tour; book in advance. *www.smokehouse.ie; tel +353 95 23739; Bunowen Pier, Ballyconneely; Mon-Fri 9am-1pm & 2-5pm*

04 LETTERFRACK ECOLOGY CENTRE

In a beautiful setting on the edge of Connemara National Park you'll find the Letterfrack Ecology Centre from where environmentalist Marie Louise Heffernan leads visitors on seashore foraging walks that cover local history and geology as well as the culinary, agricultural and medicinal uses of local seafoods.

Walks generally start at low tide on the hunt for carrageen (a common edible red shoreline seaweed), which was traditionally used for chest complaints and also makes a good gelling agent in many foodstuffs. Heading up the shore there's fucus, which can be boiled and eaten as a vegetable, and purple laver, or nori, which is typically used in sushi.

Searching rock pools for sea urchins and crabs, Marie Louise

recommends serving channel wrack (a brown alga found on rocks) with pasta or in salads, and also points out shellfish middens, heaps of discarded shells, as evidence that this form of foraging has been a vital local food source for thousands of years.

As you walk along the shore, seals playfully pop their heads out of the water and if you're very lucky, bottlenose dolphins can be seen playing in the seas. The walk finishes with a tasting of fresh seaweed, with pepper dulse, sea grass or gutweed served with crackers and cheese.

To get to Letterfrack from Ballyconneely, head north along the R341 to Clifden and then take the N59. Foraging walks run weekly on Wednesdays or by appointment. *www.theecologycentre.ie; tel +353 86 8278031; Letterfrack*

05 KILLARY FJORD SHELLFISH

It's another stunner of a drive on to Leenane where you'll find a little food trailer parked at the head of Killary Harbour. This gloriously moody steep-sided inlet is a dramatic place with an ephemeral beauty. Slicing 15km inland, it is dotted with mussel rafts, many of which belong to Simon and Kate Kennedy of Killary Fjord Shellfish.

Simon was one of the pioneers of mussel farming on the Killary, where the conditions are ideal for growing rope mussels, thanks to the unique combination of fresh and seawater, which gives the mussels a distinctive sweet flavour. Simon farms blueshell mussels on long lines submerged 8m underwater, and the food trailer is the public face of the business, where passersby can dig

into plates of steaming Killary mussels, Galway Bay clams, local razor clams and Ballynakill oysters. Plucked from the sea and simply cooked, they make a fabulous lunch while you sit at a long wooden table taking in the magnificent views.

The family live on a sheltered famine track flanking the harbour and are happy to explain the history and process of mussel farming on the Killary on a boat trip out to the long lines, returning to a converted boathouse on the shore to run through the grading, cleaning and packing of their precious cargo. *www.killaryfjordshellfish.com; tel +353 87 622 7542; Leenane; food trailer May-Oct, tours year-round by appointment only (min 10 people, but will combine smaller groups)*

06 AN PORT MÓR

Killary forms a natural border between Galway and Mayo and driving north from here on the R335 across the lonesome but spectacular Doolough Valley, the region's poignant famine history can be felt in the ruined stone cottages, sweeping slopes and inky lakes.

At the picturesque village of Louisburgh head east past Croagh Patrick, a much-loved pilgrimage mountain, and picturesque Clew Bay into Westport. This handsome Georgian town is blessed with numerous restaurants and traditional pubs, but pick of the crop for seafood is An Port Mór where chef Frankie Mallon is a great believer in supporting small local producers. Luckily, he has a bountiful selection on his doorstep.

07 Courtesy of Connemara Mussell Festival

The emphasis at An Port Mór is on local seafood and shellfish, with lobster, crab, scallops and langoustines from Clew Bay featuring regularly on the menu. Although it's a no-nonsense kind of cooking here, the flavours are big and bold and the menu creative.

Try crab cakes with seaweed polenta, king scallops with grilled fennel or the Achill Island smoked fish plate, which features wild Irish tuna, peppered mackerel, honey-roast salmon and seaweed jam. Leave a little space for a pint though, and head across the main street to the hallowed Matt Molloy's pub. *www.anportmor.com; tel +353 98 26730; 1 Brewery Place, Westport; from 5pm Mon-Sat (reservations advised)*

06 Fisherman's pub at Ballynahinch Castle

07 Connemara Mussel Festival

WHERE TO STAY
DELPHI LODGE
Built in the 1830s as a secluded sporting lodge, this charming Georgian country house is set between brooding mountains and a wild, unspoilt valley. The 1000-acre estate is famous for its fly fishing and your catch can be cooked for dinner or smoked to send home. There are just 13 rooms and convivial communal dining. *www.delphilodge.ie; tel +353 95 42222; Leenane, Co Galway*

BALLYNAHINCH CASTLE
A late 18th-cetury mansion, Ballynahinch Castle offers a touch of luxury with 48 classically styled rooms and large grounds where you can go fly-fishing or horse riding. Guests can also take a guided boat trip around Roundstone Bay to check on lobster pots, fish for mackerel and visit a deserted island. *www.ballynahinch-castle. com; tel +353 95 31006; Recess, Co. Galway*

WHAT TO DO
Take a kayaking trip along the rugged coastline from Mannin Bay (www. realadventures.ie), a nationally recognised Blueway site known for its outstanding beauty. The combination of white sands and clear waters here provide great views of the sea life below. To learn about the region's cultural heritage visit Cnoc Suain (www.cnocsuain.com) in Spiddal, a restored 17th-century hill village.

CELEBRATIONS
Taking place over four days in September, the Galway International Oyster & Seafood Festival features the World Oyster Opening Championships, cookery demonstrations, a city-wide seafood trail, plenty of live music and, thanks to those oysters, a fair bit of passion (www. galwayoysterfest.com). On the first weekend of May, the little village of Tullycross hosts the community-focused Connemara Mussel Festival: a celebration of local people, food, heritage and culture, it includes cooking demonstrations by celebrity chefs, guided seashore foraging walks and talks on conservation, heritage and archaeology. (www.connemaramussel festival.com)

Italy

EAT LIKE A VENETIAN

Hidden down the watery alleyways of Venice lies a thriving local food scene often overlooked by visitors, prizing freshness, inventive small bites and seafood.

Venice has been attracting visitors for centuries, and despite real problems today of over-tourism, rising water levels, and intrusive boats threatening the foundations of this unique floating city, the Serenissima, as it is traditionally known, is not sinking yet, nor has it become a Disney-like museum city.

While a weekend here can take in the awesome Piazza San Marco, a vaporetto ride past opulent palaces or a romantic gondola through a labyrinth of narrow canals, Venice is also becoming a surprising destination for food lovers.

While tourists often end up moaning about dining out at a trattoria with a rip-off *menu turistico*, Venetians themselves are fiercely proud of their cuisine. Eating out for the locals is much more likely to be an entertaining evening wandering around a few traditional *bacari*

NEED TO KNOW
Venice is a lagoon city: take a boat from Marco Polo Airport and use the public ferries to get around.

(wine bars), feasting off delicious *cichetti* – the Venetian take on tapas, bite-sized snacks that make use of the finest seasonal produce, such as tiny *schie* (shrimp), grilled baby cuttlefish, artichokes and radicchio, locally cured sopressa salami and Asiago cheese.

Cichetti are only the tip of Venice's unique food culture, there's artisan producers to discover, not just hidden away in the city itself, but scattered over the islands of the lagoon.

Everything comes together in the Rialto Market, where all of Venice does its morning shopping, choosing the freshest seafood from the Adriatic, vegetables grown on the lagoon, and animatedly discussing politics, football and the future of their beloved city over a glass of wine. Naturally, this food tour starts here in the market, before taking in other local spots on Venice and her surrounding islands over two to three days.

01 RIALTO MARKET

Take the traghetto public gondola across the Grand Canal from Ca' d'Oro to arrive right in the heart of the bustling Rialto Market. The earliest settlements of Venice began here and this noisy, teeming market remains the vibrant heart and soul of the city.

It is actually a maze of different markets. The *pescheria* is filled with rowdy fishmongers whose displays include wriggling eels and giant swordfish. Fruit and vegetable stalls in the *erbaria* are a cornucopia of local produce; tiny *chiodini* (nail mushrooms), late-harvest radicchio *tardivo*, rare *giuggiole* (jujube fruit). While on Ruga dei Spezieri, Spice Merchants Street, there remains Drogheria Mascari, a fragrant emporium of exotic ingredients from across the globe.

Among the market's 20-odd *bacari*, two locales stand out; Alla Ciurma where Marco Paola conjures up plump courgette flowers stuffed with anchovies and mozzarella; and All'Arco, where Francesco da Pinto slices musetto pork sausage topped with freshly grated horseradish, or fries up *coppa di testa*, (headcheese, which is pork brawn) and crunchy artichokes. *7am-1pm Mon-Sat*

02 VIZIOVIRTÙ

Delicious hot chocolate has been served in Venice since the gilded salons of Caffe Florian opened on the Piazza San Marco in 1720. But the Serenissima was never renowned for its artisan chocolate makers until Mariangela Penzo opened VizioVirtù 10 years ago.

This gourmet Aladdin's Cave may be in a quiet campo just off the Rialto bridge, but no one can ignore the tantalising aromas wafting out from Mariangela's *cioccolateria*. She creates exotic fondant truffles flavoured with everything from pumpkin or wild dill to balsamic vinegar or Mexican chillies, even tobacco. Candied fruits are taken to another gastronomic level, as glazed figs, oranges, ginger and plums are coated with intense dark chocolate. For the total experience, sit down for the daily 'chocolate tasting course' or enrol in Mariangela's Chocolate Cooking School. *www.viziovirtu.com; tel +33 041 275 0149; Calle del Pistor 5988, Castello; 10am-7.30pm*

03 OSTERIA ANTICA ADELAIDE

Antica Adelaide is the perfect symbol of the renaissance of traditional Venetian cuisine: part classic *bacaro*, part innovative trattoria. The wooden

02 Maurizio Rossi © Sustin

03 John Greim © Getty Images

01 Cantina snacks

02 Venissa food and
wine resort

03 Burano Island,
famous for lace
and biscotti

04 Cichetti counter,
Cantione Gia' Schiavi

05 VizioVirtù
chocolate display

bar heaves with locals dropping by for the honest *vino della casa* (house wine), or a fashionable glass of 'natural' wine. A counter displays *cichetti*, from *sarde in saor* (sardines marinated with onions, pine nuts and raisins) to grilled polenta topped with creamy *baccala* (salt cod), while adventurous foodies can try *nervetti* (gelatinous tendons with raw onion) or a skewer of *spienza* (spleen).

The dining room menu changes each day and diners might find tiny fried *moeche* (softshell crabs), grilled *cape lunghe* (razor clams), a steaming plate of spaghetti with succulent *canoce* (mantis shrimps), or tender cuttlefish in an ink-black risotto. The classic *fritto misto* (deep-fried seafood) is transformed into an epicurean feast, piled high with the freshest fish, crustaceans and vegetables. Buzzing everywhere is owner-chef Alvise

Ceccato, named after a Venetian Doge and on a mission to revive the Serenissima's culinary heritage. *www.anticaadelaide.it; tel +39 041 523 2629; Calle Priuli Racheta 3728, Cannaregio; 10am-3.30pm, 5.30pm-1am*

04 ALASKA GELATERIA

In Venice there is a tempting gelateria on virtually every street. But anyone tracking down Alaska Gelateria, hidden away near the picturesque Campo San Giacomo dell'Orio, is set for an assault on the senses, as the impassioned Carlo Pistacchi makes ice creams like no other.

Before you even have time to order, this eccentric reggae-loving *gelatista* will have you trying half-a-dozen spoonfuls of his latest exotic creations; artichoke with mint, arugula salad and orange, fresh

ginger, cardamom or star anise, while such classics as roasted pistachio and tangy Sicilian lemon are irresistible. All ingredients are organic: don't dare ask Carlo if there are colourants or preservatives in his creations. *Tel +33 041 715211; Calle Larga dei Bari 1159, Santa Croce; 11am-10.30pm Apr-Oct, to 7pm Nov-Mar*

05 CANTINONE GIA' SCHIAVI

Opened 120 years ago by one Giacomo Schiavi, this *bacaro* is known to all Venetians as the Bottegon – 'the storeroom'. Sandra de Respinis has been behind the bar for more than 50 years and deserves the title Queen of Cichetti.

Her speciality is rough slices of crusty bread topped off with a cornucopia of different ingredients, and Sandra has created more than 70 different recipes, creating each one

like an alchemist. She makes at least 500 *cichetti* a day, including such bites as delicious aged provolone cheese with pickled wild fennel leaves, tuna tartare sprinkled with cocoa powder or creamy gorgonzola, and crunchy apple drizzled with balsamic vinegar.

Situated on the bank of the pretty San Trovaso canal, the bar is just opposite one of the last workshops still making gondolas.
Tel +41 523 0034; Fondamenta Nani 992, Dorsoduro 992; 8.30am-8.30pm Mon-Sat

06 LE SPIGHE

Doriana Pressotto describes herself as a 'food artisan', and over 25 years her tiny *laboratorio* on the bustling Via Garibaldi, far off the tourist route near the Biennale Gardens, has metamorphosed from producing innovative homemade pasta into a unique deli that showcases her very Venetian interpretation of organic vegetarian and vegan cuisine.

Bubbly and engaging with customers, Doriana says, 'I believe in *l'energia* of my food, which is why

'I believe in *l'energia* of my food, which is why everything I cook must be eaten by the end of the day'

everything I cook must be eaten by the end of the day.' She prepares eight dishes each morning, which are sold by weight and eaten at communal tables. A typical menu could include roasted pumpkin with rosemary and thyme; courgette and basil lasagna; seaweed risotto; and a tart puntarelle salad with fermented tofu.
Tel +39 041 523 8173; Via Garibaldi 1341, Castello; 9.30am-2.30pm Mon-Sat, 5.30pm-7.30pm

07 I SAPORI DI SANT'ERASMO

At Rialto Market, stalls proudly display the sign *nostrani*, meaning 'our own'. It refers to goods that have come directly from Venice's own market garden, the lagoon island of Sant'Erasmo, where the dynamic Finotello family have a smallholding

growing such tasty seasonal vegetables as fennel, chard and asparagus on the unique salty clay soil.

The star product, though, is tiny violet artichokes, whose highly prized *castraure* (buds) are eaten raw with olive oil and Parmesan shavings. Carlo and Claudio Finotello sell their produce directly, and for anyone self-catering this is the perfect opportunity to buy from the farmer, as the Finotellos drop off by boat everyday at different spots around the city. Register on their website to order, and then choose a pick-up location. Alternatively, take the vaporetto for a day's sightseeing on Sant'Erasmo itself, as their farm is open for guided tours by appointment.
www.isaporidisanterasmo.com; tel +39 041 528 2997; Via della Boaria Vecia 6, Sant'Erasmo

08 PANIFICIO PASTICCERIA GARBO

Every hour, visitors pile out from the ferry boat that links Venice with Burano. The walk from Burano's jetty is lined with boutiques selling the island's famous lace, but rather than join everyone turning left into town, turn right along the canal until the enticing aromas of freshly baked biscotti (cookies), leads you to the door of Giorgio Garbo's old-fashioned bakery.

His speciality is *bussolà di Burano*, a compass-shaped cornmeal biscuit originally baked for fishers going to sea. While Giorgio keeps up a friendly banter with tourists in the front, local Buranelli ladies head to the backroom ovens, where a custom is unchanged for centuries; they bring the ingredients for their own secret *bussolà* recipe and pay Giorgio to bake for them.
Tel +39 041 894 6170; Fondamenta San Mauro 336, Burano; 8am-7pm

09 EOLO

Venice boasts countless cooking schools but nothing compares with a one-day lagoon cruise led by Mauro Stoppa aboard *Eolo*, his *bragozzo* (traditional wooden sailing boat).

After buying provisions at Rialto, *Eolo* sets out across the water, eventually mooring in the middle of the wetlands, as Mauro takes everyone down to the galley for a hands-on cooking lesson. His seasonal recipes range from wild cherries with tender grilled baby squids to a creamy courgette risotto. Back on deck, the crew have dressed a long table, and everyone sits down to feast from a four-course meal, perfectly paired with local wines. Afterwards you'll slowly sail back to Venice, arriving as the sun sets over San Marco.
www.cruisingvenice.com; tel +39 349 743 1552

06 Local produce at Rialto Market

07 Eating canalside in front of Cantione Gia' Schiavi

WHERE TO STAY

B&B SANDRA
Alessandra Soldi rents out three rooms of her romantic apartment for a genuine B&B experience. Guests can watch the sun setting with a glass of Prosecco from the rooftop *altana* terrace.
www.bbalessandra.com; tel +41 720 957; Corte Trapolin 2452, Cannaregio

VENISSA
On a tiny island attached to Burano, Venissa is an oasis of calm but just a 35-minute boat ride from Venice. This idyllic wine and food resort looks out over its own vineyard, with an innovative Michelin-starred restaurant.
www.venissa.it; tel +41 527 2281; Fondamenta Santa Cristina 3, Mazzorbo

WHAT TO DO

Culture lovers looking for Old Masters, such as Titian and Tintoretto, should not miss the Galleria dell'Accademia (www.gallerieaccademia.org). Visit the edgy avant-garde collection at Punta della Dogana to find Venice's modern art (www.palazzograssi.it). For an authentic local experience, book the Cichetto Row (www.rowvenice.org) to learn Venice's gondola-style rowing, ending at a waterside *bacaro* for wine and *cichetti*.

CELEBRATIONS

CARNEVALE
The biggest event in Venice's annual events calendar is its February Carnevale, a riotous festival famed for its masquerade parties. It is timed to celebrate the end of Lent and during the festivities you'll find *pasticcerie* (pastry bars) serving delicious *frittelle* (sugary fried doughnuts).

FESTA DELLA SALUTE
On 21 November Venetians celebrate the Festa della Salute, when a pontoon bridge for pilgrims stretches across the Grand Canal to the immense Chiesa della Salute, built in 1631 to commemorate the survival of the city during the plague. Try the customary *castradina* that accompanies the event, a hearty stew of salted mutton and cabbage, served in a traditional osteria such as Al Mascaron (www.osteriamascaron.it).

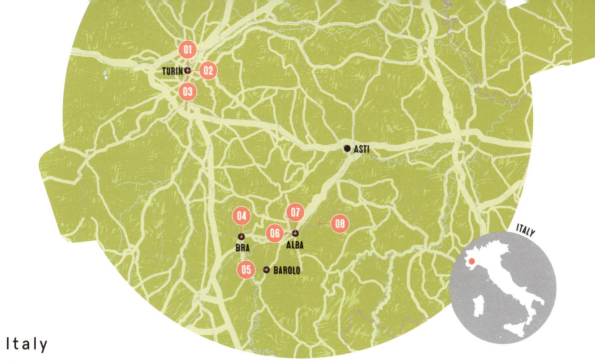

Italy

ITALIAN FOOD, THE SLOW WAY

Italy's Piedmont has an overflowing treasure trove of regional specialities, home-grown delicacies and serious culinary kudos as the birthplace of the Slow Food movement.

In a country blessed with world-famous cuisine and produce, Piedmont still stands out as a gastronomic star. This region in the northwest of Italy is rich in speciality foods and the birthplace of Slow Food – it was here in Piedmont that the idea of a movement to celebrate the pleasure and taste of food over speed and convenience was conceived – thanks to its bucolic landscape of vineyard-filled hills and deep historical links to its earthy soil. While Piedmont is deeply rooted in its food traditions, it is one of Italy's most developed and industrial regions, and it's this progressive attitude that has seen a batch of young and innovative chefs cooking up dishes melding tradition and modernity in creative and exciting ways.

The elegant city of Turin is where most Piedmont journeys kick off. It was Turin that introduced the world to its first saleable hard chocolate; gave the world Italy's famous

aperitivo (pre-dinner drink with snacks) culture; introduced us all to vermouth; and is home to Europe's largest open-air food market, Porta Palazzo.

Often touted as 'Tuscany without tourists, gourmands in the know head to Piedmont in droves to sample its beloved regional specialities and produce, which include *risotto alla piemontese* (risotto with butter and cheese), *tajarin* (a thin tagliatelle pasta), *vitello tonnato* (veal with tuna sauce), delectable soft Tomino goats' milk cheese, crunchy grissini (breadsticks), rare white truffles, Arborio rice, smooth hazelnuts and velvety gelato. Add to this two of the world's most revered wine-producing regions – Barolo and Barbaresco – and it's easy to see why Piedmont is one of the most exciting culinary scenes in Italy today.

This trail starts with a day in Turin and then heads out into the food-producing towns, villages and wine lands of Piedmont.

NEED TO KNOW
It's possible to do this 3-4 day trail by public transport, but a car offers more flexibility for the smaller towns.

02 Matteo Carassale © 4Corners

01 PORTA PALAZZO

Start your day at Porta Palazzo market, a vibrant multicultural place that sees hundreds of stalls spilling out on the Piazza della Repubblica every day, except Sunday. Stroll by glistening bright-red tomatoes, fresh figs and piles of olives, while locals fill their carts with fruit and veg, and stall-owners spruik their wares to hungry shoppers.

There's also a large indoor fish and meat market but the real reason to come here is for the covered deli and separate local and organic produce section. Wind your way around the deli picking up big bags of grissini and small wheels of soft Tomino di Talucco cheese – mainly made from goats' milk – before heading out the back to see what's in season from the farmers' organic section.
www.scopriportapalazzo.com; Piazza della Repubblica, Turin; 7am-1pm Mon-Fri, to 7pm Sat

02 EATALY

When Porta Palazzo starts packing up its stalls come midday on weekdays, make your way to one of the world's most famous 'supermarkets' – the food emporium Eataly, which was set up by one of the founders of the global Slow Food movement.

Housed in a former vermouth factory, the shelves are stocked with a staggering choice of sustainable produce from the region and the country. Cruise the aisles of bulging bags of porcini mushrooms; jars of traditional ragu; every shape, size and colour of pasta imaginable; delicate soft cheeses and decadent dark chocolate incorporating Piedmont hazelnuts. Once you've crammed your shopping bags you can prop yourself at the counter for lunch at one of the specialist eateries – dine on pizza, pasta, seafood and gelato.
www.eataly.net; tel +39 011 1950 6801; Via Nizza 230, Turin; 10am-10.30pm

03 LA DROGHERIA

You can't leave Turin without experiencing its famous *apericena* culture – an extension of the classic *aperitivo*, where instead of a small offering of complimentary snacks with your drink, you pay a little extra for a whole lot more, usually in the form of a buffet.

You'll find bars offering *apericena* throughout the city, particularly along Via Po, but one of the most impressive offerings is at La Drogheria. Housed in an old pharmacy, La Drogheria attracts a mixed crowd of locals, tourists and Turin's cool students. Drop in for a pre-dinner drink, typically a vermouth-based cocktail, such as a potent negroni (Campari, gin, vermouth), and then dig in to the heaped bowls of pasta, risottos, salads, cheeses and bruschetta.
www.la-drogheria.it; tel +39 011 812 2414, Piazza Vittorio Veneto 18, Turin; 5pm-2am

01 Wine museum surrounded by vines, Barolo

02 Truffles foraged in Alba

03 Courgette flowers, Alba

04 Colourful historic house, Alba

04 OSTERIA DEL BOCCONDIVINO

The next day, head to Bra: the town where Slow Food all started. The movement was created here in the 1980s from disenchantment with the burgeoning world fast-food scene.

A group of Italian journalists from Bra developed a manifesto and movement to promote the enjoyment and taste of food over speed and convenience, as an antidote to what was happening on a global scale. It was a way of protecting the centuries-old traditions of Italian food and promoting local production and sustainability. Today the Slow Food movement has around 100,000 members in more than 150 countries, and Bra has become a gastronomic pilgrimage site.

Spend the morning checking out the independent family-owned food shops that fill the historic centre, then visit Osteria del Boccondivino for lunch. Set within a courtyard on the first floor of the Slow Food Movement's headquarters, this is the place to really get an idea of how amazing the seasonal produce can be on the daily changing menu. Devour the fresh *tajarin* pasta with butter and sage or indulge in veal braised in a local Barolo red wine.
www.boccondivinoslow.it; tel +39 0172 42 56 74; Via Mendicità Istruita 14, Bra; noon-2.30pm & 7-10pm Tue-Sat

05 LA VITA TURCHESE

From Bra it's just a half-hour drive to Barolo in the wine region of Langhe, known for producing Italy's 'wine of kings' – full-bodied, bold, complex reds made from the nebbiolo grape.

This tiny village, home to numerous *enotecas* (wine bars) and cellars, also hosts the Museo del Vino a Barolo. Immerse yourself in viticulture history through its installations before moving on to taste test. There's nowhere more welcoming to do so than La Vita Turchese, where knowledgeable staff will guide you through your tasting and help you make your choice of the local wines before pairing a glass or two with a cheese and prosciutto plate – a lovely way to spend an afternoon and wind into the evening.
www.laviteturchese.com; tel +39 366 455 6744; Via Alba 5, Barolo; 10.30am-9pm Thurs-Sun, 2pm-7pm Mon, 2pm-9pm Wed

06 TRUFFLE HUNTING IN ALBA

Start day three bright and very early with a trip to nearby Alba where you can walk off the calories in search of Piedmont's prized *tartufo bianco* (white truffle) on a truffle hunt in this beautiful foodie town.

Thanks to its surrounding 'vegetable garden' hills, Langhe vineyards and hazelnut groves, this town has gastronomic cred in the bucketloads – not only for its revered white truffle

but also for its excellent wine, dark chocolate and gelato. November is prime truffle season and the best time of the year to head into the nearby forested hills alongside your *trifolau* (truffle hunter) guide and highly trained truffle dogs that shuffle through the woods with their noses to the ground.

The gnarly knobbly nuggets of deliciousness are buried deep beneath the earth and notoriously difficult to find. It can require hours of searching and excavation but don't dismay if you don't uncover any; plenty of local restaurants incorporate truffles into their dishes. The Alba tourist office can organise truffle hunts during the season. *www.langheroero.it; tel +39 0173 35 833; Piazza Risorgimento 2, Alba; 9am-6pm Mon-Fri, from 9.30am Sat & Sun*

07 PIAZZA DUOMO

If your truffle hunt isn't successful, you may be lucky enough to find the delicacy on the menu at one of Italy's best restaurants in Alba's main square, the Piazza Duomo.

This Michelin-starred restaurant has been going for over a decade and is headed up by chef Enrico Crippa, whose impressive resume includes being the star protégé of Gualtiero Marchesi – one of Italy's most renowned chefs and regarded as the father of modern Italian cuisine.

The menu here showcases Piedmont's premium seasonal produce, including vegetables from the restaurant's own garden. Crippa's dishes perfectly carry off new and unusual flavours while also respecting the country's culinary traditions. Book your table for lunch in advance and

expect such expertly crafted dishes as Piedmont risotto, suckling pig, scallops with black truffle, chocolate bonnet and sorrel sorbet.

If you can't score a booking here, try the equally fantastic yet more informal and relaxed La Piola downstairs, another of chef Enrico's restaurants. *www.piazzaduomoalba.it; tel +39 0173 366 167; Piazza Risorgimento 4, Alba; 12.30-2pm & 7.30-10pm Tue-Sat*

08 AL NIDO DELLA CINCIALLEGRA

To round off your trip don't miss the beautiful, quiet village of Neive. It is worthy of a stop just to wander through its pretty hilltop medieval streets with the sun setting in the afternoon over the rolling vineyards but it's also an excellent place to

06 Marco Pasqualini © Getty Images

taste-test the magnificent wines of Neive – Dolcetto d'Alba, Barbaresco, moscato and Barbera d'Alba.

The best spot to do this is Al Nido Della Cinciallegra. This unassuming *enoteca* doubles as the *tabacchiera* (convenience store) and the labels on its wooden shelves read like a who's who of the region's best wines, so it's no surprise that it's a favourite of local winemakers. Locals and drop-in tourists come here to sample the wine accompanied by a generous *aperitivo* buffet of cured meats, soft cheeses, mini quiches, salty olives and bruschetta. Taste a few wines, fill up on food, enjoy the relaxed atmosphere into the evening then grab a couple of souvenir bottles on your way out. *www.alnidodellacinciallegra.com; tel +39 0173 67367; Piazza Cocito 8, Neive; 8am-10pm*

05 View over Piazza Castello, Turin

06 Tagliolini al barolo

WHERE TO STAY

PIAZZA DUOMO
The chic minimalist rooms here couldn't be more convenient for those who have indulged in a night of degustation heaven at the attached Michelin-starred restaurant. *www.piazzaduomoalba.it; tel +39 0173 366 167; Piazza Risorgimento 4, Alba*

ALBERGO CANTINE ASCHERI
Located in central Bra and built above the wine cellars at the Ascheri family's winery, this hotel artfully mixes contemporary and industrial design. The winery was established in the late 1800s and you can peer down at the cellar vats from the hotel's lobby. Free cellar tours for guests. *www.ascherihotel.it; tel +39 0172 430 312; Via Piumati 25*

VIA STAMPATORI
A charming B&B set on the top floor of an elegant 16th-century Renaissance building, Via Stampatori is one of Turin's most peaceful and stylish places to rest your head. *www.viastampatori.com; tel + 39 339 25 81 330; Via Stampatori 4*

WHAT TO DO
Take in the 360-degree views sweeping across the Alps on the 85m-high viewing deck of Turin's iconic aluminium tower Mole Antonelliana. Piedmont is also an excellent base for outdoor activities: strap on your skis to tackle the Milky Way valleys just outside Turin, lace up your hiking boots in the Maritime Alps or jump on a bike to explore Cuneo.

CELEBRATIONS

FIERA DEL TARTUFO
One weekend in October/ November, truffle fans make the pilgrimage to Alba for the annual Truffle Festival. Sample the bounty and watch as truffle traders and buyers exchange hefty sums of cash for these prized delicacies (www. fieradeltartufo.org).

SALONE INTERNAZIONALE DEL GUSTO
Also in October, Turin's much-lauded biennial Slow Food celebration – taking place in even-numbered years – offers food workshops, tastings, and talks from artisan producers (www. salonedelgusto.it).

Italy

PUGLIA'S PEASANT CUISINE

The unsung hero of Italy's food regions, this far south pocket of fishing villages fringed by farms has its own unique take on Italian cuisine: honest, fresh and hauled from the Med.

Puglia, the foxy heel of the Italian boot, is loved for its rustic cooking as much as it is for its white-sand beaches and sultry summers. Sleepy for most of the year, in the summer months its seaside towns turn into thronged hubs as holidaymakers descend from northern Italy and the whole place takes on a carnival feel. With 800km of coastline and rolling plains that are ideal for farming, cartloads of Italy's olives, fruit and vegetables come from its sun-basked fields.

It may have long been an Italian favourite, but the region is now slowly being discovered by international tourists. It's the hobbit-friendly conical architecture, the rolling hills covered in vineyards and olive groves, the silky beaches and translucent water, the white-washed and golden-stone coastal towns perched on sea-cliffs, and the food and music summer festivals. However, it is also the cuisine. Puglia is the source of burrata, a cheese even more creamy and

delicious than mozzarella; of 'little ears' orecchiette, which is the signature local handmade pasta, so-called because of their shape; and of *friselli*, dried bread that is soaked in water and served topped with fresh tomatoes and garlic.

Long home to farming communities, Puglia is known for its *cucina povera* (peasant cuisine), whereby people make the most of local ingredients, and bottle and preserve produce over the summer to see them through the winter months. It's prime territory for vegetable creations, as well as fish and seafood, which is often eaten raw and fresh from the Mediterranean. The region is ideal for a two- to four-day food tour – you won't have to hammer across huge distances, and yet there's much to see of great variety. You can go from pasta-making in Bari's old town to a rural olive oil press with ease, while stopping to lie on a beach or explore a medieval town in between.

NEED TO KNOW
Bari and Brindisi airports serve Puglia. Trains and buses run in the region but you'll need a car for hidden corners.

01 AL TRABUCCO DA MIMÍ

Start your exploration on the Gargano peninsula in northern Puglia. This rocky promontory of land is characterised by wooded hills, sea-cliffs, and narrow coastal roads roller-coasting along its edges, and has a very different feel to the rest of Puglia.

Peculiar to the coast, as distinct from elsewhere in Puglia, are the *trabucchi* – huge wooden contraptions created from a complicated arrangement of wood beams, ropes and wheels to lower a net into the sea and catch the fish as they swim close to the coast.

Some of these you can still see working, and you can even dine on one: Al Trabucco da Mimí is just east of the coastal town of Peschici, whose buildings seem almost to tumble down the hill to the sea. The restaurant is on an old *trabucco*, jutting out over

the water, with views across twinkling Prussian-blue sea and across to locals fishing with rods from the shore. The menu is appropriately fishy, superbly fresh, and tastes all the better for its setting.
www.altrabucco.it; tel +39 0884 962 556; Località Punta San Nicola, Peschici; 12.15-2.15pm, 7-9.30pm

02 BARI FISH MARKET

Next stop is Bari, the regional capital, about two hours south along the coast. Despite its proud coastal position, 13th-century Frederick II castle and cathedral housing the remains of St Nicholas (yes, that's Santa Claus), Bari is still rather off the tourist trail.

It's a charismatic but not overtly pretty city, with one of the region's liveliest fish markets, which sets up just outside the old city right on the

harbour. It's full of fishers, loiterers, fishmongers and hangers-on, big groups of men playing cards and clusters of people around a lively bar at its centre. Well-weathered men in wellingtons stomp up and down with buckets of fish, and trays of seafood are laid out ready for sale, with well-worn scales ready to weigh out the catch.

People go crazy for sea urchins along this coast, and the spiky black balls are cut in half to display the creamy orange eggs within, ready to be scooped out and savoured on a piece of bread. In this area people like to eat raw seafood as antipasti, and at the fish market people will offer you raw octopus tentacles as a snack to go with your cold beer – the essential Bari aperitif.
Mercato del Pesce; Lungomare Augusto Imperatore; 8am-1pm

> 'People go crazy for sea urchins along this coast, scooped out and savoured on a piece of bread'

01 & 03 Local fishermen

02 Gargano peninsula

04 Taralli Pugliese – a regional savoury snack

05 Woman sits making pasta in Bari's Old Town

03 BARI VECCHIA

Next head for Bari's inner core, the Bari Vecchia (Old Town), which is a tangle of narrow lanes that resemble the maze of an Arabic medina. Ideally constructed to create shade in the summer heat, a couple of these narrow lanes are famous for their pasta makers, who sit out on the narrow lanes morning and night creating some of Puglia's most quintessential pasta shapes.

The matriarchs make the traditional local pasta, orecchiette, by hand pushing the durum flour dough (made only with water, no egg) into an almost shell-like shape, and then laying them out on large wood-framed drying racks.

This is the place to buy a bag to take home, and they'll even advise you on the kind of sauce to go with it – different pastas suit different sauces,

and orecchiette is classically eaten with *cime di rape* (turnips tops), bitter-tasting green leaves or a meaty ragu. *Via dell'Arco Basso & Via dell'Arco Alto, Bari Vecchia*

04 MASSERIA BRANCATI

From Bari, head for the bucolic area of the Valle d'Itria, less than an hour's drive away. This is one of Puglia's prettiest regions, with rolling gentle hills, small vineyards, wild flowers in the spring, and acre upon acre of twisted, ancient olive trees. Graceful white-stone towns dot the hilltops.

Most gleaming white of them all is Ostuni. From it, olive trees stretch in all directions, their silver and green leaves fluttering, their trunks like strange petrified sculpture. In recent years Italy's olive groves have been ravaged by a bacterium, *Xylella fastidiosa*, which has led to many trees dying, but

the endless groves around the Valle d'Itria have survived untainted, thanks to a strict policy of containment.

To discover more about the ancient trees and the process of obtaining the oil, you can visit a local olive press and taste the liquid gold. Corrado Rodio of Masseria Brancati, has a face burnished by Pugliese sun and a great pride in his ancient olive groves, leading visitors around to explain the process and visit some of the most spectacular trees, which date to more than 2000 years old.

You can stay at the *masseria* (farmhouse) or arrange a visit to explore the farm, with its cellar of centuries-old olive-pressing equipment, and taste what is the lifeblood of the region. *www.masseriabrancati.com; tel +39 330 822 910; Contrada Brancati; visits by appointment*

04 Federico Foto © Getty Images

05 Michael Heffernan © Lonely Planet

 CONVENTO SAN GIOVANNI EVANGELISTA

Less than an hour's drive away is the beautiful golden-stone, university town of Lecce. It's famous for many foodstuffs, such as perfect snack-fodder *rustici* (pastry puffs filled with tomato and béchamel), but perhaps the most enticing culinary adventure here is to hunt down the town's *biscotti di pasta di mandorle* – sweets made from almond paste, traditionally eaten on religious festivals.

You can still buy these from cloistered local nuns at the 12th-century convent of San Giovanni Evangelista. The nuns are not permitted to show their faces or speak to anyone outside, but still manage to keep trade going – ring the bell of the convent and you'll be able to arrange to buy some through the faceless dumb waiter, through which they'll pass out the exquisitely wrapped almond biscuits – the best time to get these is around feast days; you'll be able to spot where to go by the queue.

Via delle Benedettine, Lecce

STILE MEDITERRANEO COOKING SCHOOL

Make your last stop this excellent cookery school where you can learn to make variations on the local cuisine. The charming chef Cinzia Rascazzo, who's a local but has lived and worked in New York, is a fount of knowledge about Pugliese produce, cooking and its history, such as the time when Puglia produced olive oil in underground caverns to supply fuel to light lamps all over Europe.

You'll learn the dazzling yet simple skills of peasant cooking here, and work with superlative ingredients to make such dishes as fresh orecchiette or tagliatelle with tomato sauce, soups with *fave* (broad beans) or eggplant balls and seafood.

However, Stile Mediterraneo is unique in teaching these Puglia classics with a twist, having developed healthier slow cooking methods in place of frying. You'll learn three recipes, and have a short olive oil tasting session, plus you'll eat the dishes you've prepared; dinner includes wines specially chosen to pair with the food. The school has sites outside Lecce and in town. *www.artisansoftaste.com; tel +39 348 451 4324; Via Salandra 14*

05 – 08 Michael Heffernan © Lonely Planet

150 PUGLIA

ESSENTIAL INFORMATION

WHERE TO STAY

BORGO SAN MARCO

A short drive away from Bari, this rambling ancient farmhouse sits in rural countryside near to the coast, and has high-ceilinged, characterful rooms and a beach-style pool amid the olive groves. *www.borgosanmarco.it; tel +39 080 439 5757; Contrada Sant'Angelo 33, Fasano*

MANTATELURÈ

This 16th-century mansion in Lecce has gracious rooms set around a courtyard, and is run by restaurateur Marco Cimmino and Marta Nocco; Marco freshly bakes all the breakfast pastries for the guests. *Mantatelure.it; tel +39 08322 42888; Via Vittorio dei Prioli 42*

WHAT TO DO

The towns of Valle d'Itria, Ostuni, Martina Franca and Cisternino combine narrow white-washed alleys and ornate balconies, while the town of Alberobello, is a Unesco World Heritage site and the heartland of Puglia's local trulli architecture: it's an extraordinary cityscape, set across several small hills, where every gnomic house has a cone-shaped roof, built without using any mortar. Slow down and make the most of Puglia's white-sand beaches, which are edged by translucent, warm sea, and particularly splendid at Torre Lapillo and Baia dei Turchi, as well as the Maldives of Puglia: the very tip of Italy's heel.

CELEBRATIONS

There are *sagre* (food festivals) all year round in Puglia. These are concentrated in the summer months, when you could attend a food festival almost every night if you felt like it, with events such as the Sagra della Polpetta (Meatball Festival) in Felline in August.

Italy

EMILIA-ROMAGNA'S SOUL FOOD

Italy's most famous food exports come from this central region: Parmesan cheese, Parma ham, the world's best balsamic vinegar and, of course, ragu star in this gourmet pilgrimage.

In a country that lives, dreams and sleeps food, Emilia-Romagna has a special status, talked of in hushed, reverent tones for its ragu (of the Bolognese variety), cured meats (such as Parma ham), Parmesan cheese (also from Parma), and Modena balsamic vinegar. Emilia-Romagna is also responsible for the extraordinarily nourishing taste explosion that is golden, yolky *tortellini en brodo* (parcels of pasta in broth).

Cooking in Italy is fiercely regional. This is an exceedingly young country, only unified as a nation in 1861. Before that, it was a collection of city states. Each has its own traditions, own culture, and even its own language, so it's unsurprising that regional differences remain strong. There's even an Italian word for the fierce local pride *campanilismo*, which roughly translates as

NEED TO KNOW
Starting in Bologna, with its international airport, this 2–3 day trail is quite easy to do by train, as well as car.

believing your bell tower is the best of the lot.

However, even if people from different regions are convinced that theirs is the best cuisine in the country, they will all pay Emilia-Romagna the respect it deserves. If pressed, most Italians will even concur that, after their parents' house, this is the source of Italy's most spectacular gastronomy.

Emilia-Romagna is notable also for the sheer number of premium specialities that it packs into its small area, which are easy to explore by train as well as car. It's thus easy – or rather, a must – to take a lazy food-themed journey to try some of these at their source. Besides food, you'll delight in its fiendishly handsome cities and lushly rolling, village-dotted countryside, and wonder at how few tourists have discovered this astoundingly well-kept secret.

01 LA VECCHIA SCUOLA BOLOGNESE

Emilia-Romagna's russet-bricked university capital, Bologna, is known as 'La Grassa' (the fat one). It's a city that loves sausages, salami and cheese, and is the birthplace of the meaty, hearty ragu sauce known the world over as bolognese (but which is a pale imitation of the original).

But Bologna is not only a place to delight your taste buds, but an autumnal-hued, historic city, with a skyline pierced by medieval towers and kilometres of colonnaded porticos. It's as famous for its left-field intelligentsia and anarchist bent as it is for its freshly handmade tortellini (pasta parcels) and tagliatelle.

What better setting in which to learn to cook Emilia-Romagnan style? Start your culinary odyssey by learning a skill that will stay with you

forever: how to cook ragu just like *nonna* (grandma) at La Vecchia Scuola Bolognese. At this long-established cookery school, you can learn how to make the traditional rich meat sauce and a lasagne to warm the cockles of your heart in a two-hour course (in Italian or English).

www.lavecchiascuola.com; tel +39 051 649 1576; Via Galliera 11; 10am-3pm Mon, to 9.30pm Tue-Fri, to 10pm Sat

02 OSTERIA DELL'ORSA

All over Italy, unassuming, blink-and-you'd-miss-them trattorias are serving up some of the most spectacularly delicious meals in a simple down-to-earth atmosphere.

They're all entirely different and yet resolutely similar, with wood-lined interiors, a few higgledy-piggledy pictures, checked or white tablecloths, a notable dearth

of airs and graces, and the family split between the kitchen and front of house.

Bologna's Osteria dell'Orsa is exactly this kind of stuck-in-time place whose fame has grown through word of mouth. It's a hidden-away trattoria in Bologna's backstreets, where the pasta is freshly handmade by the family in the morning and laid out in trays ready for the day.

In the simple interior, where narrow beams of sunlight sneak in through the windows, the food you eat here will linger in the memory for years as one of the most wonderful meals you've ever had. Not just the light yet substantial punch of *tortellini en brodo*, but the slow-cooked rabbit, which is sprinkled with rosemary and salt and roasted at a low heat for hours to produce a remarkably tender tasting and aromatic meat.

01 Cycling in Bologna

02 Performing quality controls on wheels of Parmesan cheese

03 Parmesan cheese curd

04 Parma hams are marked with a hot iron

Finish off with a beautifully confected panna cotta, one of the classic Italian trattoria desserts, and accept a digestif of herb-infused liqueur to send you on your way. *www.osteriadellorsa.com; tel +39 051 231 576; Via Mentana 1; noon-midnight*

03 ACETAIA DI GIORGIO

Half an hour by train or car from Bologna, the next great foodie stop is the city of Modena, famous for its rich, dark gold that sweetens salads and funks up the world: balsamic vinegar.

The best place to buy it is directly from one of its Modena makers, where the world's best balsamic goes under the official title *aceto balsamico tradizionale di Modena*. When the door opens at the grand, petal-pale villa of Acetaia di Giorgio, you'll be struck by the sweet, acidic scent of fermenting vinegar. This has been a family-run business for generations and if you book a visit, the Barbieri family will talk you through the fermentation process step by careful step.

The vinegar is aged in a series of oak barrels for a minimum of 12 years, and, at the more sublime end of the scale, for more than 25. You'll get to taste a series of sweetly sharp vinegars, a world away from the supermarket version you may have previously drizzled on your lettuce, and then have the chance to buy some of the world's most sublime balsamic to take home with you. *www.acetaiadigiorgio.it; tel +39 059 333 015; Via Sandro Cabassi 67; visits by appointment*

04 DON PAPI

Next, try some fast food Emilia-Romagna-style, in the form of *gnocco fritto* at Don Papi trattoria in the charming town of Reggio Emilia.

Reggio Emilia is a 15-minute train ride from Modena; slightly longer by car. With its pretty piazzas and laidback traffic, this town is also considered the best place to ride a bike in the whole of Italy. Don Papi is known for its takes on *gnocco fritto*, but also serves up plenty of other regional specialities, such as *capeletti zucca* ('little hats' pasta filled with pumpkin).

Gnocco fritto is a light-as-air fried dough parcel that varies in shape and size according to the local village or town tradition but, whatever its dimensions, its an indulgent eat. It's often served as antipasto, with a wafer-thin sliver of *prosciutto crudo* (smoked ham) draped over it, ideally washed down with some local Lambrusco wine. *www.donpapi.it; tel +39 0522 442189; Viale Piave 4; noon-2.30pm Tue-Fri, 7.30pm-10.30pm Tue-Sat*

05 SALUMERIA GARIBALDI

A half-hour hop from Reggio, notably handsome Parma is particularly pleased with itself, and understandably so. Few provincial towns can say they have contributed quite so much to global gastronomic enjoyment.

It's full of stately buildings and kempt piazzas, but the real reason to come here is to try the local Parma ham and taste nuggets from the great golden wheels of Parmesan cheese. Not only these, but the town is responsible for creating the delicious concoction beloved Italy-wide, Parmigiana – a dish made from layers of fried aubergine and tomato sauce, topped with parmesan cheese. Shops groan with premium foodstuffs and this is the place to stock up with goodies to take home.

Salumeria Garibaldi is one of the town's most venerable delicatessens, where the window display is resplendent with a row of dangling haunches, and the counter is backed by more of the same. You can sample crumbly golden morsels of Parmesan before selecting your favourite to be wrapped so you can squirrel it home, and self-caterers can buy luscious portions of Parmegiana here too. *www.salumeriagaribaldi.com; tel +39 0521 235606; Via Garibaldi 42; 8am-8pm Mon-Sat*

06 ANTICA CORTE PALLAVICINA RELAIS

In a country where salami is a fine art, the Spigarolis who run Antica Corte occupy a special place in the cured meat canon. On the flat plains around Parma, they produce some of the region's most famous salami in their cellars, in a sprawling mansion on the banks of the river Po.

Surrounded by bucolic grounds filled with cows, horses, and geese, this 1320 homestead is famous for its *culatelli di zibello* – 'little bums', parcels of firm cured meat wrapped in a pig's bladder. Aged in the farm's chilly, humid cellars, the cold, foggy winters of the region are what give this ham the edge.

The meat is wrapped in twine, which gives the *culatello* its signature pear shape, and the painstaking, elaborate production method includes massaging the parcels and leaving them to rest. The result is a velvety, aromatic meat, the special taste of which makes it one of Italy's

06

most sought after artisanal creations.

Massimo and Luciano Spigaroli took over the farm more than 20 years ago, where their great-grandfather had worked first as a sharecropper and then as a tenant. They honed the process and now cure meats for clients as diverse as Armani and Prince Charles. They run a superlative restaurant, and you can stay at the farm. However, you can get a taste for their creations and gain an understanding of the process by arranging a visit, which will involve exploring the cellars and all-important tastings, accompanied by focaccia and Fortana wine.
www.anticacortepallavicinarelais. com; tel +39 0524 936539; Strada del Palazzo Due Torri 3, Polesine Parmense; tours Sat & Sun Feb–Dec

05 Modena, home to the world's best balsamic vinegar

06 Preparing the capeletti zucca pasta, a regional speciality

WHERE TO STAY

TORRE PRENDIPARTE
This is no ordinary B&B. Here you get a three-floor suite to yourself, inside one of Bologna's extraordinary, historic medieval towers. *www.prendiparte.it; tel +39 335 561 6858; Piazzetta Prendiparte 5, Bologna*

CANALGRANDE HOTEL
This elegant place in Modena is a former monastery with nothing monastic about it. The palatial, baroque surroundings have lashings of old-money atmosphere, chandeliers, sparkling gilt, marble and terraces. *www.canalgrandehotel.it; tel +39 059 217 160; Corso Canalgrande 6, Modena*

ANTICA CORTE PALLAVICINA RELAIS
Outside Parma, this is where the Spigarolis produce their marvellous speciality cured-meat parcels, *culatelli,* with several elegant rooms in the 14th-century farmhouse. *www.aticacortepalla vicinarelais.com; tel +39 0524 936539; Strada del Palazzo Due Torri 3, Polesine Parmense*

WHAT TO DO
One of Bologna's great non-culinary pleasures is to climb the 97.6m-high Torre degli Asinelli, one of Le Due Torri – two of the tallest medieval towers in the city. From here, you'll get helicopter-high views across the russet roofs of the city. While you're in the region, also take a detour off the foodie trail to see the glittering Byzantine mosaics at Ravenna (to the east of Bologna and about an hour by train), one of Italy's many wonders, dating from the fifth century.

CELEBRATIONS
The Festival del Prosciutto di Parma in September is devoted to ham, with street stalls, tastings and factory visits (www.festivaldelprosciutto diparma.com). October's Mortadello Bò in Bologna is another Italian cured meat fest (www.mortadellabo.it). There's also the three-month arts celebration that is Bè Bolognæstate, with performances and concerts from June to September (agenda. comune.bologna.it/ cultura/bolognaestate).

Tyrrhenian Sea

05 MONDELLO

PALERMO

07 06 04 01

08 SCOPELLO

09 ERICE 03 02

NUBIA TRAPANI

10

11 MARSALA

ITALY

Italy

FLAVOURS OF NORTHWEST SICILY

Floating at the crossroads of the Mediterranean, Sicily is infused with ancient colonial influences and its fragrant northwest cuisine has a distinctly Arabian-scented heart.

A feast for the senses and a world apart from the rest of Italy, the gorgeous island of Sicily has long seduced travellers with its unique and richly varied cuisine. Mediterranean climate and a dramatic mix of landscapes account in part for Sicily's culinary wealth. The ever-present sea serves up swordfish, tuna, sardines, sea urchins, squid and other seafood delights, while the mountainous interior provides fertile ground for such savoury ingredients as wild fennel, mushrooms, olives and capers, along with the ricotta cheese, almonds, pistachios and citrus that find their way into iconic Sicilian desserts like cannoli, cassata and *granite*.

Even more important to Sicily's complex culinary culture is the island's plum position at the crossroads of the Mediterranean. Starting with the ancient Greeks and Phoenicians who colonised the island in the 7th century BC, successive waves of invaders – Romans,

Byzantines, Arabs, Normans, Aragonese, and Spanish – have come and gone, each leaving their mark on the Sicilian table.

This tour focuses on Sicily's northwest, between Palermo and Marsala, where the Arab influence is most strongly felt. Many key ingredients of the region's cuisine arrived with the North African Muslims, whose 9th- to 11th-century Palermo emirate laid the groundwork for the city's Golden Age under the Norman kings. Just as the exquisite *muqarnas* carving work of Arab crafters was adopted by King Roger II and showcased alongside Byzantine religious mosaics in Palermo's Palatine Chapel, the pistachios, saffron, dried fruits, eggplant, rice and sugar cane introduced to Sicily by Arab colonisers were adopted by subsequent generations and are recognisable in modern-day Sicilian dishes – from Trapani's fish couscous to Erice's marzipan sweets.

NEED TO KNOW
International flights land in Palermo, where this 2-3 day trail starts. Hire a car to get out of the city.

01 COOKING WITH THE DUCHESS, BUTERA 28

Get into the Sicilian foodie mood with a cooking class led by the charming multilingual Duchess of Palma, Nicoletta Polo Lanza Tomasi, who invites aspiring chefs into her 18th-century waterfront palazzo in Palermo's Kalsa district. Participants harvest herbs from the palazzo's gardens, cook together in the gorgeous tile-walled kitchen and accompany Nicoletta to buy ingredients at local markets. *www.butera28.it/cooking-with-the-duchess.php; +39 333 316 5432; Via Butera 28, Palermo*

02 MERCATO DI BALLARÒ

Snaking for several blocks through the Albergheria neighbourhood, Palermo's most colourful market throbs with activity from the crack of dawn. Crammed with food stalls, bustling with recent Tunisian immigrants and cacophonous with vendors singing their wares' praises in Sicilian dialect, it bears as much resemblance to a North African bazaar as to a European market.

Food carts in Piazza Carmine sell *pane e panelle*, a snack with Saracen roots, long popular with working-class Palermitans for its low cost and high caloric content. The basic version consists of savoury *panelle* (chickpea fritters) loaded onto a sesame-seed roll with a squeeze of lemon. Optional add-ons include *crocchè* (potato croquettes flavoured with parsley or mint) and *melanzane* (fried eggplant slices); the latter two items are affectionately nicknamed *cazzilli* (little penises) for their short cylindrical form, and *felle* (butt cheeks), thanks to their appearance when placed together in pairs. *Via Ballarò & Via Collegio di Maria al Carmine, Palermo; 7am-7pm Mon-Sat, to 1pm Sun*

03 TRATTORIA AI CASCINARI

For a perfect lunch break, seek out this unpretentious neighbourhood eatery, 1.5km northwest of Ballarò. Try to visit on a Sunday afternoon, when locals linger for hours in the labyrinth of back rooms, as waiters bustle about with plates of scrumptious seasonal antipasti and fresh seafood.

Not-to-be-missed Sicilian classics here include caponata (a sweet-and-sour mix of caramelised onions, eggplant, olives, capers and celery), *spaghetti ai ricci di mare* (spaghetti with fresh sea urchins, garlic, olive oil, parsley and white wine), *pasta con le sarde* (pasta with sardines, wild fennel, pine nuts and raisins) and *involtini di pesce spada* (thinly sliced swordfish fillets, rolled up and stuffed with local capers, olives, tomatoes and breadcrumbs). *Tel +39 0916 519804; Via d'Ossuna 43/45, Palermo; 12.30-2.30pm Tue-Sun, 8-10.30pm Wed-Sat*

01 Palermo street scene, near Il Capo market

02 Palermo street market at dusk

03 Cassata siciliana, a traditional sweet

04 Historic tuna fishery in Scopello, now a beauty spot

04 PASTICCERIA CAPPELLO

Finish the day with a pair of exquisite desserts from Palermo's Pasticceria Cappello: the *setteveli*, a multi-textured masterpiece of chocolate-hazelnut cake, with seven alternately smooth and crunchy layers, or the dreamy *delizia di pistacchio*, a granular pistachio cake topped with creamy green icing and a chocolate medallion. *www.pasticceriacappello.it; tel +39 0916 113769; Via Nicolò Garzilli 19, Palermo; 7.30am-9.30pm Thu-Tue*

05 PASTICCERIA ALBA

Frozen desserts for breakfast? Yes, they're a favourite Sicilian tradition, and on sunny summer mornings this beachfront pasticceria in Mondello, 10km north of Palermo, makes a tasty spot to savour *gelato con brioche* (a sweet roll filled with gelato) or a classic Sicilian granita (crushed ice flavoured with fresh fruit or nuts).

Sicily's medieval Saracen rulers legendarily invented a prototype of the granita by mixing snow from Mt Etna with fruit juice or rosewater; nowadays, popular flavours include *limone* (lemon), *gelsi* (mulberry), *mandorla* (almond) and pistachio. For a more savoury (but still Arabic-influenced) snack, try one of Alba's famous arancine, luscious balls of saffron-scented rice, fried to a crispy golden brown and stuffed with butter, peas, ragu (meat sauce) and other flavourful fillings. *www.pasticceriaalba.it; tel +39 0916 840444; Viale Regina Margherita di Savoia 2b, Mondello; 7am-10pm*

06 PENSIONE TRANCHINA

Superb home-cooked meals featuring local produce, artisanal olive oil and seafood from the sparkling Golfo di Castellammare are reason enough to stay at this welcoming family-run pensione one hour west of Mondello in the village of Scopello.

Hosts Marisin and Salvatore preside over a daily changing menu that features grilled tuna and swordfish alongside such iconic Sicilian starters as *busiate al pesto trapanese* (corkscrew pasta with ground almonds, garlic, tomato, basil and pecorino cheese) or *pasta con spada, menta e melanzane* (pasta with swordfish, fried eggplant, cherry tomatoes and mint). Non-hotel guests can eat here on the rare occasions it's not full (drop by to see if there's a table for the same evening), but if you want to play it safe book a room. *www.pensionetranchina.com; tel +39 0924 541099; Via Diaz 7, Scopello; dinner at 8pm*

07 PASTICCERIA MARIA GRAMMATICO

From Scopello, a tortuous but jaw-droppingly beautiful 45-minute drive leads to the hilltop town of Erice, known throughout Sicily for its sweets.

The town's star culinary attraction is the confectionary shop of chef Maria Grammatico, who entered a convent orphanage at age 11 and spent 15 years learning the nuns' pastry-making secrets.

Sumptuous display cases brim with almond pastries, *torrone* (nougat made with local pistachios, almonds and honey) and *frutta martorana* (brightly coloured miniature marzipan fruits, a Sicilian tradition with 14th-century roots in Palermo's Martorana convent). Serious sweet tooths can stick around and take a cooking class from Signora Grammatico herself. *www.mariagrammatico.it; tel +39 0923 869 390; Via Vittorio Emanuele 14, Erice; 9am-7pm Oct-Apr, open later May-Sep*

08 OSTERIA LA BETTOLACCIA

Just downhill from Erice, the city of Trapani straddles a sickle-shaped peninsula gazing across the open Mediterranean towards Tunisia. Here you'll find Osteria La Bettolaccia, a Slow Food favourite where North

'Filled with blissfully creamy, sweetened ricotta, cannoli are Sicily's quintessential dessert and meant to be eaten with your fingers'

African culinary influences are woven into Western Sicily's standout recipe, *cuscus alla trapanese*. Studded with shrimp, squid, mussels and fish, the saffron-hued couscous comes accompanied by a bowl of spicy fish broth flavoured with tomatoes, garlic and parsley; ladle the sauce onto your couscous as liberally as you like.

It's a dish so locally beloved that it has its own annual festival in nearby San Vito Lo Capo (see Celebrations). *www.labettolaccia.it; tel +39 0923 21695; Via Enrico Fardella 25, Trapani; 12.45-3pm Mon-Fri, 7.45-11pm Mon-Sat*

09 LA RINASCENTE

Enter this Trapani bakery through the side door and you'll feel like you've barged into someone's kitchen;

indeed, you have. Thankfully, owner Giovanni Costadura's broad smile will quickly put you at ease, as will a taste of his homemade cannoli.

These crunchy pastry tubes – filled with blissfully creamy, sweetened sheep's milk ricotta, then dusted with ground pistachios, chocolate bits or candied orange peel – are Sicily's quintessential dessert, tracing their origins back to the Saracen muslims who roamed this island in medieval times. Two quick pointers: cannoli are meant to be eaten with your fingers, and 'cannoli' is the plural form; if you just want one (unlikely!), ask for 'un cannolo'. *Tel +39 0923 23767; Via Gatti 3, Trapani; 9am-1.30pm & 3-7pm Mon, Tue, Thu & Fri, 7.30am-2pm Sat & Sun*

⑩ MUSEO DEL SALE

South of Trapani, an other-worldly landscape of salt pools, ancient windmills and bird-rich wetlands is home to this fascinating museum tracing the history of local sea salt production, which dates back to Phoenician times.

For millennia, Trapani's 'white gold' served both as a condiment and as a crucial preservative for fish and meat. Western Sicily's hot, dry and windy climate was perfect for drying salt, and the Saline di Trapani (Trapani Saltworks) were known throughout the Mediterranean, and included in a travelogue written by Arab scholar Muhammad al-Idrisi for King Roger II in 1154.

Local chefs still use the coarse-grained salt produced here and it's possible to buy a bag to take home for your own kitchen.
www.museodelsale.it; tel +39 0923 867 061; Via Chiusa, Nubia Paceco; 9.30am-7pm

⑪ CANTINE FLORIO, MARSALA

The Marsala region, 30km south of Trapani, is world-renowned for its oak barrel-aged, fortified wines. Available in both dry and sweet varieties, this wine is an Italian kitchen staple traditionally used in desserts, such as tiramisu and savoury dishes like veal scaloppine.

To learn all about the Marsala-making process and sample the goods, tour these venerable cellars east of town – named for Vincenzo Florio, who launched the first commercial production of Marsala in 1833. Other producers nearby include Pellegrino, Donnafugata, Rallo and Intorcia.
www.duca.it/cantineflorio; tel +39 0923 781 111; Via Vincenzo Florio 1, Marsala; English-language tours 3.30pm Mon-Fri, 10.30am Sat

05 Sicilian granita

06 The town of Marsala, famed for its fortified wine

WHERE TO STAY

BUTERA 28
Delightful multilingual owner Nicoletta rents 11 comfortable apartments in the 18th-century Palazzo Lanzi Tomasi, former home of Giuseppe Tomasi di Lampedusa, author of the classic Sicilian novel *The Leopard*. Most units sleep a family of four or more. Four apartments face the sea, most have laundry facilities, and all come with well-equipped kitchens.
www.butera28.it; tel +39-333 3165432; Via Butera 28

PENSIONE TRANCHINA
In the tiny village of Scopello, this is one of northwest Sicily's most charming family-run hotels. Friendly hosts Marisin and Salvatore offer seven comfortable rooms along with superb home-cooked meals. A leisurely downhill walk leads to Scopello's picturesque beach, backed by a rust-red *tonnara* (tuna-processing plant) and dramatic *faraglioni* (rock spires). The hilltop town of Erice is an easy day trip.
www.pensionetranchina. com; tel +39 0924 541099; Via Diaz 7, Scopello

WHAT TO DO

In Palermo, visit the Cappella Palatina, a 12th-century masterpiece of Arab-Norman architecture that glitters with stunning gold mosaics, inlaid marble floors and a honeycomb-vaulted ceiling carved in Arabic *muqarnas* style (www .federicosecondo.org). West of the city, tour Erice's Castello di Venere, a castle dramatically perched on a windswept ridgeline that was once held sacred by the ancient Phoenicians, Greeks and Romans (www.fonda zioneericearte.org/ castellodivenere.php); or hike the trails of the Riserva Naturale dello Zingaro, with museums focused on local tuna fishing and agricultural traditions (www.riserva zingaro.it).

CELEBRATIONS

COUS COUS FEST
This 10-day September event brings in chefs and musicians from around the world, with couscous-making workshops, an international couscous cook-off and free World Music concerts (www. couscousfest.it).

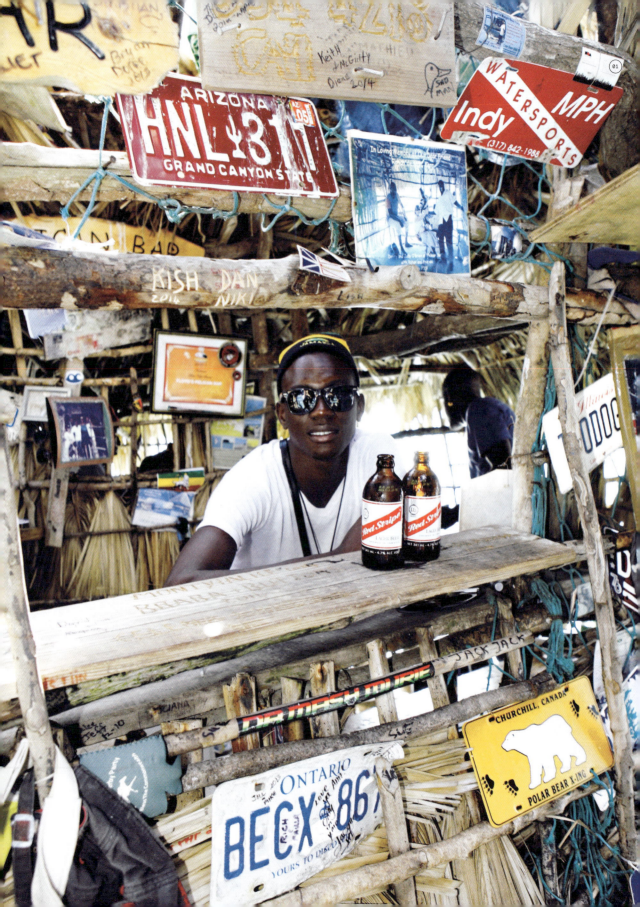

On the map:
- MAGGOTTY
- 07
- 06
- MIDDLE QUARTERS
- 08
- BLACK RIVER
- MANDEVILLE
- 02
- 01
- 05
- 04
- TREASURE BEACH
- 03
- ALLIGATOR POND

JAMAICA

Caribbean Sea

Jamaica
GRASSROOTS COOKING IN JAMAICA

Jamaica is the Caribbean's underrated culinary star, particularly around Treasure Beach where humble feasts are packed with fiery flavour, seafood and fresh produce.

In a country famed for its fleet-footed athletes and skanking reggae rhythms, Jamaica's food culture often gets short shrift. But, hidden among the drowsy beach towns and mellow mountain villages that pepper this land of easy-going-ness and irie (good-feeling) you'll find, arguably, the world's most underrated food; home-cooked, gloriously simple dishes made with hand-me-down recipes that are more likely to have been made by someone's grandma than a celebrity chef. Think marinated-to-perfection jerk chicken, beautifully tenderised goat curry, flaky meat patties, and that starch-heavy breakfast of champions (ask the sprinters) – ackee and salt fish.

The best place to dip into Jamaican food culture is in the island's bucolic southwest around Treasure Beach, a community-focused string of beach hamlets totally bereft of the edginess common in Jamaica's tougher urban enclaves. Despite a dry climate and a landscape that can pass for the African savannah in the right light, the area around Treasure Beach is popularly considered to be the breadbasket of Jamaica. Diligently irrigated fields support cassava, corn, coffee, pineapples and sweet potatoes, while the iridescent seas yield fish, much of it caught using traditional dugout canoes.

Eating in and around Treasure Beach epitomises Jamaica's ultra-laid-back approach to life. In the absence of any big international resorts, the best spreads tumble out of the humblest eating joints: a charred roadside jerk oven, a pop-up patty stall, or a tumbledown beach shack where the sound of crashing waves competes with the thud of a reggae bass. Slow food made from scratch has long been the norm in these parts. So wander over, embrace the stress-free atmosphere and learn the best ways to *nyam yuh bickle* (eat your food).

NEED TO KNOW
In a hurry? You're in the wrong place. Plan your trip around the Saturday nearest full moon, for Jake's farm banquet.

01 SMURF'S CAFE

A morning run could be in order before you decamp to Smurf's Cafe for a hearty breakfast of ackee and salt fish. Promising little from the outside, Treasure Beach's most unlikely legend lies hidden behind a scruffy breeze-block bottle shop decorated with cartoonish blue smurf motifs. Don't be put off by the dodgy design. There's nothing smurflike about the cafe out back.

Pancakes, French toast, and omelettes stuffed with callaloo (a spinach-like vegetable) adorn the simple breakfast menu, but it is the heaped plates of ackee and salt fish that attest to Smurfs' weighty local reputation. Fresh ackee is a classic only-in-Jamaica experience. Toxic when unripe, the fruit's export is carefully monitored, meaning it's difficult to sample the real thing outside Jamaica. Sautéed with salt-cod and peppers, and served

'Fresh ackee is a classic only-in-Jamaica experience. It is toxic when unripe, so the fruit's export is carefully monitored'

with sides of fried dumpling and plantain, Smurfs' ackee conspires to create a rich cocktail of Caribbean deliciousness. It's practically imperative to wash it down with a mug of the cafe's dangerously addictive Jamaican Blue Mountain coffee, home-roasted and dispensed from a smudged silver urn outside the kitchen.
Tel +876-483-7523; Ocean View Hill Dr; 6.30am-1pm

02 PELICAN BAR

Balanced on stilts above the lapping surf a kilometre off Jamaica's south coast, the Pelican is the inspired dream project of local fisher,

Floyd Forbes, who constructed his romantically dishevelled drinking joint out of old driftwood in 2001.

Decorated with rusty licence plates and other assorted knick-knacks left behind by a succession of satisfied customers, the rickety bar has built a reputation as the place to enjoy rum punches over Bloody Mary sunsets.

You'll need to charter a boat from Treasure Beach to reach the Pelican and order ahead if you want food, but the short voyage is well worth it. Adrift on a covered platform that looks like it'll take off in the next hurricane, hungry diners stand around chomping on fresh-from-

the-ocean lobster, while drinkers nurse Red Stripe beers and replay their favourite cricket moments with the local Rastas. Boats to the Pelican can usually be chartered from Frenchman's Cove beach.
Tel +876-952-3171; 10.30am-sunset

⓸ JAKE'S

A low-rise boutique hotel and restaurant abutting an attractive scimitar of sand, Jake's is the nexus of practically everything in Treasure Beach, not least the food. Lured by a pleasantly unhurried rustic-chic atmosphere, guests come here to relax, recuperate and reap various stress-relieving extras, including yoga, spa treatments and cooking classes.

But it is on Saturday nights closest to a full moon that Jake's lays down its trump card – an alfresco banquet at a local organic farm called Dool's with space for 20 guests. Pulling up chairs around a specially prepared table laid

out under some mango trees, diners chink wines glasses as a Jamaican chef rustles up local delicacies such as creole brisket marinated in Red Stripe beer. Pure magic.
www.jakeshotel.com; tel +876-965-3000; Calabash Bay; 7am-11pm

⓸ JACK SPRAT

There's a reason why the walls of quintessential Treasure Beach restaurant Jack Sprat are covered in a patchwork of retro film posters. Back in the 1970s, owner Sally Henzall's late husband, Perry Henzall, directed the seminal Jamaican movie *The Harder They Come*. Set on the beach next to Jake's (to which it is affiliated), Jack Sprat is still the nexus of the local art scene, with regular live music, movies in an outdoor cinema and beach bonfire parties.

Jack's also excels in great food – jerk chicken and conch soup are standouts – but it's the pizza that

reigns supreme. This being Jamaica, the flavours are far from conventional. Try the lobster or jerk chicken toppings by the beach, washed down with a frosty fruit smoothie.
Tel +876-965-3583; Calabash Bay; 10am-11pm

⓸ LITTLE OCHIE

The diminutive fishing village of Alligator Pond, a winding 30km drive east of Treasure Beach, is where Jamaicans go to relax at weekends and partake in the cult culinary phenomenon known as Little Ochie. Encased in a charcoal-blackened kitchen surrounded by an assemblage of paint-peeled eating shacks, this fiercely traditional restaurant sticks steadfastly to its mantra of 'keep it simple'.

The only thing that matters here is fish. First, peruse the daily blackboard menu for ideas; next, take a closer look at the catch of the day in the freezer; then, tell them how you want

it cooked. The steamed snapper and grilled lobster both have dedicated fan bases, though braver palates usually opt for a hot jerk topping heaped on crab, lobster, or shrimp. Little Ochie's refusal to stray too far from its Robinson Crusoe roots hasn't stopped it becoming one of Jamaica's few bona fide destination restaurants, luring day-trippers from as far away as Kingston. *www.littleochie.com; tel +876-852-6430; 8am until last guest leaves*

06 APPLETON ESTATE

Ever since the days when British naval officers hollered 'splice the mainbrace', the history of Jamaica has been intertwined with the history of rum. These days the drink is less about the unrefined firewater once

imbibed by sailors and more about the smooth, light and sometimes spicy spirit served up at the island's oldest distillery, the 276-year-old Appleton Estate.

Visiting Appleton, 2km east of the town of Maggotty, is as much a history lesson as a gastronomic tour. Although firmly on the tourist bus circuit these days, it's still relatively easy to reach by car or taxi via an attractive 70-minute drive north from Treasure Beach. The handsome estate sprawls across 11,000 acres and uses its sugar cane to produce 16 varieties of rum. Tours (45-minutes) include generous tastings and a free sample-sized bottle. *www.appletonrumtour.com; tel +876-963-9215; Nassau Valley; 9am-3.30pm Mon-Sat*

07 MIDDLE QUARTERS

To alleviate the head-spinning qualities of Appleton rum, you'll need to make a quick snack detour on your way back to Treasure Beach. Middle Quarters, halfway between Maggotty and Black River on the A2 road, would be just another blink-and-you'll-miss-it Jamaican settlement if it wasn't for its pepper shrimp.

The small freshwater crayfish – known as 'swimp' by locals – are caught in the nearby Black River using methods imported by erstwhile slaves from the Niger River region in Africa. While the expert fishers scour the river for the tiny crustaceans, it is left to a charismatic consortium of local women to staff a dusty line of roadside stalls where they toss the fish into bubbling cauldrons laced with spicy scotch bonnet peppers.

The cooked 'swimp' are then stuffed into plastic bags and held up like bright orange stop signs in front of practically every passing car. It's nigh on impossible to drive past. Not only is the women's sales patter engagingly humorous, the fiery 'swimp' provide an ideal antidote to a bellyful of Appleton rum.

08 SCOTT'S COVE

Scott's Cove, known colloquially as 'Border' for its location on the cusp of St Elizabeth and Westmoreland parishes, is Jamaica's food-shack capital – a high-spirited slice of roadside theatre where fish is king and haggling is the primary modus operandi. Any visitor with taste buds in southwest Jamaica should make a beeline for Border at some point to load up on the local speciality of fried snapper and bammy (a pancake made from cassava) sold from a competitive cluster of wooden stalls.

Slow your car down to jogging pace 2km south of Whitehouse and a well-stocked plate of fish and bammy will appear like Usain Bolt through your window followed by loud entreaties to buy it. Haggling is part of Border's DNA. For a more thorough exploration, get out of your car, adopt a phlegmatic air and wander through the huddle of food shacks to assess the best deals.

Most of the fish is cooked escovitch-style over open fires and marinated in a spicy vinegar containing scotch bonnet peppers. The bammy is made from grated cassava and then rolled into either balls or pancakes. It's a culinary marriage made in heaven and no true Jamaican trip is complete without trying it. Scott's Cove is located 40km northwest of Treasure Beach on the A2.

01-02 Inside the floating Pelican bar

03 Jake's boutique hotel

04 Only-in-Jamaica ackee

05 Sugar cane on Appleton Estate

06 Jack Sprat, Treasure Beach

WHERE TO STAY

JAKE'S HOTEL

Despite its inherent plushness, Jake's still manages to exude the unpretentious and rustic nature of Treasure Beach legend. Accommodation is spread around various rooms, cottages and villas, and comfortable furnishings are colourful and eclectic – imagine Gaudí meets Gauguin in a quintessentially Jamaican setting. Bonuses include a pool, art classes and an in-house literary festival. *www.jakeshotel.com; tel +876-965-3000; Calabash Bay*

MARBLUE VILLA SUITES

A small but beautiful boutique establishment located on a quiet nugget of Treasure Beach sand, Marblue offers five Babylonian villa-suites that effortlessly meld with the dreamy laid-back vibe of Treasure Beach. Aside from plush, beach-facing rooms, there's a pool, private verandas and creative meals cooked by a top-notch chef. *www.marblue.com; tel +876-965-3408; Calabash Bay*

WHAT TO DO

YS FALLS

Jamaica sports at least half a dozen Eden-like waterfalls where you can relax amid dripping foliage and do Tarzan impersonations. YS Falls might not be the quietest of the country's cascades, but it's definitely one of the prettiest, plus it's conveniently located near Appleton rum estate.

TREASURE BEACH SPORTS PARK

The place to go on a Sunday afternoon for cricket matches. Hearing the thud of leather on willow with the Santa Cruz Mountains winking in the distance is a classic only-in-Jamaica experience. Grab a pew in the wooden pavilion, order an ice-cold Red Stripe beer and listen to the locals gossiping about 'googlies' and 'lbws'.

CELEBRATIONS

Acclaimed international authors hobnob with local farmers and fishers, and there are jerk stands set up next to book stalls plying poetry at the bi-annual Calabash International Literary Festival, at Jake's Hotel in late May of even-numbered years.

The map shows numbered locations across Tokyo districts including BUNKYŌ-KU, UENO, OSHIAGE, IIDABASHI, HONGO, KORAKUEN, TAITŌ-KU, KURAMAE, JIMBOCHO, RYOGOKU, MARUNOUCHI, AKASAKA, KIYOSUMI, CHŪŌ-KU, ROPPONGI, SHINBASHI, KACHIDOKI, MINATO-KU, KOTO-KU, JAPAN. Numbered markers: 01, 02, 03, 04, 05, 06, 07, 08, 09, 10, 11, 12, 13.

Japan

A TASTE OF TOKYO'S PAST

Tokyo is a bamboozling, throbbing clash of modern and ancient, both on the streets and in the city's world-class restaurants, busy markets and traditional neighbourhood stores.

Tokyo has a desire for delicious food hardwired into its DNA. Back in the early 17th century, as Edo Castle, on the grounds of Tokyo's current Imperial Palace, rose to become the largest fortress in the world, a ravenous city of epicures gathered around it. Amazingly, given all the natural and man-made calamities that have befallen Tokyo through the centuries, in today's cutting-edge, contemporary metropolis, fragments of old Edo (Tokyo's former name) linger on. Beyond the latest novelty gadget, the blaze of neon and building-sized LCD screens, and the fluorescent flicker of subways and overhead rail stations, paper lanterns still glow, warmly lighting the way to a world of traditional dining in an Edo-era atmosphere.

Japan's capital hosts twice as many Michelin-starred restaurants as Paris – little wonder, as obsessive locals are determined to track down the ultimate purveyors of every kind of edible, from the finest ramen and soba noodles to the lightest, crispiest tempura-battered prawn, the ripest musk melon and sweetest grapes. Indeed, the city's nickname is the 'Big Sushi' since it was here that Edomae-zushi – slivers of seafood draped over pads of sushi rice, and what has become the global default for the dish – was invented in the 1820s.

This tour provides you with the inside track on historic and classic places to eat and shop for ingredients – businesses that have survived all that Tokyo could throw at them. Over four days it takes in the bayside areas of Toyosu and Tsukiji, where you'll find the brand new premises of the city's famous fish market and some of its top sushi vendors; the storied shopping districts of Ginza and Nihombashi; and the atmospheric districts of Yanaka and Asakusa where Tokyo's *shitamachi* (old city) heart still beats strong.

NEED TO KNOW
This 4-day trail is wholly based in Tokyo: use the city's stellar public transport, rent a bike or walk between stops.

01 TOYOSU MARKET
(豊洲市場)

The history of Tokyo's premier food market can be traced back to Shogun Tokugawa Ieyasu granting permission to the fishermen, who provided fish for Edo Castle, to sell their surplus near the city's Nihombashi bridge.

In 2016 the Tokyo Metropolitan Central Wholesale Market, better known as Tsukiji, is relocating to Toyosu, 2.3km from its former 80-year-old base at Tsukiji. The state-of-the-art Toyosu facility is where those keen to see the famous frozen *maguro* (tuna) auctions now have to make their way in the early hours of the morning.

Don't worry if you're not an early riser as there is still plenty to see here later in the day, although unlike at the old Tsukiji location there are off-limits areas to casual visitors so

you won't be able to wander freely. In a separate building there are retail vendors and small restaurants. *www.shijou.metro.tokyo.jp/index. html; 6-chōme, Toyosu, Koto-ku*

02 TSUKIJI OUTER MARKET
(築地場外市場)

The wholesale fish market may have relocated, but that doesn't mean the end of Tsukiji as a culinary destination. Far from it, Tsukiji Outer Market (Jōgai Shijō) has been carefully nurturing its reputation as the destination for everything and anything you might need to prepare and serve a great Japanese meal.

It's fascinating to explore the tightly packed rows of vendors here, hawking goods ranging from dried fish and seaweed to crockery and top-quality kitchen knives. Among many tempting treats are freshly shucked

oysters and fat slices of *tamagoyaki* (sweet and savoury rolled omelettes), which make delicious snacks to sample while on the go.

If you prefer to sit down there are plenty of restaurants and cafes including those at Tokyo Uogashi, a new shopping complex with a rooftop terrace overlooking Harumi-dōri. It houses scores of vendors, some of whom used to operate from the old inner Tsukiji market. *www.tsukiji.or.jp; tel +81 3 6264 1925; Information Centre Plat Tsukiji, 4-16-2 Chūō-ku*

03 TOKYO COOKING STUDIO
(東京クッキングスタジオ)

Inoue Akira is what is known as an Edo-ko (meaning Child of Tokyo), a title reserved for those born and bred in the city. And it's a classic Tokyo dish – soba noodles made from nutty

> 'At Kyūbey, sushi is served exactly as it should be: piece by piece across the counter by your own personal chef'

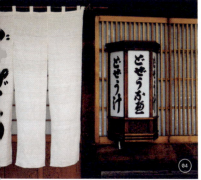

01 Cherry blossom in Ueno park, Tokyo

02 Neon nightlife

03 Locals eat at a yakitori stall

04 Traditional exterior of Komagata Dozeu

05 Chopstick maker Nakajima Hideyoshi in Tsukuda-jima

buckwheat flour – that the chef is considered a master of.

Since starting his cooking school in 2002, Inoue has taught the skill of making perfect soba to more than 20,000 food lovers in Tokyo and overseas, including to a couple of chefs who have gone on to win Michelin stars for their cooking.

Intimate soba-making workshops and general Japanese cooking classes are held in a kitchen here, a short walk north of Tsukiji Outer Market overlooking the Sumida River. *tokyo.cookingstudio.org; Hins Minato #004, 3-18-14 Minato, Chūō-ku*

04 TENYASU HONTEN
(天安本店)

Across the Tsukuda Bridge from Tokyo Cooking School is the charming residential area of Tsukuda-jima (which translates as 'Island of Cultivated Rice Fields') where it's easy to spot your next stop, Tenyasu Honten, by its weather-beaten wooden facade and giant blue *noren* (door curtain).

Since 1837 this shop has been specialising in *tsukudani* – small pieces of seafood, meat or seaweed that have been simmered in a mix of soy sauce, mirin (rice wine), salt and sugar. The kindly serving ladies who kneel on the raised tatami mat counter here will allow you taste samples of this classic Edo-era pickle so you can decide which of the smartly boxed versions to take home as a souvenir.

While in the area, also search out the 11th-generation chopstick maker and lacquerware artist Nakajima Hideyoshi. *Tel +81 3 3532 3457; 1-3-14 Tsukuda, Chūō-ku; 9am-6pm*

05 KYŪBEY
(久兵衛)

Return to the heart of Ginza for a slap-up sushi dinner at Kyūbey, served exactly as it should be: piece by piece across the counter in front of you by your own personal chef. It's very likely that genial owner Imada-san will greet you personally and share with you (in English) some of the history of this storied establishment that has been a fixture on Tokyo's dining scene since 1936.

Unlike some of its more exclusive neighbours, Kyūbey is an informal, welcoming and foreigner-friendly experience. For a special treat, order the *kaiseki* (Japanese haute cuisine) menu served on pottery crafted by famed artisan Kitaoji Rosanjin. *www.kyubey.jp; tel +81 3 3571 6523; 8-7-6 Ginza, Chūō-ku*

(06)

06 MITSUKOSHI
(三越)

Named after the first wooden bridge to be built here in 1603, Nihombashi was the location of Tokyo's fish market before it moved to Tsukiji in 1935. There are still many long-established food purveyors in this riverside area, including Japan's oldest department store, Mitsukoshi, which first opened its grand doors in 1904.

All major Japanese department stores sport extensive food halls, called *depachika*, where the grocery counters are traditionally located. Arrive here as soon as the store opens to witness the ritual bowing of the staff and calling out of 'irasshaimase' (welcome) as the first customers pass by.

This opulent food hall is where you can find prime specimens of fruit and vegetables (such as fragrant musk melons that can cost up to US$100) as well as myriad other ingredients,

'Sasa-no-Yuki translates as "snow lying on bamboo leaves", a poetic evocation of the light-as-snow tofu served here since 1691'

prepared foods and baked goods. Free samples are on offer and it's a fantastic place to come for a delicious and beautifully packaged take-out bento (boxed meal).
Tel +81 3 3241 3311; 1-4-1 Nihombashi Muromachi, Chūō-ku; 10am-7pm

07 BUDDHA BELLIES TOKYO

If you would prefer to make your own bento, head to the bookshop area of Jimbochō to find this intimate cooking school. It's run by well-travelled Akiyama Ayuko, a professionally trained sushi and *kaiseki* chef who's fluent in English and also a certified

sake sommelier. Here you can learn how to make a variety of foods for the lacquered bento box, including the rolled omelette *tamagoyaki*; other classes on offer include sushi-making.
buddhabelliestokyo.jimdo.com; 2F Uekuri Bldg, 2-4-3 Kanda-Jinbochō, Chiyoda-ku

08 NEZU-NO-TAIYAKI
(根津のたいやき)

The neighbouring districts of Nezu, Yanaka and Sendagi, collectively known as Yanesen, are charming locations to spend a day exploring. They are a living and breathing part of the *shitamachi*, or old downtown

district of Tokyo. Start by making a beeline to the takeaway counter of Nezu-no-Taiyaki to grab one of their *taiyaki* sweet pancake treats.

Cooked in a sea bream-shaped mould (the fish is called *tai* in Japanese, but the same kanji character can also mean 'happy', so when people see the fish shape the hope is they will associate it with the idea of being happy) these crispy pockets of dough are packed with *anko*, a jam made of burgundy-coloured adzuki beans.

The stall has been going strong since 1957 and the snack itself has been popular since the 19th century. Arrive early as they often sell out by noon.
1-23-9-104 Nezu, Bunkyō-ku; 10.30am-2pm, sometimes closed Mon or Tue

⑨ YANAKA GINZA
(谷中銀座)

A short walk north of Nezu-no-Taiyaki is Yanaka Ginza, a pedestrianised street of about 70 grocery stores and other shops that collectively evoke a feeling of what many of the city's retail strips would have been like a century ago.

Locals flock here to wallow in the nostalgia and make purchases from butchers, bakers and basket makers where the owners live above the shops and have been plying their trade for decades, if not longer.

The *taiyaki* hot cakes here are made in the shape of cats, which is the area's motif (because of all the local strays you'll see padding about) – look out for carved wooden cats that grace shop facades and their live inspiration, which pad along the alleys.

If you approach the street from Nippori, the nearest train station, you'll head down the Yuyake dan dan (Sunset stairs) – so-called because of the view the steps provide of the sunsets over the area.
3-13-1 Yanaka, Taitō-ku

⑩ SASA-NO-YUKI
(笹乃雪)

One train stop south of Nippori it's easy to access the venerable tofu restaurant Sasa-no-Yuki. The name translates as 'snow lying on bamboo leaves', a poetic evocation of the light-as-snow quality of the tofu served here since, incredibly, 1691.

A kimono-attired waitress will greet you on arrival, store your shoes and show you to one of the low tables on the tatami mat flooring. With some 300-plus years' experience in their cuisine, this is not the cardboard tofu of supermarkets that you may know, but a gourmet delight – particularly if you treat yourself to one of their

08 TTstudio © Shutterstock   07 Iain Masterton © Alamy

degustation menus, which can be
configured to be fully vegetarian.
Sample various versions of the
curd, some made from sesame and
arrowroot rather than soya beans,
paired with exquisite pickles, miso
and *yuzu*, a fragrant citrus.
*Tel +81 3 3873 1145; 2-5-10 Negishi,
Taitō-ku; 11.30am-8pm Tue-Sun*

⑪ IRIYAMA SEMBEI
(入山煎餅)
Asakusa was a key area for Edo-
era merchants and artisans and it's
another part of modern Tokyo where
the *shitamachi* spirit remains strong.
Iriyama Sembei has been serving
sembei (rice crackers) on an arcade
here since 1914. The rice-flour dough
used to make the fist-sized crackers
is left to mature in the sun for three

days before it is toasted golden
brown above charcoal grills and given
a finishing dip in thick soy sauce.
Watch the men here in white cotton
tops and pants, deftly processing
thousands of the crackers while sat
cross-legged in front of the coals.
*1-13-4 Asakusa, Taitō-ku; 10am-6pm
Fri-Wed*

⑫ KOMAGATA DOZEU
(駒形どぜう)
Komagata Dozeu has traded
continuously from the same location,
a short walk south of Asakusa,
since 1801. It would appear little
has changed here in more than two
centuries judging by the restaurant's
traditional exterior, hung with red
caligraphy-painted lanterns and a
blue *noren*, which leads through to

an equally Edo-evocative interior with
floor cushion seating around broad
wooden planks that act as tables.
   The speciality is the same as when
it first opened in 1801: *dojō* (loach), an
earthy-tasting, small fish with tough
bones. The restaurant's technique for
making the loach more palatable is to
gently simmer it over a small charcoal
brazier in dashi, bonito-flake broth
flavoured with soy and sake.
*ww.dozeu.com; tel +81 3 3842 4001;
1-7-12 Komagata, Taitō-ku; 11am-9pm*

⑬ OTAFUKU
(大多福)
A short walk northwest of Asakusa's
Sensō-ji is another of Tokyo's storied
old-timers. The Funadaiku family have
run Otafuku since 1915, specialising in
oden – a variety of ingredients such

as cubes of tofu, boiled eggs, chunky slices of daikon (radish), scallops and tuna, simmered here in a light soy and dashi broth that's typical of the cooking style of the Kansai area around Osaka.

The family has elevated what is a humble dish to a fine art and the whole dining experience is raised a notch or two higher by the convivial ambience of the place with its paper lanterns, hand-written menus and a tiny traditional garden with stone lantern by the entrance.

Even if you don't come here for a full meal, it's a wonderful spot for a light supper and a glass or two of *tarozake* – pine-scented sake – before bed.
Tel +81 3 3871 2521; 1-6-2 Senzoku, Taitō-ku; 5-11pm Tue-Sat, 5-10pm Sun

09 Man filleting a fish at Tsukiji fish market

10 Shoppers pause in the nostalgic shopping area of Yanaka Ginza

WHERE TO STAY
SAWANOYA RYOKAN
Family-run and providing all the hospitality you would expect of a ryokan (traditional Japanese guesthouse), the Sawanoya is a gem in atmospheric Yanaka. Some rooms have their own bath, but it's a joy to relax in the ryokan's shared cypress and eathernware baths at the end of a long day.
www.sawanoya.com; tel +81 3 3822 2251; 2-3-11 Yanaka, Taitō-ku

NUI
In a former warehouse not far from Asakusa, this stylish hostel has raised the bar for budget digs in Tokyo. There's an enormous shared kitchen and private rooms. The ground-floor cafe-bar and lounge, with furniture made from salvaged timber, is a popular local hang-out.
backpackersjapan.co.jp/ nui_en; tel +81 3 6240 9854; 2-14-13 Kuramae, Taitō-ku

WHAT TO DO
SENSŌ-JI
Tokyo's oldest temple can be traced back to AD 645, making it older than the capital itself by 1000 years. It retains an alluring, lively atmosphere redolent of Edo. Situated in Asakusa, the busy Nakamise-dōri arcade that is the traditional approach to the main temple precincts overflows with stalls selling colourful souvenirs, plus sweet and savoury treats. The main plaza holds a five-storey pagoda and a smoking cauldron of incense. (www.senso-ji.jp)

CELEBRATIONS
There's a *matsuri* (temple festival) somewhere in the Tokyo region every week and at most of them you can sample traditional foods such as *takoyaki* (battered octopus ball) and *yakisoba* (stir-fried noodles). The grandest of the city's *matsuri* is the three-day Sanja Matsuri on the third weekend of May, which attracts about 1.5 million spectators to Asakusa. During the festival a parade of *mikoshi* (portable shrines) is carried by men and women costumed in traditional dress.

Japan

FOOD FROM THE MOUNTAINS TO THE SEA

Forget everything you think you know about Japanese cuisine: the warming food of central Japan is a different beast, with mountain-foraged vegetables and lashings of local seafood.

Nagano, 250km northwest of Tokyo, is deep in the central mountainous spine of Japan. Just beyond, the mountains make a steep tumble to the Sea of Japan Sea. Long cut off from the urban centres on the Pacific coast because of the area's topography, the Sea of Japan side of the country isn't yet firmly on the tourist trail.

Travelling this region will give a new perspective on Japanese food. Think the nation's cuisine should be light and subtle? Try the belly-warming, salty hotpots and hefty buckwheat dumplings of Nagano. Nothing dainty here, but plenty of woodsy mushrooms (in autumn) and bitter shoots (in spring) foraged from the foothills. Think sushi should be as fresh as possible? Not in Toyama where the signature style is an older form of sushi, one that recalls the days when this Japanese staple was about preservation. Think *maguro* (bluefin tuna) is the

NEED TO KNOW
This 3-day trail starts in mountainous Nagano, less than 2 hours by high-speed train from Tokyo.

king of the sea? Tell that to Kanazawa, where the prized fish are fatty, winter *buri* (yellowtail) and *nodoguro* (blackthroat sea bass); the later is a curiously rich white fish from the Sea of Japan that costs more per pound at market than *maguro*.

Kanazawa was once a wealthy castle town, which developed haute cuisine to rival Kyoto's, with an emphasis on all that fresh seafood. Wash it down with premium *nihonshu* (sake) made from rice grown on the fertile plains along the coast, watered by mountain snowmelt.

This journey is designed to take three days and finish in Kanazawa. It's possible to make your way by train, bus and taxi, however hiring a car will give you the freedom to explore mountain roads and coastal detours. Be wary of driving in winter though, when snow is likely in higher elevations.

01 SANYASŌ

(さんやそう)

Start your road trip in the mountain-ringed prefectural capital Nagano, home to the magnificent Zenkō-ji temple that attracts millions of oglers a year. *Onigiri* (rice balls) are ubiquitous around Japan, but Nagano – soba (buckwheat) country – has its own kind of portable snack: *oyaki*. These palm-sized dumplings are made of fermented buckwheat flour, stuffed with all kinds of veggie fillings such as pumpkin and *nozawana* (rape leaf), then roasted.

At Sanyasō all the ingredients are fresh from local farms, because the women who run the shop are all local farmers. Assuming you got an early start, a few *oyaki* make an excellent breakfast.

Grab a seat at the one communal table and help yourself to the teapot in the centre. Sanyasō is on the road leading to Zenkō-ji, a 10-minute

'I go to the market every morning and buy what looks good. Sometimes I don't know what I'm going to make until right before dinner'

drive from Nagano Station.
Tel +81 26 235 0330; 518 Daimon-chō, Nagano; 10am-5.30pm

02 YAWATAYA ISOGORO

(八幡屋礒五郎)

A block from Sanyasō is this nearly 300-year-old spice shop. Here the speciality is *shichimi* – a blend of seven spices that the locals use to season bowls of noodles (or just about anything you like).

There are different varieties but at Yawataya Isogorō the standard blend is chilli pepper, dried orange peel, black sesame, ground ginger, Sichuan pepper, *perilla* (an Asian plant of

the mint family) and hemp seed.

The best thing about the shop, however, is that you can custom blend your own mix, adding, for example, a spicier pepper, a dash of Okinawan sea salt or swapping the orange peel for *yuzu* (Japanese citrus).

The spices come packaged in highly collectable, colourful tins. So collectable, in fact, are spices from Yawataya Isogoro that during the feudal era they were effectively considered a bribe.
www.yawataya.co.jp; tel +81 26 232 8277; 83 Daimon-chō, Nagano; 9am-6.30pm

01 History on the streets of Kanazawa

02-03 Chef at Zeniya, preparing kaga ryōri – Japanese haute cuisine

04 *Oyaki* vegetable buns at Sanyasō

03 SOBA-CHAYA GOKURAKUBŌ
(そば茶屋極楽坊)

A 30-minute drive into the mountains, along the winding Togakushi Bird Line (aka Rte 506), takes you to the village of Togakushi, inside Joshinetsu National Park. It's nationally famous for two things: *ninjitsu* (ninja arts) and soba noodles. Soba is well suited to Togakushi's high altitude and ashy soil (courtesy of the two nearby volcanoes). It was originally served to the pilgrims that came to the village's shrines and temples.

Behind Togakushi-jinja, off Rte 36, is Soba-chaya Gokurakubō – a local soba favourite that is happily off the main tourist strip. Order a classic *zaru soba* (cold noodles with sauce on the side), served on a woven bamboo tray, with a side of *sansai* (mountain vegetable) tempura.

Tel +81 26 254 3267; 3611-5 Togakushi, Nagano; 10.30am-6pm Fri-Wed Apr-Nov, from 11.30am Dec-Mar

04 MARUNAKA LODGE
(丸中ロッヂ)

From Togakushi head northeast, an hour's drive deeper into the mountains, to the hot spring town Nozawa Onsen. Marunaka Lodge is a no-frills inn that cooks up a mighty feast of traditional local fare every night for guests.

The highlight of the meal is the mushroom hotpot, a simmering cast iron pot of fungi from the surrounding hills such as *matsutake* (pine mushroom), *maitake* (hen-of-the-woods), *hiratake* (oyster mushroom), shiitake and *amitake* (Jersey cow mushroom).

You can request the mushroom hotpot year-round, but during mushroom season (October and November) the inn also leads foraging tours in the mountains nearby (not much English is spoken, but you're welcome to join all the same); in May and June, seasonal fresh mountain shoots can also be picked as part of a tour.

Tel +81 269-85-2157; 4424 Toyosato, Nozawa Onsen, Shimotakai

05 ŌTAYA
(大多屋)

Toyama is an admittedly dreary port city on the Sea of Japan, but it looms large in the world of sushi as the home of a distinct variety known as *masu-zushi* (salmon trout sushi). The trout, caught from the Jinzū River, is layered on top of a disc of vinegar-seasoned rice, wrapped in bamboo leaves and placed in a bamboo box with the lid firmly held down. The fish is pressed into the rice – this style of sushi is called *oshi-zushi* (pressed sushi) – and the vinegar in the rice cures the fish, giving it a distinct tang.

Ōtaya is far enough away from the train station to draw a strictly local clientele. The takeaway shop closes when they sell out; to avoid

disappointment, have your inn call ahead to place an order. Chopsticks, soy sauce and a little plastic knife – for cutting the *masu-zushi*, like a sushi cake, into wedges – is included.

If you're driving, consider taking the longer scenic route to Toyama via Rte 8, which runs along the sea. *Tel +81 76 425 5100; 2-19-11 Nishi-nakanomachi, Toyama; 8am-4pm*

06 SHIMA
(志摩)

Head west to Kanazawa and make a beeline for its historic geisha district, Higashi-chaya. Many of the old teahouses here ('teahouse' is the euphemism for geisha house) are now open to the public, and 200-year-old Shima, which you can tour, also

serves tea – bowls of thick *matcha* pared with *wagashi* (traditional Japanese sweets) from esteemed Kanazawa confectioner Yoshihashi.

Simple ingredients (rice, sugar and beans) are coaxed, coloured and moulded into intricate flowers that look almost too good to eat. Custom dictates that you eat the sweets first and chase it with the bitter tea. *www.ochaya-shima.com; tel +81 76 252 5675; 1-13-21 Higashi-yama, Kanazawa; 9am-6pm*

07 ZENIYA
(銭屋)

Splurge time: you can't visit Kanazawa without trying *kaga ryōri*, the local variation of *kaiseki*, Japan's haute cuisine. *Kaiseki* originated in Kyoto,

but what makes Kanazawa's version different is the city's location near the sea, which means *kaga ryōri* is full of fresh, seasonal seafood: shellfish such as *aka-gai* (ark shell) and *tori-gai* (heart clam) in spring, rock oysters in summer, *buri* (yellowtail) in late autumn and snow crab in deep winter.

At acclaimed contemporary *kaga ryōri* restaurant Zeniya, there's no menu: 'I go to the market every morning and buy what looks good. Sometimes I don't know what I'm going to make until right before dinner,' says chef Shinichiro Takagi.

He also tweaks things as he goes along, chatting with diners to learn their preferences. Zeniya has a casual atmosphere that is rare for *kaga ryōri*, though even more rare is that Takagi speaks excellent English. Check ahead that he's in town when you book, as he travels often. Reservations are a must. *www.zeniya.ne.jp; tel +81 76 233 3331; 2-29-7 Kata-machi, Kanazawa; noon-2pm, 5pm-10pm Mon-Sat*

08 ŌMI-CHŌ MARKET
(近江町市場)

This is Kanazawa's central market, in business for nearly three centuries. It's a favourite destination for local chefs, including Zeniya's Takagi, who visits around 7.30am – though you can't tell apart the chefs, in sneakers and jumpers, from the market workers.

Here you can see all the seafood and veg you ate for dinner the night before, as well as grab a filling breakfast. Look for shops selling *kaisen-don* (raw fish over rice), panko-covered croquettes stuffed with crab and shrimps, grilled squid and fresh fruit. Just don't eat and walk at the same time: it drives the market workers crazy.
35 Ōmi-chō, Kanazawa; 7am-5pm

09 TEDORIGAWA SHUZO
(手取川酒造)

Sake brewery Tedorigawa Shuzo is 15km south of Kanazawa. Here the small team makes sake in a way that blends time-honoured manual techniques and the latest technology.

The nearly 150-year-old brewery, which uses local rice and water from the holy mountain, Haku-san, was the subject of the award-winning 2015 documentary, *The Birth of Sake*. If you arrange in advance (two to three months, ideally), it's possible to take an hour-long tour of the site to see the sake-making process, followed by a tasting and opportunities to buy on-site (translator in tow). Book through Kanazawa agency, The Art of Travel. *theartoftravel.net; tel +81 76 276 3311; 41 Yasuyoshi-machi, Hakusan*

Ø5 Jigokudani Onsen's resident snow monkeys in Nagano

WHERE TO STAY
RYOKUSONE
Splash out on a room in Kanazawa's newest luxury ryokan (traditional inn). The seven rooms – including both Japanese-style futons and Western-style beds – are done up in an artful blend of contemporary and traditional design. Lavish Kaga ryori meals are served as well.
Tel +81-76-208-3999; 2-1-10-1 Tenjin-machi, Kanazawa

MARUNAKA LODGE
Cozy tatami rooms, a lounge heated with a wood-fire stove and friendly owners (in addition to fantastic food) have won this mountain inn a loyal following, so book early. There's a communal bath fed by natural hot springs.
Tel +8-269-85-2157; 4424 Toyosato, Nozawa Onsen, Shimotakai

HŌSHI
The world's oldest inn, 1300-year-old Hōshi has hot springs baths – said to have been discovered by an itinerant priest in a dream – and big seafood dinners. It's an hour's drive southwest of Kanazawa, in Awazu Onsen.
www.ryokan.ne.jp/hoshi; tel +81 76 165 1112; Awazu Onsen, Komatsu

WHAT TO DO
Visit the mountain hot spring towns of Nagano prefecture, including Nozawa Onsen and Jigokudani Onsen. The latter is Japan's famous snow monkey onsen. Here you can observe the band of furry little monkeys, who have claimed one of the steamy pools as their own. Also set aside half a day to take in Kanazawa's top sights. These include Kenroku-en, considered one of Japan's top-three gardens, where strolling paths wind around ponds and past manicured pines and traditional teahouses.

CELEBRATIONS
Kanazawa's signature festival is Hyakumangoku Matsuri and celebrates the city's historic prosperity with traditional rites such as floating lanterns down the river, plus a spirited parade of residents in 16th-century costumes. The three-day event takes place on the first weekend of June.

Jordan

LEGACY OF THE LEVANT

Jordan's pan-Arabian and Bedouin-influenced cuisine is an ever-present reminder of the complex communities who have inhabited the fertile lands of the Middle East for centuries.

A caravanserai of empires and civilisations has passed through Jordan, which sits at the heart of the Levant – a historical name for the Middle Eastern region that encompasses Jordan, Israel, Syria, Lebanon and the Palestinian territories. Nowhere is this mixed heritage more obvious than in the progressive capital Amman, where a crumbling hilltop citadel harmoniously celebrates the ruins of a Roman temple and Byzantine church alongside an Umayyad mosque of Islam.

Ancient recipes, ubiquitous spices and common ingredients unite this palm-fringed, desert-cloaked area of the world, where staples such as falafel, *shwarma* (kebab), flatbread and hummus – served in restaurants, in the home or on street corners – are as much a bedrock of society as the warm hospitality on which Jordanians pride themselves. Life here is very much intertwined with food culture, and mealtimes are an open

invitation to family and friends. The saying 'The way to the heart is through the stomach' is an Arabian saying, too.

Mediterranean-style salads, mixed grills and mezze are typical of Jordanian cuisine, infused with spices, zesty sumac and herby *za'atar*, and laced with Arabian dates, pine nuts, pistachios, chickpeas, bulgar wheat and tahini (a creamy sesame-seed paste). This pan-Arabian cuisine is complemented by the influence of nomadic cooking practices brought to Jordan by the Bedouin tribespeople that have roamed the Levantine deserts and hills for thousands of years. One-pot sharing dishes, originally intended to feed extended families as well as wayward travellers looking for shelter, are popular in Jordanian households. Lamb is highly prized for its richness, and you'll rarely find a meal here that doesn't end with a syrupy pastry or cake – a legacy of four centuries of Ottoman rule is a very sweet tooth indeed.

NEED TO KNOW
This 4-day trail can be done using public transport, with a pick-up for Feynan, but a car is helpful.

① SOUK AL KHADRA

Start your food adventure in Downtown Amman, where a cacophony of traffic, industrious locals and street vendors let you know you've arrived in the beating heart of the city. Next to the Al-Husseiny Mosque you'll find the fruit and vegetable souk, where locals come to tick off their weekly shopping list. Barrow-loads of fresh tomatoes, cucumbers, radishes, giant lettuce heads, herbs, kumquats, pistachios and dried fruits such as raisins and dates vie for attention with more unusual ingredients. Look out for bags of *mograbiah* (giant couscous), persimmons from Africa, and the rare buttery fruit *qeshta*, which looks like a scaly dragon's dropping but costs the equivalent of about £7 a pop.

Pay a visit to the stand busily dishing out *karabeej halab* – a cheap, delicious churros-like pastry snack flash-fried in oil and then dunked in syrup. Back outside, opposite the mosque, seek out the little shop with a canopy of sugar-cane grasses (similar in appearance to bamboo) where the vendor uses a clapped-out machine to freshly squeeze sugar-cane juice.

Also stop by the gentleman whipping up boiled egg sandwiches for workers from his stand on Hashemi Street. Here, fresh sesame-encrusted bread is slathered with hard-boiled egg, chilli and *za'atar* (a thyme, sumac and sesame seed-based local herb blend). *Off Hashemi St; 6am–6pm*

② HABIBAH

Jordanians will readily admit their voracious appetite for sweets, and the obsession is plain to see when you catch sight of the queue of eager punters waiting for their sweet fix at Habibah – a tiny nook in the wall selling Middle Eastern sweets and pastries in

01 Bedouin hospitality

02 Feynan Ecolodge

03 Making pitta breads at Beit Sitti cooking school

a side street near the souk. Pay your pennies at the kiosk out front and then dive in to the furnace room where giant metal platters of desserts bubble away, cooked on open flames.

If you're lucky, they'll be serving *knafeh*, a slab of crispy-top buttery sponge drenched in rose-water syrup and sprinkled with pistachio crumbs, grounded by a layer of gooey *akkawi* cheese. The yin and yang of salty and sweet makes for a unique mouthful. Paper plate and plastic fork in hand, take your snack back to the alley and perch on the wall to eat with the locals. *Al-Malek Faisal St; 9am–midnight*

③ BEIT SITTI

This intimate cooking school in the affluent suburb of Jebel Weibdeh is run by three charming sisters, Maria, Dina and Tania, as an exclusively female-run enterprise employing

women from the local community. They created the school as a tribute to their mother's memories of her own grandmother, who once used to cook up a storm in this very kitchen – Beit Sitti means 'grandmother's house'. The restored villa still feels very much like a home – near the kitchen, take a peek inside the cupboard that leads to a natural pantry, a cave-like space raised off the floor that was once used to keep meat. In the 1920s, locals in Amman still had to find inventive ways of refrigerating without electricity.

You can join them for breakfast, lunch or dinner with a hands-on session in cooking Arabic food, using seasonal vegetables picked by the women. One highlight is *ma'aloubeh* – a one-pot rice dish of cauliflower, aubergine and chicken simmered in allspice and turmeric until the cooking

05 WILD JORDAN

The next morning, head to Wild Jordan to experience a completely different side to eating in Amman. This ultra-modern organic cafe fashioned out of natural recycled materials is run in partnership with Jordan's Royal Society for the Conservation of Nature to champion a back-to-nature approach to life (the cafe is also a good place to organise park tours). On the food side, this means healthy, fresh, organic meals inspired by Jordan's wildlife and vegetation. The cafe's mantra is low fat, low carb, low calorie. Time your visit for the weekly organic Al Shams Farmers' Market held here on Fridays (11am-6pm) and you can get up close to local producers that supply the cafe.

Breakfast is particularly popular – pair gluten-free pancakes or a veggie tofu omelette with a zingy *laimon má naana* (lemon and mint slushy – you'll find this all over Jordan but hands down, Wild Jordan's is the best) for a refreshing wake-me-up. If you manage to get a table out on the terrace, you'll be treated to spectacular views of Amman's hilltop Citadel and its Roman Temple of Hercules as you eat. *www.wildjordancafe-jo.com; tel +962 79 771 1177; Othman Bin Affan St, Amman; 11am-midnight*

06 HARET JDOUDNA

After breakfast leave Amman and head south to Madaba, a slightly nondescript town famous for the Byzantine art of mosaic making, and home to one of the world's most important historical relics, the 6th century biblical Madaba Map – a preciously guarded world pilgrimage site. Madaba is also one of the best places to try traditional Jordanian food.

Flavours of the Levantine permeate

liquid has evaporated, then flipped upside down onto a communal serving dish. Another is *mouttabal*, a smoky dip made by blackening aubergine until its insides are pulp, then mixing it with tahini, lemon juice, garlic and yoghurt. *www.beitsitti.com; tel +962 777 557 744; 16 Mohammad Ali Al Sa'di St, Jebel Weibdeh*

04 SUFRA

Come night time, Rainbow St on the cusp of Downtown and Jebel Amman buzzes with bright young things gossiping with friends, enjoying the fantastically popular Syrian-owned Bakdash ice cream and trying to decide which is the best burger bar to eat at (a recent thing in Amman!). But you'll also find Sufra restaurant here, housed in a glamorous old villa and serving the best traditional Jordanian cuisine in town. So highly regarded is its food that you may spot a member of the royal family or an international ambassador dining here at the same time as you.

Ask for a table in the glass-walled back room so you can watch the in-house baker flinging parcels of freshly kneaded dough into an open-flame cauldron until the flatbreads bubble and crisp, at which point he'll retrieve them with a long stick and send them straight to your table. What to order? It's all so exquisite, cast your net wide and go for a tasting platter of hot and cold mezze, which might include *gallayeh* (a simple, spicy tomato stew that is a Jordanian staple) and *kibdeh* (chicken liver cooked with onion, garlic, coriander and lemon). *www.romerogroup.jo/sufra.html; tel +962 6461 1468; 28 Rainbow St, Amman; 1-11.30pm Sun-Thu, 9.30am-11.30pm Fri-Sat*

the walls at Haret Jdoudna, housed in a tranquil restored old house. Start with a Turkish coffee, a thick sweet brew infused with cardamom that is ubiquitous across Jordan, and then dive into hot mezze such as *sambusik* (fried pastry parcels exploding with salty local goat's cheese) and *kibbeh* (fried croquettes of bulgur wheat crammed with spiced minced lamb, onion and pine nuts). Accompany the spread with *fattoush* – a common Middle Eastern salad of lettuce, radish, cucumber, tomato and crispy pitta scraps coated in a zesty sumac dressing. Then complete the banquet with a mixed grill and *kofteh bithynieh* – tender spiced beef fillets with onions and potatoes, baked in a rich tahini sauce until bubbling and golden on top. Tahini, a creamy paste made from crushing and roasting sesame seeds, is a bedrock of cuisine across the Levant region, often used as a salad or *shwarma* (kebab) dressing and a key ingredient in hummus. *www.haretjdoudna.com; tel +962 5324 8650; Talal St, Madaba; noon-midnight*

07 ZIKRA INITIATIVE

Ripe tomatoes, ripening tomatoes and green tomatoes still to ripen… The roadside veg stalls of Jordan are aflame with crate-loads of this brightly coloured local staple, which forms the base of dozens of dishes you'll find on the table. South of Madaba near the Dead Sea, you can take part in a unique grassroots tourism exchange called the Zikra Initiative to learn how a local community in the Ghor al Mazra region of the Jordan Valley grows and harvests the tomatoes on the shores of the Dead Sea – an area with such mineral-rich soil that it is known as Jordan's bread basket.

The initiative is called Bandora Day after the traditional dish *galayet bandora* ('tomato in a pan'), a version of which you may have tried at Sufra. After the lesson in tomato farming, you'll harvest the tomatoes with villagers; then learn how to cook the dish. The local way to eat *galayet bandora* is by scooping it into bread, and it's often presented as a light meal or side dish. Funds raised

from the initiative are funnelled back into the local communities. *www.zikrainitiative.org; Ghor al Mazra, Dead Sea area*

08 FEYNAN ECOLODGE

Down a dusty road, seemingly to nowhere, 22km off the Dead Sea Highway, Feynan Ecolodge is another shining example of community tourism in central Jordan. This hotel, restaurant and activity base at the edge of the Dana Biosphere Reserve employs local Bedouins from the surrounding villages, has extremely limited electricity (though it does have hot water), and enforces a 'quiet time' policy between 10pm and 7am.

Time spent at Feynan is more fun than it possibly sounds. As well as star-gazing sessions, the lodge runs cooking classes with its chef to teach guests the ABC of Jordanian cuisine. Experience first-hand how gruelling it can be to churn chickpeas, onion, garlic, parsley and coriander into falafel mixture, which you then flick one by one into a vat of bubbling oil to flash fry until golden. To do this, you'll use a custom-designed metal scoop contraption that helps shape the ball and then propels the falafel mixture into the oil with a little ejector button, a bit like an ice cream scoop (never bind with egg; only water, you'll be told). *See Places to Stay*

⑨ BEDOUIN COFFEE CEREMONY

All roads in Jordan lead to Petra, and with good reason. But before you head there, seek out an invitation (via Feynan Ecolodge) to the disarmingly charming local Bedouin on the edge of Dana for a breakfast coffee. Unlike Turkish coffee, Bedouin coffee is commonly taken without sugar and it's a much lighter affair usually ground, roasted and brewed right in front of you over a smouldering fire pit inside the tent (don't worry; Bedouin tents are cavernous). However, like Turkish coffee it will typically still be scented with freshly ground cardamom.

The rules of coffee drinking in a Bedouin tent are many; the coffee-making equipment is highly prized, handed down over generations, and the etiquette is poetic, harking back to a time when Bedouin people roamed the country as nomads. Even today, coffee drinking is still an engrained social ritual for the Bedouin and it is said that a little bit of coffee can solve the most important things.

First things first: the coffee has to be piping hot when served. 'The coffee should scare the moustache,' says Feynan guide Suleyman in his family's Bedouin tent. To cool the coffee, you swirl it around in the cup before sipping. Each cup is just a couple of mouthfuls and while the first tipple represents hospitality, subsequent cups have different meanings. Never take more than three servings, unless you want to end your trip on a particularly sour note.

04 Unusual cooking ingredients at Souk al Khadra

05 Creamy kofteh bithynieh at Haret Jdoudna in Madaba

06 Amman's hilltop Citadel

WHERE TO STAY
LA LOCANDA
This boutique hotel in Amman's Weibdeh suburb has contemporary rooms themed around a different Arabic musician, plus a lively neighbourhood bar selling local wine and beer. *www.locandahotel.com; tel +962 6460 2020; 52 Baouniya Street, Jebel Weibdeh, Amman*

FEYNAN ECOLODGE
Dwarfed by picturesque hills on the outskirts of the Dana Biosphere Reserve, Feynan is a special spot for a contemplative stay. There's a leafy internal courtyard and cosy lounge area, and rooms come with small balconies. *www.ecohotels.me/feynan; tel +962 6464 5580; Wadi Feynan; Sep-Jun*

WHAT TO DO
AMMAN'S CITADEL
Spectacularly sited on top of one of Amman's seven hills, the Citadel ruins read like a who's who of ancient civilisations with relics of the Roman, Byzantine, Umayyad and Nabataean periods, showing just how many influences have converged on Amman over more than a millennium.

PETRA
Ancient capital of the Nabataean civilisation, World Heritage site, one of the new Seven Wonders of the World, and not forgetting *Indiana Jones* filming location – Petra has many badges of honour but to truly appreciate its scale, historical significance and sheer majesty, you need to see it in the flesh. (www.visitpetra.jo)

WADI RUM
It's not surprising that Jordan's Wadi Rum desert played Mars in the 2015 blockbuster film *The Martian*. In real life it's better, though. Giant stubby fingers of rock shoot out of the sands, dunes tower and Bedouin tents huddle amid the *siqs* (canyons). Stay at a desert camp and you'll be treated to a *zarb* – a traditional feast of lamb buried in a natural oven beneath the desert sands and slow cooked.

CELEBRATIONS
Jordan celebrates its Independence Day (from British dominion) on May 25, when bunting goes up, military parades flood the capital and a party atmosphere prevails.

Selat Utara
(North Channel)

MALAYSIA

GEORGE TOWN

CHINATOWN

COLONIAL
DISTRICT

LITTLE INDIA

03

04

01

07

05

06

02

Malaysia

PENANG'S STREET FOOD

George Town's Unesco-listed streets are an unlikely locale for Malaysia's hottest street food scene, where generations of hawkers have perfected the island's heritage cuisine.

Malaysia is the ultimate food lovers' paradise with a variety of cuisines that reflect the melting pot of races here – fabulous curries from ethnic Malays, a dozen different Chinese regional cuisines, Indian cooking that spans fierce vegetarian dishes from the south to rich kormas from the north. Ask the food-mad Malaysians where is the best place for eating out, and the unanimous answer will be their tropical island of Penang, and in particular the spectacular street food found at every corner of the ancient lanes that criss-cross George Town, which contains one of Asia's last authentic Chinatowns.

Penang became the first outpost of the British Empire in Southeast Asia when Captain Light landed here in 1786. Strategically placed on the sea routes, it quickly grew rich as a trading hub. While most of Penang remained jungle, beaches and plantations, the capital George Town became a buzzing Chinatown of temples

and mansions that was recognised as a Unesco World Heritage Site in 2008. Saved from the bulldozer, George Town is now one of Asia's hottest destinations. A local chef explains: 'This also saved our heritage cuisine because children were no longer following their parents into the family hawker stalls until the Unesco ruling started drawing in new visitors.' Everywhere you look, families of street-food cooks, from grannies through to teenagers, set up their wobbly food carts and recreate unforgettable dishes, never wavering from secret recipes that have gone unchanged for more than 50 years, passed down from generation to generation. Even their way of cooking is unchanged, from using charcoal stoves made out of an oil drum to flamboyant wok-frying over firewood that produces the mystical *wok hei* – literally 'breath of the wok' – smoky flavour that permeates so many Penang specialities.

NEED TO KNOW
Penang has its own airport; this 2-3 day trail is focused on and around George Town's heritage area.

01 CHOWRASTA MARKET

Markets are a vital part of daily life all over Penang, and the one not to miss is Chowrasta, founded way back in 1890. Situated in what was once the Indian quarter of heritage George Town (chowrasta means 'four crossroads' in Urdu), there is as much to discover in the hundreds of stalls and speciality shops that line the surrounding streets as inside the market building itself.

The four-storey 1960s bazaar has recently undergone a long-overdue makeover, greatly improving hygiene standards, but a tour of the first-floor wet market of fishmongers and butchers is still an eye-opener.

Out on the street, hidden among the hawker food stalls, fruit and vegetable, meat and fish stands of Jalan Kuala Kangsar, look out for so-called 'dry goods' vendors of preserved fish, medicinal mushrooms, salty bean-filled *tambun* biscuits, durian cake, pickled nutmeg and preserved mango. End up outside 5 Jalan Chowrasta, where each morning Lim Ah Yee attracts crowds watching him make wafer-thin rice skins that are used in the popular shrimp and bean curd *popiah* spring rolls.
Jalan Penang; 8.30am–8pm

02 DA SHU XIA SEAFOOD HOUSE

Seafood is a must in Penang and this locale, better known as Tree Shade, is a remarkable combination of restaurant and street food, with a spectacular choice of fresh fish and shellfish; softshell and flower crabs, giant tiger and mantis prawns, clams and winkles, frogs, pomfret, garupa, carp and red snapper.

Housed in a kitsch tropical cabana, its unique concept is simple; diners go straight to the kitchen where all the seafood is displayed, as at a fishmongers. You choose what you want to eat, the style you want it cooked, and ask how much it will cost.

Try softshell crab deep-fried with salted egg yolk, pomfret prepared Teochew-style (a distinctive regional Chinese cooking style) with pickled vegetables, delicate *lala* clams steamed with egg white, ginger and rice wine, finger-licking prawns sautéed in black pepper, or succulent

'Kimberley Street is considered legendary by Penangites because of the hawkers' unique interpretation of so many of the island's iconic dishes'

01 Kimberley St comes
alive at night

02 Cheong Fatt Tze
Mansion, George Town

03 Parcels of Penang
street food

04 George Town has
become a canvas for
creative street art

squid paired with the totally delicious
but pungent petai, commonly known
as 'stinky bean'.
*Tel +60 12 474 5566; 177 Lebuh
Victoria; 11.30am-3pm and 5.30pm-
10pm Thu-Tue*

03 KEDAI KOPI SIN HWA

The humble coffee shop – *kedai kopi*
in Malay, *kopitiam* in Hokkien – is
a Penang institution and, in reality,
another form of street food. The
coffee shop owner looks after the
drinks, then rents out the rest of the
space to different hawkers.

The perfect example is Sin Hwa,
on the ground floor of a Chinese
shophouse on Burma Road, a
10-minute bus ride from the heart
of George Town in the lively Pulau
Tikus neighbourhood. Locals pack
the place for noodle dishes and sticky
kueh cakes; if you come for breakfast
choose between the classic Malay
nasi lemak (coconut-steamed rice)

with *sambal ikan bilis* (anchovies),
or a nostalgic throwback to colonial
times: runny boiled eggs, toast and
kaya (coconut jam). But above all,
they line up for the man dishing
out assam laksa. Laksa is a Nyonya
(heritage fusion) soup made with
a rich coconut milk sauce, but
Penang's assam version is a tart, sour
interpretation.

The memorable recipe served
here flavours an intense rice noodle
fish soup with tamarind juice, spicy
prawn paste, crunchy cucumber and
onion. The final garnish adds mint
leaves, sliced ginger flower buds
and red chillies.

Don't expect barista coffee in any
kedai kopi. Sin Hwa, like all others,
serves a thick intense brew, the beans
roasted with sugar and margarine,
which locals often sweeten even
more with condensed milk.
*Tel +60 4228 0140; 329 Jalan
Burma, Pulau Tikus; 8.30am-5pm*

04 PENANG HOMECOOKING SCHOOL

You will find Nyonya cooking in the
three Straits Settlements where
Chinese settled along the Malay
Peninsula in the 18th and 19th
centuries – Penang, Malacca and
Singapore. Known as Peranakan
Chinese, they married local Malay
women who created a precursor of
fusion cuisine.

The problem is that blending subtle
influences and spices of Chinese
and Malay recipes has made Nyonya
a complex cuisine, with dishes that
require a long preparation time, so
you will rarely find them at street-
food stalls. As this is essentially home
cooking of family recipes, the best idea
is to book a full-immersion morning
at the cooking school of irrepressible
cookbook author Pearly Kee.

The morning begins with a tour
of Pearly's local wet market at
Pulau Tikus discovering key Nyonya

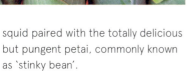

03 © David Ovada

04 © John Brunton

ingredients such as tamarind, galangal, laksa and pandan leaves, kaffir lime and torch ginger, before adjourning to her nearby home for a hands-on cooking session. Students discover heritage dishes such as curry *kapitan*, *tau eu bak* (slow-braised marinated pork belly) and *acar hu* (pickled fish), then enjoy them at lunch. *www.penanghomecookingschool. com; tel +60 16437 4380; 85 Taman Berjaya, Pulau Tikus*

05 KIMBERLEY STREET HAWKER STALLS

Legendary is the word that Penangites use when it comes to describing perhaps its most famous food street, back in the heart of George Town's Chinatown. Legendary

because most of the hawker families that colonise the street every night have been cooking their specialities for more than 50 years, and legendary because their unique interpretation of so many of the island's iconic dishes are judged to be unbeatable.

Take Lean Joo Sean, who has been setting up his *char koay teow* stall outside the Sin Guat Keong coffee shop since 1954. Assisted by his wife and wearing a distinctive chef's hat, he cooks non-stop, firing up his red-hot wok, stir-frying a magic mixture of flat rice noodles, bean sprouts, Chinese waxed sausage, mantis prawns and a secret mix of sauces and spices.

Across the street, arrive early, as Mr Por's famous duck *koay chap* sells out by around 8pm – not surprising

when you taste his bowl of intense braised duck broth, with homemade tapioca and rice noodles, every organ you can imagine from the duck, five-spice simmered hard-boiled egg and finely diced pork intestines and ears. *Kimberley Street; 6pm-midnight*

06 NASI KANDAR BERATUR

Just round the corner from Kimberley Street, the official name for George Town's most famous *nasi kandar* eatery is Restoran Liyaqat Ali, but everyone refers to it as Nasi Kandar Beratur – 'Queue-Up Nasi Kandar'. The reason why becomes apparent as soon as it opens at the surprisingly late hour of 10pm with a long line of hungry foodies snaking past the ornate Kapitan Keling Mosque.

05 xPacifica © Getty Images

06 Pete Seaward © Lonely Planet

The same family has been serving here since 1943 and the cooking of the array of complex curries with hand-ground spices that embody Penang's *nasi kandar* cuisine begins early in the morning. Although the cuisine is officially Indian Muslim it is known here as *mamak*; a rich, piquant fusion of Indian and Malay influences.

After serving a hearty portion of steamed rice it is just a question of how many of the 20-odd dishes you can squeeze onto the plate; mutton curry, beef korma, sambal squid, tangy *ayam ros* (rose chicken), crispy deep-fried fish, chilli prawns, ladies fingers, bitter gourd and long beans.
Jalan Masjid Kapitan Keling 98; 10pm–9am

07 NEW LANE NIGHT STALLS

Right by George Town's landmark high-rise Komtar building, Lorong Baru – popularly known as New Lane – is closed to traffic at 4pm each afternoon and invaded by a small army of more than 50 hawkers, who rapidly set up their rickety food carts and tempting ingredients. An hour later, charcoal is burning, woks are sizzling, smoke is swirling and pungent, delicious aromas waft everywhere.

Most important is to bag one of the wobbly metal tables: order from the stalls and they will serve you seated.

Squatting down on the pavement outside the Maxim Cafe, you'll find Ngiom Far Luan wreathed in smoke as she fans the glowing charcoal grilling her tasty sticks of pork satay, while across the street, a hawker delicately prepares vegetarian *popiah* rolls as meticulously as a Japanese sushi chef.

Finish with ice *kacang*, a mountain of shaved ice topped with *gula malaka* (palm sugar), red beans, sweet corn jelly and a kaleidoscope of syrups.
Lorong Baru, George Town; 5pm–11pm

05 Durian fruit, a common sight in Penang markets

06 A food vendor in George Town's heritage area

WHERE TO STAY

CHEW JETTY HOMESTAY
Stay with a Chinese clan family in their simple home on a wooden stilt jetty jutting out into Penang's busy harbour. www.discoverpenang. evomediatech.com/ chewjetty/; tel +60 1 343 81217; 59a Weld Quay

CHEONG FATT TZE MANSION
The magnificent 19th-century blue mansion that houses this hotel was built by a Chinese millionaire known as the 'Rockerfeller of the East'. Reserve the suite that was the ancient kitchen.
www.cheongfatttze mansion.com; tel +60 426 2006; 14 Leith Street

NATURE FRUIT FARM RESORT
In rural Balik Pulau, a 45-minute drive from George Town, this resort farm cultivates the famous durian fruit. Rent bikes to visit neighbouring Saanen Goat Farm, an organic dairy farm, and Ghee Hup Nutmeg Factory.
www.naturefruitfarm.com. my; tel +60 486 69241; 311 MK7 Kampung Genting, Balik Pulau

WHAT TO DO

In George Town, take a tour of the opulent treasure-filled Pinang Peranakan Mansion (www. pinangperanakanmansion. com.my), which offers a glimpse of the extravagant lifestyle that Penang's richest Peranakan Chinese led a century ago. Follow the Penang Street Art Trail of eye-catching murals painted by Lithuanian Ernest Zacharevic and local artists. Then step back in time with English afternoon tea in one of Asia's grandest colonial hotels, the Eastern & Oriental. Outside George Town, visit the lush Tropical Spice Garden (www. tropicalspicegarden.com) near Batu Ferringhi beach to discover the spices that flavour Penang cuisine.

CELEBRATIONS

The George Town Festival is one of Asia's major arts events, with international artists, musicians, and actors performing and exhibiting during August. The Hungry Ghosts Festival takes place in July/August and resembles a month-long Halloween, with street performances of Chinese opera, puppet shows and concerts.

Morocco

TASTING FEZ, FROM MEDINA TO MIDDLE ATLAS

The food culture and traditions of Fez and the surrounding Middle Atlas are as ancient and complex as the city's medieval medina, but easy to unlock if you know where to look.

Ochre-coloured buildings line tiny cobbled streets where donkeys and mules provide transport: things have hardly changed for a millennium in the medina of Fez. This ancient city was founded in AD 789 and is a Unesco World Heritage Site. Each neighbourhood has a mosque, fountain, school, *hammam* (traditional steam bath) and a *ferran*, the community oven. Artisans work in specific areas: tanners, copper beaters, slipper-makers, carpenters, weavers and even the last cedar-wood bucket-maker operate out of tiny stalls in the souks.

Fez lies in the foothills of the Middle Atlas Mountains in fertile soil that produces oranges, fruit, olives, wheat and grapes for wine, and its cuisine is considered the country's best. Pierce the pastry of a pigeon *pastilla*, which captures the essence of Moroccan cuisine with its meltingly tender meat, aromatic ingredients and

NEED TO KNOW
Fez medina is car-free, but this 3–4 day trail includes a day in the Middle Atlas, for which you'll need transport.

theatrical presentation parcelled up in layered filo pastry, and you'll be hooked. History provides a multitude of influences: dishes that are both sweet and savoury from Andalucía, spices from the orient, fish from the Mediterranean, dates from the desert and the favourite, couscous, with its origins here in North Africa.

Local food markets offer a sensory cornucopia that can be overwhelming – mounds of fresh, organic vegetables and barrows full of huge bunches of the freshest herbs, colourful spices, intriguing sausages, live rabbits and chickens, more than a dozen varieties of olives, a camel's head swinging on a hook, piles of glossy sweet cookies, soft goat's cheese, offal and snails, as well as local onion-and-spice-stuffed fried bread made of semolina, barley or wheat... There's only one thing for it: step into this fascinating world and taste your way through the souk.

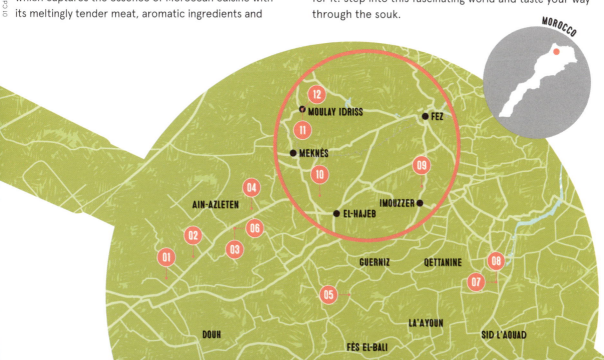

01 CAFÉ CLOCK & CLOCK KITCHEN

There's no better way to unlock the world of Moroccan cuisine than by taking a hands-on cooking course, so start your day at Clock Kitchen, set in an ancient traditional house in the Fez medina.

When ebullient owner Mike Richardson, former maître d' at The Ivy and The Wolseley in London, fancied a change of pace, he ventured to Fez to open this acclaimed cafe and kitchen beneath the minaret of the Bou Inania Medersa – one of the most important historical sites in the city.

Starting at 10am with a cup of coffee or tea, discuss your menu with chef-trainer Souad Maija. Starters could be traditional *harira* soup, a rich blend of tomatoes, chick peas, lentils and lamb. Or perhaps *zaalouk*, (roasted aubergine with spices), or *taktouka* (spiced green peppers).

Main courses of *pastilla*, couscous or tagines can be followed by honey macaroons or date and pastry rolls. Choices made, it's out into the souk with Souad to buy fresh ingredients, bargaining with the vendors and dodging donkeys.

Back in the kitchen, Souad guides you through the process of preparing and cooking a three-course lunch. Over at Café Clock, the signature dish is the now-famous and delicious camel burger – a red meat that's light and tasty, with no cholesterol. You'll be too full to eat it once you've devoured your self-made banquet, but drop by another time to test it out.

'Honey has a special place in Islam: it is used medicinally and it is also the only food eaten by recently bereaved people'

www.cafeclock.com; tel +212 535 637 855; Derb Margana, Tala'a Kebira; 10am-10pm

02 OLIVE SHOP

Work off lunch with a wander through the medina, starting with Fez's olive shops. Morocco is known for its superb olives and the hills around Fez and Meknes are covered with vast swathes of olive trees. Locals serve them with every meal as part of the array of salad starters, and in dishes such as chicken tagine with olives and lemons.

To see what all the fuss is about, head to Ghazal Miloud's olive shop

01 Royal Palace, Fez

02 Fez food market

03 Towering spices
inside a Fez souk

04 Honey-soaked
Moroccan pastries
in Fez

on Tala'a Kebira, three minutes' walk down the hill from Café Clock (there's no sign but you'll see the throngs of locals; the shop is on the left). Black and shiny, wrinkled when they're partly dried, glowing pink or green, flavoured with preserved lemon, pickled vegetables or harissa (a very hot red pepper and chili sauce), the succulent olives in this shop are presented in large dishes.

You're welcome to taste, and perhaps buy a bagful to munch while you walk.
Tel +212 535 638 780; 205 Tala'a Kebira; 10am-7pm Sat-Thu

03 COMMUNITY OVEN

You'll see – and smell – the *ferran* (community bread oven) in every district of the medina. It's always next to the hammam, so a single wood fire can heat the water for the steam bath as well as cook the loaves. Women make their bread at home,

place the dough on a tray and ask a child to take it to the oven.

The baker knows the style of each cook so there's never a mistake about which bread is taken home after baking. He is also a fount of local gossip and sometimes serves as matchmaker in the community.

To get there from the olive shop, continue down Tala'a Kebira to the Ain Azleten steps; the oven and hammam are on the right and you'll see the over fired up day and night.

04 KAAT SMEN: THE HONEY SOUK

Continue down Tala'a Kebira to this old *funduq*, or caravanserai, popularly known as the honey souk. It houses a number of small shops selling honey, *smen* (fermented butter that Moroccan cooks love to stir sparingly into tagines or couscous), and *khlie* – strips of beef dried and preserved in fat or olive oil (fried with eggs, it

makes a formidable breakfast).

A favourite is the first shop on the left, run by Hicham and his father, who are happy to give tastings of honeys such as lavender, thyme, orange blossom, mountain flowers, rosemary and eucalyptus.

Honey has a special place in Islam where it is used medicinally: carob for digestion and high blood pressure, coriander for constipation and euphorbia for sore throats. It is also the only food eaten by recently bereaved people, and Hicham is often up early to care for them and take them their honey.
Tel +212 535 634 269; Hicham Nafis Chergui; Kaat Smen, 81 Tala'a Kebira; 8am-6pm Sat-Thu

05 RUINED GARDEN

For dinner, head to this magical garden restaurant among the ruins of an old house in the medina, where chef-gardener Robert Johnstone

serves a modern take on Moroccan street food. This could mean fresh sardines rolled in a crisp couscous coating or a delicious vegetarian tagine redolent with saffron, followed by a Sephardic orange cake.

Traditionally, Moroccans eat couscous for lunch on Fridays, and if you're in town on this day of the week you can join cook Najia El Amrani in the kitchen to learn the finer points of rolling your own couscous. Najia can show you the dexterous hand and finger movements that are needed to turn the mixture into tiny balls, which are then passed through a sieve and steamed. It's easier than you think! *www.ruinedgarden.com; +212 649 191 410 or +212 535 633 066; Derb Sidi Ahmed Chaoui (next door to Riad Idrissy guesthouse); cafe 1-10.30pm; couscous rolling 10am Fridays*

06 COOKING ON THE STREET: MAKE A TANGIA

The next day, have a go at using the *ferran* you saw yesterday by joining in the tradition of cooking a tangia; a classic Moroccan dish whose name is used to describe both the meal itself and the vessel in which it's cooked – a terracotta urn (different to the better known tagine).

Set off from Bab Bou Jeloud with local foodie expert Meryem Amziane, who will guide you through the produce market to pick up meat from the butcher, plus onions, garlic and vegetables with parsley and coriander. At the spice shop, choose from warming paprika, unctuous saffron or *ras el hanout*, the spice merchant's special blend. You'll prepare the ingredients streetside and then head to the ferran where the fire attendant will place your tangia in the coals to bubble away gently, ready for collection six hours later. In Morocco the tangia is commonly a bachelors' dish: put together easily, left at the ferran to cook all day and ready to eat after work. *www.plan-it-morocco.com; +212 535 638 708*

07 R'CIF MARKET

While you're waiting for your tangia, head over to the quartier known as R'cif in the east of the medina, which boasts the best produce market in Fez. The stalls are tiny and often sell just one product: fresh fish from the coast, or snails, or camel meat, and everywhere piles of glistening vegetables and fruit.

One of the market's highlights is its pastry-makers. When you spot a large dome covered in a fine layer of dough, stop to watch the women making a

'The tangia is commonly a bachelors' dish: put together easily, left to cook all day and ready to eat after work'

05 The magnificent medersa of Bou Inania

06 Fez local in the medina

07 Tangias: Morocco's batchelor meal

delicate, soft pastry called *trid*. They take a ball of dough and some oil, stretch it out with the heels of their hands until it's very thin, then drape it over the heated dome to cook. Once done, it's layered on a platter and sold by weight. It's used in the classic dish *r'fissa*: marinated chicken and lentils on a bed of *trid*, seasoned with saffron, turmeric, ginger and *ras el hanout*, traditionally served to women on the third day after childbirth but delicious at any time.

The pastry-makers also make *waraka*, another filo-like paper-thin pastry used for *pastilla*, along with *malaoui*, a fried bread eaten plain or stuffed with onions, and the delicious *razat el kadi* that is more like a bed of noodles. Enter the medina at Bab Sid L'Aouad in R'cif and turn left to find the market.
10am-3pm Sat-Thu, 10am-noon Fri

08 B'SSARA ON THE STREET

As part of your meander through the R'cif stalls, head to this local souk snack-stop on the corner of Bab Salla; here you will find rough pottery bowls of *b'ssara* (fava bean soup). It's just a hole-in-the-wall, but serves this deliciously thick, fortifying soup with *khobz* (bread), and salt, olive oil, garlic, cumin and chilli as toppings.

To get back to the ferran to pick up your tangia, take a taxi from R'cif to Ain Azleten; walk down the steps into the medina and the *ferran* is in front of you.
Bab Salla, R'cif Market; 7am-2pm

09 DOMAINE DE LA POMMERAIE

The next day, hire a car and leave the clamour of Fez for the Middle Atlas countryside. Splendid vistas of the mountains unfold as you travel south on the N8 towards Immouzzer Kandar, famous for its trout farms. Your final destination is Domaine de la Pommeraie for cheese tasting, about an hour's drive from Fez; a farm with 12.5 hectares of fruit trees (the name means Apple Tree Farm) and a large herd of delightful Alpine goats.

The organic artisanal cheeses here are made using an old Berber method of fermentation, and cheese-maker Tarik Lechkar offers at least six varieties to savour (tasting by appointment). The *pièce de résistance* has to be the Vert de l'Atlas, a mould-induced green cheese with great depth of flavour. Children will love this farm as there's plenty of opportunity to pet the goats and run about, plus there are walking trails and cycle pathways. If you stick around long enough, the farm can also provide a delicious lunch of local produce.

It's on the P5021, heading west to Ain Chifa.
www.domainedelapommeraie.com; +212 664 904 709; Ain Chifa, Immouzzer Kandar; 10am-6pm Mon-Sun

10 CHÂTEAU ROSLANE

The Meknes region is the home of wine-making in Morocco and Château Roslane, beautifully set in landscaped gardens, is the *grande dame* of the local wine industry. It produces the vast majority of Moroccan wines – some 35 million bottles a year – and its eponymous flagship wine is the only AOP (*appellation d'origine protégée*) wine in the country.

Its full-bodied Beauvallon red is made of carignan grapes, while wine-maker Farid Ouissa has recently launched a surprisingly light, unoaked white called Solo, made of 100% sauvignon grapes, that works perfectly with a seafood *pastilla*.

A 1½ hour wine tour (book ahead)

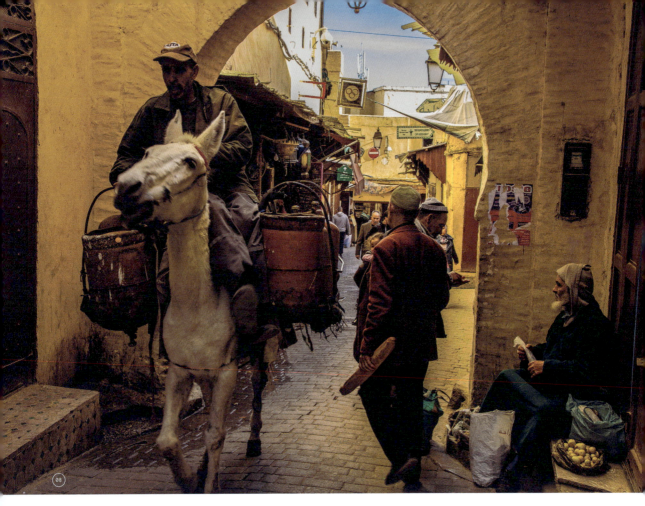

at the chateau takes in the cellars and research unit and a tasting of five or six wines.

Château Roslane is about an hour from Domaine de la Pommeraie, located between the small towns of El Hajeb and Boufakrane. *www.lescelliersdemeknes.net/en; +212 535 638 708; on the P7407 between El Hajeb and Boufakrane, Meknes*

⑪ MOULAY IDRISS OLIVE OIL PRESS

Thousands of olive trees dot the landscape in this region, and it's not surprising that almost everyone owns at least a small patch of trees. Come November, after the first of the winter rains, the harvest begins

and locals deliver their crop to the community press. In the picturesque whitewashed pilgrimage town of Moulay Idriss, half an hour north of Château Roslane, the *huilerie* is a fascinating place to visit if you can call ahead and book a tour.

Owner M Zalaghi will explain the process of crushing the olives between large woven grass discs and how he produces luscious cold-pressed extra-virgin oil with very low acidity. Taste it with local bread: its fresh, green, slightly peppery flavour is sensational. To get here, walk westwards out of town from the main square of Moulay Idriss, head under the arch and the olive oil press is on your right. *Moulay Idriss Zerhoune Huilerie; +212 600 627 561*

⑫ DAR ZERHOUNE

At the delightful Dar Zerhoune guesthouse back in Moulay Idriss's medina, you can get to grips with the finer points of Moroccan *patisserie* and breads with owner Rose Button and her manager, Hajiba.

Try your hand at mouthwatering *ghriba*, a soft-centred almond cookie, or attempt to fashion *kaab al ghazal*, shaped like curved gazelle's horns. Once made, take your efforts to the wood-fired community oven for baking. Then it's time to enjoy them with a glass of traditional mint tea on Dar Zerhoune's roof terrace with its fabulous views over the town. *www.darzerhoune.com; tel +212 642 247 793; Dar Zerhoune, 32 Derb Zouak, Tazga, Moulay Idriss*

08 Fez medina is a car-free zone; locals use horses and donkeys for transport

09 The pilgrimage town of Moulay Idriss

WHERE TO STAY

RIAD IDRISSY

This luxurious 400-year-old home has been beautifully restored to offer five bedrooms. The Ruined Garden restaurant is just next door. *www.riadidrissy.com; tel +212 649 191 410 or +212 535 633 066; Derb Idrissy*

DAR NAMIR

Food writer Tara Stevens has set up kitchen in this stylish medina house where she offers residential cooking courses tailored to your needs. Sessions cover modern Moroccan cuisine, traditional feasts, street food, pastry and bread baking, as well as Sephardic and Roman cookery. The courses also include Moroccan wine and cheese tastings. *www.darnamir.com; tel +212 691 587 751; 24 Derb Chikh el-Fouki*

WHAT TO DO

ARTISANAL AFFAIRS TOUR

Step into the workshops of traditional craft-makers, see their skills and find out about their work by meeting the artisans, picking up their tools and experiencing their daily lives in the heart of the old medina. The tours are purely educational and you won't be pressured into buying as no shopping is allowed. (www.culture vulturesfez.org)

MAGNIFICENT MEDERSAS

Don't miss the 14th century medersas (theological colleges) of Fez, where students once studied mathematics, astronomy, medicine and the Quran. Two of the best are the Bou Inania and the Attarine on Tala'a Kebira. Both are restored to their former glory, boasting carved plaster, cedar wood, intricate mosaic tiles and graceful marble fountains.

CELEBRATIONS

FÈS GOURMET

A dozen grand riad guesthouses open their doors for two weeks in March and November to cook up a storm and showcase the best of local cuisine inside some of Fez's most historic buildings. (www.armhfes.org)

FES FESTIVAL OF WORLD SACRED MUSIC

Held in May or June and now more than 20 years old, this week-long festival celebrates sacred music from around the world. (www.fesfestival.com)

08 Raquel Maria Carbonell Pagola © Getty Images

89

Haeraki Gulf

◉ LEIGH

04 06
WARKWORTH ● 05

10
08 ONETANGI
ONEROA ● ● ONETANGI
02
01 03 09
AUCKLAND
07

NEW ZEALAND

New Zealand

FLAVOURS OF THE PACIFIC

Indigenous ingredients and briny bounty from New Zealand's North Island waters help set the stage for Auckland's eclectic food scene, which sources local but thinks global.

Framed to the west and east by the waters of the Manukau and Waitemata Harbours, Auckland spreads across a narrow coastal isthmus on New Zealand's North Island. Here, one in three households owns a boat and the forest-clad surf beaches and ocean surrounding Auckland are essential to the lifestyle of the local people. The country's biggest city is also its most cosmopolitan urban area, and culinary influences from Asia, the Pacific and beyond merge with more established food traditions from earlier European settlement and New Zealand's indigenous Maori people.

Enveloped by the ocean at the edge of the globe, *kai moana* (seafood) is a true highlight of the Auckland region's food scene, and oysters farmed in the cool island waters of the Hauraki Gulf combine on restaurant menus and at farmers' markets with other seafood from around the country. Green-lipped mussels,

scallops and salmon all feature regularly, and local chefs are adept at integrating flavours, ingredients and cooking techniques from around the world.

It's a global culinary mash-up demanded by Aucklanders – despite, or perhaps because of, the country's geographic isolation, New Zealanders are among the most well-travelled people on the planet – that is being increasingly balanced by an emerging desire to buy local and eat local. Farmers' markets are booming – with stalls often helmed by recent immigrants keen to add their own spice to Auckland's cultural menu – and local wine, craft beer and coffee are all essential complements to an increasingly nuanced food scene.

Yet despite this growing sophistication, a quintessentially informal New Zealand approach to dining lingers: popular restaurants often channel a rustic laid-back vibe celebrating less complicated times.

NEED TO KNOW
To make sure you catch the weekend farmers' markets, do this 3-day trail Friday to Sunday.

01 DEPOT EATERY

Relaxed and informal, Depot Eatery in Federal St's dining precinct perfectly captures what's great about Auckland's modern restaurant scene. Chef and owner Al Brown sources produce from around the country – the menu is studded with proudly local dishes such as New Zealand lamb ribs – and the team at the raw bar are kept busy shucking briny-fresh shellfish.

Begin a leisurely lunch with the kingfish sashimi, or team sweet Marlborough *tuatua* (clams) with a glass of Quartz Reef bubbles from Central Otago. If you're looking to resurrect yourself after a big night, ease into a breakfast of Auckland's best bacon and egg sandwich, or the essential combo of coffee and *beignets* (deep-fried choux pastry). *www.eatatdepot.co.nz; tel +64 9 363 7048; 86 Federal St, Auckland City; 7am-late*

02 AUCKLAND SEAFOOD SCHOOL

About 2km from mid-town Auckland, Wynyard Quarter is a harbourside precinct of cafes, restaurants and bars with views of Auckland's iconic Sky Tower. Here you'll find the Auckland Seafood School, based at the Auckland Fish Market.

Downstairs a wet market combines with a handy provedore selling artisan produce from around New Zealand. A sunny purpose-built area upstairs hosts interactive cooking classes showcasing local seafood, such as the popular grilled seafood session that teaches barbecue-friendly recipes.

Classes are held from 6pm on weeknights and 11am at weekends, and sessions end with a sociable shared meal fuelled by New Zealand wine. *www.aucklandseafoodschool.co.nz; tel +64 9 379 1497; Level 1, 22-32 Jellicoe St, Auckland Fish Market, Wynyard Quarter*

03 16 TUN

Fragrant New Zealand hops such as Motueka and Pacific Jade are becoming renowned with craft brewers globally – the Nelson Sauvin hop even echoes the fruity profile of Marlborough's famed Sauvignon Blanc wines – and 16 Tun is an excellent spot to explore the country's booming craft beer scene.

With a strict focus on only New Zealand beers, 16 Tun's 19 taps are filled with a rotating selection of flavour-packed drops from Kiwi craft brewers such as 8 Wired, Tuatara and Garage Project. Local Auckland region brewers including Hallertau, Epic and Liberty are regulars, and a fridge full of bottles and cans creates havoc for the indecisive drinker. Fish sliders and *paua* (abalone) fritters are highlights on the food menu. *www.16tun.co.nz; tel +64 9 368 7712; 10-26 Jellicoe St, Wynyard Quarter; 11.30am-late*

01 Auckland's skyline

02 Matakana Village
Farmers Market

03 Charlie's
Gelato Garden

04 MATAKANA VILLAGE FARMERS MARKET

It's a 45-minute drive north of central Auckland to the rural settlement of Matakana, where vineyards and artisan food producers are expanding the gourmet scene around this coastal area.

On Saturday mornings, Matakana farmers market is a riverside event featuring the best of local flavours. Green-lipped mussel fritters are served with a super-fresh slice of white bread and a squeeze of lemon, and European influences shine through with buffalo cheese from the nearby Whangaripo Valley and homemade Sicilian-style sausages. Local almonds and macadamias are also harvested for oils and natural nut butters.
www.visitmatakana.co.nz/village/ farmers-market; riverside, Matakana village; 8am-1pm Sat

05 CHARLIE'S GELATO GARDEN

Around 3km south of Matakana village on the road from Auckland, Charlie's Gelato Garden is another essential stop with vineyard views. This is gelato made the old-fashioned artisanal way, crafted daily with fresh fruit including strawberries, blueberries and grapes from Charlie's own orchards and vines.

The full array of gelato and refreshing sorbetto flavours is dizzying. More than 50 in total can be served across the year, including grown-up variants such as licorice or pistachio, and seasonal surprises like mandarin or Easter egg.

Beyond the frozen attractions that usually draw queues in the height of summer, Charlie's is a well-known spot to buy the sweetest of fresh strawberries around December to January, and brilliantly indigo table grapes from late February to early May.

www.charliesgelato.co.nz; tel +64 9 422 7942; 17 Sharp Rd, Matakana; summer 9am-5pm daily, winter 10am-4pm Fri-Sun

06 SAWMILL CAFE

A scenic drive of 15km, past one of the region's best swimming beaches at Matheson Bay, links Matakana village to the coastal settlement of Leigh. In a former timber sawmill, the Sawmill Cafe is one of the best day trips from the big city.

Its rustic interior and sunny garden often host New Zealand's biggest bands and a surprising range of international acts.

The best of the cafe's wood-fired pizzas is the Gratuitous, packed with fresh fish and shrimps; an ideal match for a citrusy Pale Ale brewed at Sawmill's own microbrewery, based nearby, or wine from Matakana vineyards.
www.sawmillcafe.co.nz; tel +64 9 422

6019; 142 Pakiri Rd, Leigh; 10am-late
Dec 27-Mar & 10am-late Thu-Sun
Apr-Dec 24

07 LA CIGALE MARKET

A few kilometres east of Auckland's
waterfront, you'll find the city's
best farmers' market. Originally
envisioned as a French-style market
by Francophile Aucklanders Elizabeth
and Mike Lind, La Cigale in the central
heritage suburb of Parnell now
features many other cuisines.

On Saturday and Sunday mornings
the market is packed with locals
browsing more than 40 different
vendors. New Zealand's famed
green-lipped mussels punctuate
overflowing servings of paella,
and cured and smoked salmon
is served at the Canadian-style
Al's Deli.

Recent additions to the mix
from Serbia, Israel and Turkey
reinforce Auckland's profile as New
Zealand's most cosmopolitan city,
and *kombucha* (fermented tea) and
smoothies from Organic Mechanics
highlight a growing focus on healthy

living. Local company Ahi-Ka, for
example, sells natural tonics at
the market with health-promoting
properties. Based on traditional
Maori recipes, leaves from indigenous
plants including *kawakawa* are
combined with ginger, kale, turmeric
and wheatgrass to create these
tonics, which promote good digestion
and claim to reduce inflammation in
the body.
*www.lacigale.co.nz; tel +64 9-366-
9361; 69 St Georges Bay Rd, Parnell;
8am-1.30pm Sat-Sun*

08 DRAGONFIRED

In a compact cove framed by
scarlet-bloomed pohutukawa trees,
Dragonfired's location on Waiheke
Island's Little Oneroa beach is a
classic slice of relaxed Kiwi-style

'Te Matuku oysters are celebrated for
being sweet and creamy. Pair them
with chardonnay-infused vinegar and
a class of buttery Valhalla chardonnay'

dining. Order freshly baked pizza
from the mobile wood-fired oven,
or settle on pita bread crammed
with Mediterranean-style lamb. Sit
on Little Oneroa with sand between
your toes, or make your way a few
bays around to Dragonfired's second
location near Palm Beach.

Frequent passenger and vehicle
ferries run to Waiheke Island from
downtown Auckland; the island's laid-
back network of vineyard restaurants,
boutique olive oil producers and
arcing sandy beaches are most easily
accessible if you take a car (or bike)
or hire one on the island.
*www.dragonfired.co.nz; tel +64 21-
922 289; Little Oneroa Beach & Palm
Beach, Waiheke Island; 10am-9pm
daily in summer & 11am-7pm Fri-Sat
in winter*

09 THE SHED AT TE MOTU

Owned by the Dunleavy family – one of New Zealand's most esteemed winemaking families – Te Motu Vineyard was established in 1989 as a pioneering Waiheke winery. Stellar Bordeaux-style blends are served in the tasting room and at The Shed, Te Motu's restaurant.

In a rustic outdoor setting on the edge of a vineyard, The Shed pairs local produce with global flavours. Menu standouts include the slow-cooked lamb shoulder with biryani-spiced pilaf, and king salmon from the cool waters of New Zealand's South Island served with mandarin, sesame and ginger.

www.temotu.co.nz; tel +649 372 6884; 76 Onetangi Rd, Waiheke Island; noon-3pm daily & 6pm-late Fri-Sat

10 OYSTER INN

Farmed in the clear waters of the Te Matuku Bay marine reserve on Waiheke Island's southeast coast, Te Matuku oysters are celebrated for being sweet and creamy. The best place to eat them is either fresh from Te Matuku's Waiheke shop, or on the view-friendly deck at The Oyster Inn in Oneroa, the island's sleepy main settlement.

Pair Te Matuku oysters with a chardonnay-infused vinegar and a glass of the buttery Valhalla chardonnay from Waiheke's Man O'War vineyard, or combine local Onetangi Dark Ale with battered Clevedon oysters and wasabi mayonnaise.

The Oyster Inn also has accommodation and on summer Sunday afternoons there's often live music and entertainment from Auckland's top DJs.

www.theoysterinn.co.nz; tel +64 9 372 2222; 124 Oceanview Rd; noon-late daily Nov-Apr, closed Tue May-Oct

04 The Oyster Inn

05 Vine-strewn Waiheke Island

WHERE TO STAY

GREAT PONSONBY ART HOTEL

A short stroll from Ponsonby Rd's exciting dining scene, the convivial owners of this bed and breakfast have enlivened a gracious Victorian villa with Pacific art. Breakfasts are legendary.

www.greatpons.co.nz; tel +64 9 376 5989; 30 Ponsonby Terrace, Ponsonby

CABLE BAY VIEWS

Views of the Hauraki Gulf and well-ordered vineyards fill the horizon at these modern studio apartments. Stylish decor and interesting New Zealand art fills the spacious interiors, and it's just a short walk to two of Waiheke Island's best vineyard restaurants.

www.cablebayviews.co.nz; tel +64 9 372 2901, 103 Church Bay Rd, Oneroa, Waiheke Island

WHAT TO DO

For a different perspective on Waiheke, soar on a zipline above vineyards and native forest. It's an exhilarating soft adventure suitable for most travellers, run by EcoZip Adventures (www.ecozipadventures.co.nz). There are three separate 200m-long stretches to ride; look out to the skyline of Auckland's CBD as you're whizzing through the air.

CELEBRATIONS

AUCKLAND SEAFOOD FESTIVAL

During the last weekend of January, Auckland hosts this seafood festival in Wynyard Quarter. Top restaurants partner with vineyards for pop-up openings. Speciality NZ dishes to look out for include smoked eel and Maori-style raw fish salad. (www.aucklandseafoodfestival.co.nz)

PASIFIKA FESTIVAL

Auckland is the planet's biggest Polynesian city – 15% of the population have Pacific Islands ancestry – and in mid-March the music, culture and food of countries including Samoa, Tonga and the Cook Islands are celebrated at this South Pacific party in Auckland's Western Springs suburb. Dishes to try include *fai kai* (fish baked in coconut cream) from the tiny nation of Niue. (www.aucklandnz.com/pasifika)

Oman

SEAFOOD IN MUSCAT

With a coastline stretching more than 2000km it's only natural that local fish and lobster should star in Arabian dishes of the Omani capital, where Spice Route seasonings rule.

The breadth of natural landscapes in Oman never fails to delight. Jutting out from the Arabian Peninsula, the country's 2092km coastline is a playground for sailing fans (and their audience of somersaulting dolphins). Meanwhile the looming crags of Oman's Jabal Akhdar mountains lure hikers, and daredevils hire 4WDs for adventures in the sand dunes below. Its capital Muscat, a port city of white-washed houses, impressive mosques and gleaming royal residences, is perched on the country's northern coast at the nexus of desert, mountains and sea. Food-lovers who alight here have an extraordinary wealth of local produce at their fingertips: the spoils of fruit groves, pastures and the teeming Gulf of Oman, infused with spices from distant shores thanks to the country's swashbuckling past.

Omani dishes derive their warmth from a blend of pepper and turmeric. The heat builds slowly; it's rare to find truly fiery food here. For centuries, Omani sailors were active traders along the Spice Routes and today, ginger, cloves, turmeric, pepper and other seasonings continue to add piquancy to stews and curries. Zanzibar in particular has left an imprint: the East African archipelago was under the control of the Sultanate of Oman for more than 150 years.

But it's fresh seafood that enjoys top billing on local menus. Omani lobster is justly famous across the Arabian Peninsula for its succulence. Squid and *hamour* (white-fleshed grouper or codfish) adorn many a barbecue.

Meanwhile kingfish, hauled into Muscat's port, is a favourite ingredient for Omani stews.

Inland of Muscat, bananas, pears and figs are grown in the foothills of the Al Hajar mountains. But Oman's king of fruits is the date, a cornerstone of Oman's legendary hospitality when served with coffee.

NEED TO KNOW
This 3-day trail heads out into the mountains around Muscat on the final day, for which you'll need a car.

01 KARGEEN CAFFE

Beneath the glow of brass lamps and among polished wooden furnishings, Kargeen Cafe is an atmospheric spot to experience Omani hospitality over expertly brewed coffee and a traditional breakfast. Following local tradition, eggs are a key part of breakfasts at Kargeen, along with rounds of flat *rukhal* bread, *zaatar* (a Middle Eastern herb blend), *mahyawa* (umami-rich fish sauce), cheese and more, all washed down with sturdy coffee. 'The time of simmering usually decides the strength of the coffee,' explains chef Hussain. 'The longer you simmer, the more bitter it will be.'

The blend of spices used in Omani coffee, *qahwa*, varies among families and each chef has their own preference. 'I add a pinch of saffron and cardamom powder to the mix,' says Hussain. 'In the pot, I add two to three teaspoons of rose water.' The resulting infusion is the perfect fuel to explore Muscat.
www.kargeencaffe.com; tel +968 2469 9055; Al Bashair St; 8am–midnight Sat-Thu, noon-midnight Fri

02 SULTAN QABOOS PORT MARKETS

Hail a cab for the 15-minute ride to Sultan Qaboos Port, ground zero for Muscat's seafood scene. Start by exploring the fish market, with its lively open-air stalls where everything on display is caught from the Gulf of Oman by local fishermen. Vendors holler about their haul of barracuda, buyers barter over piles of squid, and kingfish is sawn into slabs.

At the far end of the fish market, follow a doorway into the covered fruit and vegetable market, where figs, ginger and pomegranates are arranged in colourful mounds. This juicy produce is all grown locally around Jabal Akhdar, the 'Green Mountain' west of Muscat. Around 23,000 pomegranate trees bloom in this part of Oman, which flushes pink and gold when the fruit comes into season in September and October. Locals even credit the fruit with the longevity of pomegranate farmers.
Sultan Qaboos Port, Mutrah; 6am-noon Sat-Thu

03 MUTRAH SOUK

A 10-minute walk south of the food markets lies the striking gateway to Mutrah Souq, a glittering emporium of traditional Omani crafts, clothing and snacks. Start by refreshing yourself in the excellent cafe above the souk entrance, Al Corniche: wash down rice-stuffed vine leaves with a cooling blend of pressed lemon

02 © Anitta Isalska

> 'Hot date syrup was once used as a weapon, dumped through the fortress's grates to scald would-be invaders'

Ø1 View of Muscat's old town

Ø2 Fisherman at Sultan Qaboos Port

Ø3 Decadent dessert at Juniper Restaurant atop Jabal Akhdar

Ø4 Oman's ubiquitous date palms

and mint. Then follow the crowds into the souq for dessert: the main atrium (shortly after the entrance) has several sweet-toothed gift stalls including Omani Halwa Corner.

Unlike many Middle Eastern *halwas*, which have a fine-grained texture and a sesame base, Omani *halwa* is an altogether stickier affair. This gelatinous sweet is more akin to Turkish delight in texture, made from a rolling boil of wheat starch, rose water, sugar and saffron.
Mutrah Souk, Mutrah; 7am-1pm & 5-10.30pm

Ø4 BAIT AL BILAD

Take a 25-minute taxi southeast from Muscat to Qantab village for a traditional Omani cookery class with Blue Ocean Oman. The venue, Bait al Bilad ('the village house'), is tucked in among a scattering of whitewashed

fishing houses and holiday homes in tiny Qantab. 'Move around the hot surface, don't touch the same spot twice,' instructs Anna, the class leader, who is translating for two local chefs commanding the kitchen.

The first lesson is cooking Omani flatbreads by dotting dough quickly around a hot griddle. For experts, it involves a deft flick of the wrist; beginners are more likely to wad clumps of dough unevenly on the surface. Top of the menu is kingfish curry: hunks of this tuna-like meat are plunged into coconut milk broth, which billows steam fragrant with turmeric, ginger and pepper. The resulting stew is served in gargantuan portions in the shady inner courtyard of Bait al Bilad.
www.oceanblueoman.com/cooking-classes; tel +968 9612 5091; Qantab village beach; book in advance

Ø5 BLUE MARLIN

Stroll along the sandy beach in Qantab before hailing a taxi for the marina, back in the direction of central Muscat. For tourists, yacht-lovers and fishermen, this is the gateway to Muscat's shoal-rich waters. For some, that means *dhow* (traditional boat) cruises of the Gulf of Oman on the lookout out for pods of spinner dolphins; for others, deep-sea fishing.

Blue Marlin is an exceptional seafood spot in the marina, where you can feast on catch of the day overlooking boats that bob in the inky waters. Its seafood platters are heaped with whole lobster tails, sweet and smoky from the barbecue, plus gamey kingfish, prawns and reef cod, garnished with lemon butter and rice.
www.marinaoman.net; tel +968 2474 0038; Marina Bandar Al-Rowdha; 8am-11pm

03 Courtesy of Alila Jabal Akhdar Hotel

04 © Anitta Isalska

06 NIZWA SOUK

Make an early start for the final day of your Omani food odyssey. More than 35 varieties of dates glisten in Oman's market stalls and the best selection is in Nizwa, the former Omani capital about 1.5 hours outside of Muscat. In the heart of the town lies Nizwa Souk, aglitter with enamelled khanjar daggers and traditional pottery.

For sweet-toothed travellers, the highlight is the Date Souk, a friendly dried fruit emporium that offers complimentary coffee while you decide on your favourite variety of date. Paler *khalas* dates have a melt-in-the-mouth caramel quality, while popular *farth* dates are chewier and dark chestnut in hue. Mix it up with dates stuffed with almonds, rolled in sesame, or dunked in chocolate.

The curious history of this super-sweet fruit can be explored nearby at Nizwa Fort, a 17th-century castle with a bird's-eye view over the surrounding valleys. Omanis joke that they're sweet with their enemies, and they mean it quite literally – hot date syrup was used as a weapon, dumped through the fortress's grates to scald would-be invaders. In more peaceful times, it was used to sweeten drinks, much as it is today.

Oman is light on public transport, so you're best off hiring a car to get to Nizwa or taking a guided excursion (for certain mountain roads around Jabal Akhdar, you'll need a 4WD). *Nizwa Souk, Nizwa; 9am-1pm & 5-8pm Sat-Thu, 5-8pm Fri*

07 JUNIPER RESTAURANT

Half an hour north along a winding road, head up to the cooler temperatures of Jabal Akhdar, a fertile territory for fruit-growing – look out for date plantations as you drive. Atop the mountain, Jabal Akhdar Hotel's Juniper Restaurant has a terrace with a big mountain panorama.

Try its sumptuous Omani lobster, served with buttered mange tout and tomato-flavoured *freekeh* (a green wheat). As you tuck in, contemplate the bounty of the surrounding hills: it's not just dates, but also pomegranates, pears, almonds, plums and a host of other foods that thrive here. *www.alilahotels.com/jabalakhdar; tel +968 2534 4200; Alila Jabal Akhdar Hotel; Plot No.4 Al Roose, Jabal Akhdar, Nizwa; 7am-11pm*

08 UBHAR RESTAURANT

Drive back into Muscat, aiming to miss the rush-hour traffic. Before you hit the centre, swap seafood for Oman's most legendary celebration dish to round off your gourmet weekend. *Shuwa* takes slow-cooking to a new level: a whole lamb wrapped in banana leaves is lowered into an outdoor pit and slow-cooked for anything between 24 hours and three days.

This ceremonial roasting often occurs just before Eid al Fitr, the culmination of Ramadan, Islam's month of dawn-until-dusk fasting. Ubhar Restaurant serves up this butter-soft meat in a hospitable setting, just near Muscat's palatial opera house. *ubharoman.com; tel +968 2469 9826; Al Sarooj Road, Muscat; 12.30-3.30pm & 6.30-10.30pm*

05 Local man looks out over the Gulf of Oman

06 Mountain views from Alila Jabal Akhdar Hotel

07 Dates stuffed with almonds

WHERE TO STAY

TULIP INN

This mid-range choice has a pleasing central location, friendly staff and cosy, colourful furnishings. *www.tulipinnmuscat.com; tel +968 2447 1500; Way 3504, Al Khuwair, Muscat*

AL BUSTAN PALACE

East of central Muscat, this resort omits no extravagance. From the eye-popping architecture of its glittering atrium to spacious rooms overlooking an infinity pool fringed with palms: a stay worthy of the Sultan himself. *www.ritzcarlton.com; tel +968 2479 9666; Al Bustan Street, Quron Beach, Muscat*

WHAT TO DO

BAIT AL ZUBAIR MUSEUM

Time-travel through five millennia of Omani history at this diverting cultural museum. Highlights include a dazzling collection of jewellery and traditional weapons. (www. baitalzubairmuseum.com)

SNORKELLING THE GULF

Peer into a colourful undersea paradise by snorkelling off the coast of Muscat. Coral Ocean Tours pairs guided snorkelling with a short dolphin-spotting cruise. (www. coraloceantours.com)

ROYAL OPERA HOUSE

Even if you can't stop for a show, Muscat's regal opera house is worth a visit for a peek at its Burmese teak, Italian marble and Omani palace-themed interior. Arrive early to be ushered in for daily guided tours of the building. (www.rohmuscat.org.om)

CELEBRATIONS

MUSCAT FESTIVAL

An annual cultural festival hits the Omani capital in mid-January. Expect fireworks at focal locations Al Amerat Park and Al Naseem Park, cycling races, and cookery demonstrations (www. muscat-festival.com).

EID AL FITR

It's worth timing a trip for the festivities that mark the end of the Muslim month of fasting. On Eid al Fitr, the fast is broken with a ceremonial sweet date followed by shuwa lamb. Eid usually falls around July, though it gets earlier every year (in 2017 it's at the end of June).

Peru

LIMA, CAPITAL OF NEW ANDEAN CUISINE

A new generation of innovative local chefs has transformed Peruvian cuisine and firmly cemented Lima as the most exciting place to eat in South America.

Crossroads of the Americas, Lima was stirring up sublime eats long before it became a celebrated world gastronomic capital. Founded in 1535, Peru's colonial capital has a history of innovation, starting with when it wedded indigenous traditions with the Spanish palette. The arrival of many others – including African, Japanese, European and Chinese people – has introduced many more styles and flavours into the mix.

Dynamic and diverse, Lima is something of a natural laboratory for fusion. Over the past 400 years, Andean stews have mingled with Asian stir-fry techniques, and Spanish rice dishes have absorbed flavours from the Amazon, producing the country's famed *criollo* (creole) cooking. Most recently, a generation of experimental young innovators are elevating Lima's culinary scene to gastronomic heights. None are more celebrated than Gastón Acurio, the first top-tier

NEED TO KNOW
Lima is a big city so be prepared for long ambles between stops on this 3-4 day trail, or grab taxis.

chef to put local flavours front and centre. International visitors who once made a beeline for Cuzco and Machu Picchu are now finding more reasons to linger in the country's rough-around-the-edges capital. From the battered counters of simple *cevicherías* serving lime-marinated fish with chillies and onions to exclusive restaurants reinventing molecular cuisine, this is a food lover's paradise. This trail takes you from Lima's historic core out to the well-heeled suburbs of Miraflores and Barranco.

Lima's coastal location translates to a bounty of fresh seafood, while market stalls reflect Peru's astonishing geographic diversity. Wake up early and wander to see the breadth of stalls stacked with pyramids of tropical fruit, a rainbow of Andean potatoes and burlap bags of quinoa. Market visits run one-part sensorial immersion to two-parts exploration. So pack your appetite and practise the word *yapa*; it means more please.

PERU

01 02
LIMA CENTRO
EL AGUSTINO
LA VICTORIA
SAN MIGUEL
JESÚS MARÍA
LINCE
MAGDALENA DEL MAR
03
SAN BORJA
06 05
11 SURQUILLO
08 04
MIRAFLORES
PACIFIC OCEAN
12
07
BARRANCO SANTIAGO DE SURCO
09 10

01 LA CASA DE LA GASTRONOMIA PERUANA

This new museum in Lima's historic downtown district is dedicated to celebrating the country's complex culinary heritage, and a fitting place to whet your appetite for Peruvian cuisine.

Panels present the diet of the Incas, who were the creators of Machu Picchu and the empire builders who dominated Peru from after AD 1100 until the arrival of the Spanish; the different regional cuisines, and the staggering influence immigration has had on Peruvian cooking.
Tel +51-321-5627; Conde de Superunda 170; 9am-5pm Tue-Sun

02 MUSEO DEL PISCO

The educational aspect of this wonderful bar might get you in the door, but it's the congenial atmosphere and outstanding mixologists that will keep you here. The Museo del Pisco offers Peru's signature drink, a grape brandy, in its many forms and most tempting incarnations. You might start with the classic pisco sour, blended with fresh lime, egg white and bitters. Up the ante with one of the original creations with ginger, fresh fruit or herbs.

The bar occupies the Casa del Oidor, a gorgeous 16th-century mansion that once welcomed the celebrated General José de San Martín, who was instrumental in the struggle to liberate South America from Spanish rule in the 19th century. You'll find the museo on the far side of Lima's central Plaza de Armas.
museodelpisco.org; tel +51-993-500-013; Jr Junín 203; 10am-10pm

03 ASTRID Y GASTÓN

Peru's fabled novoandina cuisine was the first Andean movement to enliven typical ingredients by presenting them in a new light, using new cooking techniques and ingredient combinations. Gastón Acurio's flagship restaurant, run by Lima native Diego Muñoz, is the standard-bearer of this food movement in Lima and a culinary tour de force.

The seasonal menu features traditional Peruvian fare, but it's the exquisite fusion specialities that seal the sublime fine-dining experience. The 28-course tasting menu showcases the depth and breadth of possibility here — just do it.

Guests may be treated to a kitchen visit to watch white-coated armies assembling plates with tweezer-fine precision. The setting is a historic mansion in the upmarket suburb of

Miraflores, with multiple dining rooms and sterling service, including a helpful sommelier.
www.astridygaston.com; tel +51-442-2775; Av Paz Soldan 290; 12.30-3.30pm & 6.30pm-midnight Mon-Sat

04 MERCADO SURQUILLO

Want to see how Lima eats? Start your second day of food touring with a wander among the throngs at this labyrinthine market. You'll see a stunning variety of Peruvian produce such as dragon fruit, guava, sweet mango, half a dozen banana varieties, and fruit with no name in English, stacked high alongside displays of medicinal herbs, with dedicated areas for meat, fish and seafood. The market is in the district of Surquillo, which adjoins Miraflores.
Paseo de la Republica block 53; 8am-5pm

05 AL TOKE PEZ

Before sunrise, chef Tomás Matsufuji (a Peruvian of Japanese descent) browses Lima's fish market for the day's catch. In his modest shop, it's filleted, marinated and served up as super-fresh ceviche. Arrive early to score one of the half-dozen stools that line the battered counter.

The daily *menú*, or set lunch, focuses on Limeño classics prepared with precision. Expect a heaping plate of *chicharron de marisco* (fried seafood), ceviche and seafood rice. The shop is a 10-minute walk north of Surquillo market.
Av Angamos Este 886; 11.30am-3.30pm Tue-Sun

06 RESTAURANT HUACA PUCLLANA

Dine with a view of the illuminated ruins at Huaca Pucllana, an adobe ceremonial centre dating from AD 400 that is ensconced in Miraflores. This sophisticated eatery serves up a skillfully rendered array of contemporary Peruvian dishes ranging from *lomo saltado* (beef stir fry) to seafood chowders. But come here for the grilled *cuy* (guinea pig) – a traditional food that is native to the Andes and an ideal source of protein. Raised in country kitchens on grain, nothing could be more organic and natural, though the thought of it leaves some tourists a little squeamish. Save room for a pisco and lemon parfait.
www.resthuacapucllana.com; tel +51-445-4042; Gral Borgoño cuadra 8; 12.30pm-midnight Mon-Sat, to 4pm Sun

07 LA BODEGA VERDE

Spend day three of your Lima tour in the city's southern district of Barranco. Located in the Museum of Contemporary Art, this indoor-outdoor cafe and gallery is a pleasant spot to linger after a morning spent browsing the exhibits.

Order a milkshake made with *lucuma* (a local creamy orange fruit), or an organic Peruvian coffee. Sweets, such as carrot cake, are especially good. The enclosed park setting is one of the few places in the city where you will see local families spread out relaxing.
Tel +51-248-8559; Av Grau 1511; 8am-8pm

08 CHOCO MUSEO

You don't need a golden ticket to access this chocolate factory producing organic and fair-trade treats. The beans-to-bar workshop, offered every afternoon, takes visitors into the kitchen to craft handmade chocolates and concoct Mayan hot cocoa from scratch.

The Amazon Basin offers an ideal climate to grow cocoa and Peru has produced cocoa for the past century, yet until recently chocolate production had fallen into decline. Now entrepreneurs and cocoa farmers are looking into how to make high-quality chocolate a key industry for the country. The factory is about a 10-minute walk from the Museum of Contemporary Art.
www.chocomuseo.com; tel +51-014-773-584; Av Grau 264; 11am-10pm

09 ISOLINA

In Peru, *criollo* (creole) cooking is the fusion of native ingredients (potatoes, chillies, seafood) with the disparate cooking styles of conquerors, slaves and immigrants brought together over many centuries. At Isolina, you'll find home-style *criollo* food at its best. The restaurant doesn't shy away from tripe and kidneys, but also offers loving preparations of succulent ribs, *causa*

escabechada (whipped potatoes with marinated onions) and vibrant green salads on the handwritten menu.

Family-sized portions come in old-fashioned tins, but you could also make a lighter meal of starters such as marinated clams or ceviche. If you like your food *picante* (spicy), tell them to turn up the heat by asking for your meal *a la Limeña*.
Tel +51-247-5075; Av San Martín 101; 10am-midnight

⑩ JUANITO'S
A leftover 1960s leftist haunt, this worn-in woody bar is one of the mellowest haunts in Barranco, a suburb known for its nightlife. Decorated with a lifetime's worth of theatre posters, now it's the spot where writers swig *chilcanos* (pisco and

'In Peru, *criollo* cooking is the fusion of native ingredients with the disparate cooking styles of conquerors, slaves and immigrants'

ginger ale) and deconstruct the state of humanity. Juanito's is on the far side of Parque Barranco but there's no sign; look for the crowded room lined with wine bottles.
Av Grau 274; 11.30am-2am Mon-Sat, noon-midnight Sun

⑪ EL PAN DE LA CHOLA
In South America, finding real, crusty whole-grain bread is rarer than striking gold. Enter this small brick cafe baking four scrumptious varieties,

with organic coffee from the Peruvian Amazon, Greek yoghurt, and cakes and desserts. There's European-style seating at big wooden tables; grab a sandwich or share the tasting plate with bread, olives, hummus and fresh cheese. If it's a nice day, try walking the coastal route back towards central Lima when you're done (it's a couple of kilometres), browsing gardens along the cliff tops, or you could grab a bicycle from a rental stand en route.
Av La Mar 918; 8am-10pm Tue-Sat

⑫ CENTRAL

Part restaurant, part laboratory, Central reinvents Andean cuisine and rescues age-old Peruvian edibles you'd find nowhere else. Dining here is an experience, evidenced by the tender native potatoes served in edible clay. Chef Virgilio Martinez wants you to taste the Andes. He paid his dues in Europe and Asia's top kitchens, but it's his work here that dazzles.

Seafood – such as the charred octopus starter – is a star, but Andean classics like suckling pig deliver, served with pickled vegetables and spiced squash. A menu supplied by sustainable fish and a rooftop herb garden enhance the ultra-fresh appeal. *centralrestaurante.com.pe; tel +51-242-8515; Santa Isabel 376; 12.45-3.15pm & 7.45-11.15pm Mon-Fri*

04 Gaston Acurio – the Peruvian chef behind Astrid y Gastón

05 Peruvian potato cakes

06 Amazonian aguaje fruit at a Lima market stall

WHERE TO STAY
HOTEL DE AUTOR
A B&B dream stay on a quiet cul-de-sac, with utterly personalised service. Antique maps and travel tomes kindle inspiration for your journey throughout Peru. Rooms are spacious, with balconies and clawfoot tubs. *www.hoteldeautor.com; tel +51-681-8074; Av 28 de Julio 562B, Quinta Bustos, Miraflores*

CASA CIELO
A beautiful boutique hotel that's centrally located, offering top-notch service and great value. The look is modern Andino: ceramic bulls and photographs from Mario Testino, a Lima local, adorn the neutral walls. *www.hotelcasacielo.com; tel +51-242-1127; Calle Berlin 370, Miraflores*

WHAT TO DO
PARAGLIDING
From the Miraflores cliff tops, exhilarating paragliders soar over coastal skyscrapers and glide above the surfers; beginners can join a tandem paragliding session with Peru Fly (www.peru fly.com).

FUNDACIÓN MUSEO AMANO
This quiet mansion holds one of Peru's finest private collections. Private, by-appointment-only tours peruse exquisite pottery from Chimú and Nazca cultures and the most intricate textiles you may ever lay eyes on, produced by the coastal Chancay culture. (www.museoamano.org)

MUSEO MARIO TESTINO (MATE)
This museum in Barranco celebrates native son and world-renowned fashion photographer Mario Testino. The permanent exhibition includes iconic portraits of Princess Diana, Kate Moss and notable actors. There are also beautiful portraits of Andean highlanders. (www.mate.pe)

CELEBRATIONS
One serious eating event, Mistura is Lima's prestigious week-long international food fair held in September. Tickets allow visitors to taste an astonishing array of delicacies, from samples of the finest restaurants to the best street food (mistura.pe).

Map labels: MIRAGAIA, FONTAÍNHAS, RIBEIRA, Rio Douro, VILA NOVA DE GAIA, PORTUGAL

Portugal

INSIDE THE CAFES & TASCAS OF PORTO

Performing a fine balancing act between traditional and progressive, casual and fancy, Portugal's northerly wine city has become renowned for superb seasonal and slow fare.

Porto has some of the country's richest pickings when it comes to food. Why? Just look around you. This soulful city in Portugal's northeast reclines on the banks of the mighty Rio Douro, which meanders east to its namesake wine region, ribbed with steep, terraced vineyards that yield citrusy whites, gutsy reds and the world's finest ports (this sweet fortified wine can only officially be called port when it is produced right here in the Douro Valley). The Atlantic hammers Porto's coast to the west, bringing the freshest fish and shellfish to tables across the city; while the mountains and fertile valleys of the Trás-os-Montes roll out east, producing exceptional cured meats in *fumeiros* (smokehouses) and pungent cheeses made from goat's and ewe's milk.

Top-quality regional produce features not only on the menus of cosy, wood-beamed taverns and gourmet restaurants with

twinkling views of the medieval Ribeira district, but also in backstreet delis, cafes and on market stalls. Seasonal and organic are more than just buzzwords here, with chefs taking pride in local sourcing – from the guy rustling up *tripas à moda do Porto* (offal and white bean stew) in the little family *tasca*, to riverside wine bars with an intimate vibe and *petiscos* (tapas).

Eating out in Porto can be as casual or as elaborate as you wish, but it's rarely formal – even at the pinnacle. Much-lauded chefs such as Rui Paula, Pedro Lemos and José Avillez have upped the gourmet ante, reinventing traditional Portuguese dishes with prowess, flair and the lightest of imaginative touches. Wherever you go, you'll find the emphasis is on slow food and unfussy flavours. And naturally, this being Porto, these are matched by some knockout Douro wines and port from grand lodges established by 17th-century British merchants.

NEED TO KNOW
This 2-day trail loops Porto's central neighbourhoods: it's a compact city and very walkable.

01 Joyfull © Shutterstock

PORTUGAL 223

01 CAFÉ MAJESTIC

An entire culture revolves around coffee in Porto, and every local has a soft spot for one particular cafe, but Café Majestic is a name that crops up time and again. Push open the door of this belle époque coffee house and it's as though the clocks stopped in 1920 – with cherubs frolicking on mirrored walls, opulently gilded woodwork and gold-braided waiters.

Artists, philosophers and writers – including JK Rowling in the midst of penning *Harry Potter* – have gathered here over the years. And there's no place like the Majestic for easing into the morning over potent coffee and still-warm *pastéis de nata*, custard tarts sprinkled with cinnamon. Go local and order, say, a *cimbalino* (espresso) or a latte-like *galão*, served in a tall glass with frothy milk. *www.cafemajestic.com; +351 222 003 887; Rua Santa Catarina 112, Aliados & Bolhão; 9.30am-midnight Mon-Sat*

02 MERCADO DO BOLHÃO

Head five minutes northeast to reach the 19th-century, wrought-iron Mercado do Bolhão.

At its lively best on Friday and Saturday mornings, the market hums with vendors doing a brisk trade in local produce – ripe fruit, tangy raw sheep's cheese from the Alentejo, Atlantic-fresh fish, glossy olives, smoked meats and sausages made with every bit of the pig except the oink, plus pulses, lentils, *tremoços* (lupin beans) and great fat bulbs of garlic.

Make a morning of it and linger over a glass of sparkling *vinho verde* and a tasting plate of cheese, olives and ham at the market's hole-in-the-wall Bolhão Wine House, run with a passion by Patrícia and Hugo in their grandmother's old florist shop. *Tel +351 222 009 975; Rua Formosa, Aliados & Bolhão; 7am-5pm Mon-Fri, 7am-1pm Sat*

03 CENTRAL CONSERVEIRA DA INVICTA

While you're in this neck of town, squeeze in a mooch along Rua Sá da Bandeira, right next to the market, where old-fashioned grocery stores are a blast of nostalgia. They are piled to the rafters with beans, nuts and pulses, *bacalhau* (dried salt cod), piri-piri chilli peppers and the like.

Strolling further south brings you to Central Conserveira da Invicta, where the walls are a mosaic of tins of fish in colourful retro wrappings. Here you can stock up on tinned tuna, *bacalhau* and sardines as well as Portuguese wine, port, oils and preserves. *Tel +351 912 833 884; Rua Sá da Bandeira 115, Aliados & Bolhão; 10am-8pm Mon-Sat*

04 CAFÉ DE SANTIAGO

Wander east along the Rua de Passos Manuel to reach Café de Santiago. The *francesinha* here is legendary and

with good reason. If you're planning on tackling this gut-busting monster of an open sandwich, come very hungry.

Since 1959, the good folk of Porto have been pouring in for this winning combo of wood-fired bread, *linguiça* (smoked cured pork sausage with garlic and paprika), roast meat and ham, topped with cheese and a fried egg and drenched in rich beer sauce. You might have to wait for it, but it's worth it, we swear.
www.cafesantiago.pt; tel +351 222 055 797; Rua de Passos Manuel 226, Aliados & Bolhão; 7.30am-11pm Mon-Sat

05 LEITARIA DA QUINTA DO PAÇO

Continue west along Rua de Passos Manuel, bearing left onto Rua de Avis, then right onto Rua de Santa Teresa to emerge at this slick *café-patisserie*, with a nod to its 1920s origins as a dairy in the backlit photos

gracing the walls. A cheeky slice of Paris in Porto, the cafe is renowned for its éclairs. And what éclairs! These deliciously crisp, light choux-pastry numbers come in flavours from zesty lemon to blue cheese, apple and fennel, and chocolate with port wine. Chances are you won't stop at one.
www.leitariadaquintadopaco. com; tel +351 222 084 696; Praça Guilherme Gomes Fernandes 47, Aliados & Bolhão; 9am-8pm daily

06 TABERNA DO LARGO

Swinging south leads you to this *tasca* (tavern) in the Ribeira neighbourhood, which hooks you the instant you walk in. Perhaps it's the aroma from the deli counter as you pass through to snag a table out back – your eye alighting on a succulent ham or an unctuous mountain cheese. Perhaps it's the soulful glow of lamplight cast across cheek-by-jowl tables, or the warm welcome from Joanna and Sofia.

A lot of attention to detail has gone into the menu, with hand-picked wines marrying beautifully with tapas-sized dishes and tasting plates. Be it meltingly tender black pork from the Alentejo, black sausage from the Beira, feisty Douro peppers, oven-baked *alheira* sausage from the Minho, or Algarvian salt-cured tuna, the food is delicious, generous and prepared with a pinch of love.
Tel +351 222 082 154; Largo São Domingos 69, Ribeira; 5pm-midnight Tue-Thu, 5pm-1am Fri, noon-1am Sat & Sun

07 TAYLOR'S

Ruby, vintage, aged tawny or white; mellow and nutty, complex, sweet or fruity – whatever your preference, no visit to Porto is complete without a port tasting. To race back to the 17th-century origins of port wine production, cross the Ponte de Dom Luís I to reach the Vila Nova de Gaia

neighbourhood. Here imposing port lodges open their doors for tours of barrel-lined cellars and tastings.

Picking just one is tricky, but venerable, British-run Taylor's has been decanting some of the Porto's finest since 1692. Hour-long tours (€5) give an insight into Douro Valley grape varieties and take in the staggering cellars, piled high with huge barrels, including a whopper containing 100,000L of late bottled vintage. Your visit will finish in the refined Library Room, with a tasting of three ports – an extra dry white, a late-bottled vintage and a 10-year-old tawny.
www.taylor.pt; tel +351 223 742 800; Rua do Choupelo 250, Vila Nova de Gaia; 10am–6pm Mon–Fri, to 5pm Sat & Sun

08 FLOR DOS CONGREGADOS

Back on the other side of the river, slip down a lane off the regal beaux-arts Avenida dos Aliados to reach Flor dos Congregados – a rustically beamed, stone-walled tavern that looks like it has been teleported from a wooded mountainside. A deeply satisfying

lunchtime treat here is the 'Terylene' – slow-cooked, marinated pork in a bun – which pairs superbly with a glass of sparkling red Tinto Bruto wine.

The family that runs the place likes to keep the blackboard menu simple – fresh fish, veal cooked until tender in wine, and smoky, smooth-textured *alheira* sausage. Using season-driven recipes handed down over generations, this is good honest Portuguese grub at its home-cooked best.
Tel +351 222 002 822; Travessa dos Congregados 11, Aliados & Bolhão; 6.30–11pm Mon–Wed, noon–3pm & 6.30–11pm Thu–Sat

09 PROVA

As the setting sun warms the medieval facades of the Ribeira district, follow the lead of wine-loving locals and head to Prova. Wine bars are two a penny in Porto but this one is different; this one has Diogo Amado, whose enthusiasm for wine is contagious and knowledge unsurpassed. A crisp, citrusy white from the Alentejo, a spritzy *vinho verde* from the rain-drenched hills of the Minho, a noble red from the Dão,

or a robust, oak-aged wine from the terraced slopes of the Douro – you'll find some of Portugal's best here, along with appetising tapas, mellow jazz beats and a nicely chilled vibe.
Tel +351 916 499 121; Rua de Ferreira Borges 86, Ribeira; 5pm–midnight

10 DOP

Just around the corner is DOP, a stylishly minimalist address that breathes new life into the historic walls of the Palácio das Artes. Much-feted chef Rui Paula heads up the kitchen. The menu speaks of a chef who loves his country and takes pride in careful sourcing. Rui allows each ingredient to take centre stage in dishes that walk a fine tightrope between tradition and creativity, such as perfectly roasted kid goat, creamy lobster rice or codfish prepared with precision and flair.

The seasonal tasting menu is the way to go, with a nod to the techniques, textures and flavours that underpin modern Portuguese cuisine.
Tel +351 222 014 313; Largo São Domingos 18, Ribeira; 7.30–11pm Mon, 12.30–3pm & 7.30–11pm Tue–Sat

05 Courtesy of Leitaria da Quinta do Paço

WHERE TO STAY
GALLERY HOSTEL
For a little luxury on a budget, this hostel is a winner with its sunny conservatory, terrace, cinema room, lounge bar, shared kitchen and free walking tours. The hostel is bang in the heart of the hip Rua Miguel Bombarda, a street lined with independent galleries, boutiques and boho-flavoured bars. *www.gallery-hostel.com; tel +351 224 964 313; Rua Miguel Bombarda 222, Miragaia*

ROSA ET AL
This midrange hotel occupies a gorgeous townhouse, with six plush, wood-floored suites, spa treatments, a first-rate restaurant and a lovely garden out back. *www.rosaetal.pt; tel +351 916 000 081; Rua do Rosário 233, Miragaia*

WHAT TO DO
For a culture fix, Porto's hulking hilltop Sé cathedral, where Prince Henry the Navigator was baptised in 1394, is unmissable, as is the dazzlingly baroque Igreja de São Francisco, embellished with nearly 100kg of gold leaf. For staggering views of the city reduced to postcard format, head up to the Jardim do Palácio de Cristal, a botanical garden spread lushly across the heights of Massarelos.

CELEBRATIONS
The *tripeiros* (Porto locals) need little excuse to celebrate. The biggest parties are in summer, kicking off with the culture-packed Serralves em Festa (www.serralves. pt) in early June – a free two-day festival with 200 events skipping from contemporary dance to theatre, cinema and photography exhibitions. Midsummer madness ensues for the head-hammering Festa de São João later that month, when the city erupts into music, competitions and riotous parties; this is also when merrymakers pound each other on the head with squeaky plastic mallets (you've been warned).

07 GM Photo Images © Alamy

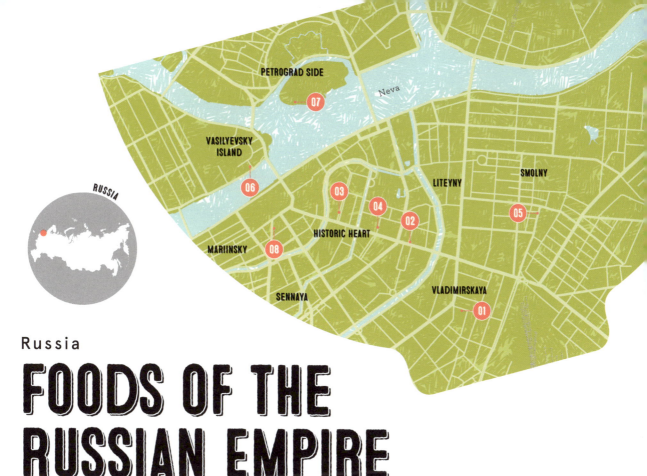

MARIINSKY

VASILYEVSKY ISLAND

PETROGRAD SIDE

Neva

LITEYNY

SMOLNY

HISTORIC HEART

SENNAYA

VLADIMIRSKAYA

RUSSIA

07
06
03
04
02
05
08
01

Russia

FOODS OF THE RUSSIAN EMPIRE

A keen sense of heritage is a key ingredient for chefs in Russia's imperial capital St Petersburg, where classic dishes from empire days are being lovingly reinvented.

Known affectionately as Piter to its fiercely loyal and largely free-thinking residents, St Petersburg is a grand city that never fails to impress. A succession of tsars commissioned fabulous palaces and cathedrals from top European architects of the day to grace its streets. Contemporary economic titans have followed suit sponsoring a treasure trove of arts and culture, not to mention an inventive and delicious food scene. Stereotypes that you might have about dull and stodgy Russian food are blown away here. Locals prize a good meal and define it by the talents of the chefs and the ambience of the restaurant rather than the prices on the menu.

Using fresh ingredients and inventive combinations, the city's best chefs are reviving traditional classics at the same time as creating contemporary dishes that build and improve on past culinary glories.

The former imperial capital's food scene is wide open to visitors: you can serve yourself in modern, pleasant *stolovaya* (canteens) or glam it up for grand restaurants dripping in Tsarist splendour. Not only is this your chance to discover the wonderful heritage of the Russian kitchen, but also the cuisines of the former Soviet Union's satellites in Central Asia and the Caucuses. It's as likely that you'll leave Piter with a taste for the Georgian cheese bread *khachapuri* and the thick rice and meat stew *kharcho* as for bliny (buckwheat pancakes) and borsch (beetroot soup).

This trail makes for a perfect weekend in St Petersburg. Your initial culinary explorations can easily be confined to its historic heart, which revolves around Nevsky Prospekt. On your second day, cross the Neva River to explore the dining scene elsewhere in the city – notably on St Petersburg's islands.

NEED TO KNOW
St Petersburg is a large metropolis: you'll need to negotiate the city's metro system to get about on this 2-day trail.

01 KUZNECHNY MARKET

At St Peterburg's premier fresh produce market you're sure to be enticed by the colourful displays of top-grade fruit, vegetables, dairy goods and other staples.

Wandering the brightly lit aisles of this grand covered market, your progress will be slowed by vendors offering samples of, among other things, pickled garlic and cucumbers, dripping slices of honeycomb, creamy yoghurt and smoked cheese.

The 21st century quietly slips away and it's easy to imagine the author Fyodor Dostoevsky – who lived his final years in a flat (now a museum), an apple's throw from Kuznechny – browsing the stalls and sizing up the grapes or freshly butchered meat as he mulled the plot of *The Brothers Karamazov*.
Kuznechny Pereulok 3; 8am-8pm

02 KUPETZ ELISEEVS

A short stroll up Vladimirsky Prospekt will bring you to Nevsky Prospekt, the city's most famous boulevard. Your destination is the dazzling food hall and dining complex of Kupetz Eliseevs. Opened at the start of the 20th century when the city was besotted with all things art nouveau (known in Russia as *style moderne*), this was the Eliseevs brothers' flagship operation, with little expense or design flourish spared in its construction.

Massive plate-glass windows provide glimpses of the ornate interior of stained glass, chandeliers, polished brass and a giant pineapple palm. The exterior is no less lavish, graced with four allegorical sculptures representing industry, trade and commerce, art, and science. Recently restored to its former glory, Kupetz Eliseevs is packed with covetable Russian branded goods including blends of tea, caviar and handmade chocolates as well as delicious freshly baked breads, cakes and pastries. Animatronic figures dance in the window displays and there are pleasant cafes in the food hall as well as the former wine cellar.
kupetzeliseevs.ru; tel +7 812 456 66 66; Nevsky Prospekt 56; 10am-11pm

03 PYSHKI

Food businesses from Soviet times, when St Petersburg was called Leningrad, are thin on the ground today. One proletarian survivor, hailing from 1958 and marooned on what has morphed into one of the city's fanciest retail streets, is the doughnut cafe Pyshki. It's a combination of nostalgia and

'The best way to taste caviar is to transport a small mound to the side of the hand and then eat it directly off your skin'

01 St Isaac Cathedral, St Petersburg

02 The Hermitage, Winter Palace

03 Local delicacy at Caviar Bar & Restaurant

04 Pyshki's beloved doughnuts

05 Fish speciality, Koryushka

thriftiness that sees a constant line of babushkas and families at the counter exchanging a handful of roubles for their freshly fried, sugar-dusted doughnuts and milky coffees. Gastronomy it ain't, but beloved it certainly is – so much so that it's a protected landmark. It's about a 15-minute walk west down Nevsky Prospekt from Kupetz Eliseevs. *Bolshaya Konyushennaya Ulitsa 25; 9am-8pm*

04 CAVIAR BAR & RESTAURANT

For the classic Russian pre-dinner aperitif, throw on your glad rags and make your way to the Belmond Grand Hotel Europe, just off Nevsky Prospekt and a bolthole for the rich and famous since 1830. In its Caviar Bar & Restaurant, a sommelier of sorts can advise on the dozen or so

varieties of sustainably sourced fish eggs on offer, including *malossol* beluga, *astrakhan* and Siberian *oscietra*, and even rare golden caviar from Russia's Far East.

The sturgeon's roe is served in the traditional manner with bliny, *smetana* (sour cream), chopped egg and other condiments. Even so, the best way to taste caviar is by using the mother-of-pearl spoon to transport a small mound to the side of the hand and then eat it directly off your skin.

Chase the morsels with a shot or two of *polugar* – a spirit distilled from bread and available in six varieties made especially for hotel. Alternatively, allow the sommelier to wheel up the trolley packed with flavoured vodkas or pour you a glass of champagne.

While at the hotel also take a peek into its historic L'Europe

restaurant with its stunning art nouveau decor – the Sunday brunch here is fit for a tsar. *www.belmond.com/grand-hotel-europe-st-petersburg/restaurants_caviar_bar; tel +7 812 329 6000; Belmond Grand Hotel Europe, Mikhailovskaya Ulitsa 1/7; 5pm-11pm Wed-Sun*

05 MECHTA MOLOKHOVETS

It's another step-back-in-time moment at 'Molokhovets' Dream', an understated dining room where the menu takes its inspiration from Elena Molokhovets, whose *A Gift to Young Housewives* was Tsarist Russia's most popular cookbook and manual of household management, reprinted 28 times between 1861 and 1914.

This is the ideal place to sample definitive versions of borsch and beef stroganoff, as well as less frequently

04 © Simon Richmond

05 © Simon Richmond

seen dishes such as goose breast in forest berry sauce and veal cutlets in mushroom ragu. The speciality of the house is *koulibiaca*, a golden pastry pie of fish or rabbit, ideally preceded by *kissel*, a deliciously sweet soup of berries and wine.
www.molokhovets.ru; tel +7 812 929 2247; Ulitsa Radishcheva 10; noon-11pm Mon-Fri, 2-11pm Sat & Sun

06 RESTORAN

On day two, head to Vasilyevsky Island. Peter the Great originally intended this triangular isle in the Neva River delta to be the heart of his city. As such, it is among St Petersburg's oldest neighbourhoods – especially at the eastern tip known as the Strelka (meaning 'tongue of land'), which is crammed with

institutions and museums including the fascinating Kunstkamera housing Peter's very own collection of ghoulish monstrosities.

Perhaps not the best appetiser for a meal, the Kunstkamera is nonetheless opposite one of the city's most enduring modern Russian restaurants, simply entitled Restoran. Stylish, spacious and not so formal to be off-putting, this is a great spot for a relaxed meal of haute Russe cuisine.

Delicious renditions of bliny, *pelmeni* (dumplings) and *solyanka* (a meat and vegetable soup) are served alongside fancier dishes such as duck baked with apple or whole baked sterlet poached in white wine and herbs. Desserts include a superb *mille-feuille* 'Napoleon'. In the winter,

a fire keeps it all cosy, while in the summer the centuries-old, thick walls make it cool as a cave.
Tel +7 812 327 8979; Tamozhenny Pereulok 2, Vasilyevsky Island; noon-11pm

07 KORYUSHKA

Ginza Project is one of St Petersburg's leading operators of restaurants, with concepts ranging from modern Russian to Japanese. One of its most famous ventures is the retro-Soviet Mari Vanna, which has outlets in London and New York, as well as St Petersburg's Petrograd Side.

However, for Georgian dishes and a chance to eat a local fish, opt for Koryushka. The restaurant is named after the smelt, a small fish that is native to the city's rivers and served here in a variety of ways such as pickled, deep fried in batter or in a crunchy coating of nuts.

Super-fresh salads are served alongside memorable Georgian staples such as slices of fried aubergine wrapped around walnut butter, *satsivi* (a chicken and nut-sauce dish), and a variety of *khachapuri* breads.

The icing on the cake is Koryushka's sublime location on Zayachy Island next to the Peter and Paul Fortress, offering a panoramic view of the Hermitage across the Neva River. *en.ginza.ru/spb/restaurant; tel +7 812 917 9010; Petropavlovskaya Krepost 3, Zayachy Island; noon-1am*

08 COCOCO

Sergey Shnurov, lead singer of massively popular Russian ska-punk band Leningrad, together with his wife Matilda, pioneered the farm-to-table concept in St Petersburg with their restaurant Cococo. What you get here are inventive modern Russian dishes with a twist.

Plates are playful and inspired in their use of seasonal, organic and locally sourced products. Take their version of sushi, using local cuts of fish and rye bread instead of vinegared rice, or the beef sirloin served in a sauce made from kvass, a fermented beverage also made from bread. Cococo's famous dessert 'My mother's favorite flower' resembles a smashed chocolate plant pot, filled with ice cream topped with chocolate 'soil'. *www.kokoko.spb.ru; tel +7 812 579 00 16; Voznesensky Prospekt 6, W Hotel; noon-midnight Sun-Thu, noon-last guest Fri & Sat*

06 Kupetz Eliseevs' opulent food hall and dining complex

WHERE TO STAY
SASHA & ANDREI HOMESTAY
If there are more convivial hosts than Italophiles Andrey and Sasha in St Petersburg we have yet to find them. The energetic couple extend the warmest of welcomes at their three eclectically decorated apartments dotted around the city centre. Socialising is encouraged and freshly made bliny and vodka shots are usually served on arrival. *asamatuga@mail.ru; tel +7 812 315 3330; Nab Kanala Griboyedova 51*

RACHMANINOV ANTIQUE HOTEL
Feeling like a secret place for those in the know, this ideally located boutique hotel behind the Kazan Cathedral in St Petersburg's historic heart offers great value for money. It's got a pleasant old-world feel with hardwood floors, attractive Russian furnishings in the public areas and guest rooms individually painted by a local artist. *www.hotelrachmaninov .com; tel +7 812 327 7466; Kazanskaya Ulitsa 5*

WHAT TO DO
THE HERMITAGE
The geographic and tourism centrepiece of the city is one of the world's greatest art collections, partly housed in the baroque Winter Palace and the extraordinary ensemble of buildings that surround it. No other institution so embodies the opulence and extravagance of the Romanov dynasty. You could easily spend a whole day here and across Palace Square at the 20th-century and contemporary art galleries of the Hermitage's newest venture in the revamped east wing of the General Staff Building. (www. hermitagemuseum.org)

CELEBRATIONS
Victory Day on May 9 is a day of huge local importance, when residents remember the 900-day Nazi blockade of St Petersburg. Crowds assemble at Piskaryovskoe Cemetery in the north of the city to commemorate the victims, and there is a huge parade along Nevsky Prospekt followed by fireworks over the Neva River in the evening.

Scotland

EATING AT THE ENDS OF THE EARTH

Scotland's Outer Hebrides islands are a remote food frontier, where people live off the land and seafood plays a starring role in traditional produce and briny local dishes.

Sprinkled like stepping stones across the North Atlantic, the Outer Hebrides – or the Western Isles as they are also known – are a world unto themselves. Though proudly part of Scotland, this 130-mile-long string of wee isles is deliciously unique. Remote and rugged, they dance to their own gently lilting Gaelic tune, rising up to barren mountains and fringed by some of the most dazzling white beaches you'll ever clap eyes on. This is a land defined by the elements, changing tides and weather that can do a U-turn in the blink of an eye – from the swirling mists and howling winds of a 'dreich' day bleached of colour to blinding sunshine.

As in much of Scotland, the food here is nourishing, warming and redolent of peaty land and briny sea. Life here is that bit closer to nature and this is reflected in what lands on your plate and in your glass. Expect to try some of the freshest fish and shellfish you'll ever taste –

NEED TO KNOW
From mainland Scotland fly to Benbecula Airport, at the start of this 2-3 day trail: car hire is essential.

winkles plucked from crystal-clear rock pools, plump, sweet cockles and mussels gathered from craggy shorelines lashed by turquoise sea, meaty wild salmon and trout fished from jewel-coloured lochs, king scallops, langoustines, lobster and crab. Like seafood? You're going to love it here.

Slow touring is the only way to discover the nooks and crannies of these misty, rainbow-draped islands. A road trip takes you along winding, single-track lanes past small crofts and flocks of inquisitive sheep – in no hurry to make way for the odd passing car. Between compelling glimpses of dunes swathed in lush machair (dune grasslands), seals bobbing out at sea and wild, Tolkienesque landscapes, you'll be tempted to stop at little bakeries, distilleries and smokehouses where locals keep a tight grip on family tradition, restaurants that play up slow food and beaches ripe with foraging potential.

01 David A Johnson © Getty Images

SCOTLAND

08
07 ● MIAVAIG   ● STORNOWAY
06   Lewis and
             Harris

ATLANTIC
OCEAN

05 ● TARBERT

04 ● LEVERBURGH

03
North   ● LOCHMADDY
Uist

02
BALIVANICH ●   01   Isle of Skye

01 MACLEANS BAKERY

The flimsy-looking plane skitters along the runway as you touch down on the island of Benbecula and outside looms lonely moor, a piercing blue sea and almost total silence. Just north of the airport on the B892 Balivanich-Benbecula road is family-run MacLeans Bakery, where you can stop off at the shop to buy perfectly crisp oatcakes and biscuits, fresh bread and cakes. Locals rave particularly about the oatcakes, which brothers Ewen and Alan have been baking according to a traditional recipe for the past 15 years. Pair them with smoked fish. *Tel +44 1870 602659; Uachdar Balivanich, Benbecula; 8am-3pm Mon-Fri, to 2pm Sat*

02 HEBRIDEAN SMOKEHOUSE

From the bakery, take a short northerly drive and cross the causeway to the neighbouring island of North Uist and the Hebridean Smokehouse – keep your eyes peeled; it's on the left. Among the peat bogs and glittering lochans of North Uist, this smokehouse is kid-in-candy-shop stuff for anyone into seafood.

Locally cut peat provides the mellow smoky flavour for fish and shellfish caught by its small inshore fleet – the freshness and quality is second to none. The aroma hits you like a crisp left hook the moment you step into the shop. Then you're drawn to the counter selling melt-in-the-mouth smoked scallops, fleshy salmon smoked with peat and beech wood, plump mackerel fillets, kiln-roasted lobster tails and smoked salmon pâté. Be sure to visit the viewing gallery for a peek at the slicing and smoking process. *www.hebrideansmokehouse.com; tel +44 1876 580209; Clachan, Locheport, Isle of North Uist; 8am-5.30pm Mon-Fri, 9am-5pm Sat*

03 COCKLE BAY

Your next stop is in Berneray, an island linked to North Uist by another causeway. Ah Berneray! Tacked onto the top of the Uists, this dinky island is in many ways the Outer Hebrides in microcosm, with its brooding high moors and lochs, *machair*-cloaked dunes and the staggeringly lovely, three-mile West Beach thrashed by Atlantic waves.

When the tide is low, this is a cracking island for a spot of coastal foraging. Cockle Bay, the inlet immediately to the west of the causeway, has some of the richest pickings. In-the-know locals come here to gather the cockles that lie buried a couple of inches beneath the sand – a chink against rake means you have struck bivalve gold.

There are few simpler pleasures than securing a rake and bucket and joining them in their search for some of the plumpest, sweetest cockles

 caption marker: ⑬

you are ever likely to taste – each one a pure, bursting mouthful of the sea. Mussels also cling to the rocks on this beach and can simply be picked by hand.

⑭ THE ANCHORAGE

From Berneray take the one-hour ferry to Leverburgh in South Harris on the island of Harris, where you'll be greeted by a harbour lined with colourful lobster pots. Otters can occasionally be sighted splashing around in the water here.

Lobster is the star of the menu at the Anchorage, right next to the ferry slipway. It's unassuming on the face of things, sure, but don't let that put you off – there's a reason why almost every table is taken at this place even in the low season. Besides broad views out to sea, it serves deeply satisfying portions of fish and chips, butter-soft scallops, sweet local lobster and giant langoustines – all

locally caught, all uniformly delicious. *Tel +44 1859 520225; The Pier, Leverburgh, South Harris; noon-3pm & 7-11pm*

⑮ SOCIAL DISTILLERY

Heading north, Tarbert is home to the Social Distillery, which hit the ground running when it opened in autumn 2015. Its single malt isn't ready just yet – first bottling will be in 2019 – but in the meantime the distillery is tapping into the growing market for craft gins.

The Isle of Harris Gin is an ode to the sea, with subtle notes of juniper, angelica, coriander, bitter orange peel and liquorice, as well as the distinctive flavour of sugar kelp hand-harvested by a local diver. Hook onto one of the 1¼-hour tours (£10) for a peek behind the scenes and a tasting. The quickest way to reach the distillery from Leverburgh is to drive along the west coast, but don't pass up the opportunity to take the dramatic

Ø1 South Harris beach, looking towards Eigg and Rhum

Ø2 Daily island ife on Harris

Ø3 Callanish Standing Stones on Lewis

Golden Road. This single-track road spectacularly twists and turns along the island's fjordlike east coast, rippling through moonlike rockscapes of naked gneiss rock, pockmarked with *lochans* (small lakes). You'll want to pause for photos on almost every corner. *East Loch, Tarbert; www. harrisdistillery.com; tel +44 1859 502212; tours 11am Wed, Thu & Sat*

06 ABHAINN DEARG

A highly scenic drive north takes you through the dramatic mountains and loch-speckled heights of North Harris, before swinging west to the swooping beaches and azure waters of Carnish in Lewis. Toast your good fortune at having arrived in this

'Berneray is a cracking island for coastal foraging. In-the-know locals come here to gather the cockles that lie buried in the sand'

sensational setting with a wee dram at Abhainn Dearg. In 2011, the distillery produced the first single malt whisky in the Outer Hebrides since 1829.

Still in its infancy, it is the brainchild of Mark Tayburn (Marko), who saw the potential of the mineral-rich waters flowing down from the Uig hills. Hook onto one of the half-hourly tours (£3) for the inside scoop. *www.abhainndearg.co.uk; tel +44*

1851 672429; Carnish, Isle of Lewis; 11am-1pm & 2pm-4pm Mon-Sat

07 AUBERGE CARNISH

Oh wow, what a view! The sea vistas are never short of extraordinary in the Outer Hebs, but at this timber-framed boutique hotel and restaurant perched on the edge of Uig Sands they are mind-blowing. Pull up a chair in the sleek restaurant, decked out

04 Cody Duncan © Alamy

in aqua-blue and white, with picture windows allowing you to swoon over the same coloured sea and sand.

As for the food, it's hard to beat in these parts. Chef Richard puts his own spin on French techniques combined with Hebridean ingredients, using seasonal produce sourced on the island. Together with his wife Jo-Ann, he brings dishes to the table that are full of robust flavours. You could begin with smoked haddock risotto with parmesan, then move onto flaky fillet of cod with smoked mussels in a creamy dill sauce. Fish takes centre stage, but mains such as loin of Lewis lamb with shiitake and brandy sauce are also impressive. Book ahead. *www.aubergecarnish.co.uk; tel +44 1851 672459; 5 Carnish, Uig*

08 UIG LODGE SMOKED SALMON

Follow the narrow road northeast from Carnish for three miles to reach this Victorian lodge, the romantic vision of Sir James Matheson who owned the Isle of Lewis when the lodge was built in 1876. Affording spectacular views of Uig Bay, it has been owned by the Green family since 1981. Guests staying the night can fish in the clean lochs and river pools whose waters drain out to sea. Prime salmon fly-fishing season runs from 1 June to 15 October, while sea trout and brown trout can be caught between 15 March and 16 October.

Quality shines through in the oak-smoked Atlantic salmon sold unsliced or hand-sliced here. It's so darn delicious, in fact, that it has won the lodge a Great Taste Golden Fork Award for speciality producer of the year. *www.uiglodge.co.uk; tel +44 1851 672396; Uig; 9am–5.30pm Mon–Fri*

04 Woman looks out to sea, Berneray Hostel

WHERE TO STAY

BERNERAY HOSTEL

At the budget end of the spectrum is the basic but atmospheric Berneray Hostel, which offers dorm beds housed in a pair of restored blackhouses right by the fabulous sweep of East Beach, and camping close to sand dunes. It's an incredibly peaceful spot, and otters and seals can sometimes be spotted splashing around out at sea. *www.gatliff.org.uk; tel +44 845 293 7373*

AUBERGE CARNISH

A petite boutique hotel with a big view of a big arc of white sand, Auberge Carnish is set on a working croft. The rooms have been stylishly designed with natural materials and soothing colours, and come with little luxuries such as Hebridean seaweed bath products. *www.aubergecarnish. co.uk; tel +44 1851 672459; 5 Carnish, Uig*

UIG LODGE

The breathtaking Atlantic views from Uig Lodge are said to have inspired author Arthur Ransome to pen *Great Northern?* – the final book in Ransome's *Swallows and Amazons* series of children's books – in 1947. Retaining plenty of Victorian character, rooms are bright and spacious with pine trappings and tartan-style fabrics. *www.uiglodge.co.uk; tel +44 1851 672396; Uig*

WHAT TO DO

With *machair*-swathed dunes, white-sand beaches, moorland and lochs, the 7.5-mile Berneray Circuit Trail (www. isleofberneray.com) is an excellent intro to the area. Ponder the mysteries of prehistory at the Callanish Standing Stones (www. callanishvisitorcentre. co.uk) on Lewis, which form one of the most complete stone circles in Britain.

CELEBRATIONS

July is the time for festivals: Highland games, performing arts, music and workshops come to the Sail Stornoway Maritime Festival (www.sailstornoway. co.uk); Berneray leaps to life and its population swells for Berneray Week, with an upbeat mix of music, *ceilidhs*, crafts and a sandcastle building competition.

INDIAN OCEAN

BEAU VALLON ● — 03
02 — ● VICTORIA
01

Mahé

ANSE BOILEAU ●

04 — ● ANSE ROYALE

05
BAIE LAZARE ●

SEYCHELLES

Seychelles

TROPICAL TASTES OF A CREOLE SPICE TRAIL

Centuries of French, African and Indian influence have fired up the Seychelles cooking pot to create a tasty Creole cuisine of aromatic curries grounded by tropical produce.

Palm-fringed beaches, a verdant mountainous interior, and all the activities you could ask for – swimming, snorkelling, hiking, fishing... The main island of Mahé (pop 79,000) in the Seychelles, an Indian Ocean archipelago off the coast of Africa, couldn't be a more postcard-perfect tropical getaway. But it's the colourful Creole language and food that really sets the island apart. Understandably, Mahé is a popular holiday destination, one that caters to international palates. But pass by the hotel buffets, seek out smaller eateries and you'll be rewarded with a spicy taste of local life.

A mélange of historical influences combined to create the Creole cooking that characterises Mahé today. The island was uninhabited when the French first settled here in the 1770s. Under French and then English rule, plantations cultivated spices such as nutmeg, cloves, cinnamon and pepper in addition to coconut palms, rice and sweet potatoes. African influence came in part from the indentured former slaves brought to the Seychelles in the 1800s. Indian and Chinese minorities also arrived to work, many from neighbouring Mauritius. All left their own tasty legacy.

Expect fish, fish and more fish on the menu. Multicoloured longboats and net trawling still provide an abundant catch for local markets and eateries. Look for snapper, jobfish, parrotfish, grouper, tuna, shark, kingfish and barracuda, to name but a few. Expect coconut-milk-spiked curries or fine French sauces to accompany the catch, or find it simply grilled over coconut husks, with a garlic, ginger and chilli paste. Accompaniments include rice, and *chatinis* (chutneys) made from pumpkin or papaya.

Starting in the bustling capital city of Victoria, this tour takes you from the beach to the verdant interior and wild west coast.

NEED TO KNOW
Mahé is hilly, with limited transport, but driving (left side!) is easy enough. Rent cars from Victoria airport.

01 Justin Foulkes © Lonely Planet

01 VICTORIA MARKET

Mahé's capital city of Victoria only has a population of about 26,000, but it seems like they all come through the market on a busy Saturday. You'll see every shade of skin and hair colour imaginable, but the African influence is felt most strongly here.

By 6am fishermen have set up stalls with their day's catch, an astonishing array of seafood. Local women banter back and forth in the native Creole (most residents speak Creole, French and English) while selling piles of tropical fruits and vegetables.

Spice vendors hope their wares' pungent aromas will draw you in. Look for local specialities such as the bright red, apple-sized jamalac fruit, with its sweet-sour tang and water-chestnut-crunch. And this is the place to stock up on cinnamon, pepper and sarongs to take home.

Market St, Victoria; 9.30am-5pm Mon-Fri, 9am-noon Sat

02 MARIE ANTOINETTE

Original Marie Antoinette owner Kathleen Foneska was awarded for her contribution to tourism on Mahé, the country's largest economic sector today. Her son Roy and his partners carry on her welcoming tradition more than 50 years later at this gracious, fine-dining Creole institution.

The restaurant occupies a plantation-era home, filled with antiques juxtaposed with tropical furnishings and long-time, good-humoured waitresses that keep things light. Try the tasting menu for a little of everything – fried parrotfish, tasty aubergine fritters, papaya chutney… The more adventurous can request fruit bat – a local delicacy – instead of the prawn stew.

Wash it down with the local lager, Seybrew, before you tuck into caramelised bananas for dessert. On the way out, say hello to the resident giant tortoises in the yard.

These 100-plus-year-old behemoths are indigenous to an outlying Seychelles island.

www.marieantoinette.sc; tel +248 4266 222; Serret Rd, Victoria; noon-2.30pm & 6.30pm-10pm Mon-Sat

03 BOATHOUSE RESTAURANT

After an afternoon spent on Beau Vallon Beach, kick back with a Creole supper at the Boathouse. You can feel the ocean breezes coming through the open walls at this casual bar-restaurant across the street from the sand.

The evening meal is served buffet-style and includes fresh salads such as smoked fish, bitter melon, patrol (a slightly bitter gourd in the cucumber family) and papaya. Typical mains might be octopus curry and grilled tuna and snapper: the 'Creole salsa' is made with several locally grown chilli varieties, so watch the heat!

www.boathouseseychelles.com; tel +248 4247 898; N Coast Rd, Beau Vallon; 9am-5.30pm & 7.30-10.30pm

04 JARDIN DU ROI

Five generations of the same French-English family have served as caretaker for this 25-hectare traditional homestead that was once a spice plantation. Today it is a culinary garden of Eden set high up a mountainside.

Six different trails lead past medicinal herbs, tropical orchards, palm forests and flower gardens, which are also home to a dozen or so giant tortoises. Spice plants are too many to count: pepper, nutmeg, cinnamon, cloves, coffee, patchouli, lemon grass – the list goes on. A plant checklist and the odd interpretive sign helps keep you oriented.

Once you've tired, stop for lunch at the little cafe where local Creole cooks conjure up dishes using site-picked ingredients, such as banana leaf-baked jobfish, coconut cream curry and citronella iced tea.

Tel +248 4372 313; Les Canelles & Sweet Escott Rds, Anse Royale; 10am-5pm

05 ANSE SOLEIL CAFE

Another day, another beach. Anse Soleil is a small-but-gorgeous sandy crescent backed by bamboo groves, palm trees and granite boulders.

It's prime snorkelling and sun-lolling territory, while the cafe at the north end of the beach is known for its idyllic thatched-roof deck overlooking the water, and a slightly surly owner. Never mind that; the seafood is some of the freshest around because they buy directly from local boats. For an early dinner, plump for the grilled whole fish, lobster or fruit bat. Note the restaurant's road is private; do not park here unless you're heading straight to eat. Anse Soleil is 5 miles west of Anse Royale.

Tel +248 4361 700; Anse Soleil Rd; noon-8pm

01 Fish barbecue on Beau Vallon beach

02 Coconuts and spices for sale at Victoria Market

03 Marie Antionette restaurant

WHERE TO STAY

LE MERIDIEN FISHERMAN'S COVE

This hotel occupies an enviable spot at the west end of Beau Vallon Beach, with low-lying bungalows by the sea. A fine seafood restaurant, laid-back bar and infinity pool all overlook turquoise waters. *www.lemeridien fishermanscove.com; tel +248 4677 000; Bel Ombré Rd, Beau Vallon*

HANNEMAN HOLIDAY RESIDENCE

Expect personal attention from the helpful owner-manager at these seven self-catering apartments, a 10-minute walk above the beach. Though quite a climb, the hillside locale provides panoramic vistas. To cool off, there's a central courtyard pool. *www.hanneman-seychelles.com; tel +248 4425 000; off N Coast Rd, Beau Vallon*

ANSE SOLEIL BEACHCOMBER

Simple rooms set right on the beach: what more could you want? You'll feel warmly welcomed at this small family-run hotel with a great location. All the self-catering apartments, deluxe and standard rooms include private terraces. *www.ansesoleil beachcomber.com; tel +248 4361 461; Coast Rd, Anse Soleil*

WHAT TO DO

BEAU VALLON BEACH

Beau Vallon, 5km northwest of Victoria, is the longest and, arguably, the prettiest stretch of sand on Mahé. The beach fronts a tiny town centre from where kayaking, Hobie Cat sailing and snorkelling boat trips are available.

STE ANNE NATIONAL MARINE PARK

Snorkeling is a must-do on Mahé and Ste Anne National Marine Park is fins down the best site for spotting colourful fish because of its pristine reefs and varieties of coral. Mason's Travel (masonstravel.com) offers excursions with a picnic lunch.

CELEBRATIONS

During the last week in October, the Festival Kreol (Creole Festival) takes over Mahé's capital Victoria for a six-day celebration of Creole food, music, art and folk dance.

Slovakia

A SHEPHERD'S TOUR OF SLOVAKIA

Slovakia is a European nation that retains a village feel, with hearty country cooking built on dairy from precious sheep flocks, freshly baked breads and local farmers' produce.

An understated beauty, Slovakia is dotted with rolling foothills and alpine mountains where rural traditions and folkways still hold sway. A shepherd's heart beats in this tiny Central European nation. Even in the many cafes of the capital, Bratislava, you can feel the village influence; a hearty peasant dish *bryndzové halušky* (dumplings with sheep's cheese and bacon bits) is considered a national treasure.

It was back in the late Middle Ages when Walachian settlers first brought their sheep husbandry skills to the central Slovak hills. Sheep's milk products remain the most important Slovak agricultural product still today. Farmers fought for – and won – the right to an EU-protected geographical designation for *bryndza* (a soft, slightly acidic sheep's cheese with a wonderfully pungent flavour), not unlike champagne in France.

In addition to the fine, spreadable *bryndza*,

sheep dairies produce semi-hard *oštiepok* by working the lump cheese further, shaping it into fancy moulds and smoking it to infuse it with an earthy flavour. Or it's steamed, strung into strips and rolled or braided to create semi-hard *paranica* cheese with a subtle, creamy texture.

Originally shepherd's terms, *salaš* (sheepfold) and *koliba* (shepherd's hut) now both refer to rustic country restaurants, by far the best places to sample hearty Slovak fare such as *demikát* (a thick cheese soup), *kapustnica* (sour cabbage and sausage soup, *bryndza*-topped *halušky* (gnocchi-like potato dumplings) and *pirohy* (moon-shaped dumplings a bit like the more well known Slavic pierogi). Your tour starts in the capital, with its pedestrian-friendly old town and castle, before venturing out to the countryside where you'll find bucolic views and a warm welcome in the heart of local cheese production.

NEED TO KNOW
Bratislava makes a good base for this 2–3 day trail but Vienna, 66km away, may be easier to fly into.

01 BRATISLAVA FLAGSHIP RESTAURANT

Because of its emphasis on everything homemade, Flagship should be your first stop on the evening of your arrival. Locals and visitors alike are attracted to the reasonable prices and to the elaborate interior that replicates a street-front in old Bratislava.

You can buy acacia honey and blackcurrant wine, among other local products, at the Shop of the Good Shepherd before having a seat. Take your time with the menu, which includes a detailed glossary of local food terms and light-hearted look at the historic making of the national dish *bryndzové halušky* – complete with old photos of shepherds tending their flocks and playing their flutes in the field.

All the various dumplings, noodles and breads are made on the premises and the cheese comes

'Until the 1990s, there were few supermarkets in Slovakia, and today fresh markets remain popular year-round'

from localfarms. The combination of *halušky* and *pirohy* provide an excellent introduction to local Slovak cuisine: opt for the version sprinkled with shredded *oštiepok* in addition to *bryndza*.
www.bratislavskarestauracia.sk; tel +421 917 927 673; Námestie SNP 8, Bratislava; 10am-midnight Mon-Sat, noon-midnight Sun

02 MILETIČOVA MARKET

Morning time is the busiest at any local market, and Miletičova is no exception. You'll find the little old *babkas* (grannies) and young mothers alike trolling the covered aisles for

fresh vegetables early on a Saturday.

The place is not the newest or the shiniest, but it does have the freshest offerings. Look along the edges of the market for the booths selling dairy – including sheep's milk and cheeses. The smoked variety comes in some interesting decorative shapes here, made using hand-carved wooden moulds.

You'll also find pastries for a breakfast snack. If you really want to go all out, order a *langoš* – hot, deep-fried dough best topped with garlic oil, sour cream and shredded cheese. Until the 1990s, there were few supermarkets in Slovakia; shopping was

done separately at dried goods stores, bakeries and butcher shops, and fresh markets remain popular year-round. *Miletičova Ulica 821; 8am–7pm*

03 CHEF PARADE

Appropriately close to the market, don your apron at Chef Parade to learn the basics of Slovak cooking (taught in English). You begin in the late morning so that a couple of hours later you can finish by eating the tasty lunch you created. Menus vary but will always include three courses.

You might get your hands dirty kneading the dough for dumplings or slicing the sausage for sour cabbage soup. If you're lucky, for dessert you'll be making *lokše* – thick potato pancakes served with sweet cheese, strawberry jam or poppy seeds and nuts. Advance reservations required. *www.chefparade.sk; tel +421 948 234 553 Miletičova ulica 60*

04 BIOFARMA PRÍRODA

After lunch pay a visit to Biofarma, 27km north of Bratislava, to experience the origins of ingredients like those you cooked with. This working organic farm has more than 100 sheep, as well as pigs, horses, goats, ducks, rabbits and one very friendly dog.

Families often bring their children here to provide a glimpse into what rural life is like. Stop by the bakery (closes 5–6pm) to see the wood-fired oven or to buy a fresh loaf or smoked cheese. Then tour the dairy barn before enjoying the nature trail; this site was once a botanical garden.

For dinner the *koliba*, occupying an old log chalet, is perfect for a rustic meal. Start with plate *z mliečnice* (a mixed cheese plate from the sheep dairy) and Biofarma's site-made spreadable cheese, smoked *oštiepok* and string

varieties of the cheese. The mutton *gulaš* (stew) is a real treat. *www.biofarma.sk; tel +421 918 280 546; Botanická Záhrada, Stupava; 10am–9pm*

05 EXPOZÍCJA JÁNOŠÍK A TERCHOVÁ

The next day, the country calls. The small town of Terchová is a world away, but barely more than two hours' drive from the city. Here beneath the Malá Fatra mountains, you start to be able to see the challenges the environment created for agriculture.

The Janošík and Terchová Exposition is an excellent place to learn more. This small museum is lined with exhibits on folk culture, shepherding practice and traditional cheese-making. The old photos offer an especially evocative glimpse into the past. Look for the wooden implements used in the sheep

03 Hemis © Alamy

dairies, along with the traditional embroidered clothing the men wore. Those and the flutes and horns on display are still used in folk dances today. Also at the museum, you'll find information about Janošík, the Slovak 'Robin Hood', of fact and fiction. *pmza.sk; Sv. Cyrila a Metoda 960, Terchová; 9am-4.30pm Tue-Sun Jun-Aug, 9am-3pm Tue-Sun Sep-May*

06 SALAŠ KRAJINKA

You know the cheese must be fresh when you can see the lambs and ewes through the windows in the rustic restaurant. You can witness various stages in the cheese-making process at this highly regarded Liptov dairy.

While you're here, shop for not only the impressive cheeses but also butter churns, whey dippers and mugs – all hand-carved from wood, just like those in the museum. Lunch provides

the opportunity to taste some hard-to-find classics, such as *žinčica*, a sour-milk drink prized by old-timers, as well as modern creations, such as *bryndza* soup with bacon and onions.

Look for the fluffy sheep symbol on the menu for dishes made with local ingredients, such as *halušky* with homemade sausage... Lamb choices abound – a relative rarity in Slovakia as the animals are valued most highly for their milk and wool. Try it in goulash soup, stewed with rosemary and red wine or fried schnitzel-style as a steak. *www.salaskrajinka.sk; tel +421 918 964 800; off E50, 2km east of Ružomberok; 10am-9pm*

07 KOLIBA GRETA

Take the afternoon to enjoy the beautiful Liptov Valley, surrounded by five different mountain ranges. Driving the back roads you'll often find

individual farmers selling their cheese from roadside stands. Astride the large reservoir Liptovská Mara (20km east of Ružomberok) sits your final destination.

Greta is another traditional restaurant, but the chefs here often switch things up by offering themed evenings (Saturday is a barbecue party). Tasty roast pork, duck and trout dishes are always on the menu. If you aren't sheep-cheesed out, try the *oštiepok* baked in puff pastry and served with salad. Sour milk gives the *pirohy* here a unique flavour, and it's also a good spot for *bryndza* with grilled bacon. Traditionally costumed waiters and folk music are a big part of the draw, so don't expect a quiet night on summer weekends. *www.kolibagreta.sk; tel +421 445 540 040; Liptovská Sielnica 270, Liptovská Sielnica; 8am-10pm*

01 Steps leading
up to Bratislava
Castle

02 Salaš Krajinka,
a Liptov Valley
restaurant and
dairy farm

03 Street food in
Bratislava

04 Bratislava Old
Town's main square

05 Local honey at
Miletičova Market in
Bratislava

WHERE TO STAY
PENZÍON VIRGO
Bold colours and Baroque-inspired wallpaper spice up the otherwise standard modern rooms at this old-town B&B. Genuine espresso with the breakfast buffet is a true perk. Apartments come with kitchenettes and terraces. *www.penzionvirgo.sk; tel +421 220 921 400; Panenská 14, Bratislava*

HOTEL AVANCE
Creamy neutrals complement sleek, black accents, creating a sense of upscale luxury just steps from the pedestrian centre in Bratislava. It boasts a miniature spa with Jacuzzi tub and massage treatments in addition to a restaurant. *hotelavance.sk; tel +421 259 208 400; Medená 9, Bratislava*

HOTEL KOLIBA GRETA
Choose from double rooms upstairs in the grand main log chalet or opt for a two-storey suite in a shared log cabin at this Liptov Valley restaurant/hotel. Accommodation is simple, but spotless. A large green yard out back leads to the waters of Liptovská Mara reservoir. *www.kolibagreta.sk; tel +421 445 540 040; Liptovská Sielnica 270, Liptovská Sielnica*

WHAT TO DO
MUSEUM OF THE LIPTOV VILLAGE
When the Liptovská Mara was flooded, many old buildings were moved here to create an open-air museum. Tour everything from a Renaissance chateau to a rustic village home. Horses, goats and sheep help bring the village to life here. (www.liptovskemuzeum.sk)

GINO PARADISE BEŠEŇOVÁ
Soak in one of several large indoor and outdoor pools at this thermal hot spring spa, 13km southeast of Liptovská Sielnica. A couple of tall waterslides up the adrenaline level. (www.ginoparadise.sk)

CELEBRATIONS
On a long weekend in July, thousands flock to Terchová to celebrate the Janošík Days folklore festival. Highlights include traditional shepherd songs and dances, and there are Slovak foods and crafts. (www.janosikovedni.sk)

05 PailDetail © Alamy

Ø5

South Africa

REINVENTING WEST CAPE TRADITIONS

At the southern tip of Africa, Cape Town chefs have created a progressive food scene by revisiting ancestral traditions and respecting the cape's rich natural resources.

South Africa's Mother City, established in 1652, Cape Town is home to soaring Table Mountain, golden beaches, bountiful vineyards and an urban landscape that is both multicultural and design savvy. The city's original raison d'être was as a food and watering station for the boats of the Dutch East India Company, and it's still hard to imagine a more delicious location in the whole of Africa than Cape Town.

The Dutch settled slaves here from the Malay Archipelago among other places, laying the basis for the unique Cape Malay dishes that are an integral part of the modern food landscape alongside practically every other type of cooking you can think of.

Capetonian chefs have some incredible produce to work with: freshly harvested fish and seafood such as

NEED TO KNOW
This trail can be done in 4 days, but dedicate as much time as possible: Cape Town's surroundings are a gourmet delight.

crayfish, kingklip and the meaty snoek; succulent cuts of game including springbok that are seasoned and tossed on African-style *braais* (barbecues) or dried into deliciously moreish biltong; and a cornucopia of fruit and vegetables ripened to perfection in the warm southern sun. Innovative cooks also tap into the ancient foraging ways of the indigenous Khoe-San people to incorporate into their menus unusual ingredients such as the leaves and flowers of fynbos, the unique range of plants that flourish in the Western Cape.

This culinary tour begins in the City Bowl, where Cape Town was conceived and began to flourish soon after the arrival of the Dutch, then takes you beyond the city's suburbs and out to the Western Cape. Here you'll find 300-plus-year-old Winelands, a windswept coastline and charming fishing villages.

01 COMPANY'S GARDEN

In 1652 the splendid Company's Garden was essentially a farm. In the 19th century the gardens began to take on the pleasurable shape they have today, although the new VOC Vegetable Garden section is inspired by the original market garden.

Next to the Vegetable Garden the shaded Company's Garden Restaurant is a chic and calm place for breakfast – try the French toast made with banana bread, bacon, strawberries and maple syrup. For a light lunch go for their twist on *bobotie*, a Cape Malay classic marrying curried minced beef or lamb with a savoury egg custard; here it's served in a sandwich or rolled in a roti with sides of homemade chutney and *sambal* (pickles).
www.thecompanysgarden.com; tel +27 21 4232919; Queen Victoria St; 7am–6pm

02 LEKKA KOMBUIS

Lekka Kombuis chef Gamidah Jacobs has lived her whole life in the Bo-Kaap. This district of vividly painted, low-roofed heritage buildings on the northeastern slopes of Signal Hill (a five-minute walk from the Company's Garden) is where freed slaves settled after emancipation in the 1830s.

South Africa's Cape Malay population is descended from these Asian and African slaves. They are mainly Muslim people with a distinctive cooking culture, blending the tastes of the colonial Dutch with the mildly spicy Malay styles of their forefathers. Gamidah will take you shopping for spices at Atlas Trading Company, where the Ahmed family have been serving Bo-Kaap residents since 1946, before heading to her turquoise-painted home on the other side of historic Wale St to start her Lekka Kombuis (meaning 'tasty kitchen' in Afrikaans) cooking class.

With well-practised movements of her fingers Gamidah will demonstrate how to make dishes such as *samoosa* (triangular pockets of crisply fried flaky pastry stuffed with spiced potato or minced meats); *dhaltjies* (chickpea flour fritters also known as chilli bites); and a fragrant Cape Malay chicken curry. It's Cape Malay home cooking at its finest.
www.lekkakombuis.co.za; tel +27 21 423 3849; 81 Wale St

03 HONEST CHOCOLATE CAFE

It's a short stroll to another historic building that once was a mortuary but is now home to the contemporary art gallery Commune.1, as well as Honest Chocolate Cafe. The driving forces behind this artisan chocolate shop are founders Anthony Gird and

01 & 03 Oep Ve Koep
restaurant, Paternoster

02 Oranjezicht City
Farm market

04 Vegetables growing
at Company's Garden

05 Waitress at
Africa Cafe

Michael de Klerk, who craft small batches of their sweet treats using traditional methods such as hand tempering the chocolate on a granite slab tabletop.

The raw cacao is ethically sourced from Ecuador, and their products are processed-sugar free, using agave nectar to add sweetness. Even the wrappings, decorated with art from local illustrators, are made from eco-friendly paper.

The cafe is a chocoholic's dream, with the bean sold in liquid, solid, ice cream and cake form – there are even vegan and gluten-free options. Wednesday to Saturday evenings it also runs an intimate bar, specialising in artisan gin-based cocktails, at the back of the building's secluded courtyard. *www.honestchocolate.co.za; tel +27 76 765 8306; 64A Wale St; 9am-5pm Mon-Sat*

04 AFRICA CAFE

Located on a corner of Heritage Square lies a complex of Cape Georgian and Victorian buildings that includes, in its courtyard, a fruit-bearing vine that has grown here since the 1770s. Here, brightly painted Africa Cafe has been doing exactly what it says in its tagline – 'serving Africa on a plate' – to great acclaim since 1992.

The business was started by inter-racial couple Portia and Jason de Smidt, two years before the end of apartheid, in their home in the bohemian suburb of Observatory. In their current home it's certainly touristy, but still one of the best places to sample dishes from across the continent including ostrich curry from Botswana, Moroccan herb relish, Congolese spinach, sweet potato and cheese balls from Malawi and Senegalese stuffed papaya.

Come with a hearty appetite: you can eat as much as you like of the set feast while the talented staff go on song-and-dance walkabout around the tables mid-meal. *www.africacafe.co.za; tel +27 21 422 0221; 108 Shortmarket St, City Bowl; 6-11pm Mon-Sat*

05 ORANJEZICHT CITY FARM MARKET

Among the abundant crop of farmer and artisan food markets sprinkled across Cape Town and its surroundings, the one not to miss is that run by Oranjezicht City Farm (OZCF) every Saturday at Granger Bay.

From this location you'll have a grand view of Table Mountain and the lower slope suburb of Oranjezicht, named after the original farm established here in 1709. By the early 20th century the once-large farm had disappeared,

swallowed up by urban development, leaving the small Homestead Park and a forlorn bowling green. In 2013 a group of local volunteers began to transform this into the current farm, which is attractively laid out and sells produce alongside many other edible goodies at the weekly market.

Even if you miss the market, the OZCF farm (8am-4pm Mon-Sat) is well worth visiting to get an insight into the urban farming movement that's taken a grip in Cape Town. *www.ozcf.co.za; Granger Bay, V&A Waterfront, Beach Rd; 9am-2pm Sat*

06 GREENHOUSE

Amid the Milky Way of Capetonian star chefs, Peter Tempelhoff shines brightly. His culinary imagination runs riot at this elegant restaurant in the Cellars-Hohenort hotel in Constantia, an affluent and long-established suburb hugging the southern slopes of Table Mountain.

Look out for edgy but also fun creations such as 'Release the Kraken' – ethically sourced octopus and gamefish served amid swirling dry ice and bursts of ginger-infused octopus ink. Vegetarians are offered a dedicated menu that includes equally wacky creations such as 'Mushrooms & Things' in which fungi are artistically mixed with strawberry, fruit beer, peas and truffle.

Don't miss the 'Four Degrees of Cheese' dessert, in which prized cheeses from the Cape Winelands are prepared at four temperatures ranging from a freezing ice cream to a silky soufflé. *www.collectionmcgrath.com; tel +27 21 794 2137; The Cellars-Hohenort, 93 Brommersvlei Rd, Constantia*

07 VELD & SEA

The Khoe-San people foraged along the Cape's coast millennia ago, but it took a visiting Japanese traveller in 2012 to open Roushanna Gray's eyes to the contemporary culinary possibilities of the multiple kinds of seaweed as well as mussels on her local Scarborough beach.

A creative foodie, Roushanna has been integrating indigenous edible plants into her cooking for a decade, since joining her mother-in-law Gael Gray to run the Good Hope

06 © Simon Richmond

Gardens Nursery near the entrance to Cape Point. Lately she's ploughed her passion into her Veld & Sea business, offering fynbos and coastal foraging tours. You'll learn sustainable techniques for harvesting various types of seaweed, shellfish and fynbos followed by a hands-on cooking course by the beach, in which you might make lasagne with kelp or a face mask using a variety of seaweeds.

Check Roushanna's blog for dates of the tours, which are dictated by the tides, and details of her collaborations with local chefs on pop-up dinner events. goodhopenursery.wordpress.com; tel +27 72 234 4804

08 OEP VE KOEP

It's an invidious task to choose from the multitude of fantastic culinary road trips that you could make from Cape Town. However you're unlikely to be disappointed by a drive up the west coast to postcard-pretty Paternoster, where rustic whitewashed cottages frame the beach and fishermen haul in crayfish and other seafood.

This is the landscape that inspired maverick chef Kobus van der Merwe, author of the cookbook *Strandveldfood*, to create dishes that are both strictly seasonal and 'hyper-local'. In a beachcomber-decorated courtyard, accessed from his mum's quirky corner store Oep Ve Koep, your tastebuds will be treated to dishes such as springbok carpaccio with dune celery, a snoek *bobotie*, pickled *veldkool* (sea asparagus) with lava jam, and Saldanha Bay mussels in a tea-smoked yellowtail broth. Bookings are essential for lunch. www.facebook.com/oepvekoep; tel +27 22 752 2033; St Augustine Rd, Paternoster; 9am-2.30pm Wed-Sat, 9am-noon Sun

06 Coastal foraging with Roushanna Gray, Veld & Sea

WHERE TO STAY

LA GRENADINE

Expats Maxime and Mélodie ladle on the Gallic charm at these imaginatively renovated former stables. The garden planted with fruit trees is a magical oasis, the lounge is stacked with books and vinyl LPs, and breakfast is served on actress Mélodie's prized collection of china. The location in Cape Town's Gardens area is a short stroll from the City Bowl. www.lagrenadine.co.za; tel +27 21 424 1358; 15 Park Rd, Gardens

ABALONE HOUSE

Local celebrity chef Reuben Riffel has one of his restaurants at this five-star guesthouse in Paternoster. The rooms have artsy touches and there is a spa and plunge pool. www.ablonehouse.co.za; tel +27 22 752 2044; 3 Kriedoring St, Paternoster

WHAT TO DO

TABLE MOUNTAIN

Around 600 million years old, and a canvas painted with the rich diversity of the Cape floral kingdom, Table Mountain is truly iconic. You can admire the showstopper of Table Mountain National Park from multiple angles, but you really can't say you've visited Cape Town until you've stood on top of it. Riding the cableway up Table Mountain is a no-brainer; the views from the revolving car and the summit are phenomenal. Once you are at the top there are souvenir shops, a good cafe and some easy walks to follow (www.tablemountain.net).

CELEBRATIONS

A street parade and party, Tweede Nuwe Jaar (Cape Minstrel Carnival) on 2 January is when the satin- and sequin-clad minstrel troupes traditionally march through the city from Keizersgracht St in the City Bowl to the Bo-Kaap. There also smaller marches on Christmas Eve and New Year's Eve nights. At the end of May, the Mother City goes even more gourmet than usual when the four-day Good Food & Wine Show checks into the Cape Town International Convention Centre (www.goodfoodandwine show.co.za).

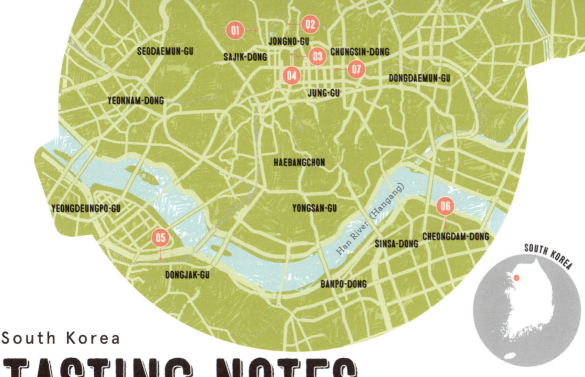

South Korea

TASTING NOTES FROM THE HAN RIVER

Kimchi may be a Unesco-listed pickle with a museum to its name, but there's far more to Korean cuisine. Head for Seoul, where the dynamic dining culture celebrates old and new.

At the cutting edge of fashion and technology, but also deeply traditional, Seoul is one of Asia's most dynamic cities, sporting serene temples and grand palaces as well as mountain trails, 24-hour markets and an awesome culinary scene. Capital of Korea for more than 600 years, this is a city where royal tastes demanded – and received – the finest foods and most intricate preparations.

It's also where common folk indulged their appetites with hearty dishes bursting with flavour and healthy ingredients. There is so much more to Korean food than the spicy cabbage pickle of kimchi and the barbecue charred beef ribs of *galbi*, and Seoul delivers it all with unique dishes available here from across the Korean peninsula.

Seoul's population of more than 10 million is perpetually on the go, their engines stoked by thousands of delicious places to eat.

At unpretentious establishments you sit on floor cushions while motherly figures in caps and aprons dish up bubbling tofu-laden stews or steaming bowls of noodles.

At fancier places you can sizzle prime cuts of beef or pork at a table barbecue, and be amazed at the overflowing abundance of *banchan* (side dishes).

Wherever hunger strikes there's sure to be something appealing nearby to eat, be it piping hot *hotteok* (sweet pancakes filled with brown sugar and cinnamon) from a street stall, or the ultimate energy booster – the chicken, ginseng and herbal soup *samgyetang*.

The following culinary tour can be done in a weekend, taking you both sides of the mighty Han River that splits Seoul roughly into the ancient northern side and the modern southern side.

NEED TO KNOW
Parts of this 2-day city trail are walkable; Seoul also has a user-friendly, excellent subway system.

(02)

01 TONGIN MARKET
(통인시장)

Traditional shopping arcades are an increasingly rare sight in Seoul, yet one that is not only surviving but thriving is Tongin Market, a short walk west of the royal palace Gyeongbokgung.

About half way along the retro arcade, in business since 1941, is the Lunch Box Cafe where, for the equivalent of just a few dollars, you'll get a plastic tray and 10 coin tokens that can be exchanged with market vendors for nibbles such as *jeon* (pan-fried vegetables), *jijim* (vegetable pancakes), *gimbap* (rolls of rice and rainbow strips of veggies wrapped in dried seaweed) and *tteokbokki* (chewy bullets of rice cake, simmered in a sweet, spicy sauce).

Make a full meal of it back at the cafe by using more of your tokens or pay for rice and seaweed soup; the kimchi is free.

'Traditional shopping arcades are an increasingly rare sight in Seoul, yet one that is not only surviving but thriving is Tongin Market'

tonginmarket.co.kr; tel +82 2 722 0911; 18 Jahamun-ro 15-gil, Jongno-gu; market 9am-6pm Mon-Fri, 9am-1pm Sat, cafe 11am-4pm Mon-Fri

02 CHA MASINEUN TTEUL TEAHOUSE
(차마시는뜰)

East of Gyeongbokgung are Bukchon's hilly streets lined with some 900 *hanok* (traditional Korean homes). Single storey, made of wood with broad tile roofs and a central courtyard, several *hanok* have been adapted into guesthouses, shops and cafes such as the charming Cha Masineun Tteul, which translates as

'a garden where people drink tea'. There is indeed a lovely interior courtyard garden with a lotus-filled pond. Swivel your head and the equally appealing view from the cafe's front window is of the palace and hills of central Seoul.

It's a relaxing place to chill over a traditional Korean infusion, such as chilled *omijacha*, a five-flavour berry tea. The drink's vivid red colour contrasts perfectly with the buttery yellow of the house speciality: *hobak sirutteok*, a feather-light pumpkin rice cake served fresh from the steamer. *Tel +82 2 722 7006; 26 Bukchon-ro 11na-gil, Jongno-gu; 10.30am-10pm*

03 MUSEUM KIMCHIKAN
(뮤지엄김치간)

Kimjang, the collective practice of making kimchi, was heritage-listed by Unesco in 2013 and in 2015 this museum opened to celebrate the quintessential Korean pickle. Its high-tech, interactive displays provide an opportunity to learn more about this culinary classic, which is not just made from cabbage: this style of pickling with *gochujang* (chilli paste) and other spices can be done to almost any vegetable in any season.

Different parts of the country also have their own variations of kimchi. A digital installation in the main hall shows exactly how it's done, and there are audio guides in English, Chinese and Japanese to help you decode other exhibits. With advance reservation, and as long as there's a minimum of five people, you can take part in a variety of kimchi-making classes that are held here, too.

The museum is a block behind the Templestay Information Centre in the heart of the Insa-dong.
www.kimchimuseum.co.kr; tel +82 2 6002 6456; Insa-dong maru Level 4-6, 35-4 Insadong-gil, Jongno-gu; 10am-6pm Tue-Sun

04 BALWOO GONGYANG
(발우공양)

Stroll downhill from Bukchon to the Templestay Information Centre opposite the Buddhist temple Jogye-sa. On the centre's fifth floor is Balwoo Gongyang, a serene restaurant founded by the respected Buddhist nun and dietician Dae Ahn to serve temple cuisine. *Balwoo Gongyang* translates as 'monastic formal meal' which sounds unpromising, but in the capable hands of Dae Ahn's team reveals itself as heavenly vegetarian cuisine with subtle flavours and a pleasing mix of textures.

Ingredients are seasonal but you may find among the dishes a delicate salad with bellflower roots and pine-nut dressing, or fried shiitake mushrooms in sweet-and-sour sauce. Steamed sticky rice with gingko nuts and black sesame seeds arrives wrapped in a lotus leaf. Part of the 15-course 'enlightenment' meal is *yeongwachae*, a whole lotus blossom topped with vegetables, and *bulgogi*, a dish made of beans that mimic the texture of beef.
Tel +82 2 2031 2081; 56 Ujeongguk-ro, Jongno-gu; 11.40am-3pm & 6-8.50pm

05 NORYANGJIN FISH MARKET
(노량진수산시장)

It's hardly worth going to bed if you want to experience Noryangjin Fish Market in full flight: auctions to the retail and restaurant sector start around 1am. However, business goes on around the clock at this market

05 John Steele © Getty Images

south of the Han River so it's no problem to turn up later in the day, as many locals do, wanting to sample Seoul's freshest fish and seafood.

The 700 stalls and numerous restaurants that make up the market are housed in a new multistorey state-of-the-art complex next to their old home. Apron-clad vendors will happily help you select from live crabs, prawns, the dark-orange and -red *meongge* (Korean sea squirt; very much an acquired taste) or prepared platters of *hoe* (raw fish slices).

Adventurous eaters can give *sannakji* a go – chopped baby octopus, its tentacles still wriggling as you chew it down. For an extra fee, restaurants in the market will serve what you've bought with a variety of side dishes or cook your purchase for you. There's an open eating area on the top floor with great views across Seoul.
www.susansijang.co.kr; tel +82 2 814 2211; 688 Nodeul-ro, Dongjak-gu; 24hr

06 JUNG SIK
(중식)

Since 2009 chef Jung Sik Yim has been wowing local epicureans with a very 21st-century take on Korean cooking. Having honed his culinary skills at top New York City restaurants, Jung Sik has brought to Seoul a sublime multi-course dining experience that combines traditional ingredients with the cutting-edge methods of molecular gastronomy.

The restaurant may be based in Seoul's ritzy Gangnam-gu, an area made famous by pop star Psy's catchy dance tune, but there is no horsing around with the flavours or presentation here.

Top-quality ingredients have been sourced from across the country, with a focus on Jeju-do, Korea's largest island and a tropical holiday destination that is well known for its delicious seafood and black pork belly.

Save room for Jung Sik's desserts, beautiful creations such as 'Cherry Blossoms' – a bowl of light pink sponge dotted with spots of whipped cream, cherry gel'ee, passion fruit, a spoonful of tangy cherry sorbet and a branch of dark chocolate. Book at least one month in advance to be sure to get a table.
jungsik.kr; tel +82 2 517 4654; 11 Seolleung-ro, 158-gil, Gangnam-gu; noon-3pm & 5.30-10.30pm

07 GWANGJANG MARKET
(광장시장)

Gwangjang Market dates back to 1905 and has been in its current home since 1962. On two crossed alleys running through the market's ground floor are hundreds of street food vendors, alongside kimchi and fresh seafood stalls.

Specialities here include *hotteok* (sweet pancakes filled with brown sugar and cinnamon) and the

savoury mung bean pancakes *nokdu bindaetteok*. Watch the female cooks prepare the *bindaetteok* from soaked mung beans that are ground between revolving millstones into a thick batter, mixed with bean sprouts, green onions and garlic before being fried into delicious, crispy, golden patties not unlike giant hash browns.

A more healthy option is *bibimbap*, a bowl of rice topped with vegetables, meat and *gochujang* (a chilli sauce); and the similar *boripab* where steamed barley replaces the rice. All the ingredients are combined before eating.

The atmosphere sizzles in the evenings when hordes of office workers come here to fuel up on the hearty food and shots of *soju* (a potent spirit alcohol) or mugs of *makgeolli* (a milky rice wine).
88 Changgyeonggung-ro, Jongno-gu; 8.30am-10pm

05 Bukchon Hanok Village, Seoul

06 Auction at Noryangjin Fish Market

WHERE TO STAY
RAK-KO-JAE
(락고재)
A beautifully restored *hanok*, with an enchanting garden that's modelled after a Japanese ryokan. The guesthouse's mud-walled sauna is included in the prices, as is breakfast and dinner.
www.rkj.co.kr; tel +82 2 742 3410; 19 Bukchon-ro, 6-gil, Jongno-gu

MINARI GUEST HOUSE
(미나리하우스)
Located near the street art of Ihwa-maeul, the four appealing rooms at this modernist house sport minimalist design and arty touches. Breakfast is served in a lovely gallery cafe on the ground floor that opens out onto a spacious tiered garden.
www.minarihouse.com; tel +82 70 8656 3303; 3 Ihwajang 1nagil, Jongno-gu

WHAT TO DO
Walk part or all of the 14th-century Seoul City Wall, which runs for 18.6km connecting the peaks of Bukaksan (342m), Naksan (125m), Namsan (262m) and Inwangsan (338m) on the north side of the Han River. Six out of eight of the original fortress gates remain, the most famous of which are the Great South Gate Sungnyemun (commonly callled Namdaemun) and the Great East Gate Heunginjimum (Dongdaemun), near the futuristic, Zaha Hadid-designed Dongdaemun Design Plaza. The panoramic views of Seoul from atop the hills make the effort of climbing up well worth it. (seoulcitywall.seoul.go.kr)

CELEBRATIONS
One of the best times to visit Seoul is in May in the run-up to the spectacular Lotus Lantern Festival (Yeon Deung Hoe). It's during this month that Buddha's birthday is celebrated with masses of coloured paper lanterns decorating all the major temples of the city. The highlight, held the weekend before Buddha's birthday, which is calculated according to the lunar calendar, is a huge daytime street festival and evening lantern parade – the largest in South Korea. (www.llf.or.kr)

06 © Getty Images

CASTELLFULLIT DE LA ROCA · · · BESALÚ
05 · 07
06 · OLOT · SANTA PAU
04
03
02 · VIC · GIRONA
08

SPAIN

01 · BARCELONA

MEDITERRANEAN SEA

Spain

A CATALAN FOOD LESSON

Between the shining stars of Barcelona and Girona, rural Catalonia is an enthralling gourmet destination where traditional recipes and fertile volcanic soils are inspiring chefs.

Landscape and history find rich expression on the Catalan plate. This fiercely distinct region of Spain encompasses an astonishing range of landscapes, from the sun-kissed Costa Brava to the Pyrenees, where lonely Romanesque monasteries are perched in wild valleys. *Mar i muntanya* (sea and mountain) dishes reflect the opposing extremes of Catalonia's terrain, uniting produce scooped from the coast with meat farmed in Pyrenean pastures. Bright flavours such as tomato and red peppers are omnipresent, their tang complemented by fragrant nuances of almond and dried fruit: legacies of Muslim rule in the Iberian Peninsula from the seventh century. The best dishes marry tart flavours with earthy notes to wondrous effect.

Catalan cuisine has risen to global stardom and in 2016 the region was crowned European Region of Gastronomy, while Michelin-starred Girona restaurant El Celler de Can Roca continues to top best-restaurant lists. But some gastronomic enclaves remain relatively unknown outside Spain, such as Garrotxa with its *cuina volcànica* (volcanic cuisine). Here in this bucolic area of the Catalan Pyrenees, hills and valleys have been sculpted by volcanoes that now slumber. The fertile, ashy soil is credited for the quality of local produce: turnips, truffles and chestnuts add depth to pork, while nut and herb liqueurs moisten the palate between forkfuls. Dishes are awarded a *cuina volcànica* mark to indicate locally sourced status and inventive use of traditional ingredients.

The promise of bulging *botifarra* (sausage), rich mountain cheese and lovingly seared vegetables is sure to set your appetite ablaze. This gastronomic adventure will guide you from fresh seafood to the robust flavours of Catalonia's volcanic landscape over the course of three days.

NEED TO KNOW
This 3-day trail starts in Barcelona but focuses on small-town Catalonia: rent a car for ease of travelling.

02

⓵ MERCAT DE LA BOQUERIA

Begin in Barcelona with an amuse-bouche of Catalan flavours at historic food hall La Boqueria. A market has stood here since the 13th century, though the hall housing it today is a mere 160 years young.

The market is beloved of visitors, and you'll understand why with your first glance at produce ranging from grab-and-go *cargols* (snails) to slabs of goat's cheese and glistening cured meats. Follow local rhythms to find the best food: tourists tend to cluster at the main entrance, so don't get distracted by the rainbow of smoothie stalls.

Find more elbow room (and local shoppers) by ploughing into the further realms of the market. Arrive early, as La Boqueria is hugely popular with tour groups, and don't miss taking away some *jamón ibérico* – rather than grabbing a package, find a vendor shaving off melt-in-mouth

'Chef Fina aims to express the richness of the surrounding Garrotxa scenery through the finest produce grown in the volcanic soil'

slices of this protected-status ham on demand. But sometimes, the crowds have the right idea. Pinotxo Bar (pinotxobar.com) is wildly popular, with local legend Juanito Bayen among the friendly crew dishing up plates of stewed chickpeas, washed down with generous glasses of wine. As you're by the Balearic Sea, we'd advise balancing on a stool here to sample fresh mussels, razor clams and *xipirons amb mongetes* (squid with beans).
boqueria.info; tel +34 933 18 25 84; La Rambla 91, Barcelona; 8am-8.30pm Mon-Sat

⓶ CASA RIERA ORDEIX

Leaving Barcelona, head for the spirited town of Vic about an hour's drive north. Among its labyrinthine old-town streets, you won't fail to notice weighty truncheons of meat hanging in deli windows. This treasured delicacy is *llonganissa*, first mentioned in the 14th century, gilded with protected status, and only produced in and around Vic.

Delve into centuries of *llonganissa* history at Casa Riera Ordeix, a factory with attached deli and one of only a handful of authorised local producers. Its experienced sausage

02 LOOK Die Bildagentur der Fotografen GmbH © Alamy

makers trust the old methods, which you can find out about on an hour-long tour behind the scenes.

Pere, who has been making *llonganisses* for an impressive 32 years, explains that carefully chosen meat is mixed with diced bacon, sea salt and black pepper. The mixture is allowed to rest for a weekend and then packed into natural casing, tied with twine and hung to dry.

'The drying process can last from three to six months depending on the size and climate,' says Pere. The result is a glistening cured meat that makes your mouth water with every bite (and there'll be many – this chewy sausage is a workout for your jaw).

Maribel, another factory worker who has hand-wrapped *llonganissa* sausages for a grand total of 29 years, finds them delicious with sugar and quality champagne, a mouth-watering mix of salty and sweet.

www.casarieraordeix.com; tel +34 938 89 30 34; Plaça del Màrtirs 14, Vic; one-hour tours 9am-noon & 3-5pm Mon-Fri, by prior arrangement Sat & Sun

03 EL JARDINET

Appetite whetted, sit down for a feast in the heart of medieval Vic. Restaurant El Jardinet serves up some of the best regional dishes in a charming setting (including terrace for sunny days).

Tuck into *fideuà*, fine wheat noodles strewn with seafood, or juicy Iberico pork, lightly braised. If you feel inspired by the peaceful garden, you're in good company – the locally loved 20th-century 'Prince of Catalan Poets' Josep Carner spent time here.
www.eljardinetdevic.com; tel +34 938 86 28 77; Carrer dels Corretgers 8, Vic; 1-3.30pm & 8.30-11pm Tue-Sat, 1-3.30pm Sun

04 CAN XEL

The terrain begins to ripple with valleys and triangular hills on the approach to the Garrotxa's volcanic region, a 45-minute drive north from Vic. This fertile area is the heartland of *cuina volcànica*, famed for its full-bodied flavours.

Your first stop is in Santa Pau: a tiny village famous for its *fesol* (plump white beans), cherished by local chefs because of the way they absorb flavour while retaining their shape.

The best spot to try them is Can Xel: order a plateful of *botifarra amb fesols de Santa Pau*, in which beans accompany a succulent Catalan sausage with serious pedigree: *botifarra* dates almost to Roman times, with its recipe of lightly spiced pork little changed since then.
www.canxel.com; +34 972 68 02 11; Carretera Santa Pau, Santa Pau; 1-3.30pm & 8.30-11pm Mon, Tue & Thu-Sat, 1-3.30pm Sun

05 MUSEO DEL EMBUTIDO

Next, bite off a hunk of sausage history in the village of Castellfollit de la Roca, a 20-minute drive north of Santa Pau (in the northern part of the volcanic zone). For more than 20 years, this pint-sized museum, based on the premises of local cured meat experts J Sala Riera, has been laying bare the mysteries of medieval sausage-making, with displays of stuffing tools from across the centuries, photographs of workers in the company's 150-year history, and opportunities to sample various meaty treats at the end.

The village, perched precariously on a basalt cliff, also offers spectacular views of the surrounding region. *Tel +34 972 29 44 63; Carretera de Girona 10, Castellfollit de la Roca*

06 LES COLS

Take the road back into Olot, a 15-minute drive, but detour to Les Cols before you reach the centre. Fina Puigdevall, the chef at this revered slow-food restaurant, is something of a culinary poet.

Fina aims to express the richness of the surrounding scenery through the finest produce grown in the volcanic soil, especially mushrooms, nuts, and root vegetables.

Without exception, the results are inventive and delicious, such as Catalan classics *calçots* that are served tempura-style. Robust vegetable flavours, a calling card of *cuina volcànica*, come through in ice creams flavoured with pumpkin, while Garrotxa's very own black truffles

add smokiness to cheeses and game. Finish with ratafia, a herbal liqueur made from macerated green nuts, another iconic product of Garrotxa's volcanic soil. *www.lescols.com; tel +34 972 26 92 09; Carretera de la Canya, Olot; 1-3.30pm & 8.30-10.30pm Wed-Sat, 1-3.30pm Tue & Sun*

07 LA CÚRIA REIAL

Bid goodbye to *cuina volcànica* in style by stopping in picturesque Besalú, en route back to your Barcelona starting point.

Restaurant La Cúria Reial is as extraordinary for its views as its food: it overlooks the fortified bridge, an emblem of this medieval town. Savour mushroom-strewn terrines and expertly cooked game, finished off with jasmine-crowned melon soup. *www.curiareial.com; tel +34 972 59 02 63; Plaça Libertat 8-9, Besalú; 1-3.30pm & 8.30-10.30pm Wed-Mon*

08 ROCAMBOLESC

Head south from Besalú for your final stop, Girona. On the outskirts of this romantic city, the culinary legends at El Celler de Can Roca stir up sensational Catalan cuisine – the only snag is the 11-month waiting list.

More accessible to casual gourmands is Rocambolesc, on the left bank of the Onyar in central Girona. This is the dessert-focused brainchild of Jordi Roca, one of the three brothers behind three-Michelin-star El Celler. Jordi dreamed of a dessert trolley trundling around Girona, but when the practicalities proved bothersome, he established this ice cream place instead.

This dessert experience feels both sophisticated and gleefully childlike. Ice cream flavours include chocolate dark enough to blot out the sun, zesty strawberry, and violet, with up to 35 toppings to adorn each cloud-like serving.

Find space in your luggage for Rocambolesc's jars of sweets or a box of absurdly tall cupcakes, which tower with frosting, French-style *macarons* and chocolate baubles. *www.rocambolesc.com; tel +34 972 41 66 67; Carrer de Santa Clara 50, Girona; noon-9pm Sun-Thu, to 11pm Fri & Sat*

Ø5 Riverside scene, Girona

WHERE TO STAY
MIL ESTRELLES
Dream deeply in a historic farmhouse, stargaze through the ceiling of a clear plastic bubble-room, or luxuriate in a floatarium at this enchanting couples-only retreat, 20km northwest of Girona. *www.milestrelles.com; tel +34 972 59 67 07; La Bastida Borgonyà*

HOTEL LA PERLA
Bed down in the volcanic heart of Garrotxa at this cosy hotel in Olot. From kid-friendly playrooms to local ingredients sizzled lovingly in the restaurant, this simple place extends a warm welcome to guests. *www.laperlahotels.com; tel +33 972 26 23 26; Carretera la Deu 9, Olot*

WHAT TO DO
FLYING OVER GARROTXA
Garrotxa's tempestuous scenery is easy to enjoy on rambles and cycle rides. For a truly staggering panorama, take to the air on a hot-air balloon. Vol de Coloms in Olot leads 90-minute joy-flights over the hills, including a glass of bubbly to steady your nerves. (www.voldecoloms.cat)

MUSEU D'ART, GIRONA
Easy-to-ramble Girona, with almost every medieval laneway crammed with historic sights and galleries, is a bona fide banquet of cultural attractions. One of the most memorable is the Museu d'Art, with its extensive range of regional art from Romanesque sculpture to Modernism, via vast Gothic oil paintings. (www.museuart.com)

CELEBRATIONS
MERCAT DEL RAM
The streets surrounding vast Plaça Major in Vic are overrun with farm-fresh produce at Easter time in the run-up to Palm Sunday. Farmers haul their cheeses down from the Pyrenees, home-bottled liqueurs are laid out, and there'll be no shortage of *llonganissa* sausage. Look out for horse-riding displays, cattle shows and a host of other events exhibiting rural life in Catalonia. (www.vicfires.cat)

Spain

PINTXOS AND MICHELIN STARS IN SAN SEBASTIÁN

Gastronomic superstardom comes as second nature to the people of Spain's northern Basque Country, where even the local tapas – known as pintxos – are like art on a plate.

There may be bigger and better-known culinary hotspots, but few cities are as food crazy as San Sebastián (known as Donostia in the Basque language). Set on an idyllic bay in the Basque Country of northeastern Spain, this gracious belle époque resort is a food-lover's dream date, offering everything from multi-Michelin-starred restaurants to magnificent *pintxos* (Basque tapas) and stunning seafood.

The city has long been a bastion of Basque culture, and its vibrant food scene reflects that. Culinary traditions, safeguarded by the city's unique gastronomic societies, are deeply entrenched even as they're being updated for the 21st century. The *nueva cocina vasca* (New Basque cuisine) movement emerged here in the late 1970s, and today the city's trail-blazing chefs continue to innovate and push boundaries. As a result, San Sebastián and

01 Justin Foakes © Lonely Planet

NEED TO KNOW
San Sebastián's Parte Vieja is best enjoyed on foot; this 2–3 day trail is perfect for non-drivers.

its environs boast four of the world's top 20 restaurants and more Michelin stars per capita than almost anywhere else on earth.

But eating well here is not all about multi-course tasting menus and haute cuisine. One of the city's quintessential experiences is bar crawling around the Parte Vieja, filling up on *pintxos*. These magnificent one-plate wonders are a central feature of the city's culinary landscape and are enjoyed as much by socialising locals as visiting tourists.

Fuelling San Sebastián's insatiable appetite for fine food is a ready supply of fresh ingredients. From the sea come *antxoas* (anchovies), *merluza* (hake) and *bacalao* (salted cod), a mainstay since it was introduced by Basque fishermen in the 15th century. Inland, verdant hills provide lush grazing ground for livestock – *txuleta* steak is a prized Basque speciality – and a rich assortment of seasonal fruit and veg.

01 BOTANIKA

Before embarking on your culinary adventures, treat yourself to breakfast at this laid-back cafe. Housed in a residential block by the river, it's a popular spot with a leafy courtyard and a sunny, art-filled interior. The cafe specialises in vegetarian food and has many local fans.

If you don't make it for breakfast, come late afternoon when everyone from parents with toddlers to laptop-wielding students and gossiping shoppers stops by for a coffee or glass of something stronger.
Tel +34 943 44 34 75; Paseo de Arból de Guernica 8; 9am-11pm Mon-Thu, to midnight Fri & Sat, 10am-10pm Sun

02 MERCADO DE LA BRETXA

After breakfast follow the river down to the Parte Vieja, and, on its eastern side, the Mercado de la Bretxa. The market, which is centred on a small, neo-classical shopping mall, is serious foodie territory and many local chefs come here to stock up on their daily provisions.

Outside, farmers' stalls are laden with brightly coloured regional produce: tomatoes from neighbouring Getaria, black Tolosa beans, *guindilla* peppers from Ibarra, *idiazábal* cheese. Inside, in the basement of the main building, local fishmongers put on an impressive display with trays full of monkfish, Aguinaga *elvers* (eels), hake and, of course, the omnipresent *bacalao*.

Also in the basement you'll find richly stocked butchers' stalls adorned with hanging *jamon* (ham) and strings of Basque *chistorras* (cured sausages). *Alameda del Boulevard*

03 SAN SEBASTIÁN FOOD

For a memorable introduction to the local cuisine, sign up for a class at San Sebastián Food's gleaming cooking school. One of the most popular courses, and one of several to include a guided market visit, is the Pintxo Masterclass. Led by expert Basque chefs, this hands-on session covers the tricks and techniques behind some of the city's trademark *pintxos* (tapas), including the legendary 'Gilda'. This spicy combination of anchovies, manzanilla olives, and *guindilla* peppers was created in 1946 at the Bar Casa Vallés and named after the Rita Heyworth film, which was a big hit at the time and one of the few 'hot' movies to have survived Franco's censorship. The cooking school is a short walk south of Bretxa market. *www.sansebastianfood.com; tel +34 943 42 11 43; Hotel Maria Cristina, Paseo de la República Argentina 4*

04 LA CUCHARA DE SAN TELMO

For a rousing finale to your day, head to the Parte Vieja for a pintxos bar crawl. One of the joys of eating in San Sebastián is that you don't have to

01 A handful of pintxos

02 Bodegón Alejandro

03 Sublime
cheesecake,
La Viña

04 Artful pintxos,
San Sebastián

dine at a Michelin-starred restaurant to sample superb contemporary cuisine. If you know where to go, you can tuck into innovative high-end food for no more than the price of a drink. Take this place. A small, unfussy bar that serves superb cooked-to-order *pintxos*.

Dishes such as *carrillera de Ternera al vino tinto* (calf's cheeks braised in red wine) and *foie salteado con compota de manzana* (foie gras with apple compote) are mini-masterpieces of modern Basque cooking with superb ingredients and sumptuous flavours. *www.lacucharadesantelmo.com; Calle de 31 de Agosto 28; 7.30-11pm Tue, noon-3.30pm & 7.30-11pm Wed-Sun*

05 LA VIÑA

Ask a local and they'll tell you that the art to a successful bar crawl is to have one, maximum two, *pintxos* at any one place. Most bars have their own speciality and that's the one to

go for. Just down the road from La Cuchara, La Viña is a traditional wood-clad bar that's been in the same family since it opened in 1959. It serves excellent seafood *pintxos* but its main claim to fame is its celebrated *tarta de queso* (cheesecake).

Every morning batches of this wobbly, caramel-coloured delicacy are cooked and left to cool in baking tins strewn across the bar. The recipe is a jealously guarded secret but whatever they make them with, the resulting cakes are sublime: light, creamy, and sweet without ever being too cloying.

The *tarta* will round off your day nicely but, quite frankly, it's pretty fabulous any time. *www.lavinarestaurante.com; tel +34 943 42 74 95; Calle de 31 de Agosto 3; 10.30am-5pm & 6.30pm-midnight*

06 BODEGÓN ALEJANDRO

The next day, head back in the Parte Vieja for a sit-down lunch affair at this casual, much-lauded restaurant. Bodegón Alejandro is part of local food history: it was here that the triple Michelin-starred chef Martin Berasategui got his first taste of kitchen life, working alongside his mum and aunt in what was then his parents' restaurant.

Nowadays, it's one of several eateries managed by Andoni Luis Aduriz, the superstar chef-patron of Mugaritz, the world's sixth best restaurant. And while the menu here is more down to earth, chef Inaxio Valverde cooks a very popular line in Basque seafood with dishes such as cod with crab stew, squid in its own ink, and baked lobster. *www.bodegonalejandro.com; tel +34 943 42 71 58; Calle de Fermín Calbetón 4; 1-3.30pm Tue & Sun, 1-3.30pm & 8.30-10.30pm Wed-Sat*

03 © Lorna Parkes

04 © Lorna Parkes

07 SIDRERÍA PETRITEGI

The Basque Country has long been a centre of cider production (*txotx* in Basque). Records refer to it as far back as the 11th century, and it's said that in the 17th and 18th centuries Basque seafarers would take more cider than water on their ships in the hope that the vitamins it contained would stave off scurvy.

To test its medicinal properties for yourself, head to Sidrería Petritegi, a traditional cider house in the hills 5km southeast of San Sebastian. One of the few cider houses open year round – most fling their doors wide from January to April when the annual batch of cider is cracked open – it offers guided tours and tastings, as well as a classic cider-house menu of cod omelette, *bacalao* or hake, *txuleta* steak, and cheese with quince jelly and walnuts.

But the star of the show is the strong, still cider, which barmen skillfully squirt from huge barrels directly into your tankard. Be warned, though, it can get messy, and as

the cider flows, be prepared for the fact that your night might end in a drenching.
www.petritegi.com; tel +34 943 45 71 88; Petritegi Bidea 8, Astigarraga; 1-3.30pm & 8-10pm Fri-Sun, 8-10pm Mon-Thu

08 MAISOR

Some 25km west of San Sebastián, Getaria is a charming fishing village renowned for its seafood restaurants and *txakoli* wine. This sparkling white is produced in the nearby hills and, with its low alcohol content and crisp dry flavour, makes an ideal accompaniment for *pintxos*. But it's the sea that's the historical lifeblood of Getaria, and its fishing fleet continues to ply the cold Cantabrian waters trawling for turbot, mackerel, sea bream and sardines.

A local speciality are anchovies, salt-cured and preserved by hand at Maisor, a family-run canning outfit down at the harbour. Maisor is open for guided visits (during shop opening times but best on weekday mornings) and runs hands-on workshops (reservations required) where you

can learn all about the traditional techniques they use to salt, bone, and pack the fish.
maisor.com; tel +34 943 14 09 93; Edificio Astillero, Puerto 3, Getaria; shop 10.30am-2pm & 4-7pm Jun-Oct, see website for low-season hours

10 ELKANO

Round off your visit to Getaria with a meal at Elkano, a much-revered local institution. This superb seafood restaurant has been thrilling diners since 1964 and under its second-generation owner, Aitor Arregui, it recently earned its first Michelin star.

Unlike many of the area's starred eateries, it's kept things traditional and still specialises in seasonal fish prepared with disarming simplicity. Its signature dish, *rodaballo* (turbot), is cooked on an open-air charcoal grill, served whole. Another Basque classic to try is *kokotxas pil pil*, hake throats served in an emulsion of their own gelatin, with olive oil, parsley and garlic.
www.restauranteelkano.com; tel +34 943 14 00 24; C Herrerieta 2, Getaria; 1-3.30pm & 8-10.30pm Wed-Mon

ESSENTIAL INFORMATION

WHERE TO STAY

PENSIÓN AIDA
An excellent *pensión* over the river from the Parte Vieja. Rooms are bright and bold, full of exposed stone, and everything smells fresh and clean. The communal area, with sofas and mountains of information, is a further plus. *www.pensiones conencanto.com; tel +34 943 32 78 00; Calle de Iztueta 9*

PENSIÓN AMAIUR
The young, friendly owners of this old-town guesthouse have created something different, with a charming cottage-chic look, colourful wallpaper and bathrooms in Andalucían blues and whites. *www.pensionamaiur.com; tel +34 943 42 96 54; Calle de 31 de Agosto 44*

WHAT TO DO

PLAYA DE LA CONCHA
Curving around the bay, Playa de la Concha is one of Europe's finest city beaches. In summer, thousands take to its golden sands as crowds of locals, tourists and out-of-towners stroll along the beachfront promenade.

MONTE IGUELDO
Head to the summit of Monte Igueldo for inspiring views over the city's spectacular bay, coastline and surrounding mountains. The best way to get there is via the funicular to the Parque de Atracciones at the top. (www.monteigueldo.es)

SAN TELMO MUSEOA
Recently reopened after major renovation work, this museum is dedicated to Basque culture and society. Exhibits range from historical artefacts to modern art. (www.santelmomuseoa.com)

CELEBRATIONS
Summer events include the July Heineken Jazzaldia jazz festival, and Semana Grande – a week-long August jamboree culminating in a spectacular fireworks display. In September, Hollywood hotshots rock into town for the International Film Festival. The winter highlight is the Festividad de San Sebastián (20 January), an event featuring drummers in 19th-century military garb, ladies in traditional costume and men dressed as cooks.

Ø7 © Lorna Parkes

Ø7

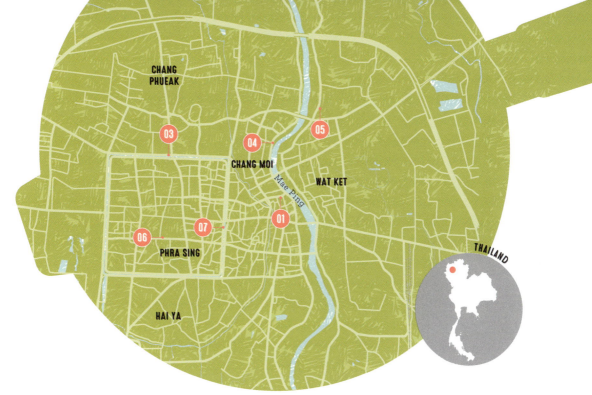

Thailand

NORTHERN TRIBAL ROOTS

Long before Siam became Thailand, Chiang Mai was the capital of a northern tribal kingdom with a distinct cuisine. Know where to look, and you can still find it there today.

Every year, millions of people flock to Thailand's jungles and beaches, unaware that the Thai kingdom is actually two nations squeezed into one. The Kingdom of Siam, which gave the world green curry, snooty felines and celebrity twins, is actually a central Thai creation, founded in Thonburi on the banks of Bangkok's Chao Phraya river.

The north was, until 1775, a completely separate entity, the homeland of the Lanna people, with their own language, culture, customs and, most importantly, cuisine.

The bulk of the dishes that people immediately think of as Thai – green curry, red curry, pad Thai – are actually from the central school, cooked up in the lowlands and transported north and south by Siamese empire-builders. In the process, many of Thailand's regional cuisines were cleansed from the national menu. But not all; around Chiang Mai, one-time capital of the Lanna kingdom, an ember of culinary pride still lingers, in rich chilli pastes and 'jungle' curries that recall Lanna's ancient origins as a tribal society in the rainforests of the north.

The foundation of Lanna cuisine is *nam prik*, actually a whole family of incendiary pastes made with pounded chillies. Some incarnations of this fiery flavour infuser are used as a dip; others are added to soups and stews for extra vitality. The second foundation stone of Lanna cooking is pork – a clear nod to Lanna's hill tribe origins – which crops up in everything from stir-fries and stews to *sai oua*, the northern Thai sausage. Three days following this trail in and around Chiang Mai will give you enough time to push back a few culinary boundaries and gain an understanding of this unique regional cuisine.

NEED TO KNOW
Chiang Mai is a 70-minute flight from Bangkok. Once there, you won't need a car for this 2-3 day trail.

01 TALAT WARAROT

For your first introduction to northern Thai cooking, rise early and join the crowds of eager shoppers at Talat Warorot, Chiang Mai's frenetic 'wet and dry' market, which is an easy walk east from the old city via Pratu Tha Phae city gate.

In the central atrium of this covered food market you'll find a maze of stalls selling the essential ingredients for northern Thai cooking. But ignore the piles of dried herbs, spices and fungi for the time being, and seek out the spicy roasting smells that will lead you to your real objective – *sai oua*, the famous spicy sausage of northern Thailand.

Rolled up like an English Cumberland on steroids, this pork delight is prepared with prime cuts of pork belly, to maximise flavour, and stuffed with lemongrass, galangal,

chillies and a generous helping of red curry paste, like a curry in a sausage skin. You'll find the city's best *sai oua* at a tiny stall called Dom Rong; just follow your nose, and the crowds of old ladies queuing up for their daily *sai oua* fix.
Thanon Chang Moi; 6am-5pm

02 TONG TEM TOH

After a busy morning in the rush and bustle of Talat Warorot, flag down a *rót daang* (red truck) and head to Thanon Nimmanhaemin, the posh part of town. This is not the most immediately obvious place to score authentic Northern Thai cuisine, but Tong Tem Toh sticks to its Lanna roots while surrounding restaurants serve every cuisine under the sun to tempt the tourist trade.

Set in a modest teak house with a garden terrace, this is where the

next generation break from classes at nearby Chiang Mai University to feast on home-style northern cooking.

Everything here is done well, but special commendation goes to the *kaeng hang lay*, a rich pork stew infused with flavours that flow across the border from Myanmar. Flavoursome pork belly cuts swim with peanuts and ginger shreds in a dense chestnut-coloured sauce made sweet and sour with tamarind paste.

After lunch, it's worth strolling south a few blocks to sample another Chiang Mai staple – a fruit smoothie from I-Berry (off Soi 17, Thanon Nimmanhaemin), the juice-bar owned by Thai comedian Udom Taepanich, made gloriously cool with scoops of homemade fruit sorbet.
Tel +66 53 894701; Soi 13, Thanon Nimmanhaemin; 11am-9pm

02 Tuui & Bruno Morandi © 4Corners

'Rolled up like a Cumberland on steroids, *sai oua* is stuffed with lemongrass, galangal, chillies and red curry paste'

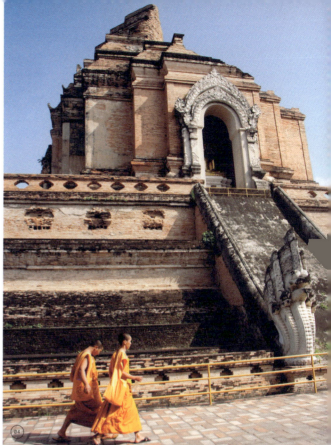

04 Julia Hiebaum © Alamy

03 Catherine Sutherland © Lonely Planet

05 Atid Kiattisaksiri © Getty Images

01 & 05 Celebrating Songkran festival

02 Wat Phra That Doi Suthep

03 Sai oua, a spicy sausage and regional food

04 Monks walk by Wat Chedi Luang

03 TALAT PRATU CHANG PHEUAK

As darkness falls, it's time to pay homage to the latest empire exerting its influence on the cuisine of Chiang Mai. Since the Northern Thai capital became the favourite destination for Chinese backpackers, the city's Thai-Chinese dining has gone from strength to strength, and the Talat Pratu Chang Pheuak night market – an easy stroll north from the Old City – is home to one of the finest dishes of them all.

Finding the best *kow kah moo* (slow-braised pork leg with rice) in Chiang Mai is easy. Just look for the 'Cowboy Lady' in her distinctive Stetson hat, and pull up a plastic chair in her corral. At this modest food stall, the whole family is set to work stewing a mountain of pork legs in a rich broth scented with Sichuan pepper, cinnamon, star anise and Golden Mountain Sauce – Thailand's favourite soy condiment.

Within seconds of sitting, a plate of tender pork will arrive at your table, layered over rice with steamed greens and pickled mustard leaves.
Thanon Mani Nopharat; 6pm-10pm

04 TALAT MUANG MAI

After the rich flavours of the preceding day, start the morning with a palate cleanser. Thanks to the Royal Project, founded in 1969 to give hill tribe farmers an alternative crop to opium, Chiang Mai is the fruit basket of Thailand. The cream of the crop is delivered fresh to the waterfront every morning at Talat Muang Mai, the city's bustling fruit market.

Here you'll find every fruit under the tropical sun: lychees as fat as duck eggs, mountains of pineapples, mangoes and pungent durians, candy-red rose apples, and some of the sweetest mangosteens, passion fruit and rambutans in Asia. Look out for stranger delights such as other-worldly dragonfruit and *salak* – a curious fig-like fruit covered in scaly snakeskin.
Thanon Praisani; open 24hr

05 KHAO SOI LAM DUAN FAH HAM

For lunch, leave the comforts of the old city behind and take a *rót daang* to Thanon Charoenrat on the east bank of the Mae Ping river, a residential enclave that is renowned for serving the best *kôw soy* in the city. What is *kôw soy*? Only the most famous Northern Thai dish of them all! This lip-smacking blend of coconut milk, chilli, turmeric, Thai seasonings and both soft and crispy fried egg noodles is the perfect representation of Chiang Mai's position at the crossroads between north and south Thailand and the more restrained seasonings of mainland China.

Your destination for a lunch to remember is an anonymous-looking family-run canteen by the road side. The 'Khao Soi Lam Duan Fah Ham' sign is easy to miss, so look instead for the lunchtime queues, then grab any seat you can find and order the house *kôw soy*. It's rich, aromatic and full of flavour, served with a side of picked vegetables, creating a delightful mixture of flavours and textures on the palate. And it's cheap; so cheap, you'd be forgiven for ordering a second bowl, and maybe even a third.
352/22 Thanon Charoenrat; 9am-4pm

06 HUEN PHEN

You'll have time for a bit of *wat-*hopping before supper, so make the most of it at Wat Chedi Luang, the most atmospheric of the city's many monasteries. By serendipity, you are now just a couple of blocks from Huen Phen, one of the best places in town for a full-on Northern Thai feast. By day, this is a low-key canteen, but at night the antique-filled dining room behind creates a surprisingly romantic setting for some of Chiang Mai's best Northern Thai cooking.

This is a place to order a bit of everything, from highly spiced jungle curries – prepared with plenty of curry paste, but no coconut milk – to neat bundles of rice steamed with spiced pigs' blood. One must-try is *nam prik ong*, a northern-style curry paste with ground pork, dried chillies and tomato, served as a dip for a platter of local vegetables. The texture is a little like bolognese; the flavour is like a torpedo exploding in a spice market.
Tel +66 53 277103; 112 Thanon Ratchamnkha; 8am-3pm & 5-10pm

07 CHIANG MAI THAI COOKERY SCHOOL

Before leaving Chiang Mai, it makes sense to gain a little northern cooking know-how. Chiang Mai is Thailand's cooking course capital, and while most courses focus on central Thai standards, the masterclasses run by celebrity chef Sompon Nabnian offer a chance to delve deeper in the cooking traditions of the north. Classes run from 4pm to 8pm and the menu includes northern staples such as *nam prik ong* and *kaeng hang lay*.
www.thaicookeryschool.com; tel +66 53 206388; 47/2 Th Moon Muang

06 Lanna-run stall at Talat Pratu Chang Pheuak night market

07 Durian fruit on a market stall

08 Umbrella maker, Chiang Mai

WHERE TO STAY

AWANA HOUSE
Small, cosy and great for families, Awana scores highly for its friendly service, perky decor (check out the wall murals), swimming pool and perfect location close to the Pratu Tha Phae city gate. *www.awanahouse.com; tel +66 53 419005; 7 Soi 1, Thanon Ratchadamnoen*

MO ROOMS
Eccentric and arty, Mo Rooms offers truly imaginative spaces, themed around the Chinese zodiac by different Thai artists. *www.morooms.com; tel +66 53 280789; 263/1-2 Thanon Tha Phae*

ANANTARA RESORT & SPA
Resorts don't come much swankier than the Anantara, a design-magazine vision of natural hardwoods enveloping the teak mansion that used to house the British consulate, with fine-dining in two elegant restaurants, set in a Zen-inspired garden. *chiang-mai.anantara. com; tel +66 53 253333; 123 Th Charoen Prathet*

WHAT TO DO

Chiang Mai is famed for its monasteries, called *wats*, which stud every other block inside the ruined medieval city walls. Some, like Wat Chedi Luang and Wat Phra Singh, are national treasures dripping with gold. Others are delicate jewel boxes, inlaid with intricate mosaics and crowned by gilded timbers that morph into writhing naga serpents. Perhaps the definitive Chiang Mai monastery experience is the pilgrimage to Wat Phra That Doi Suthep, with a perfect stupa crowning the sacred mountain to the east of the old city.

CELEBRATIONS

The Lanna people love to party, and at no time is this more apparent than at Songkran in April, when every man, woman and child in Chiang Mai grabs a hosepipe or water-pistol, drenching passers-by in water to mark the coming of the Northern Thai New Year. There's no excuse for not taking part, so throw on some old clothes, leave your water-sensitive tech in the hotel and, well, dive in.

01

Turkey

ISTANBUL'S KEBAP TRAIL

Think kebab is just kebab? Think again. In Turkey's most atmospheric city this beloved daily staple runs the gamut from spicy meatballs to grilled offal, bridging divides across the city.

It may not be the modern capital, but few would dispute İstanbul's claim to be Turkey's major city. A magical place where East (Asia) meets West (Europe) and where tradition effortlessly coexists with modernity, İstanbul has a cuisine that is as rich as the city's history and as diverse as its heritage (and that's really saying something). Within this cuisine, one dish reigns supreme: the kebap.

It's hard to overstate the local passion for skewers of grilled meat. Served in homes, from street stalls and food stands, in traditional *kebapçıs* (kebap joints) and in upmarket *restorans* (restaurants), kebaps are a daily staple for many and a lasting passion for most. There are innumerable versions but the most popular are the *şiş kebap* (small pieces of lamb grilled on a skewer), döner kebap (wafer-thin slices of lamb cooked on a revolving upright skewer and often served

stuffed in a bread roll with salad); *şiş köfte* (meatballs wrapped around a flat skewer and grilled); and the decadently rich *İskender* (Bursa) kebap (döner served on crumbled pide bread, topped with yoghurt and served with tomato and butter sauces).

This kebap trail starts in the Old City's Bazaar District and kicks on to Beyoğlu across the Golden Horn on its second day, visiting traditional produce markets, popular shopping strips, food stands, *kebapçıs* and *ocakbaşıs* (kebap restaurants where the meat is cooked in front of diners on long hearths covered by a copper hood). The simple eateries in the Bazaar District largely cater to the shopkeepers, artisans and porters who ply their traditional trades around the Grand Bazaar, and like the bazaar they are only open from Monday to Saturday. You'll find these Beyoğlu traders open on Sundays.

NEED TO KNOW
This 2-day trail is city-based and focuses on İstanbul's tourist-friendly districts: use public transport.

02

01 SPICE MARKET (MISIR ÇARŞISI)

Vividly coloured spices sourced from every corner of the globe are displayed alongside piles of jewel-like *lokum* (Turkish Delight), glistening sun-dried apricots and freshly roasted nuts at Turkey's most famous produce market. Head here in the morning when local housewives visit their favourite merchants to stock up on pantry essentials and trade good-humoured repartee – later in the day tour groups predominate and the shopkeepers can be harried. *www.misircarsisi.org; Eminönü; 8am-7.30pm daily*

02 HASIRCILAR CADDESİ

After stocking up on spices, dried fruits and local gossip, you'll almost inevitably exit the western gate of the market and plunge into the mercantile mayhem of Hasırcılar Caddesi. This is sacrosanct turf for

İstanbullus, a narrow, Ottoman-era laneway crammed with shops, cheap eateries, artisans' workshops and one of the city's most exquisite mosques, the Rüstem Paşa Camii.

Popular purchases include freshly roasted coffee beans from Kurukahveci Mehmet Efendi, pressed beef preserved in garlic and spices from Namlı Delicatessen and the city's best baklava from Develi – there are a few tables in the latter for mid-morning pastries and glass of tea. Other stores sell everything from kebap skewers to *isot biberi* (dried pepper), which is used in many meat dishes. *9am-5pm Mon-Sat*

'There aren't many dishes as polarising as liver. Turkish enthusiasts love to eat the pungent offal grilled, fried or even raw'

03 KILIÇÇLAR CADDESİ

Leaving the Spice Bazaar precinct, continue up atmospheric Mahmutpaşa Yokuşu, a winding street crammed with shoppers, street vendors and heavily laden porters. Hundreds of these porters carry heavy *fardels* (bundles) on their backs, navigating the narrow laneways of the bazaar district to deliver goods from warehouses and workshops to shops. This is hard work that builds big appetites, and the porters all have their favourite eateries in the district, most of which specialise in kebaps.

Head to Kılıççlar Caddesi – a street behind the Nuruosmaniye Mosque

02 © Virginia Maxwell

01 Istanbul's
Süleymaniye Mosque

02 Boza drinks lined
up on the counter,
Vefa Bozacısı

03 Butcher shop
in Kadınlar Pazarı
(Women's Market)

04 Man sitting inside
Rüstem Paşha Mosque

to find popular foodstands offering döner kebap, *dürüm* kebap (succulent grilled meat rolled in thin *lavaş* bread) and *kokoreç* (seasoned lamb intestines stuffed with offal, grilled on a skewer and served in bread).
Lunchtimes Mon-Sat

04 GAZIENTEP BURÇ OCAKBAŞI

From Kılıççlar Caddesi, follow the crowds into İstanbul's famous Grand Bazaar (Kapalı Çarşı). There's plenty to purchase in this atmospheric Ottoman-era marketplace – most notably gold and silver jewellery, finely woven textiles and rugs of every description – but many locals head here to eat rather than shop. Lunchtimes can be chaotic, with hungry shopkeepers, workers and shoppers flocking to the food stands and eateries tucked into laneways and hidden in *hans* (caravanserais).

On one of those laneways is

popular Gazientep Burç Ocakbaşı, a simple place where the *usta* (master chef) expertly grills meats over coals. Regulars swear by his Adana kebap (a spicy version of *şiş köfte*), but all of the grilled meats here are delicious.
Parçacılar Sokak 12, off Yağlıkçılar Caddesi, Grand Bazaar; noon-4pm Mon-Sat

05 VEFA BOZACISI

After enjoying your simple lunch in or around the Grand Bazaar, make your way to the nearby Süleymaniye Camii, one of the city's most magnificent mosques. From its front plaza, follow narrow Ayşekadin Hamamı Sokak down into the residential Vefa neighbourhood, which is filled with pretty Ottoman-era timber houses that are slowly being restored to their original glory.

Occupying pride of place on

the district's main shopping strip is the bar Vefa Bozacısı, a city institution established in 1876 that has changed little in the ensuing century.

It specialises in *boza*, a viscous tonic made with water, sugar and fermented barley. Topped with dried chickpeas and a sprinkle of cinnamon, *boza* has a reputation for building strength and virility, so can be a handy pick-me-up after a busy morning spent exploring the bazaars.
www.vefa.com.tr; tel +90 212 519 4922; 66 Vefa Caddesi; 8am-midnight

06 KADINLAR PAZARI

Most visitors to İstanbul know about the Spice and Grand Bazaars, but few have heard of Zeyrek's Kadınlar Pazarı (Women's Market), a small shopping district nestled in the shadow of the Aqueduct of Valens.

This majestic stone aqueduct was commissioned by the Roman

03 © Virginia Maxwell

04 Mark Read © Lonely Planet

emperor of the same name in the 1st century AD and is one of the city's most prominent landmarks – cross the major thoroughfare of Atatürk Bulvarı, walk through the Fatih Anıt Park and continue under the aqueduct's arches to find the market.

Here, sheep and goat carcasses swing in the breeze in front of traditional butcher shops, ready to be transformed into kebap dinners by local residents.

Tubs of spices, sheep heads (popular in soup) and dried vegetables used to make dolmas (vegetables stuffed with rice and herbs and then baked in the oven) are other popular offerings.

Also on this street is one of the best meat restaurants in the Old City, Sıırt Şeref Büryan Kebap, which is known for its melt-in-your-mouth *büryan* (lamb slow-cooked in a pit). *İtfaiye Caddesi, Zeyrek; daily*

⑦ HAMDI RESTAURANT

Hamdi Arpacı is one of İstanbul's great success stories. Arriving in the metropolis from the small town of Birecik in Turkey's southeast, he set up a ramshackle kebap stand in the parking lot next to Eminönü's New Mosque in the late 1960s and slowly built a loyal customer base of local shopkeepers and tradespeople.

Over the years, these local customers were joined by people from across the city, lured by his tender, expertly spiced and grilled meats. Today, Arpacı presides over three restaurants, the best known of which is located next to the Spice Market, where your day kicked off.

As well as a menu filled with every possible style of kebap, the restaurant offers panoramas of the Old City and Beyoğlu skylines from its top-floor dining space; book in advance to score a terrace dinner

table with a dress-circle view. *www.hamdi.com.tr; tel +90 212 444 6463; Kalçın Sokak 11, Eminönü; noon–11pm daily*

⑧ BALIK PAZARI

Sundays are quiet in many of the Old City's neighbourhoods, so it makes sense to spend the second day of your kebap trail across the Galata Bridge in Beyoğlu, a high-octane shopping and entertainment district that is often referred to as 'the modern city'. Its main thoroughfare, the 1.4km-long pedestrianised İstiklal Caddesi, is popular for both promenading and shopping and is frantically busy every day of the week.

At its heart is the Balık Pazarı (Fish Market), a 19th-century structure incorporating two handsome shopping arcades as well as an open-air laneway where fresh produce is sold. Food stands near the entrance offer *kokoreç* and freshly fried *midye tava* (skewered mussels), and the alluring produce stands and stores are crammed with fresh fish, cheese, caviar, fruit, bread, vegetables, pickles and sweets.

Şahne Sokak, off İstiklal Caddesi, Beyoğlu; daily from 8am

09 ASMALI CANIM CİĞERİM

There aren't many dishes as polarising as liver. Enthusiasts (many of whom seem to live in Turkey) love to eat the pungent offal grilled, fried or even raw; the rest of us can't think of anything less appetising. If you're a liver-lover, you'll want to head to this Beyoğlu institution near the Tünel end of İstiklal Caddesi, a short walk from the Balık Pazarı.

Here, cubes of fresh liver are grilled on skewers and wrapped in hot *lavaş* bread with your choice of sumac-dusted onion, rocket (arugula), spicy *ezme* (tomato paste) and herbs. Food is enjoyed with an *ayran* (salted yoghurt drink) – the traditional accompaniment to any kebap meal and one of the city's signature snacks.

Tel +90 212 252 6060; Minare Sokak 1, Asmalımescit, Beyoğlu; noon-midnight

10 ZÜBEYIR OCAKBAŞI

There are thousands of kebap restaurants in İstanbul, but few are as beloved as Zübeyir. A huge, perennially packed place spread over two floors, it features two *ocakbaşıs* on which simply sensational chicken wings, lamb chops and kebaps sizzle.

To garner a true appreciation of the kebap-master's art, request a seat near the *ocakbaşı* so you can watch the meats being prepared and then expertly grilled over coals – it will be a fitting finale to your trail.

www.zubeyirocakbasi.com.tr; tel +90 212 293 3951; Bekar Sokak 28, Beyoğlu; noon-midnight daily

Ø5 Teahouse inside the Grand Bazaar

WHERE TO STAY

HOTEL IBRAHIM PASHA

An exemplary boutique hotel, this Old City offering has stylish rooms and welcoming communal areas including a lounge with fireplace and a rooftop terrace bar with views of the Blue Mosque. *www.ibrahimpasha. com; tel +90 212 518 0394; Terzihane Sokak 7, Sultanahmet*

10 KARAKÖY

This recently opened İstanbul outpost of the mega-glam Morgans portfolio of boutique hotels is on the Beyoğlu side of the Galata Bridge. It offers well-appointed rooms, a stunning foyer lounge and an impressive restaurant. *www.morganshotelgroup. com/originals/10-karakoy; tel +90 212 703 3333; Kemeraltı Caddesi 10, Karaköy*

WHAT TO DO

SÜLEYMANIYE MOSQUE

This 16th-century imperial mosque near the Grand Bazaar was commissioned by Süleyman I, known as 'The Magnificent', and it certainly lives up to its patron's name. Don't miss the rear garden terrace with its Golden Horn view, or the tombs of Süleyman and his adored wife Roxelana in the cemetery. (Professor Sıddık Sami Onar Caddesi; sunrise to sunset)

RÜSTEM PAŞA MOSQUE

Hidden on an elevated platform above the Hasırcılar Caddesi shopping strip, this diminutive mosque dates from 1560 and was commissioned by Rüstem Paşa, son-in-law and grand vizier of Süleyman the Magnificent. A showpiece of the best Ottoman architecture, it is clad inside and out with exquisite İznik tiles.

CELEBRATIONS

Food is an important part of the holy month of Ramazan (Ramadan). After fasting from sunrise to sunset, devout Muslims break their fast at often-eleborate *iftar* meals. Some Old City restaurants offer special *iftar* menus that non-Muslims are welcome to sample, and the three day Şeker (Sugar) Bayramı festival celebrating the end of Ramazan involves the copious consumption of sweet treats such as baklava.

USA

EXPLORE NEW YORK'S JEWISH CUISINE

Brought to the Big Apple by Eastern European Jews, what was once a cuisine for poor Lower East Side immigrants has been revitalised by a new generation of New York chefs.

In typical New York fashion, locals often describe their home town as the centre of the universe. Hubristic? Maybe. But a visit to this metropolitan melting pot is always epic, thanks to the nearly 8.5 million diverse people who live, create and dine exceptionally here. When it comes to food, the city offers no shortage of adventures, but New Yorkers reserve a special place in their hearts for the briny, creamy, tangy, crisp and soul-satisfying flavours of the city's Jewish cuisine.

Between 1880 and 1920, more than a million Eastern European Jews immigrated to New York's Lower East Side – a staggering addition to an already overcrowded neighbourhood. Impoverished though they were, generations of Jewish mamas toiling in dilapidated tenement kitchens turned out schmaltz-glistening staples while urging their children to '*esn, esn!*' ('eat, eat!'). On the streets, a clamouring riot of pushcarts

NEED TO KNOW
This 2-day trail homes in on Lower East Side, the Union Square area and Brooklyn: walk and take the G train.

peddled pickles, bagels and loaves of impossibly dark rye bread. And local Jewish butchers and fishmongers helped to introduce the joys of smoked meat and cured fish to the city.

Over the decades the community spread, leaving a trail of iconic eateries in its wake – delicatessens such as 2nd Avenue and Carnegie, smoked fish legends Barney Greengrass and Zabar's, and minuscule knish bakery Yonah Schimmel's.

In recent years, a new crop of young Jewish restaurateurs has taken up the reins. Equally inspired by their culinary heritage and the global food scene, they are revitalising timeworn Jewish classics for a new generation. From their commitment to craftsmanship and sourcing quality ingredients to their whimsical remixing of flavours – think challah bread pudding and smoked meat-topped eggs benedict – their food exemplifies the reverential-yet-playful approach that makes 'eating Jewish' in New York so exciting.

01 Olimpio Fantuz © 4Corners

① RUSS & DAUGHTERS

Start the morning the traditional Jewish way: with bagels and lox. Down on Houston Street, the Russ family has been slinging smoked and cured fish since 1914. New York theatre legends like Zero Mostel and Molly Picon were once regulars, nudging past the throngs of customers to the fish counter for a bagel topped with paper-thin slices of belly lox (salmon cured with salt) and a slick of cream cheese.

Today, fourth-generation owners Joshua Russ Tupper and Niki Russ Federman are bringing their family's Smithsonian-knighted heritage into the 21st century. Take a chance on the cheekily named 'Super Heebster' bagel, topped with whitefish and baked salmon salad, a constellation of tiny, wasabi-infused fish roe and horseradish dill cream cheese. Prefer to eat your fish sitting down? Head around the corner to the recently opened Russ & Daughters Café on Orchard St, which serves all the fixings plus first-rate *latkes* (crispy fried grated potato pancakes). *russanddaughters.com; tel +1 212 475 4880; 179 E Houston St; 8-8pm, to 7pm Sat, 5.30pm Sun*

② KATZ'S DELICATESSEN

Noodle around the Lower East Side's vintage clothing stores and art galleries, then walk back to Houston to squelch it mightily with a pastrami sandwich from this landmark delicatessen. There's nothing contemporary about Katz's vintage neon signage, cash only policy or 128-year old process of curing and smoking meat – it takes pride in doing things the old fashioned way. But the amply stuffed sandwiches are too heavenly to miss.

Remember the sultry 'I'll have what she's having' scene from the 1989 romantic comedy *When Harry Met Sally*? It was filmed at Katz's. *katzsdelicatessen.com; tel +1 212 254 2246; 205 E Houston St; 8am-10.45pm Mon-Wed, 8am-2.30am Thu, 8am-midnight Fri-Sat, 12am-10.30pm Sun*

③ BREADS BAKERY

Meander your way uptown to Union Square. When snack time hits, head directly to 16th Street. Opened by Israel-born baker Uri Scheft in 2013, Breads Bakery is already an institution. People flock here for multi-seeded challah (a braided, egg-enriched loaf of bread) and marzipan *rugelach* (a small, twisted pastry). But Scheft's *pièce de résistance* is his *babka* – a yeasted cake-bread hybrid that dates back to 19th-century Eastern Europe. Made with laminated dough and swirled with an innovative combination of Nutella and chocolate chips, Breads' version is a buttery revelation. *breadsbakery.com; tel +1 212 633 2253; 18 E 16th St; 6.30am-9pm Mon-Fri, to 8pm Sat, 7.30am-8pm Sun*

④ MILE END

Follow the gravitational pull of smoked meat to Brooklyn where, since 2010, Montreal natives Noah and Rae Bernamoff have served haute Eastern European fare with a Québécois accent.

Savour your morning coffee with cream cheese, tomato and capers on a sesame bagel from Black Seed Bagel (a noveau Jewish bakery also founded by Bernamoff). True to Montreal style, they are boiled in honey water and crisped in a wood-fired oven.

Pair that with a platter of smoked meat hash, which studs a sizzling jumble of potatoes and onions with generous cubes of brisket and a fried egg. The meat is inspired by 88-year-old Montreal-based Jewish delicatessen Schwartz's, but the dish is totally original. *mileenddeli.com; tel +1 718 852 7510; 97A Hoyt St, Brooklyn; brunch 8am-4pm Mon-Fri, 10am-4pm Sat-Sun, dinner 5pm-10pm Sun-Wed, 5pm-11pm Thu-Sat*

05 BROOKLYN FARMACY

Walk 20 minutes south and west past the brownstones and boutiques of Cobble Hill to this soda fountain store. Brooklyn Farmacy remains true to the revitalised 1920s-era apothecary shop in which it is housed – right down to the penny tile floors, vintage medicine cabinets and marble counter.

Sibling-owners Peter Freeman and Gia Giasullo serve handcrafted sundaes and floats, but the menu's true highlight is their egg cream, a frothy cocktail of milk, chocolate syrup and seltzer water first concocted by Jewish Lower East Side soda jerk Louis Auster in 1890. Brooklyn Farmacy's take on the Jewish elixir comes garnished with a pretzel rod – it's sweet-meets-salty perfection. *brooklynfarmacyandsodafountain. com; tel +1 718 522 6260; 513 Henry St, Brooklyn; 7.30am-10pm Mon-Thu, to 11pm Fri, 10am-11pm Sat, 10am-10pm Sun*

06 PECK'S HOMEMADE

Take the G train four stops to this artisanal food shop in Brooklyn's Clinton Hill. Owner Theo Peck has serious culinary *yichus* (pedigree): his great grandfather founded Ratner's, a famous kosher dairy restaurant that served the Lower East Side for 97 years.

Peck, who opened his store in 2013, keeps this heritage close to heart, peppering the menu with updated Jewish classics. Snag a backyard table and slurp a bowl of richly flavoured matzo-ball soup dressed up with tender bites of chicken confit. Finish the meal with a couple of Peck's crisp-edged coconut macaroons. *peckshomemade.com; tel +1 347 689 4969; 455A Myrtle Ave, Brooklyn; 7.30am-9pm Mon-Fri, 8am-9pm Sat, 9am-7pm Sun*

01 View of Brooklyn Bridge from Dumbo, Brooklyn

02 Exterior of Katz Deli

03 Classic pastrami sandwich, Katz Deli

WHERE TO STAY

THE BOWERY HOTEL
Once known as NYC's downtrodden skid row, Bowery is now an avenue of downtown cool and this hotel fits right in. *www.theboweryhotel.com; +1 212 505 9100; 335 Bowery*

WYTHE HOTEL
History, location and a refined hipster aesthetic combine in this hotel, which is situated in a revamped, 1901 barrel-and-cask factory on the Brooklyn waterfront. *wythehotel.com; +1 718 460 8000; 80 Wythe Ave*

WHAT TO DO

Deep dive into the Lower East Side's vibrant past with a guided tour of the Tenement Museum (tenement.org), then take in the flora and incredible views on the High Line (thehighline.org), a 1.45-mile-long public park set on a disused railroad.

CELEBRATIONS

EGG ROLLS, EGG CREAMS & EMPANADAS FESTIVAL
The Lower East Side's Jewish, Chinese, and Puerto Rican cultures come together for this June block party. Celebrate with live klezmer music and sample the festival's namesake foods. (eldridgestreet.org)

GREEK JEWISH FESTIVAL
Kehila Kedosha Janina, an 89-year-old Jewish-Greek synagogue (the only one in the western hemisphere) hosts this May festival, with pastries, live music, dancing, and crafts. (kkjfestival.com)

03 Sivan Askayo © Lonely Planet

USA

CREOLE COOKING AND A CAJUN FAIS DO-DO

Louisiana is a sizzling cooking pot of immigrant and colonial influences, which manifest in New Orleans' local take on Creole cuisine, and in the bayous of nearby Cajun Country.

New Orleans is a city with deep international roots. Ornate balconies and wrap-around porches evoke the grand cities of Europe, while bright Creole cottages inspire thoughts of the Caribbean. Beyond New Orleans, southern Louisiana hugs the Mississippi as it twists past grassy levees and restored plantations. Then there's Cajun Country: a landscape soggy with lush waterways and marshy bayous where residents gather for crawfish boils and toe-tapping live music carried by fiddles, accordions and yelps.

The culinary scene's exuberant heritage can be traced back to the region's convivial Creole and Cajun settlers. Historically, Creoles were the locally born, city-dwelling descendants of two groups: Europeans, primarily from France and Spain, and African slaves – all arriving, generally, before the Louisiana Purchase in 1803 when the United States bought the land from France. Creole

cooking is marked by the use of sauces, herbs, fresh seafood and tomato-based dishes, with West African, Caribbean and Native American influences and local ingredients. Cajuns, on the other hand, are descendants of French refugees who fled Canada's maritime provinces, known as Acadie, after the British conquered the region in the 1700s. A contingent of Acadians settled in southern Louisiana and their simple 'country' food embraces seafood, meat and sausages, and one-pot meals.

The Mississippi River is the rough divide between the Creole cuisine of New Orleans and the Cajun dishes of the bayous and Louisiana prairie. In New Orleans, fourth- and fifth-generation locals gather at beloved Creole restaurants, many owned by the same families for decades. Rather than being trapped in the past, creative chefs are today energising the dining scene, adding gourmet and global twists to Cajun and Creole classics.

NEED TO KNOW
New Orleans has its own airport. This 3-day trail includes a day in Cajun Country, for which you'll need a car.

01 Jordan Banks © 4Corners

01 SOUTHERN FOOD & BEVERAGE MUSEUM

To kick off your southern food journey head to New Orleans' Southern Food & Beverage Museum in Central City, which charts the culinary heritage of the southern US states. In the mid-1800s, this spot housed the vibrant Dryades Market, a farmers' market that catered to African Americans and Jewish, German and Italian immigrants.

Highlights include artefacts from Antoine's – the oldest continuously operating restaurant in the US run by the same family – which opened in New Orleans in 1840, and a replica of the French Quarter's still-standing Old Absinthe House as it appeared in the 1890s.

At one time this potent green liquor, infamous for its alleged hallucinogenic properties, was so beloved by the fun-loving New Orleans locals that the city became the absinthe-drinking capital of the US.
natfab.org; tel +1 504 569 0405; 1504 Oretha C Haley Blvd; 11am-5.30pm Wed-Mon

02 DOOKY CHASE

For lunch head to Dooky Chase in the Tremé – New Orleans' oldest African American neighbourhood. In 2016 chef Leah Chase, who's still in the kitchen in her 90s, was given a lifetime achievement award by the US's prestigious James Beard Foundation, and her Creole food is the real deal: stuffed peppers, stuffed jalapenos and stuffed chicken, stews, jambalaya and oyster dressing.

This typical New Orleans cuisine has French and Spanish roots, as well as African influences, and derives primarily from urban settlers, white and black, and their descendants.

A community gathering spot in the Tremé since 1941, Dooky Chase has hosted civil-rights leaders and presidents. Hot sausages and fried chicken hold court at the robust lunch buffet in a dining room outfitted with colourful African American art.

Also on the menu is red beans and rice, a simple dish traditionally served across New Orleans on Mondays – laundry day for homemakers who were then too busy to cook.
www.dookychaserestaurant.com; tel +1 504 821 0600; 2301 Orleans Ave, Tremé; 11am-3pm Tue-Fri, 5-9pm Fri

03 PARKWAY BAKERY & TAVERN

Round off day one with a New Orleans classic: the po'boy. This messy sandwich of French bread – baked locally and slightly chewy – stuffed

'According to legend, lobsters followed the Acadians south when they fled Canada in the 1700s'

01 New Orleans' French Quarter

02 Louisiana sugarcane estate, Laura Plantation

03 Wood-fired oyster roast, Cochon Butcher

04 Dining on Freret Street

with roast beef, fried oysters or fried shrimp, was born during the Depression when two former streetcar workers opened a coffee and sandwich shop during a New Orleans streetcar transit strike. The two filled their bread with beef gravy and sliced potatoes and gave them free to strikers, and so a New Orleans food legend was born.

The best are dressed with mayonnaise, tomato, shredded lettuce and pickles. Today, Parkway Bakery & Tavern in Mid-City is famed for its roast beef po'boy; a gravied mess on a crusty bun. For dinner, squeeze into the vintage tavern and enjoy a cocktail with your meal, or order at the counter at the back and join a communal table. Napkins are an absolute necessity.
www.parkwaypoorboys.com; tel +1 504 482 3047; 538 Hagan Ave, Mid-City; 11am-10pm Wed-Mon

04 NEW ORLEANS SCHOOL OF COOKING

Start your second day at the popular New Orleans School of Cooking in the French Quarter for a lesson in Cajun and Creole cooking. Pre-book a hands-on class or join the daily Food, Fun & Folklore cooking demo – a 2½-hour session with a living-room feel, in which chefs entertain students with stories tied to regional and culinary history while preparing a meal of classic southern Louisiana fare. This is a great opportunity to see how locals prepare gumbo, a spicy, full-bodied stew served over steamed rice, typically overflowing with seafood, sausage or chicken. The stew's thick dark gravy is sometimes made with okra, a vegetable with a gummy pod brought to New Orleans by West African slaves. Jambalaya, a rice dish that resembles Spanish paella, is another class favourite. The demo finishes with a chance to eat the meal that you've just watched being cooked up.
www.neworleansschoolofcooking. com; +1 504 525 2665; 524 St Louis St, French Quarter

05 COCHON BUTCHER

Succulent slices of tender roast beef tumble from the bun. Fried eggs, messy cheeses and kicky sauces slather their way onto Instagram feeds. Yep, the sandwich is king at Chef Donald Link's rustically chic deli, butcher shop and wine bar in the Warehouse District. It's a simple but satisfying dinner after an afternoon wandering nearby museums.

House-made meats and sausages are the all-stars at the butcher shop, which sells Cajun favourites such as andouille sausage, a spicy smoked

pork sausage often found in gumbo, and tasso, a tasty cured pork used to flavour gumbo, jambalaya, and red beans and rice.
www.cochonbutcher.com; +1 504 588 7675; 930 Tchoupitoulas St, Warehouse District; Mon-Thu 10am-10pm, to 11pm Fri & Sat, to 4pm Sun

06 FRERET STREET

End the day with a trip to Freret St, where a clutch of hopping new restaurants, bars and music venues strut their stuff. Located in the University District in New Orleans' Uptown, it's a fun place to wander in the evening.

Named for 19th-century cotton baron William Freret, the street was a prosperous commercial strip in the 1920s and 1930s. White flight, violent crime and extensive Hurricane Katrina damage drove out these businesses, and 10 years ago the street was in a state of serious decay. In 2007, a few committed locals started the Freret St Market. Two years later, entrepreneurs Neal Bodenheimer and Matthew Kohnke opened a craft cocktail

bar, Cure (www.curenola.com), in a 100-year-old former fire station.

With Cure's success, development snowballed and today 19 new restaurants, bakeries and watering holes are open between Jefferson Ave and Napoleon Ave, making Freret St one of the city's biggest post-Katrina success stories.
www.thenewfreret.com; Freret St, Uptown, University District

07 LAURA PLANTATION

The next day, hit the road and head west into the southern Louisiana countryside, following the Mississippi upriver. In Vacherie, about 50 miles from New Orleans, you'll find Laura Plantation, a unique sugarcane estate established in 1805 and managed by four generations of Creole women (unlike many of its neighbours, which were Anglo-owned).

Today, tours explore the canary-bright Big House and the slave cabins, and explain how Louisiana sugarcane has historically been used to make products such as cane syrup and molasses. Depending on the season,

you may see sugarcane as it's planted, growing or harvested. Cane syrup and cane molasses are sold on-site.

To see how sugarcane is used to make rum, continue on to Donner-Peltier Distillery (www.dp-distillers.com) down the road in Thibodeaux. Its Rougaroux rum is named for a legendary swamp werewolf.
www.lauraplantation.com; tel +1 225 265 7690; 2247 Hwy 18, Vacherie; tours 10am-4pm

08 FRENCH PRESS

Take a road trip down bayou backroads to Lafayette, where breakfasts (served til 2pm) at French Press are a party on the plate – or as the Cajuns might call it, a *fais do-do*. Take the Sweet Baby Breesus, named for New Orleans Saints football quarterback Drew Brees: three buttermilk biscuits layered with Steen's cane syrup, bacon and fried boudin balls. Boudin is a popular Cajun sausage – often sold at mom-and-pop convenience stores – made from pork scraps, seasonings and rice stuffed into pig intestines.

Order this artery-clogging ensemble with an equally indulgent side of cheddar cheese grits (coarsely ground grains cooked with water and typically served as a side dish in the South). Distressed walls, exposed piping and decorative typeface pieces keep the restaurant, a former printing plant, invitingly shabby.
www.thefrenchpresslafayette.com; tel +1 337 233 9449; 214 E Vermilion St, Lafayette; 7am-2pm Mon-Fri, 9am-2pm Sat & Sun

09 BREAUX BRIDGE CRAWFISH BOIL

According to legend, lobsters followed the Acadians south when they fled Canada in the 1700s – shrinking during their long swim to Louisiana's bayous. Resembling tiny lobsters, crawfish, also called mudbugs, are served fresh-boiled or as pre-peeled tail meat. The latter is mixed into jambalaya or smothered in a stew-like gravy to make a local dish called étouffée.

Crawfish are popular in season from early December to mid-July. If you can, finangle an invitation to a crawfish boil; a community gathering where crawfish and Cajun seasonings are tossed into a giant pot and typically boiled with potatoes and other vegetables.

For the next best thing, drive 9 miles east from Lafayette to the Fruit Stand in Breaux Bridge – dubbed the Crawfish Capital of the World – for the commercial version of a crawfish boil. Eat your crawfish on-site or get a sack to go. How to eat 'em? As Cajuns say: 'Pinch de' tail and suck de' head.'
www.thefruitstandinc.com; tel +1 337 332 4636; The Fruit Stand, 200 W Mills Ave, Breaux Bridge; 11am-8pm

05 Louisiana crawfish boil

06 Sandwich, Cochon Butcher

WHERE TO STAY

LE PAVILLON
Smile at the man in the top hat then stride into this grand but never-too-serious hotel in the Central Business District. Ghost stories and a nightly spread of peanut butter and jelly sandwiches add to the fun.
www.lepavillon.com; tel +1 504 581 3111; 833 Poydras St, New Orleans;

BAYOU CABINS
Themed cabins draped with bright Christmas lights hug Bayou Teche in Breaux Bridge. After check-in, hosts Rocky and Lisa Sonnier share a platter of homemade boudin.
www.bayoucabins.com; tel +1 337 332 6158; 100 W Mills Ave, Breaux Bridge

WHAT TO DO

In New Orleans, hop the St Charles Avenue Streetcar from Canal St to explore the Warehouse District, home of the top-notch WWII Museum (www.nationalww2museum.org) and engaging Ogden Museum of Southern Art (www.ogdenmuseum.org). A longer ride travels through the lush Garden District. To experience live roots music and southern dancing, pay a visit to the Blue Moon Saloon (www.bluemoonpresents.com) in Lafayette.

CELEBRATIONS

With themed parades, wild costumes, a long-running history and a global reputation for excess, Mardi Gras season in New Orleans – stretching from January into February – is one for the bucket list (www.mardigrasneworleans.com). Food stalls are a highlight at Jazz Fest in late April (www.nojazzfest.com). The Po'boy Festival in November features po'boys from New Orleans' best restaurants (www.poboyfest.com). In May, head to Breaux Bridge to celebrate mudbugs at the Crawfish Festival (www.facebook.com/BreauxBridge CrawfishFestival).

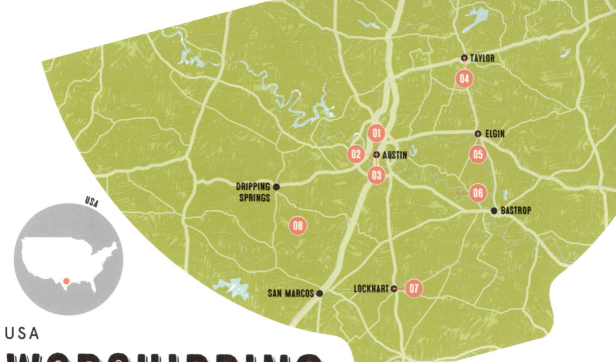

USA

WORSHIPPING THE TEXAS BBQ PIT

Simple smoking practices and family recipes have given barbecue a divine status in Central Texas, where huge slabs of meat are served the traditional way in rustic shacks.

Country is a way of life as much as a place. Even if most Texans now live in urban areas, they're influenced by the state's agriculture-rich, roping-and-riding heritage. Even in the hip state capital Austin, people still wear cowboy boots and jeans and eat barbecue while listening to live music. So let the screen door slam behind you, eat some 'Q and meet some locals. Folks 'round here are mighty friendly.

If Texas had a state religion, it would be BBQ. At last count – and yes, Texas counts these things – the Lone Star state had more than 4,200 barbecue outlets. Meats and methods vary regionally, but it's the simple smoking of Central Texas that is most revered. The meat market tradition here began in the late 1800s. German and Czech immigrants who opened groceries with butcher counters found not all the cuts sold. So they smoked the remaining bits or made sausages out of them.

When hungry itinerant farm workers came in and made a meal of the smoked meats – along with crackers and pickles from the store shelves – a legend was born.

Some of the oldest barbecue joints retain a rustic air. In Austin, a new era of pit masters attracts crowds willing to wait in line for as much as five hours. A few things are always true: barbecue means the meat is cooked low and slow – for as long as 14 hours. Seasoning means a dry rub (a salt-and-pepper mix with onion powder, garlic, chilli powder or other secret ingredients). If sauce is available, it will be on the side. Beef brisket, pork ribs and homemade sausage are the holy trinity of Central Texas 'Q. Lots of places still serve on butcher paper. Not all offer utensils – or alcohol (some places let you BYO beer). Side dishes are extremely simple. Note that Monday is a day of rest, when almost every place worth worshipping closes.

NEED TO KNOW
Hire a car at Austin-Bergstrom International Airport; all stops are within 50 miles of there.

01 WRIGHT BROS BREW & BREW

Austin's best locally crafted coffee and beer are on offer at this hip hangout, which is also the sole purveyor of award-winning Kerlin BBQ's *kolaches*. Imagine fluffy Czech-inspired rolls stuffed with tender, smoky brisket and cheddar cheese. Egg-and-pepper jack cheese, or spinach-and-goat's cheese varieties are also available.

But barbecue for breakfast, who can resist? We recommend coming early and taking yours, along with your brew of choice, to go so you can fortify yourself while waiting in line at the next stop, a half mile down the road. *www.thebrewandbrew.com; tel +1-512-493-0963; 500 San Marcos St, Austin; 8am-midnight*

02 FRANKLIN BARBECUE

The celebrity superstar of the barbecue scene, Aaron Franklin boasts a book, a TV series and a coveted James Beard award to his credit. A bevy of magazines and blogs have named this unassuming barbecue joint, which started as a food truck, best in the land. Expect impossibly juicy turkey and pulled pork, snappy sausage with a pepper kick and oh-so-tender brisket with a crispy bark of fat. If you're lucky, you'll get to sample some of the 'burnt ends' that get cut off.

Every day lines form hours ahead of opening. Expect to wait three to five hours (lunch-only served). Staff sell sodas and many patrons come prepared with coolers stocked for a little day-drinking. Sometimes

'Every day lines form hours ahead of opening. Staff sell sodas and many patrons come prepared with coolers for a little day-drinking'

an entrepreneur is on hand to rent camp chairs; best bring your own, it's a long wait. *www.franklinbarbecue.com; 900 E 11th St, Austin; 11am-sold out Tue-Sun*

03 FREEDMEN'S BAR

Spend the afternoon at the Bob Bullock State History Museum, learning about the immigrants who brought their BBQ techniques to Texas, until you feel peckish again. End your day at the historic 1869 Freedmen's Bar, which was once a general store owned by a former slave. The quirky antiques repurposed

02 Courtesy of Franklin Barbecue

01 Texas cowboys
on a ranch

02 & 04 Aaron
Franklin at the pit;
typical meat feast,
Franklin Barbecue

03 Barbecue served
on butcher paper,
Smitty's Market

into tables hark back to that era.

Set the mood with an Ol' Schmokey to drink: bourbon, orange, pecan-smoked bitters and oak smoke. The holy trinity of meats is stellar here, but Freedmen's offers an expansive array of smokehouse flavours. Barbecued pork belly or gargantuan beef ribs, anyone?

Among the sides, the smoked pickled jalapeños and grilled coleslaw stand out. And don't forget the smoked banana pudding for dessert. You can enjoy these eclectic offerings inside, or out at picnic tables in the beer garden.
www.freedmensbar.com; tel +1 512 220 0953; 2402 San Gabriel St, Austin; 11am-midnight Thu-Sat, 11am-10pm Sun, Tue & Wed

04 LOUIE MUELLER BARBECUE

The Mueller family barbecue dynasty began in 1949 when Louis opened his grocery store in small-town Taylor.

Gradually the place became all about the meat. Son Bobby took over until his death in 2008 and today grandson Wayne mans the pit. Granddaughter LeAnne and other grandson John own their own renowned BBQ trucks in Austin (La Barbecue and John Mueller Meat Company, respectively). However, the original is worth the drive 35 miles northeast of Austin.

Hear the slamming of the screen door and watch people filling glasses with sweet tea – you can easily imagine the place back in the day. Pains have been taken so that the dining room expansion blends seamlessly with the original smoky walls and exposed brick. No wonder the place has cameoed in several movies.

The brisket here is super moist, and the sauce... oh the sauce – it's thin, but meaty, almost jus-like

with peppery overtones and scant tomato taste.
www.louiemuellerbarbecue.com; tel +1-512-352-6206; 206 W 2nd St, Taylor; 11am-6pm Mon-Fri, 10am-6pm Sat

05 SOUTHSIDE MARKET

Among the oldest butcher shop/ barbecue joints in the region, Southside (1882) is also one of the few that still has a genuine market attached. After lunch in Taylor, drive the 16 miles south to do some shopping at this institution in Elgin.

Choose from the shelves filled with homemade seasoning rubs, hot and barbecue sauces and wood chips for the fire. Meat-wise, the Elgin outlet is best known for its 'hot guts' (a spicy sausage). If you live in the USA it's good news, as the sausage and brisket can be ordered for nationwide delivery for when you get back home. If not, grab the dried goods and

settle for a recipe T-shirt listing the essential ingredients for barbecue: 'Quality Meat, Dry Rub, Texas Post Oak, Time.'
www.southsidemarket.com; tel +1 512 281 4650; 1212 Hwy 290 E, Elgin; 8am-8pm Mon-Fri, to 9pm Sat, 9am-8pm Sun

06 SHELLERS BARRELHOUSE BAR

A further drive 18 miles south brings you to the picturesque Hill Country town of Bastrop. Here historic old homes compete with eclectic main-street boutiques for attention. A few miles outside town, Lost Pines Resort & Spa provides a rural escape — and a chance for more barbecue.

On-site Shellers Barrelhouse Bar evokes everything Texas with its cowhide-covered chairs and live country and western music on Friday and Saturday. Here you have the chance to try some of the Southside Market sausage you were eyeing earlier in the day. In a nod to tradition, it is served with sautéed peppers, smoked

mustard and German potato salad.
lostpines.hyatt.com; tel +1 512 308 1234; 575 Hyatt Lost Pines Rd, Lost Pines; 3pm-midnight Mon-Thu, 11am-1am Sat, 11am-midnight Sun

07 SMITTY'S MARKET

The state legislature has officially named Lockhart (30 miles southwest of Bastrop) the barbecue capital of Texas, with four smokehouses to its name. But for our taste, it's Smitty's Market that has the most soul.

Here the line snakes through the back door into the smoke-blackened, cave-like pit room where you order by the pound (or fraction thereof), not the plate. Emerging into the dining hall you pay (cash only) and queue again for drinks and sides before heading to communal tables. Sauce is available if you ask, but forks aren't.

Look for traditional cuts such as pork shoulder clod on the menu. Back in the 1990s, a now-resolved family feud resulted in a split: the owning family's daughter retained this building and her brothers relocated the original business,

Kreuz Market, across town.
www.smittysmarket.com; tel +1 512 398 9344; 208 S Commerce, Lockhart; 7am-6pm Mon-Fri, to 6.30pm Sat, 9.30am-6.30pm Sun

08 THE SALT LICK BBQ

Consider a hike through Lockhart State Park before you mosey along to dinner in Driftwood, 30 miles west of Bastrop. Set amid the gently rolling farmland south of Austin, everything about this place says country.

It's not just the setting that's different: here meats are seared and grilled over an open pit like the owners' ancestors did it when they crossed the country looking to farm in the 1800s. If you're in a group, it's worth ordering family-style for all-you-can-eat brisket, ribs, sausage, coleslaw and beans. For dessert, try a helping of the homemade pecan pie or blackberry cobbler. You can bring your own beer, or buy a bottle of wine at the adjacent winery. Cash only.
www.saltlickbbq.com; tel +1 512 858 4959; 18300 FM 1826, Driftwood; 11am-10pm

ESSENTIAL
INFORMATION

WHERE TO STAY

AUSTIN FOLK HOUSE B&B
Fun and folksy rather
than prim and proper,
this comfortable bed and
breakfast holds a wide
appeal. Rooms occupy a
historic house in a leafy
neighbourhood near the
University of Texas.
*www.austinfolkhouse.
com; tel +1 512 472 6700;
506 W 22nd St, Austin*

SOUTH CONGRESS HOTEL
The stylish, contemporary
rooms here are locally
designed, meshing
perfectly with the hotel's
mid-century mod facade.
Staying on South Congress,
you're in the heart of
Austin's hippest district.
*www.southcongresshotel.
com; tel +1 512 920 6405;
1603 S Congress Ave, Austin*

**HYATT REGENCY LOST
PINES RESORT & SPA**
Horseback riding, hiking
and a lazy river pool are
all part of the adventure
at this 400-acre resort.
It's rural but certainly not
rustic, and the rooms here
are all laid-back luxury.
*www.lostpines.hyatt.com;
tel +1 512 308 1234; 575 Hyatt
Lost Pines Rd, Lost Pines*

WHAT TO DO

**BOB BULLOCK STATE
HISTORY MUSEUM**
Texas music, football, cattle
drives and the oil and gas
industry are all among
the subjects of engaging
exhibits here. Look for
the histories of the early
European settlers who
introduced their ways of
cooking to the state (www.
thestoryoftexas.com).

LOCKHART STATE PARK
Numerous short
hikes criss-cross this
forrested, 260-acre park,
which encompasses a
meandering stream called
Clear Creek. The park
hosts frequent events
and there's a swimming
pool for cooling off in
summer. (http://tpwd.
texas.gov/state-parks/
lockhart)

CELEBRATIONS

One weekend in April,
Austin Food & Wine
Festival invites top
local and state chefs to
show off their cooking
during parties, tastings,
demonstrations and
competitions. Barbecue,
of course, is usually
well represented.
(www.austinfoodandwine
festival.com)

USA

MAINE'S ATLANTIC WAY

Lobster shacks, seafood baskets and warming chowders are a way of life in coastal Maine, where lobster is so ubiquitous it was once the preserve of the poor.

The southern coast of Maine wears its maritime heart on its windblown sleeve. Fog-draped lighthouses dot the coast. Fishing boats cruise island-speckled bays. Lobster pounds and clam shacks jostle for attention along the US 1 highway: lobster alone comprises 13.5% of the value of state exports. Once so common it was considered suitable only for the poor or prisoners, lobster today is a global delicacy. In 2014, Maine lobstermen hauled in more than 124 million pounds of the crustacean, valuing nearly $460 million.

Why do lobsters thrive here? Thank the rocky coastline, which offers hiding places for young lobsters, and effective protection measures that Maine lobstermen have implemented to prevent over-harvesting. In this area of the USA you'll find that fish, oysters and clams are often fried, arriving with a simple side of French fries, coleslaw and tartar sauce. Lobsters are steamed or broiled and

NEED TO KNOW
To get to any of Maine's coastal lobster shacks, you'll need a car. This trail will take 3 days.

typically served with a side of drawn, or melted, butter.

Every self-respecting coastal town from Kittery north to Calais has a scruffy lobster shack not far from the local dock – they're great places to slurp thick seafood chowders and savour warm lobster rolls. In the past decade, innovative chefs in Portland - southern Maine's urban anchor - have embraced all that is fresh and local while adding global kick, making it a highly respected centre of gastronomy for a town of such a small size (population 66,000). The buzziest restaurants cluster in and around the Old Port district downtown. Allagash Brewing Co jump-started the craft beer scene when it began operations in 1995 and today the town is heaving with microbreweries. For road trippers, travel in Maine is best enjoyed from late May through to October, as many businesses close in colder months.

01 Portland Press Herald © Getty Images

02 Justin Sullivan © Getty Images

01 LOBSTER SHACK AT TWO LIGHTS

Red picnic tables overlook a craggy coast. A majestic lighthouse breaks the skyline. And a brigade of red food trays overflows with lobster rolls, clam chowders and crinkle-cut fries. Yep, you're stepping into a postcard at the Lobster Shack at Two Lights, perched beside the Atlantic Ocean in Cape Elizabeth, 8 miles south of Portland.

It's a scenic spot where you will bump elbows with other diners, but the crowds add to the sense of fun at this third-generation lobster shack.

Lobster rolls here are simple and traditional: a hotdog bun lined with lettuce, stuffed with fresh lobster meat and topped with mayo and a pickle slice. Drizzle some drawn butter for a whoosh of extra flavour. *www.lobstershacktwolights.com; tel +1 207 799 1677; 225 Two Lights Rd, Cape Elizabeth; late Mar-late Oct 11am-8pm daily, to 8.30pm Jul & Aug*

02 LUCKY CATCH CRUISES

You can live the life of a lobsterman – if only for 90 minutes – as a passenger aboard the Lucky Catch, a commercial lobster boat. Cruises depart throughout the day from Long Wharf in downtown Portland's Old Port district and head into Casco Bay to pull up lobster traps. During the trip, crew-members show passengers how to bait and set traps and how to rubber-band lobster claws.

Captain and owner Tom Martin calls these excursions 'trap-to-table' experiences because guests can eat the day's lobster catch at Portland Lobster Company. After paying the wholesale price for the lobster, carry your precious cargo in hand over to the restaurant. 'You can put a whole meal together for 10 bucks', enthuses Martin. *www.luckycatch.com; tel +1 207 761 0941; 170 Commercial St, Portland; May-Oct, check website for schedule*

03 DUCKFAT

As you cosy into your seat at the bar, pause to appreciate the view into the kitchen. That's where, as they say, the magic happens. The restaurant is tiny, holding just the bar, a long counter and a few tables, but the food packs a punch: everything that can be fried is done so in delicious duck fat.

First up? Handcut Belgian fries. These wickedly good potatoes arrive in a paper cone along with the dipping sauce of your choice. The *poutine* French fries beckon with duck-juice gravy, cheese curd and a sunny-side-up egg if you want it (and you do).

Duckfat opened in 2005, kick-starting Portland's swift rise as one of Northeast USA's top food destinations. Award-winning chef Rob Evans and wife and co-owner Nancy Pugh source locally, from the bread to the produce to the duck eggs to the beer. *www.duckfat.com; +1 207 774 8080; 43 Middle St, Portland; 11am-10pm*

01-02 Harbor Fish Market, Portland

03 Cape Elizabeth, Maine

the building sits on top of water.'

The variety of seafood for sale is impressive: if it lives in the sea, you'll probably find it here. On any given day, the market displays on average 15 varieties of oysters. For meals to go, staff can pack a cooler for a road trip or cook a lobster for you to take away.

Ready to tackle your first boiled lobster? Then bib up and follow these instructions: twist the skinny legs then slurp out the meat. Next, twist off the claws. After breaking the claws with the cracker, dip their meat in drawn butter. Savour the exquisite flavour. Next, twist the tail until you break it. Remove each flipper, extract the meat. And yes, you made a mess, but it's totally expected.

www.harborfish.com; +1 207 775 0251; 9 Custom House Wharf, Portland; 8.30am-5.30pm Mon-Sat 9am-4pm Sun

04 TWO FAT CATS BAKERY

Don't believe in love at first sight? Then you've never gazed at a whoopie pie inside the cozy confines of Two Fat Cats Bakery. Boasting a fluffy layer of marshmallow buttercream sandwiched between chocolate snack cakes, this Maine speciality is a flirt. Call it the Oreo cookie of your dreams.

Made fresh each morning, whoopie pies and other classic American desserts are the focus at this 10-year-old bakery two blocks east of the Old Port district. Think red velvet cupcakes, mixed berry pie and three-level vanilla cake with lemon custard, all of it made from scratch.

As for whoopie pies, they became Maine's official state treat in 2011 (with blueberry pie taking the honours for official state dessert). Popular in Maine as well as the Pennsylvania Amish country, the treat earned its name, we hear, because Amish farmers yelled 'whoopie!' when finding one in their lunch pail.

www.twofatcatsbakery.com; tel +1 207 347 5144; 47 India St, Portland; 8am-6pm Tue-Fri, to 5pm Sat, to 4pm Sun

05 HARBOR FISH MARKET

Entering Harbor Fish Market is an adventure for the senses. There's the chatter of people and the action of traders steaking fish with sharp knives. You'll hear the sounds of the skinning machine and confront four large, bubbling lobster tanks as you enter. And did we mention the smell? Wrap up warm, because the sheer volume of ice can make the place quite damp.

Co-owner Mike Alfiero has been running the market with his family for 50 years and says the location is unique. 'It's like going back in time. We're in a building that's over 200 years old and we're literally on a wharf, which means

06 SUSAN'S FISH-N-CHIPS

Mmm, chowder. Or *chowdah* as they say in New England. The best of these milk- or cream-based soups burst with local seafood. Chowders trace back to 16th- and 17th-century English and French coastal villages. New World settlers created their own variations based on local bounty. Today, most are prepared with potatoes and onions.

What you won't taste in New England clam chowder? Tomatoes. Tomatoes are found in Manhattan clam chowder, a soup created in New York City and deemed inferior by self-respecting New Englanders. For her seafood chowder, Susan Eklund of Susan's Fish-n-Chips combines her thick and creamy fish and clam chowders with shrimp, scallops and lobsters – all fresh and local. Slurp it from a bread bowl or sprinkle it with crackers.

03 Joe Dube @ 500px

At this come-as-you-are locals' joint just outside downtown Portland, you can also enjoy free coffee with your meal, scoop tartar sauce from a mason jar and, in summer, bite into fried lobster on a stick. www.susansfishnchips.com; tel +1 207 878 3240; 1135 Forest Ave, Portland; 11am-8pm

07 CENTRAL PROVISIONS

The red-brick Central Provisions is Portland's latest It Girl. Long lines; plenty of media attention. The critics also love it and so should you - as locals will attest, this ingénue earns the kudos.

The menu changes daily, spotlighting seasonal fare, while a thoughtful wine list and craft cocktails keep diners well watered. Small plates embrace the salt of the earth and the sea, such as local caviar, Otter Cove oysters and sea urchin.

This Old Port restaurant, an inviting spot for a top-notch dinner, sits inside one of the city's oldest buildings, built in 1828. On your visit, angle for a seat overlooking the line

'It's like going back in time. We're in a building that's over 200 years old and we're literally sitting on top of water'

chefs in action. In warmer months, look for locally sourced blueberry desserts. Local oysters are on the menu year-round. Co-owner Paige Gould's recommendation for food lovers is to take advantage of the local seafood while in Maine. 'The Casco Bay produces the most beautiful fish', she says – a result of its nutrient-rich cold water. www.central-provisions.com; tel +1 207 805 1085; 414 Fore St, Portland; 11am-2pm, 5pm-midnight

08 HARRASEEKET LUNCH & LOBSTER

Preppies, pop your collar. You've reached nirvana. Snap a selfie beside the 16ft-high duck boot at the flagship store of beloved outdoor and hunting retailer LL Bean in Freeport,

then drive to the South Freeport marina for lunch at Harraseeket Lunch & Lobster.

This red-and-white icon is hard to miss. A classic Maine lobster pound, it's more formal than a lobster shack but certainly not fancy. Lobster pounds traditionally hold lobsters in tanks with circulating water and sell the crustaceans by weight. Take a moment to enjoy the picturesque collection of yachts resting on the water before placing your order for a seafood basket and fried onion 'middles' at the front window.

For steamed clams or live or boiled lobsters, walk around the corner of the building to the lobster pound. If the picnic tables are full, dine off the hood of your car like a local. Harraseeket is BYOB so bring your favourite Maine beer for the meal. *www.harraseeketlunchandlobster. com; tel +1 207 865 4888; 36 S Main St, South Freeport, Freeport; lunch 11am-7.45 pm, to 8.45pm mid-Jun-Aug, lobster from 7am*

09 BREWERIES OF ONE INDUSTRIAL WAY

You'll hear the rumours about Epiphany well before your arrival at Foundation Brewing Company, an innovative microbrewery producing brown ales, IPAs and farmhouse brews. The farmhouse beers are inspired by *saisons*, which were beers that farmers in Belgium and northern France once brewed for themselves from ingredients on-hand. The golden-orange Epiphany, a double IPA, wins acolytes with its juicy blend of citrus, tropical fruit and pine.

'Epiphany is about the aroma and the flavour that you can get out of the hops,' explains co-owner John Bonney. You might taste pineapple and mango on the nose, then get a little bit of pine in the back. The bad news? It sells out.

Fortunately, several other craft beers are on tap at the thriving collection of breweries bordering Industrial Way, a strip of warehouses 20 minutes from downtown Portland. Foundation shares space with Austin Street Brewing and it can be a convivial scene, with food trucks (typically Thursday to Saturday) and patio lounging.

For your last afternoon, start at Foundation, hit Austin Street then cross the street to Belgian-style powerhouse Allagash Brewing. From here, it's half a mile to DL Geary Brewing Company, which kick-started the Portland microbrewery scene. *www.foundationbrew.com; tel +1 207 370 8187; Foundation Brewing Company, 1 Industrial Way, Portland*

04 Lobster Shack at Two Lights, outside Portland

05 Freshly baked whoopie pies, Two Fat Cats Bakery

06 Lobster for the pot, Harbor Fish Market

WHERE TO STAY

PORTLAND HARBOR HOTEL
Rooms at this classically styled hotel on Fore Street overlook either Casco Bay or courtyard gardens. In the centre of the Old Port action, the hotel is an easy walk from boutiques, galleries, top restaurants and the wharves. *www.portlandharbor hotel.com; tel +1 207 775 9090; 468 Fore Street, Portland*

HARRASEEKET INN
Afternoon tea in the lobby is a thoughtful touch at this classic white clapboard inn within walking distance of the LL Bean flagship store in Freeport. The inn is named for the nearby Harraseeket River. According to lore, the name Harrasseeket stems from a Native American term meaning River of Many Fish. *www.harraseeketinn.com; tel +1 207 865 9377; 162 Main St, Freeport*

WHAT TO DO

Wander the galleries and indie shops in the Old Port district then pop into the Portland Museum of Art (www. portlandmuseum.org)

to admire its American art collection, which includes works by local Maine artists Winslow Homer, Louise Nevelson and Andrew Wyeth. For an active afternoon, hop a Casco Bay Lines ferry (www.cascobaylines.com) to Peaks Island where you can explore by bike or kayak. In Freeport, the massive LL Bean flagship store awaits. Shop, listen to a 'fish tank' talk, learn to make knots or shop til you drop – the store is open 24/7.

CELEBRATIONS

Drive north to Yarmouth in mid-July for the Clam Festival, serving 6,000lb of clams (www. clamfestival.com). Craft brewers from across the Pine Tree State and New England share their sudsy creations at the Portland Brew Festival on Labor Day weekend in early September (www. portlandbrewfestival. com). In mid-October, watch lobster chefs in action, join a beer and whisky crawl and sample Maine's finest foods at Harvest On the Harbor (www.harvestontheharbor. com) in Portland.

PACIFIC OCEAN

Ka'ie'iewaho Channel

SUNSET BEACH

KAHUKU

07 06 05

HALE'IWA

WAIALUA

08 09

WAHIAWA

PACIFIC OCEAN

PEARL CITY

KANE'OHE

'AIEA

KAILUA

HONOLULU 04

03 10

WAIKIKI

KAHALA

01

02

Kaiwi Channel

USA

USA

HAWAII'S ORIGINAL FUSION TRADITIONS

Local Hawaiian food is a far cry from the touristy luau feasts: it's about fresh farm produce, ancient multicultural recipes and even a unique local brand of haute cuisine.

Flung so far west of the US mainland, Hawaii feels like another country. The most geographically isolated place on the planet, this Polynesian archipelago has evolved unique flora and fauna, soulful cultural traditions and a diverse cuisine unlike any other.

The first arrivals in the Hawaiian Islands were Polynesian voyagers whose double-hulled outrigger canoes were stuffed with plants such as breadfruit, taro and coconuts, as well as pigs and chickens. Beginning in the 18th century, European and American explorers, whalers and missionaries dropped off livestock and exotic fruits and vegetables in Hawaii. Next came 19th-century sugar plantation workers hailing from China, Japan, Korea, the Philippines and Portugal. Each wave of immigrants brought their own food traditions and ingredients, adding to the multicultural mixed plate that now represents local cooking. To think of it another way, Hawaii

was experimenting with fusion food more than a century before it became trendy. In the 1990s, a dozen star local chefs elevated island flavours to create the haute Hawaii Regional Cuisine (HRC), which continues to evolve today, everywhere from fancy restaurant kitchens to food trucks.

With its mix of fine dining, family restaurants and vibrant markets, O'ahu is the best island for travellers to take a big bite of Hawaii's one-of-a-kind food culture. This has little to do with touristy luau feasts. Instead, local food (meaning island-style dishes only found in Hawaii) is all about neighbourhood kitchens serving mixed plate lunches, *pupu* (appetisers) devoured with friends at raucous sports bars, roving food trucks and, most of all, bountiful farmers' markets. For a sweet ending after a hot day at the beach, nothing beats a shave ice from a roadside stand – simple, cheap and guaranteed to bring out smiles of warm *aloha* in everyone.

NEED TO KNOW
To take advantage of the Saturday farmers' market, be sure to follow this 2-day trail over a weekend.

① HOUSE WITHOUT A KEY

After a long transoceanic flight, the first thing you'll want to do after arriving in Honolulu is stick your toes in the sand. Do that with a cocktail in hand on Waikiki Beach. Named after a Charlie Chan detective novel, the romantic House Without a Key is the perfect sunset-watching spot, with open-air tables on the beach. Hawaiian musicians strum guitars and ukuleles while graceful dancers perform the hula with the ocean and palm trees as a backdrop.

This beach bar serves elegant Pacific Rim fusion cuisine, but also makes some of the islands' best mai tais (a tropical cocktail of rum, lime and orange juices and orgeat syrup – a sweet almond syrup).

www.halekulani.com; tel +1 808 923 2311; Halekulani, 2199 Kalia Rd, Honolulu; 7am–9pm

② KCC FARMERS' MARKET

Many of O'ahu's best-loved farmers, fishers, ranchers, artisanal food producers, and street-food chefs gather every Saturday morning near Diamond Head, just east of Waikiki. Join the crowds of locals and tourists who come to sample island-harvested goodness, from Hawaiian sea salt and wild honey to tender greens grown by local Nalo Farms on O'ahu's Windward Coast.

For Native Hawaiian flavours, look for vendors selling fresh *poi*, a staple side dish made from pounded taro root, and coconut cups full of *'awa* – a mildly sedating drink extracted from Polynesian kava plants.

It's worth getting here early to watch the chefs' cooking demonstrations as you sip hot or iced Hawaii-grown coffee.

http://hfbf.org; tel +1 808 848 2074; Kapiolani Community College (KCC), 4303 Diamond Head Rd, Honolulu; 7.30am–11am Sat

③ CHINATOWN

After exploring the farmers' market, hit Waikiki Beach for fun in the sun. When your stomach starts to growl again, head to the city's historical Chinatown neighbourhood.

Once a notorious red-light district for sailors arriving at Honolulu Harbor, modern Chinatown has eclectic art galleries, antiques shops and boutiques, street-corner *lei* makers and pan-Asian restaurants.

For a full-on sensory experience – sniffing whole fish caught just that morning or exotic fruit such as durian and rambutan – step inside the O'ahu Market, dating from 1904. Nearby at Chinatown's maze-like Kekaulike and

'Matsumoto's little tin-roofed grocery store busily serves more than a thousand cones of shave ice every day'

01 Waikiki Beach, Honolulu

02 Tropical fruits for sale

03 Tiki carvings on O'ahu

04 Cake from Kahuku Farms' cafe

05 Catch of the day is hauled through Honolulu's Chinatown

Maunakea marketplaces, cooks whip up budget-priced meals of spicy noodles, sour soups, salty rice plates and more.
O'ahu Market, 145 N King St, Honolulu; open daily

04 ALAN WONG'S

One of the founding chefs who influenced Hawaii Regional Cuisine, Alan Wong roots his cooking in Hawaii's multiethnic plantation-era heritage. At his eponymous restaurant in downtown Honolulu, tucked away inside a nondescript office building, the chef spotlights local farmers and ranchers and seafood delicacies from across the Hawaiian Islands.

Splurge on a tasting menu of Big Island lobster, twice-cooked *kalbi* (Korean-style) short ribs and ginger-crusted *onaga* (long-tail red snapper). For dessert, spoon into silky *haupia* (coconut-cream) sorbet served in a chocolate shell and drizzled with *liliko'i* (passion fruit) sauce. Book ahead for a table, because this place is always popular.
www.alanwongs.com; tel +1 808 949 2526; 1857 S King St, Honolulu; 5pm-10pm

05 KAHUKU FARMS

Get up early on Sunday morning for a bewitchingly beautiful circle-island drive. Cruise over the mountaintop Pali Hwy (Hwy 61) to the serene Windward Coast. Wind past aquamarine bays, white-sand beaches and coastal lookouts all the way to Kahuku, a rural community of farms and ranches where food trucks serve plates of hot, garlicky buttered prawns at the side of the highway.

Kahuku Farms is your destination to get in touch with what Hawaiians lovingly call *'aina* (land). Reserve ahead for a one-hour tour, which guides you past fields of tropical fruits and vegetables, or just swing by the farm's cafe for a tropical-fruit smoothie and grilled homemade banana bread.

Kahuku honey and pineapple-papaya jam make *'ono* (delicious) souvenirs to take home.
www.kahukufarms.com; tel +1 808 628 0639; 56-800 Kamehameha Hwy (Hwy 83), Kahuku; 11am-4pm Wed-Mon

06 TED'S BAKERY

On O'ahu's famous North Shore, surfing is the way of life. Pull over at Sunset Beach, a tempting spot for swimming and snorkelling in summer or for watching big-wave riders in winter. Across the street, Ted's Bakery dishes up local-style mixed plate lunches,

each so huge it could probably feed two people (or one ravenous surfer). Dig into mini mountains of chicken *katsu* (cutlets), flaky mahi-mahi (dolphinfish) or *loco moco* (two scoops of white rice topped with a hamburger patty, a fried egg and gravy).

But the best reason to stop here is for a slice of pie: chocolate-macadamia nut, strawberry-guava, *liliko'i* cheese pie and *haupia* sell out quickly, so don't arrive late in the day. Chow down outside at picnic tables or head back to the beach for a sunny picnic.
www.tedsbakery.com; +1 808 638 8207; 59-024 Kamehameha Hwy (Hwy 83), Hale'iwa; 7am-8pm

07 MATSUMOTO'S SHAVE ICE
Everybody who visits the North Shore winds up eventually in Hale'iwa, where food trucks line the slow-moving, two-lane highway through town. You're here for the shave ice, Hawaii's version of a snow cone/slushy drenched with sugary syrup in a rainbow of flavours.

Open since the 1950s, Matsumoto's little tin-roofed grocery store busily serves more than a thousand cones every day (yes, really), so lines can be long. Order your shave ice with condensed milk, sweet azuki beans, or *mochi* (pounded rice cakes) for an extra kick.
www.matsumotoshaveice.com; tel +1 808 637 4827; 66-111 Kamehameha Hwy (Hwy 83), Hale'iwa; 9am-6pm

08 WAIALUA SUGAR MILL
A few miles down the road from Hale'iwa, Waialua is a sleepy town. Although its booming sugar plantation days are long gone, Waialua is making a comeback with boutique farms growing coffee, chocolate and more. In the town centre, its historic sugar mill has been refashioned into a shopping centre for locally made goods.

Stop for a cup of Waialua-grown coffee and to sample dark chocolate and cacao nib bars. Local convenience stores sell bottles of Waialua Soda made with all-natural tropical flavours such as *liliko'i*, mango and pineapple.
www.waialuasugarmill.com; 67-106 Kealohanui St, Waialua; 8am-5pm

09 DOLE PLANTATION
As you circle back to Honolulu you'll drive across endless green fields in central O'ahu. In the 20th century, much of what you see was exclusively used to grow pineapple. James Dole planted the first pineapple plants here in 1900 and his enterprising idea later grew into an international business empire.

What was once a small fruit in the

1950s on the Dole Plantation became a tourist extravaganza in the 1980s. Today all the tour buses pull over here and you should too, if only to taste the frozen pineapple concoction called 'Dole Whip'. Take a walking tour of the bountiful gardens and get an up-close look at blossoming coffee trees, spiky pineapple plants, alien-looking cacao pods and more. *www.dole-plantation.com; tel +1 808 621 8408; 64-1550 Kamehameha Hwy (Hwy 99), Wahiawa; 9.30am-5pm*

⑩ HAWAIIAN FOODS

Back in Honolulu, this neighbourhood restaurant is the place to try authentic Hawaiian specialities. Run by the same family since 1950, Hawaiian Foods serves oven-roasted *kalua* pig, *laulau* (pork, chicken or fish wrapped inside taro or ti leaves and steamed) and poke (cubed raw seafood mixed with flavourings such as soy sauce, sesame oil, seaweed or roasted *kukui* nuts).

Plate lunches all come with *poi*, rice, *haupia* and *lomi* salmon (diced salmon with tomatoes, green onions and hot pepper flakes). Get your order to go and eat it on Waikiki Beach at sunset for a delicious last memory of Hawaii's local food, which is 'broke da mouth' (literally, so good it breaks the mouth, as the Hawaiian pidgin saying goes). *www.hailishawaiianfood.com; tel +1 808 735 8019; 760 Palani Ave, Honolulu; 10am-7pm Tue-Sun*

06 Train takes visitors on a tour of the pineapple farm at Dole Plantation

WHERE TO STAY
MOANA SURFRIDER
Open since 1901, this was the very first resort hotel for tourists on Waikiki Beach. Staying here feels like stepping back in time, but with all the modern amenities such as swimming pools and a spa. *www.moana-surfrider.com; 2365 Kalakaua Avenue, Honolulu*

THE MODERN HONOLULU
Away from the tourist hubbub, this minimalist modern boutique hotel is an oasis that puts you closer to the Honolulu dining scene – its restaurant overlooks the harbour and Iron Chef Morimoto mans the helm. *www.themodernhonolulu.com; 1775 Ala Moana Boulevard, Honolulu*

MALAEKAHANA BEACH CAMPGROUND
You'll feel like a castaway when you pitch your tent or park up your campervan by the beach at Malaekahana State Recreation Area on O'ahu's pretty Windward Coast. Or stay in a plantation-style hut. *www.malaekahana.net; 56-335 Kamehameha Highway, Laie*

WHAT TO DO
In Honolulu, tour 'Iolani Palace (www.iolanipalace.org), the only royal palace in the USA, and the fascinating Hawaiian history and cultural exhibitions at the Bishop Museum (www.bishopmuseum.org). O'ahu's most visited attraction is Pearl Harbor, which played a pivotal role in WWII; reserve in advance to tour the USS Arizona Memorial (www.nps.gov/valr). East of Waikiki Beach, the protected marine reserve of Hanauma Bay is a top snorkelling spot.

CELEBRATIONS
HAWAII FOOD & WINE FESTIVAL
In October, top chefs Alan Wong and Roy Yamaguchi head an all-star line-up during this two-week festival spread across four islands. (www.hawaiifoodandwine festival.com)

WAIKIKI SPAM JAM
In late April or early May, this street food festival celebrates the tinned meat that Hawaii has not been able to live without since US troops first imported it during WWII. (www.spamjamhawaii.com)

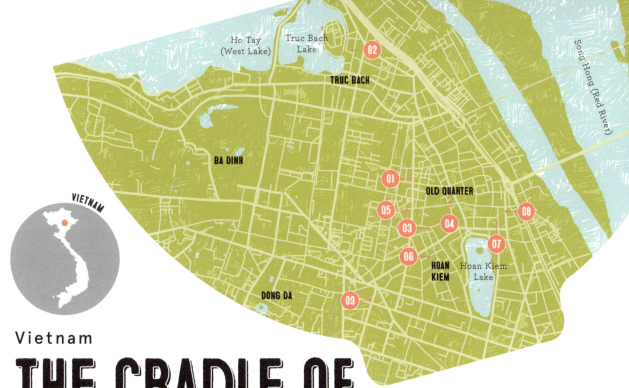

Vietnam

THE CRADLE OF VIETNAMESE CUISINE

Vietnam's complex cuisine is distinctly local but also a product of centuries of outside influence, and nowhere is this more celebrated than on Hanoi's cacophonous streets.

Hanoi's importance on Vietnam's culinary stage is unrivalled. Shaped by centuries of foreign domination, and often overlooked in favour of bigger, brasher Ho Chi Minh City in the south, this compact, elegant capital is responsible not just for the ideology that's shaped modern-day Vietnam, but also for Vietnamese food as we know it. As the cradle of Vietnamese civilisation, Hanoi is the birthplace of some signature national dishes that have become synonymous with Vietnamese food worldwide, such as *pho* and *bun cha*. Many of the foreign influences that filtered down to the rest of the country did so through here.

The food of Hanoi, whether it's a single dish cooked in a hole-in-the-wall over a charcoal brazier, or a refined multi-course fusion extravaganza, is the product of centuries of miscegenation, a palimpsest of colonial influences and culinary infiltration by Vietnam's neighbours. From the conquering Mongols came beef; Chinese domination contributed cooking techniques such as stir-frying; the French brought baguettes, dill, coffee and wine. Chillies, flat noodles, and coconut milk crossed over from Cambodia, Laos and Thailand. Yet this melange of influences, notable for the abundant presence of fresh herbs, merged into a cuisine uniquely its own. It's governed by the principles of freshness, variety and harmony of textures and flavours, a balance of five fundamental tastes: sweet, salty, spicy, bitter, and sour, and a regional, seasonal availability of ingredients. At its heart, Hanoi is a city of gourmands and there's no better place in Vietnam for street food. This tour focuses on the labyrinthine Old Quarter – the city's commercial heart for six centuries – which holds the key to Vietnamese cuisine, and also the adjacent French Quarter.

NEED TO KNOW
Hanoi's Old Quarter is chaotic, yes, but also a wonderful place to wander on foot. This trail deserves 4 days.

01 BANH CUON GIA TRUYEN

In this little shop, Tran Thi Van – a third-generation banh cuon master – ladles scoops of rice-flour batter onto the steamer, covers it with a lid for a few seconds and then deftly lifts the gossamer-thin white sheets onto a tray, using a bamboo stick. She then fills each one with minced wood-ear mushrooms and seasoned ground pork, adds a generous sprinkle of deep-fried shallots and the tender rolls are ready to be dipped in *nuoc cham* (the most common of Vietnamese dipping sauces).

Some customers come here for a rare Hanoi delicacy, found in very few *bahn cuon* joints: *ca cuong* (giant water bug), steamed, cut up and served in fish sauce. For wartime residents of Hanoi, it represents the nostalgic taste of childhood, when people made use of any protein they could get. *Tel +84 4 280 108; 14 Pho Hang Ga; 10am-9pm*

'The secret of *pho* is the clear broth, made with marrow-rich beef bones simmered for hours to give it that earthy sweetness'

02 HANOI COOKING CENTRE

Banh Cuon Gia Truyen is one of the favourite breakfast stops of Dinh Phung Linh, one of the chefs at Hanoi Cooking Centre, where foodies can get a hands-on introduction to dishes from Hanoi, the Northern Highlands and the spicy seafood from the coast, or be initiated into the secrets of *nem* (spring roll) making.

For Dinh, the food itself is only part of the experience; he is keen for students to understand the history, culture and traditions behind the cooking methods and every dish. In addition, Dinh organises street food tours, with market visits to complement the cooking classes. Not only does he teach you to identify various exotic ingredients and what can be used as a substitute back home, but he actively encourages visitors to try some of Hanoi's lesser-known culinary delights: chicken testicles, sautéed silkworms and frogs. *www.hanoicookingcentre.com; tel +84 4 3715 0088; 44 Chau Long Street*

03 BUN CHA DAC KIM

At lunchtime, Hang Manh Street in the Old Quarter is fragrant with the mouth-watering aroma of pork patties and slices of pork belly being grilled over hot coals. The cook tosses

02 Matt Munroe © Lonely Planet

03 Matt Munroe © Lonely Planet

the freshly grilled pork into a bowl, alongside a bowl of *nuoc mam cham* (fish sauce) with sliced carrot and papaya and proceeds to place plates of *bun* (rice noodles), fresh herbs, chillies and deep-fried *nem cua be* (pork and crab spring rolls) in front of customers, who spill out onto the pavement.

This Vietnamese take on barbecue originated in 1950s Hanoi, and while every Hanoi neighbourhood now has its *bun cha* joint, this is one of the oldest, with the descendants of the original owner running the show.

Make sure you come to the right restaurant, as there's an impostor with the same name.
Tel +84 4 828 5022; 1 Hang Manh; 11am-5pm

04 MY GA TAN

Walk along Hang Can Street and you'll see rows and rows of empty soft drink cans with chicken feet sticking out of them in a tangle of herbs. Not the most appetising dish, at first glance, but if you resist the temptation to keep on walking and perch at one of the plastic tables at Thu Anh Nguyen's stall, she'll upturn the can into your bowl, and you will be blown away by the tenderness of the meat.

The poussin is kept in a can to retain all of its juices and the herbal broth it's steamed in; its flesh and the broth come out almost black, with an extra tangy kick delivered by the accompanying dash of kumquat juice/ salt paste.

This relative newcomer on the streets of Hanoi hails from China, showing the continuing influence of Vietnam's powerful neighbour. The broth is said to have powerful restorative properties, and is a hangover cure to boot.
Tel +84 96 670 2692; 50 Hang Can; 5-11pm

05 PHO GIA TRUYEN

Every morning, a queue of locals forms at this drab-looking spot in the Old Quarter. They wait patiently as the cook lowers strips of beef into the cauldron to cook for a few seconds before ladling the fragrant broth over bowls of noodles topped with chopped spring onions.

Bowl in hand, customers then perch on stools to slurp *pho* in silence. The beef noodle soup dish is ubiquitous all over Vietnam but believed to have originated in Hanoi with the coming of the French. The secret is in the clear broth, made with marrow-rich beef bones simmered for hours to give it that earthy sweetness. The name *pho* is thought to be a corruption of 'feu', as in 'pot au feu' or beef stew, with beef becoming more widely consumed in northern Vietnam under French colonial rule.
Tel +84 4 380 0126; 49 Bat Dan; 7am-11pm

06 Hoang Dinh Nam © Getty Images

06 MADAME HIEN

In the heart of the Old Quarter, this century-old colonial villa with louvred shutters once belonged to François Charles Lagisquet, the 19th-century architect of the Hanoi Opera House, and is occupied once more by a Frenchman – chef Didier Corlou.

In its current incarnation it's a fine dining venue, a tribute to his wife's ancestral cuisine, named after her grandmother, with only a touch of French culinary influence. Dine on *cha ca* (grilled fish with galangal), or *pho* foie gras with lemongrass with the knowledge that both Ho Chi Minh and the king of Spain were once hosted within these very walls.
www.verticale-hanoi.com; tel +84 4 3938 1588; 15 Chan Cam; 11am-11pm

07 GREEN TANGERINE

Quite the opposite of Madame Hien's exploration of traditional Vietnamese recipes, at Green Tangerine the marriage of two chefs has resulted in the melding of French and Vietnamese cuisines with the focus on French dishes with a Vietnamese twist instead.

Chefs Stéphane Yvin and his wife Huong, who hails from a family of chefs, have been perfecting their craft through more than a decade of experimentation. Their 'innovation menu' changes every six months, and diners may be treated to such fusion experiments as duck breast with young green rice in coconut milk, king prawns with rum, and mango salad. There's a separate Vietnamese

tasting menu also, with refined takes on *pho bo* and *ca qua* fish in tamarind sauce, with flambéed banana the only concession to Western tastes.
www.greentangerinehanoi.com; tel +84 4 3825 1286; 48 Hang Be; 11am-11pm

08 CAFE LAM

As one of Hanoi's oldest cafes, Cafe Lam is as much a landmark as a destination for those craving a caffeine hit. This one-room joint, frequented by loyal local customers, was a gathering place for students and artists in the 1950s – the turbulent transition time when French rule was on its way out and Ho Chi Minh was on his way in – and its walls are adorned by artworks

given to proprietor Nguyen Lam by his then customers.

Vietnamese brew tends to be drip-filter robusta (a strong, full-bodied, slightly bitter coffee), sweetened with condensed milk, and that's what Mr Lam serves, along with *ca phe sua da* (iced coffee). Introduced to Vietnam by the French in the 19th century, coffee plantations sprang up all over the Vietnamese highlands, and Hanoi remains the king of coffee shops. *www.cafelam.com; tel +84 4 3824 5940; 60 Nguyen Huu Huan; 6.30am–10.30pm*

⑨ QUAN AN NGON

With its yellow awnings and food stalls lining the courtyard to create a market-like atmosphere, Quan An Ngon bridges the gap between street stall and restaurant. It's also one of the very few places in Vietnam where diners can find classic dishes from Vietnam's three regions, as befitting a capital city worth its salt.

Feast on crispy *banh xeo* (filled pancake) from Central Vietnam, Northern *xoi ga* (chicken sticky rice) and *cha ca Hanoi* (Hanoi-style fish marinated in galangal and turmeric and served with dill). Then come back for Southern *ca tho to* (caramelised fish in clay pot), *canh chua* (sweet and sour soup with pineapple, tamarind and tomatoes), Saigon-style *chao long* (rice porridge with pig's liver) and a riot of *goi cuon* (translucent spring rolls) from all over the country, dipped in tangy *nuoc cham*. *www.ngonhanoi.com.vn; tel +84 4 3942 8162; 18 Phan Boi Chau; 7am–9.45pm*

06 Street vendor selling vegetables off their bicycle

WHERE TO STAY
MAISON D'ORIENT
This intimate 12-room hotel, designed by a young Vietnamese architect and decked out with handmade furniture and French colonial armchairs, is tucked away in a small cul-de-sac just out of the French Quarter. *www.maison-orient.com; tel +84 4 3938 2539; 26 Ngo Huyen*

ESSENCE HANOI HOTEL
All dark wood and muted colours, this contemporary boutique hotel maintains a tranquil ambiance in the very heart of the Old Quarter, with custom bathtubs and good views of the historic city centre from its top floor. *www.essencehanoihotel. com; tel +84 4 3935 2485; 22 Ta Hien, Hang Buom*

WHAT DO DO
On Tran Hung Dao, Hoa Lo Prison – aka the 'Hanoi Hilton' – is a sobering reminder of the sub-par conditions in which Vietnamese political prisoners were held by the French colonialists. During the Vietnam War, US senator John McCain was a prisoner here. Alternatively, to see the man who's shaped Vietnam's destiny and who continues to exert his influence posthumously, visit the Ho Chi Minh Mausoleum in Ba Dinh Square, where lines of reverent Vietnamese file past the embalmed body in the stark marble tomb, watched over by crisply uniformed guards. Head to Hoan Kiem Lake early in the morning for a glimpse of traditional Vietnamese life – locals practising tai chi and street vendors getting into position. A red wooden bridge takes you to the 18th-century Jade Mountain Temple on a small island, dedicated to the victory of General Tran Hung Dao over the Mongols in the 13th century.

CELEBRATIONS
The Water Puppet Festival is a unique part of Tet celebrations held at the 11th-century Thay Pagoda, 30km west of Hanoi. The wooden puppets bob about the watery stage in the lake, with puppeteers practising this uniquely Vietnamese, millennia-old craft while hidden behind a bamboo screen.

FOOD TRAILS

First Edition
Published in November 2016 by Lonely Planet Global Limited
CRN 554153
www.lonelyplanet.com
ISBN 9781786571304
© Lonely Planet 2016
Printed in Malaysia
10 9 8 7 6 5 4 3

Managing Director Piers Pickard
Associate Publisher Robin Barton
Art Direction Daniel Di Paolo
Commissioning Editor Lorna Parkes
Editors Karyn Noble, Rebecca Tromans
Cartographers Wayne Murphy, Corey Hutchison
Pre-press Production Graham Parsons
Print Production Larissa Frost, Nigel Longuet

Thanks to Jessica Cole, Barbara di Castro

Authors Isabel Albiston (Argentina), Brett Atkinson (New Zealand, Southwest Australia), Carolyn Bain (Denmark), Amy Balfour (Maine, New Orleans –USA), Sara Benson (Hawaii - USA), Joe Bindloss (London – England, Chennai – India, Thailand), Abigail Blasi (Delhi – India, Puglia & Emilia-Romagna – Italy), John Brunton (Bali – Indonesia, Venice – Italy, Malaysia), Kerry Christiani (Germany, Portugal, Scotland), Gregor Clark (Canada, Lyon – France, Sicily – Italy), Lisa Dunford (Seychelles, Slovakia, Texas – USA), Janine Eberle (Tasmania - Australia), Duncan Garwood (San Sebastián – Spain), Trent Holden (Melbourne – Australia), Anita Isalska (Oman, Catalonia – Spain), Anna Kaminski (Vietnam), Leah Koenig (New York – USA), Virginia Maxwell (Turkey), Carolyn McCarthy (Chile, Peru), Daniel McCrohan (China), Rebecca Milner (Central Japan), Kate Morgan (Piedmont – Italy), Karyn Noble (Greece), Etain O'Carroll (Ireland), Lorna Parkes (Jordan), Brandon Presser (Iceland), Helen Ranger (Morocco), Kevin Raub (Brazil), Simon Richmond (Tokyo – Japan, Russia, South Africa, South Korea), Brendan Sainsbury (Jamaica), Luke Waterson (Southwest England), Nicola Williams (Paris, Dordogne – France)

Lonely Planet offices
USA
230 Franklin Road, Building 2B, Franklin, TN 37064 T: 615-988-9713

IRELAND
Digital Depot, Roe Lane (off Thomas St), Digital Hub, Dublin 8, D08 TCV4

STAY IN TOUCH lonelyplanet.com/contact

Paper in this book is certified against the Forest Stewardship Council™ standards. FSC™ promotes environmentally responsible, socially beneficial and economically viable management of the world's forests.